The Complete 30-Day Whole Foods Cookbook

600 Delicious Compliant Everyday Recipes for Lifelong Health and Food Freedom

Laura J. Davis

Copyright© 2021 By Laura J. Davis All Rights Reserved

This book is copyright protected. It is only for personal use. You cannot amend, distribute, sell, use, quote or paraphrase any part of the content within this book, without the consent of the author or publisher.

Under no circumstances will any blame or legal responsibility be held against the publisher, or author, for any damages, reparation, or monetary loss due to the information contained within this book, either directly or indirectly.

Disclaimer Notice:

Please note the information contained within this document is for educational and entertainment purposes only. All effort has been executed to present accurate, up to date, reliable, complete information. No warranties of any kind are declared or implied. Readers acknowledge that the author is not engaged in the rendering of legal, financial, medical or professional advice. The content within this book has been derived from various sources. Please consult a licensed professional before attempting any techniques outlined in this book.

By reading this document, the reader agrees that under no circumstances is the author responsible for any losses, direct or indirect, that are incurred as a result of the use of the information contained within this document, including, but not limited to, errors, omissions, or inaccuracies.

Table of Content

30-Day Whole Foods Meal Plan Challenge 1

Chapter 1 Eggs 8

Scrambled Eggs with Mushrooms and Greens 8
Perfect Jammy Eggs 8
Bacon and Brussels Sprouts Frittata 8
Southwest Scrambled Eggs with Avocado 9
Egg Salad with Fresh Dill 9
Turkish-Inspired Poached Eggs 9
Buffalo Chicken and Veggie Frittata 10
Light Taco Breakfast Casserole 10
Mushroom, Leek, and Spinach Frittata 10
Eggs with Cabbage and Prosciutto 11
Deviled Eggs with Smoked Paprika 11
Baked Sausage Scotch Eggs 11
Classic Shakshuka 12
Egg Florentine Cups 12
Bistro Curly Endive and Egg Salad 12
Charred Tomatillo Salsa Over Omelet 13
Smoky Shrimp Omelet with Arugula 13
Bacon and Kale Frittata 14
Persian Herby Frittata 14
Scrambled Egg with Salmon 14
Sweet Potato Stacks with Hot Sauce 15
Baby Spinach and Tomato Frittata 15
Soft-Boiled Scotch Eggs 15
Butternut Squash Frittata 16
Bacon, Spinach, and Tomato Breakfast Salad 16
Fried Eggs with Veggie 17
Scrambled Eggs Breakfast Tacos 17

Chapter 2 Breakfasts 18

Green Vegetable and Fruit Smoothie 18
Summer in A Glass 18
Southern Fall Smoothie 18
Sausage with Eggs and Home Fries 18
Mango and Pistachio Millet with Raspberry 19
Southwest Egg Breakfast Bowls 19
Fingerling Potatoes with Spring Asparagus 19
Cherry and Banana Cocoa Smoothie 20
Potato Croutons 20
Poached Pear 20
Hearty Pacific Northwest Mushroom Hash 20
Chia Seeds Pudding 21
Potato, Sausage and Bacon Breakfast Bites 21
Skillet Potatoes with Herbs 21
Spinach and Arugula Breakfast Hash 21

Chapter 3 Beef 22

Beef Brisket with Celery Root Slaw 22
Beef Short Ribs with Cauliflower Rice 22
Citrus Beef Short Ribs 23
Beef Short Ribs with Vegetable and Parsley 23
Picadillo-Style Beef Chuck Roast 23
Churrasco with Chimichurri 24
Fajita Beef Skillet Over the Cauliflower 24
Meat Loaf with Sweet-Sour Glaze 24
Slow Cooked Beef Short Ribs 25
Sirloin with Beans 25
Beef and Sweet Potato Chili 25
Slow-Cooked Shawarma 26
Hot Beef Arm Roast 26
Mici with Mustard Dipping 26
Cuban Beef and Bell Peppers 27
Beef Arm with Mushrooms and Snow Peas 27
Sirloin, Zucchini, and Mushroom Stir-Fry 27
Beef Brisket Braised with Potatoes 28
Asian Beef and Zucchini Noddles Soup 28
Russian Beef Stew Meat 28
Borscht 29
Catalina Beef Tacos 29
Beef Stroganoff with Coconut Sour Cream 30
Basil Sirloin Medallions with Veggie 30
Beef Short Ribs with Two Mushrooms 31
Grilled Beef Skirt 31
Mushroom Stuffed Sirloin Roulade 32
Beef Hamburger Soup 32
Pineapple Beef Steak Kabobs 33
Tender Beef Pot Roast 33
Stuffed Bell Peppers with Beef 33
Thai-Style Beef Curry with Green Beans 34
Braised Beef Brisket 34
Beef Steaks with Garlic-Shallot Purée 34
Steak Fajita Bowls with Veggie 35
Mongolian Beef and Mixed Greens 35
Indian Masala Steak Stir-Fry 35
Black Pepper Beef and Coleslaw Stir-Fry 36
Sirloin Steak and Broccoli Stir-Fry 36
Balsamic Chuck Roast and Veggies 36
Seared Sirloin Steak with Asparagus 37
Pan-Seared Beef Rib-Eye with Arugula 37
Traditional Picadillo 38
Herb Beef Eye of Round Roast 38
Pepperoncini-Flavour Skirt Steak 39
Steak au Poivre with Green Peppercorn Sauce 39
Ritzy Short Rib Ragù 40
West African Suya Stir-Fry 40
Bacon-Wrapped Beef Meatloaf 41
Hawaii Lazy Moco 41

Chapter 4 Pork ... 42

Balsamic and Herb Pork Tenderloin ... 42
Pork Tenderloin with Squash and Shallots ... 42
Garlicky Pork Butt Roast with Collards ... 42
Baby Back Ribs with Brussels Sprouts ... 42
Pork Loin and Vegetable Yellow Curry ... 43
Teriyaki Pork Tenderloin ... 43
Coriander-Crusted Pork Tenderloin ... 43
Cabbage and Pork Sausage Casserole ... 44
Pork with White BBQ Sauce and Collard Greens ... 44
Herb Pork Loin and Spiced Cauliflower ... 45
Korean-Style Pot Roast with Jicama Salad ... 45
Pork Sausage ... 45
Walnut-Crusted Pork Tenderloin with Greens ... 46
Pork Loin with Potato and Fruit Smash ... 46
Pork Loin Back Ribs with Mole Verde ... 46
Pork Char Siu with Vegetable Medley ... 47
Cider-Brined Roasted Pork Tenderloin ... 47
Pork Chops with Sweet Potato Colcannon ... 48
Pork Tenderloin and Bell Pepper Stir-Fry ... 48
Spaghetti Squash with Pork Arrabbiata Sauce ... 48
Pork Loin Chops with Zucchini Noodles ... 49
Baby Back Ribs with Spiced Rub ... 49
Bavarian Pot Rump Roast ... 49
Pork Shoulder with Pear Sauce ... 50
Traditional Caldo Verde ... 50
Pork and Veggie Stuffed Cabbage ... 51
Pork Loin Chops with Watermelon Salad ... 52
Potato, Pork Sausage, and Kale Soup ... 52
Pork Patties with Ginger Sauce ... 52
Mojo Pork Shoulder ... 53
Rosemary Pork with Red Potatoes ... 53
Pork Shoulder Curry with Asparagus ... 53
Basil Pork Tenderloin and Cauliflower Curry ... 54
Pork Chops with Parsnip Purée ... 54
Pork Shoulder with Butternut Squash ... 54
Pork Sausage Potato Hash ... 55
Pork Chops with Spiced Applesauce ... 55
Pork Scaloppini with Cremini Mushrooms ... 55
Spice-Crusted Roast Pork Tenderloin ... 56
Pork Shoulder Lettuce Wraps with Salsa ... 56
Pork Carnitas ... 57
Green Chile Pork Shoulder ... 57
Cider Pulled Pork Butt ... 57
Chili Verde Pork Tenderloin ... 58
Pork Sausage with Sweet Potatoes ... 58
Pork Chops with Mashers and Pesto ... 59
Apple-Pork Chops and Spinach ... 59
Tarragon Grilled Pork Chops ... 60
Dried Apricot Stuffed Pork Chops ... 60

Chapter 5 Lamb ... 61

Marinated Lamb Leg ... 61
Tahini Lamb with Almonds and Parsley ... 61
Curried Lamb and Potatoes ... 61
Garlic-Roasted Leg of Lamb Roast ... 62
Lamb Loaves with Cauliflower and Apricots ... 62
Green Curry Lamb Stew Meat ... 62
Pomegranate Braised Lamb Shanks with Almonds ... 63
Lamb Chops and Potatoes with Pesto ... 63
Tunisian-Style Lamb and Squash Stew ... 64
Gyro-Inspired Skillet Sausages ... 64

Chapter 6 Fish and Seafood ... 65

Shrimp Gumbo with Cauliflower ... 65
Shrimp with Vinaigrette and Salad ... 65
Balsamic-Glazed Salmon and Sweet Potatoes ... 65
Shrimp and Vegetable with Lemon Sauce ... 66
Green-Chile Squash with Seeds-Crusted Fish ... 66
Zucchini-Wrapped Cod Fillet with Brussels Sprouts ... 66
Sheet Pan Shrimp with Roasted Broccoli ... 67
Shrimp and Vegetable Sauce over Squash ... 67
Mediterranean Calamari with Veggie ... 67
Pink Shrimp and Tomatoes with Pesto ... 68
Sea Scallops and Veggie with Aioli ... 68
Shrimp on Cauliflower Grits with Bacon ... 68
Dijon Salmon with Cashews ... 69
Cod Fillet with Spinach Cream Sauce ... 69
Salmon Fillet with Lemon-Basil Pesto ... 69
Paprika Salmon ... 70
Salmon Fillet with Mustard-Dill Cream Sauce ... 70
Toasted Coconut Salmon Fillet ... 70
Ceviche with Avocado ... 71
Sole Fillet with Olives, Pistachios, and Tarragon ... 71
Salmon and Bluebrry Salad in Avocado Boats ... 71
Seared Scallops with Bacon and Spinach ... 72
Citrus Cod with Spinach ... 72
Pan-Seared Cod Fillet ... 73
Light Tuna Lettuce Wraps ... 73
Shrimp with Mashed Potatoes ... 73
Sweet and Sour Red Snapper ... 74
Pan-Seared Sea Scallops with Orange Sauce ... 74
Pineapple Salmon Fillet ... 74
Shrimp and Fish Cakes with Snap Peas ... 75
Cassava-Crusted Calamari ... 75
Asian Shrimp and Zucchini Noodles ... 75
Shrimp with Pine Nuts ... 76
Fish Fillet en Papillote ... 76
Mussels and Squash in Spicy Tomato Sauce ... 76
Lemon Dill Salmon Fillet ... 77
Scallops with Ginger-Blueberry Sauce ... 77
Ginger Snapper Fillet with Shiitake Mushrooms ... 77
Mexican-Style Tuna Boats ... 78
Lobster Mac Skillet ... 78
Jamaican Jerk Salmon with Fruity Salsa ... 78

Ahi Tuna with Tangy Fruit Salsa	79
Citrus-Ginger Glazed Halibut Fillet	79
Harissa Salmon Fillets with Warm Salad	79
Speedy Shrimp Scampi	80
Cod Fillet in Tomato and Pepper Sauce	80
Salmon with Cauliflower and Spinach Salad	80
Fish en Papillote	81
Basil Roasted Salmon Fillet with Broccoli	81
Thai-Style Red Curry Shrimp	81
Fish and Vegetable Stir-Fry	82
Cod Fillet with Olive Relish and Pilaf	82

Chapter 7 Poultry 83

Stuffed Bell Peppers with Turkey	83
Chicken Tikka Masala with Cauliflower Rice	83
Zucchini-Basil Chicken Thighs Hash	83
Southwest Turkey Legs with Fruit Salad	84
Italian Turkey Meatballs with Marinara Sauce	84
Instant Pot Turkey Chili with Avocado	84
Skillet Buttered Chicken Thighs	85
Patrick's Golden Chicken Fingers	85
Chicken Breast with Ginger and Basil	85
Orange Chicken Breast with Cauliflower Rice	86
Chicken with Red Bell Pepper	86
Fresh Rosemary Whole Chicken	86
Turkey and Veggie Chili	87
Cajun Chicken Wings	87
Chicken with Jerk Rub	87
Hawaiian Chicken and Pineapple Burgers	87
Kung Pao Chicken Lettuce Cups	88
Whole Chicken with Steak Spice	88
Chicken Meatballs with Tomato Cream Sauce	88
Mustard Chicken Salad Lettuce Cups	89
Poultry Breast-Asparagus Roll-Ups	89
Greek Whole Chicken and Potatoes	89
Salsa Verde Chicken Breast	90
Turkey Tenderloins with Pepper	90
Stir-Fried Chicken Breast and Bok Choy	90
Spanish Chicken Breast Cauliflower Skillet	90
Whole30 Fauxsole Verde con Pollo	91
Piri Piri Whole Chicken	91
Chicken with Sweet Potatoes and Mushrooms	92
Green Chile Chicken Thigh Stew	92
Chicken with Kielbasa Stuffed Mushrooms	92
Mojo Roast Chicken Wings	93
Tangy Chicken Skewers	93
Onion Chicken Meatballs	93
Turmeric Chicken	94
Butter Chicken Thighs	94
Asian Chicken Curry with Bok Choy	95
Oregano Chicken Thighs with Parsnips	95
Chipotle Chicken with Roasted Tomatoes	96
Herby Roast Chicken and Vegetables	96
Chicken Thighs and Artichoke Stew	96
Lemony Chicken with Green Beans	97
Thai Curried Chicken Bowls	97
Turkey Meatballs with Squash	97
Chicken Legs with Artichoke and Olives	98
Chinese Five-Spice Chicken Wings	98
Grapefruit Whole Chicken	98
Roasted Pepper Chicken Breast	99
Chicken Legs Cacciatore	99
Comforting Chicken Breast Fricassée	99
Sticky Apricot Chicken Drumsticks	100
Garlic Herb Chicken and Vegetable	100
ChickenWings with Green Chile Sauce	100
Italian Chicken Thighs with Fennel	101
Creamy Spinach Artichoke Chicken Breast	101
Skillet Seasoned Chicken Piccata	101
Smoky Butternut Spanish Chicken Meatballs	102
Chicken Stir Fry with Green Beans	102
Chicken Breast Schnitzel	102
Chicken Thighs with Walnuts	103
Turkey Stuffed Bell Peppers with Guacamole	103
Garlic Chicken Thighs Primavera	103

Chapter 8 Vegetables and Sides . 103

Cabbage, Carrot, and Cashew Slaw	104
Spicy Broccoli, Mushrooms, and Squash	104
Grilled Lemony Asparagus	104
Oven-Roasted Cauliflower	104
Balsamic and Wine-Glazed Red Onions	105
Pan-Roasted Brussels Sprouts and Butternut Squash 105	
Oven-Roasted Spaghetti Squash	105
Smashed Potatoes with Dried Herb	105
Twice-Fried Green Plantains	106
Sautéed Lemony Kale with Almonds	106
Green Beans with Bacon	106
Grilled Zucchini with Italian Herbs	106
Butter Parsley Stuffed Mushrooms	107
Paprika Cashews	107
Sweet Potato Croutons Baked	107
Garlicky Cherry Tomatoes	107
Loaded Roasted Carrots with Ginger Sauce	107
Golden Oven Fries	108
Balsamic Sweet Potato and Brussels Sprouts	108
Brussels Sprouts and Shallots Bowl	108
Pumpkin-Spiced Sweet Potato	108
Warm Fennel Olives	109
Whole Roasted Hot Spiced Cauliflower	109
Celeriac, Carrot, and Potato Pot Roast	109
Chili Brussels Sprouts	110
Golden Onion Rings with Aioli	110
Chili Roasted Zucchini Slices	110
Super Easy Zucchini Noodles	110
Sautéed Kale with Pine Nuts	111
Sweet Potatoes Mash	111
Broccoli Soup	111
Zucchini Ribbons	112
Green Beans with Almonds	112
Carrots with Fennel and Shallots	112

Red Cabbage with Apple and Bacon	112
Brussels Sprouts with Lemon Tahini	113
Sautéed Lemony Kale	113
Kale with Garlic	113
Chile Roasted Sweet Potatoes	113
Baby Beet and Red Cabbage Salad	113
Parsnips with Lemony Dill	114
Zucchini with Basil	114
Quick Sugar Snap Peas	114
Sweet Potato and Cauliflower Mash	114
Pistachio Over Kale Salad	114
Balsamic Roasted Root Veggie	115
Curry Carrot and Sweet Potato Soup	115
Green Beans with Almond	115
Greek Spiced Potatoes	115
Romaine Heart with Tahini Dressing	116
Butternut Squash and Kale Salad	116
Mustard Brussels Sprout Slaw	116
Red Curried Cauliflower	116

Chapter 9 Salads and Wraps 117

Tropically- Inspired Chicken Salad	117
Barbecue-Pulled-Chicken Lettuce Wraps	117
Toasty Sesame Chicken Wraps	117
Mediterranean Chicken Breast Wraps	117
Teriyaki Skirt Steak Wraps	118
Bacon, Egg, and Veggie Salad	118
Mexican Picadillo with Lettuce	118
Hot-and-Sour Salmon Fillet Salad	119
Prosciutto and Shrimp Cabbage Cups	119
Roast Beef and Avocado Salad Wraps	119
Vegetable Wraps with Lemony Zucchini Dressing	119
Pork, Apple, and Fennel Radicchio Wraps	120
Chicken Breast, Bacon and Kale Salad	120
Lime Watermelon Salad	120
Balsamic Tomato Salad	120
Greek Olives Salad	121
Cilantro-Lime Pork Tenderloin Salad	121
Tangy Brown Rice Salad with Jalapeño	121
Jerusalem Veggie Salad	121
Chicken Breast Salad	122
Oregano Lamb Chop Salad	122
Smoked Salmon Salad	123
Broiled Salmon Steak Salad	123
Oven-Roast Vegetable Salad	123
Kale and Green Olives Salad	124
Asian Cabbage Salad	124
Rosemary Cauliflower	124
Salmon and Baby Yellow Potato Salad	124
Tomato and Cucumber Salad	125
Beef Steak Fajita Salad	125
Carne Asada Salad	125
Fattoush	126
Oregano Chicken Breast and Kale Salad	126
Chicken Thighs Taco Salad	126
Pork and Olives Greek Salad	127
Chimichurri Pork Shoulder and Cabbage Salad	127
Mediterranean Chicken and Veggie Salad	127
Potato Salad with Chicken Sausage	128
Steak Salad with Charred Onions	128
Turkey Meatball and Lemon-Avocado Salad	128
Chicken Larb Salad	129
Warm Chicken Romaine Salad	129
Chicken, Watermelon, and Spinach Salad	129
Fruity Chicken Chopped Salad	130
Italian Chopped Salad with Grated Yolk	130
Ahi Tuna Mango Poke	130
Mayo Chicken Salad	131
Beef Taco Salad	131
Balsamic Peach Arugula Salad	131
Tuna, Snow Pea, and Broccoli Salad	132
Shrimp and Mango Salad	132
Beef Steak and Broccoli Salad	132

Chapter 10 Soups, Stews, and Noodle Bowls 133

Chili Beef with Sweet Potato	133
Brazilian Cod and Shrimp Stew	133
Curry Pork and Carrot Noodle Bowls	133
Thai Chicken and Potato-Noodle Bowls	134
Steak, Mushrooms, and Rutabaga-Noodle Bowls	134
Smoky Scallop and Zucchini Noodle Bowls	134
Mexican Shrimp and Zucchini Noodles Soup	135
Pork and Carrot-Noodle Bowls	135
Vegetable Soup with Basil-Nuts Pesto	135
Pork Tenderloin and Pepper Paprikash	136
Spring Asparagus Cream Soup	136
Mexican-Style Pork Shoulder Stew	136
Beef and Root Vegetable Stew	137
Moroccan Beef Meatball Stew	137
Pork Shoulder and Green Chile Stew	137
Chicken, Bacon and Mushroom Soup	138
Italian Beef and Veggie Soup	138
Carrot-Parsnip Soup with Bacon Crumble 10	138
Italian Chicken Sausage Soup	138
Gazpacho Shrimp and Zucchini Noodle Soup	139
Southwest Chicken and Potato Noodle Bowl	139
Chinese-Style Egg Drop Soup	139
Roasted Veggie Soup	139
Italian Chicken and Vegetable Soup	140
Thyme Chicken and Zoodle Soup	140
Chicken Thighs and Dumplings Soup	140
Chicken Sausage and Kale Stew	141
Beef and Bell Pepper Soup	141
Beef Fajita Soup	141
Turkey Sausage and Root Vegetable Soup	141
Creamy Broccoli and Kale Soup	142
Sweet Potatoes Pork Stew	142
Butternut Squash Pureed Soup	142
Simple Egg Drop Soup	142
Chicken and Vegetable Soup	143

Matzo Ball Soup with Dill and Parsley 143
Autumn Pumpkin Chili 143
Spicy and Sour Shrimp Soup 144
Pork and Napa Cabbage Soup............................ 144
Lush Chicken and Carrot Stew 144
Chicken Breast and Avocado Soup 145
Silky Broccoli Soup... 145
Cauliflower Soup with Sausage and Spinach...... 145
Turnip Leek Soup 146
Almond Chicken and Sweet Potatoes Stew 146
Winter Greens and Potato Soup........................... 146
Pork Loin Stew 147
Lush Shrimp Coconut Bowl 147
Mexican-Style Chicken Soup................................ 147

Chapter 11 Sauces, Dressings, and Dips 148

5-Ingredient Mayonnaise 148
Eggless Mayonnaise 148
Caesar-Style Salad Dressing 148
Ketchup For Whole30.. 148
Creamy Caramelized Green Onion Sauce 148
Arugula and Walnut Pesto.................................... 149
Jalapeño and Seeds Harissa Sauce 149
Asian Barbecue Sauce 149
Chile-Grapefruit and Cilantro Vinaigrette............. 149
Lemon Tahini Sauce 150
Strawberry-Chile Summer Vinaigrette 150
Sherry-Citrus Vinaigrette 150
Tangy Barbecue Sauce 150
Cashew Ranch Salad Dressing 151
Citrus-White Miso Dressing 151
Punchy Fig-Balsamic Dressing............................. 151
Almond Butter-Chile Sauce 151
Hot BBQ Tahini Sauce.. 151
Light Garlic Paste 151
Oil-Free Herb and Pine Nuts Pesto 152
No-Oil Great Red Sauce....................................... 152
Rich Cashew Cream Sauce 152
Roasted Red Peppers Sauce 152
Roasted Red Bell Pepper Sauce.......................... 153
Delicious Steak Sauce.. 153
Caramelized Garlic Paste 153
Mexican Guacamole 153
Spanish Romesco Sauce 154
Flavorful Ginger Sauce... 154
Simmered Classic Chili... 154
Versatile Chimichurri... 154
Dump Ranch Dressing 155
Homemade Fiery Cocktail Sauce......................... 155
Whole30- and Paleo-compliant mayonnaise........ 155
Salsa Sauce 155
Sunshine Dip 156
Pearl Onion, Mushroom, and Caper Sauce......... 156

Chapter 12 Spices and Rub 157

Vibrant and Umami-Rich Spice Blend 157
Go-To Spice Rub for BBQ 157
Super Spicy Jerk Rub... 157
Italian-Style Umami Spice Blend 157
Adobo Spice Blend 157
Bagel Be Gone Spice Blend 157
All-Purpose Blackening Spice 158
Montreal Steak Spice Blend 158
Asian-Style Umami Spice Blend........................... 158
Mexican Taco Seasoning 158
Spicy Seeds Blend 158
Shawarma Spice Blend 10 158

Chapter 13 Basics 159

Chicken Bone Broth.. 159
Marinated Red Onion 159
Beef Bone Broth 159
Clarified Butter.. 159
Smoky Hot Pepitas 160
Roasted Chicken Breasts and Thighs 160
Speedy Mayo Base 160
Compound Butter 160
Oven-Roasted Spaghetti Squash......................... 161
Raspberry and Rosemary Smash 161
Freshly Lemon Brewed Iced Tea......................... 161
Garlic Confit Baked... 161
Citrus Zinger... 161
South Africa Fruity Rooibos Iced Tea 161

Chapter 14 Beverages 162

Pickled Red Onion.. 162
Bubbly Melon-Berry Lemonade 162
Pink Fizzy Mocktail 162
Iced Peach Tea... 162
Choco-Vanilla Rooibos Hot Tea 162
Blood Orange and Lime Paloma 163
Peach-Orange Agua Fresca................................. 163
Raspberry-Lime Sparkling Water 163
Watermelon Puree and Lime Sparkling Water 163
White Tea and Fruit Sangria 163
Refreshing Mocktail Mule 163

Appendix 1: Measurement Conversion Chart..... 164
Appendix 2: Recipe Index.................................... 165

30-Day Whole Foods Meal Plan Challenge

Meal Plan	Breakfast	Lunch	Dinner	Motivational Quotes
Day-1	Spinach and Arugula Breakfast Hash	Citrus Beef Short Ribs	Shrimp with Vinaigrette and Salad	It does not matter how slowly you go, as long as you don't stop.

Time It Wisely

Eating the Whole30 way for a month is a commitment, and it may require some planning. I purposefully started mine after the holiday rush when I knew there wouldn't be too many celebrations, holidays to work around. Find a time that works for you, but don't use Thursday's happy hour as an excuse to put it off.

Day-2	Potato, Sausage and Bacon Breakfast Bites	Southwest Turkey Legs with Fruit Salad	Curry Pork and Carrot Noodle Bowls	Don't let a stumble in the road be the end of your journey.

Make a Plan, and Stick with It

The key to a successful diet is to plan so that no obstacle comes as a surprise. Get sweet cravings at work? Pack your meals and plenty of snacks ahead of time so you're not going hungry. Know you'll be eating out with a friend this week? Scope out the menu for compliant options before you go.

Day-3	Chia Seeds Pudding	Curried Lamb and Potatoes	Sautéed Lemony Kale with Almonds	Don't dig your grave with your own knife and fork.

Take a Closer Look at Nutrition Labels

Sure, it's easy to avoid the junk food aisle—but what's eye-opening is the number of artificial–read: not compliant–ingredients lurking in inconspicuous foods like processed meat. Spoiler alert: There are tons of added sugar hiding in your sliced ham. Carefully inspect your food for sneaky sugars like sucrose, dextrose and maltodextrin. Unsure of an ingredient? Say hello to Google search.

Day-4	Turkish-Inspired Poached Eggs	Meat Loaf with Sweet-Sour Glaze	Mediterranean Chicken Breast Wraps	When you eat crap, you feel crap. Keep going.

Leap, and the net will appear.

Give Yourself a Break

For most people, completing this 30-day meal plan successfully will come down to a choice of what is most important to you: spending less money on groceries or spending less time in the kitchen. For me, given my schedule during the week, I decided I would rather spend more money on time-saving ingredient shortcuts, such as pre-cut vegetables and rotisserie chicken.

| Day-5 | Potato, Sausage and Bacon Breakfast Bites | Balsamic and Herb Pork Tenderloin | Mexican Shrimp and Zucchini Noodles Soup | Take it one meal at a time. |

Discover New Recipes

It is the perfect time to have fun by trying new recipes. I discovered so many new favorites during the course of my 30-day Whole Foods. They all have recook value and I keep them in my personal recipe book and keep coming back to them every time I cook.

| Day-6 | Buffalo Chicken and Veggie Frittata | Instant Pot Turkey Chili with Avocado | Oven-Roasted Spaghetti Squash | When you feel like quitting, think about why you started. |

Remind Yourself It's Only 30 Days

There are days you're going to want to quit. As inspiration, I would go back to these words: "Don't you dare tell us this is hard. Beating cancer is hard. Birthing a baby is hard. Losing a parent is hard. Drinking your coffee black. Is. Not. Hard." You are worth 30 days of trying something new. Armed with these tips, I know you can do it.

| Day-7 | Green Vegetable and Fruit Smoothie | Pepperoncini-Flavour Skirt Steak | Balsamic-Glazed Salmon and Sweet Potatoes | If not now, when? |

Don't Binge Before You Start

"I'll start my diet on Monday" is something we all say to justify eating whatever we want. I've found that this is especially true for those who know they're going to be doing the 30-day Whole Foods and have set a date. While it's not a diet, it does still give people the feeling the world is ending and they need to cram as much food that they won't be eating into their mouth as fast as possible before they start. Don't do this. Just don't.

| Day-8 | Southwest Scrambled Eggs with Avocado | Chicken with Red Bell Pepper | Sheet Pan Shrimp with Roasted Broccoli | Fall seven times, stand up eight. |

Order First at the Restaurant, No Regrets

When you go out to eat, pick a healthy option and then put the menu down. When you stare at the menu, you can easily second guess yourself, and it can trigger you to veer off course. People also change their minds when they see or hear what others have ordered. Be firm and stay committed to your plans. Be the first to order and feel great about what you ordered.

Day-9	Light Taco Breakfast Casserole	Tahini Lamb with Almonds and Parsley	Bacon, Egg, and Veggie Salad	Every step is progress, no matter how small.

Do Make a Few Freezer Meals Before You Start

I'm not saying slave away in the kitchen stock piling freezer meals for all 30 days, but I do think having a few things ready to go is beneficial. If you have some spare time, make a casserole or meatballs and put them in the freezer for the days when you get home late, didn't get to the store or simply just don't feel like cooking. For even less work, throw a soup in the crock pot and freeze it in individual portions when it's done.

Day-10	Chia Seeds Pudding	Paprika Salmon	Thai Chicken and Potato-Noodle Bowls	One pound at a time.

Raid Your Cabinets

Junk food sitting around is junk food just waiting to be eaten. If it's within sight or within reach you're just asking for unnecessary temptations and tests of willpower. Before you start, go through your cabinets, cupboards and refrigerator. Toss out, freeze, pack away or donate anything that you don't need this month.

Day-11	Southern Fall Smoothie	Pork Loin Back Ribs with Mole Verde	Prosciutto and Shrimp Cabbage Cups	A year from now, you will wish you started today.

Don't Put Yourself in Tempting Situations

I'm not asking you to be a hermit and tuck yourself away in a dark basement for a month, but I am telling you to be cautious of the situations you willingly put yourself in. That means don't agree to go to your favorite restaurant where you always get fried chicken and waffles and think you will eat Whole Foods . Even if you might be able to, it's a risk that's not worth taking yet.

Day-12	Potato Croutons	Ritzy Short Rib Ragù	Pink Shrimp and Tomatoes with Pesto	With the new day comes new strength and new thoughts.

Have Strategies in Place for Your Social Life

Like I said, I'm not asking you to be a recluse. You don't have to avoid leaving the house, you just have to be smart about it! If you want a date night with your significant other, great! Do your research first and find a place you'll both be happy eating at.

Day-13	Scrambled Egg with Salmon	Whole Chicken with Steak Spice	Chinese-Style Egg Drop Soup	Quit slacking and make shit happen.

No Fake Treats

No recreating desserts or chips or cake or whatever. I just saw a pin for a Whole30 mocha and the article suggested adding ungodly amounts of cacao and using coconut milk to make froth to recreate your chocolatey, sugary morning drink at the coffee shop. Ummmmm no.

Day-14	Potato, Sausage and Bacon Breakfast Bites	Korean-Style Pot Roast with Jicama Salad	Twice-Fried Green Plantains	The past cannot be changed, the future is yet in your power.

Identify Your Personal 'Food With no Brakes' and Avoid Them

What foods are triggers to old binging or mindless eating habits are different for all of us. While some people are totally fine having almond butter here or there on fruit, it's a food I couldn't keep in the house.

Day-15	Mango and Pistachio Millet with Raspberry	Tahini Lamb with Almonds and Parsley	Mediterranean Calamari with Veggie	There's no such thing as failure: either you win, or you learn.

Leftovers, Leftovers, Leftovers

Leftovers will become your best friend. If you want an easy way to meal prep, doubling the batches of dinners you make and making that be your meal prep is a good way to go about it. It will help you reduce time spent on the whole one day meal prep strategy. Other than that, leftovers take the thinking out of what you're going to have for lunch tomorrow and make life (and decision making) a lot easier.

Day-16	Hearty Pacific Northwest Mushroom Hash	Skillet Seasoned Chicken Piccata	Dijon Salmon with Cashews	You will never win if you never begin.

Budget and Shop the Sales

It's no secret that healthy food is more expensive. It sucks, I know. I hate it too. But there's smart ways to shop so eating well doesn't have to break the bank. Some staple items like ghee, flours/starches, coconut aminos, and high quality oils will be necessary expenses but don't let the sticker shock scare you. Most of these things will last you a while.

Day-17	Potato Croutons	West African Suya Stir-Fry	Spring Asparagus Cream Soup	You are your only limit.

Physically Move Your Scale Out of Eyesight

So many people struggle with the rule forbidding you to weigh yourself. Even if you think you won't be tempted, you totally will be when day 20 rolls around and you're feeling ahhh-mazing. To avoid this problem all together, just do yourself a favor and put your scale up in a closet or in the trunk of your husband's car or on a high shelf in the garage.. anywhere but on the bathroom floor where you've weighed yourself everyday for years.

Day-18	Sausage with Eggs and Home Fries	Baby Back Ribs with Spiced Rub	Brussels Sprouts and Shallots Bowl	Success is no accident: it is hard work and perseverance.

Don't Make Weight Loss the Main Goal

If you're overweight, then yes losing weight is going to help make you healthier in the long run. But you shouldn't start this program with weight loss being your primary desired outcome. Health first, weight loss second.

Day-19	Green Vegetable and Fruit Smoothie	Brussels Sprouts and Shallots Bowl	Vegetable Wraps with Lemony Zucchini Dressing	What you plant now, you will harvest later.

Exercise

Moving around just helps us feel better. It relieves stress and boosts our mood. Even if it's just for a short walk outside, getting your mind off all things in a way that benefits your body can be really helpful.

Day-20	Southwest Egg Breakfast Bowls	Chicken with Kielbasa Stuffed Mushrooms	Lobster Mac Skillet	If you know you can do better, then do better.

Change Your Mindset

Think positively going into this. This is something to celebrate! No grumbling before even starting. Celebrate and get excited about the fact that you're taking control. You picked YOU and that's super awesome. No more passively letting things happen to you anymore. You're now in the front seat.

Day-21	Fingerling Potatoes with Spring Asparagus	Pan-Seared Beef Rib-Eye with Arugula	Mediterranean Calamari with Veggie	Never let your fear decide your future.

Sip on Herbal Teas

Non-caffeinated teas are a fun way to experience different tastes without eating garbage. Buy a tea sampler and instead of mid-meal snacks, drink some tea instead. Some of my favorite flavors are peppermint, rooibos, rosehip, lemon balm, and ginger.

Day-22	Baked Sausage Scotch Eggs	Cabbage and Pork Sausage Casserole	Creamy Broccoli and Kale Soup	It is never too late.

Eat More Soup

Counter to drinking meals from a cup, which tend to be full of sugars and mindlessly consumed, soup has been shown to be incredibly satiating. I love soup because you can make a ton of it, it's a great way to extend food, it's inexpensive, bone broth is a superfood, and you can pack a ton of vegetables into every bite.

Day-23	Mango and Pistachio Millet with Raspberry	Hawaiian Chicken and Pineapple Burgers	Greek Olives Salad	Leap, and the net will appear.

Keep it Simple.

Don't over meal plan or plan overly ambitious meals. Find recipes with 3-4 ingredient that you can mix-n-match throughout the week.

Day-24	Skillet Potatoes with Herbs	Green Curry Lamb Stew Meat	Balsamic Roasted Root Veggie	The secret of change is to focus all of your energy not on fighting the old, but on building the new.

Emergency Meals.

Have emergency food on hand! Things like hard-boiled eggs, salad mix and compliant dressing or a compliant rotisserie chicken will be your best friend. In a pinch I'll even eat an avocado.

Day-25	Bacon and Kale Frittata	Pork Shoulder Curry with Asparagus	Beef and Root Vegetable Stew	You get what you focus on, so focus on what you want.

Figure Out Your Go-To Foods:

Foods like eggs, frozen precooked shrimp, and frozen blueberries. By keeping all of these things in stock, I could whip up a quick meal if I didn't feel like cooking something huge. And the frozen blueberries were an awesome snack when I was feeling like I wanted some ice cream.

Day-26	Chia Seeds Pudding	Garlic Chicken Thighs Primavera	Pork and Olives Greek Salad	Yes, I can.

Eat Enough Protein

I notice that when folks cut out their morning toast, they forget to double up on their eggs. Most people are not eating enough protein. If you aim for at least 20% of your calories from protein on a 2,000 calorie diet, that's 100 grams. This means 4-6oz of eggs, fish, red meat or poultry at each meal. Animal protein is incredibly satiating, and full of easily absorbed vitamins and minerals. (Don't confuse grams of protein with weight of meat, these are different values.)

Day-27	Baby Spinach and Tomato Frittata	Beef Brisket Braised with Potatoes	Autumn Pumpkin Chili	Don't stop until you're proud.

Take it Easy on Fruit

you're trying to change your relationship with food and for many, this means turning off your sweet tooth. Swapping candy for multiple servings of fruit a day will not help you break your sugar addiction. Fruit is sugar. Dried fruit is even more concentrated sugar. Keep your fruit intake to one or two servings a day.

Day-28	Poached Pear	Pineapple Salmon Fillet	Fruity Chicken Chopped Salad	A little progress each day adds up to big results.

Avoid Drinking Your Meals

Although smoothies are technically allowed, I am not a fan of drinking calories. Science shows that your brain's normal satiety signals are bypassed when you gulp instead of chew. This means, people don't account for those calories later in the day, and end up eating more. Do yourself a favor, wake up five minutes earlier and make yourself some eggs or reheat some leftovers instead of bringing a smoothie along for your commute.

Day-29	Egg Florentine Cups	Italian Chicken Thighs with Fennel	Sautéed Kale with Pine Nuts	It has to be hard so you'll never ever forget.

Avoid Meal Fatigue.

It's not all about sweet potatoes, bacon and avocado. Do some pre-work and save recipes so you aren't stuck eating the same thing every day.

Day-30	Mango and Pistachio Millet with Raspberry	Asian Shrimp and Zucchini Noodles	Carne Asada Salad	If you have discipline, drive, and determination …nothing is impossible.

Sit Longer with Your Food

Sit down, relax, and appreciate your meal. Rushing to get the food down and watching TV while surfing Facebook is not going to help you change your relationship with food. Have a conversation with someone instead of staring at a screen. Give yourself a full 20 minutes to let your brain's satiety signals kick in before you rush up for seconds.

Chapter 1 Eggs

Scrambled Eggs with Mushrooms and Greens

Prep time: 10 minutes | Cook time: 9 minutes | Serves 2

- 2 tablespoon cooking fat
- ½ onion, finely chopped
- ½ bell pepper, any color, cut into strips
- 1 cup sliced button, cremini, or portabella mushrooms
- 1 cup chopped greens (kale, spinach, chard, or mustard greens)
- 6 large eggs, beaten
- 1 avocado, split lengthwise, pitted, peeled, and diced
- ¼ teaspoon salt
- ¼ teaspoon black pepper

1. Heat a large skillet over medium-low heat. Add the cooking fat and swirl to coat the bottom of the pan. When the fat is hot, add the onion, bell pepper, and mushrooms and cook, stirring, until the onions are translucent, 4 to 5 minutes.
2. Stir in the greens and cook until they begin to wilt (the time will vary depending on the type of green). Add the eggs and cook, stirring frequently and scraping the bottom and sides of the pan to prevent sticking, until the eggs are scrambled, fluffy, and still look wet but not runny, 5 to 7 minutes.
3. Remove the pan from the heat, top with the diced avocado, season with the salt and pepper, and serve.

Perfect Jammy Eggs

Prep time: 5 minutes | Cook time: 7½ minutes | Serves 6

- 1 tablespoon kosher salt
- 6 large eggs

1. Fill a medium saucepan with 2 quarts water, add the salt, and bring to a gentle boil over medium-high heat. Prepare a large bowl of ice water.
2. Carefully add the eggs to the boiling water and cook for 7½ minutes, adjusting the heat as necessary to prevent the water from boiling too rapidly and cracking the eggs. Immediately remove them from the water with a slotted spoon and gently transfer them to the bowl of the ice water. Let them rest for 1 minute.
3. Transfer the eggs to a cutting board. They will continue to cook in the shells, so work quickly. With the end of a butter knife, gently crack the shells, immediately peel the eggs, and cut each in half. Serve.

Bacon and Brussels Sprouts Frittata

Prep time: 10 minutes | Cook time: 33 minutes | Makes 1 (9-inch) frittata

- 5 slices bacon, chopped into 1-inch pieces
- 12 large eggs
- ¼ cup full-fat coconut milk
- 1½ teaspoons fine Himalayan salt, divided
- 1 teaspoon ground black pepper
- 1 teaspoon dried dill weed
- ½ onion, sliced
- 2 cups shredded Brussels sprouts
- 1 tablespoon Dijon mustard
- 1 tablespoon avocado oil

1. Preheat the oven to 350ºF (180ºC).
2. Heat a 9-inch oven-safe skillet over medium heat. Add the bacon pieces and cook, stirring occasionally, for 10 minutes, or until the bacon begins to crisp up.
3. In the meantime, in a large mixing bowl, whisk together the eggs, coconut milk, 1 teaspoon of the salt, the pepper, and the dill until light yellow, smooth, and frothy. Set aside.
4. When the bacon is done, add the onions and Brussels sprouts to the skillet. Mix well, cover, and cook for 3 minutes. Stir in the mustard, oil, and remaining ½ teaspoon of salt until well combined.
5. Pour in the egg mixture and cook undisturbed for about 5 minutes, until the edges begin to look cooked and dry and are separating from the skillet.
6. Carefully transfer the skillet to the middle rack of the oven. Bake for 15 minutes, then check for doneness. When the center is set, meaning it does not jiggle when the skillet is moved, the frittata is done. After 15 minutes, check every 2 minutes until it is set.
7. Remove the skillet from the oven and let the frittata cool for a few minutes.
8. Run a spatula around the edge of the frittata and a little under it to make sure it has not stuck to the skillet. To flip it out of the skillet, put a plate or cutting board over the top of the skillet and, in one swift motion, quickly flip it over. Cut the frittata into eight equal slices.
9. Store leftovers in an airtight container in the fridge for up to 1 week. Enjoy cold or reheat in a preheated 350ºF (180ºC) oven for 8 minutes.

Southwest Scrambled Eggs with Avocado

Prep time: 5 minutes | Cook time: 5 minutes | Serves 2

1 avocado, split lengthwise, pitted, and peeled	6 large eggs, beaten
2 tablespoons cooking fat	1 teaspoon salt
	½ teaspoon black pepper
	1 cup Salsa

1. Set the avocado halves flat side down on a cutting board and cut into thin slices.
2. Heat the cooking fat in a large skillet over medium heat. In a mixing bowl, whisk the eggs with the salt and pepper. When the oil is hot, add the eggs and cook, stirring and scraping the bottom and sides of the pan to prevent burning, until the eggs are scrambled, fluffy, and still look wet but not runny, 5 to 7 minutes.
3. Divide the eggs between 2 plates, top with the avocado, and spoon the salsa evenly over both portions.
4. Serve with steamed spinach and pan-fried plantains; or last night's leftover veggies and a side of berries.

Egg Salad with Fresh Dill

Prep time: 5 minutes | Cook time: 12 minutes | Serves 4 or 5

10 large eggs	Vidalia onion
⅔ cup whole30- and paleo-compliant mayonnaise	½ cup finely chopped fresh dill
½ cup finely chopped	½ teaspoon kosher salt, plus more as needed

1. Fill a large bowl with ice and water and set it nearby.
2. Bring a large pot of water to a boil over high heat. Using a slotted spoon, slowly lower the eggs into the water, being careful not to crack them on the bottom of the pot. Cook the eggs for exactly 12 minutes for hard yolks and whites. Transfer the eggs to the ice bath and let cool for at least 5 minutes.
3. Peel the eggs. Using a cheese grater, grate each egg into a medium bowl. (Alternatively, you can push them through the holes of a wire rack to quickly "chop" them.)
4. Add the mayonnaise, onion, dill, and salt. Stir to thoroughly combine. Taste and adjust the salt as desired. Serve, or cover and store in the refrigerator for up to 5 days.

Turkish-Inspired Poached Eggs

Prep time: 10 minutes | Cook time: 8 minutes | Serves 2

¼ cup ghee	For The "Coconut "Fauxgurt":
1 teaspoon Aleppo pepper	1 (13½-ounce / 382.7-g) can full-fat coconut milk, refrigerated overnight
1 garlic clove, finely chopped	2 probiotic capsules (not pills or tablets)
4 large eggs	
½ cup torn fresh dill, for garnish	

Make the Coconut Fauxgurt
1. Without shaking the can, carefully open it and spoon 1 cup of the solidified white cream into a mason jar (save any remaining coconut cream and the coconut water left in the can for another use). Add the contents of the probiotic capsules to the jar and stir together with a nonreactive spoon (such as one made from plastic or wood). Cover the jar with cheesecloth and let stand at room temperature for 48 hours, until slightly thickened. Transfer the fauxgurt to the refrigerator until ready to use. (It will keep in the refrigerator for up to 5 days.)

Make the Eggs

2. In a small saucepan, stir together the ghee and Aleppo pepper. Melt the ghee over medium-low heat, about 3 minutes. Reduce the heat to its lowest setting to keep the mixture warm until ready to serve.
3. In a small bowl, whisk together 1 cup "fauxgurt" and garlic. Set aside.
4. Bring a medium saucepan of water to a very gentle simmer, around 185°F, over medium heat.
5. Crack an egg into a fine-mesh strainer set over a bowl and give it a swirl to separate any of the scraggly whites. Using a large spoon, swirl the water in the pot to create a vortex. While the water is swirling, carefully add the egg. Repeat this process with each egg until they are all in the pot. Cook until the egg whites are firm and the yolks are still soft, 4 to 5 minutes. Stir the water occasionally to keep the eggs from coming in contact with the bottom of the pot.
6. Using a slotted spoon, carefully remove each egg from the water and transfer 2 eggs to each serving bowl, making sure not to puncture the yolks. Spoon the garlicky "fauxgurt" over the top of the eggs and drizzle with the Aleppo-spiced ghee. Garnish with the dill and serve immediately.

Buffalo Chicken and Veggie Frittata

Prep time: 10 minutes | Cook time: 20 minutes | Serves 8

2 tablespoons extra-virgin olive oil
¼ cup diced yellow onion
2 stalks celery, diced
1 clove garlic, minced
1½ cups shredded cooked chicken
10 large eggs
⅓ cup Whole30-compliant hot sauce, plus more for serving
¼ teaspoon salt
¼ teaspoon cayenne pepper
Sliced green onions (optional)

1. Preheat the oven to 400ºF (205ºC).
2. In a 10-inch cast iron or other ovenproof skillet, heat the olive oil. Add the onion, celery, and garlic. Cook, stirring frequently, until tender, 5 to 7 minutes. Remove from the heat. Spread in the skillet and top with the chicken.
3. In a large bowl, whisk together the eggs, hot sauce, salt, and cayenne. Pour over the chicken. Bake until the middle is set, 15 to 20 minutes.
4. Let stand for 10 minutes. Run a knife around the edge of the pan. If desired, top with the green onions and additional hot sauce. Cut into wedges.

Light Taco Breakfast Casserole

Prep time: 15 minutes | Cook time: 40 minutes | Serves 8

2 tablespoons extra-virgin olive oil
½ cup diced yellow onion
1 pound (454 g) lean ground beef or turkey
1 teaspoon Whole30-compliant chili powder
½ teaspoon onion powder
½ teaspoon garlic powder
½ teaspoon dried oregano
¼ teaspoon smoked paprika
¼ teaspoon ground cumin
¾ teaspoon salt
10 large eggs
¾ cup Whole30-compliant salsa, plus more for serving (optional)
½ teaspoon black pepper
1 avocado, halved, pitted, peeled, and sliced (optional)
Chopped fresh cilantro (optional)

1. Preheat the oven to 350ºF (180ºC).
2. In a large skillet, heat 1 tablespoon of the olive oil over medium-high heat. Add the onion and meat. Cook, stirring with a wooden spoon to break up the meat, until browned, about 10 minutes. Add the chili powder, onion powder, garlic powder, oregano, paprika, cumin, and ¼ teaspoon of the salt. Stir and set aside.
3. Crack the eggs into a large bowl; whisk until blended. Add the remaining ½ teaspoon salt, the salsa, and the pepper. Stir to combine.
4. lightly coat the sides and bottom of a 2-quart baking dish with the remaining 1 tablespoon olive oil. Spread the cooked meat and onion on the bottom of the pan. Pour the egg mixture over the meat. Bake for 30 to 35 minutes, until cooked through.
5. Let stand for 10 minutes before serving. Run a knife around the edge of the dish. Cut into squares. To serve, top with avocado slices, salsa, and/or cilantro, if desired.

Mushroom, Leek, and Spinach Frittata

Prep time: 10 minutes | Cook time: 10 minutes | Serves 2 or 3

2 medium leeks (white and light green parts only)
6 large eggs, lightly beaten
1 tablespoon full-fat coconut milk
2 teaspoons fresh thyme, finely chopped, or ½ teaspoon dried thyme, crushed
¼ teaspoon salt
¼ teaspoon red pepper flakes
2 tablespoons extra-virgin olive oil
1½ cups sliced fresh mushrooms
1 (about 6-ounce / 170-g) bag baby spinach, roughly chopped
1 clove garlic, minced
2 tablespoons thinly sliced green onions

1. Trim the roots and wilted leaves from the leeks. Cut the leeks in half lengthwise, then cut them crosswise into ¼-inch-thick pieces. Rinse well with cold water. Drain and dry the leeks and set aside.
2. Preheat the broiler. In a medium bowl, combine the eggs, coconut milk, thyme, salt, and red pepper flakes; set aside.
3. Heat the olive oil in a large oven-safe skillet over medium heat; add the leeks and mushrooms and cook, stirring frequently, until softened, 5 to 8 minutes. Add the spinach and garlic and let the spinach wilt for 30 seconds.
4. Pour the egg mixture into the skillet and cook over medium heat. As the egg mixture sets, run a spatula around edge of skillet, lifting the cooked egg so the uncooked egg flows underneath. Cook until the egg is beginning to set (the surface will still be moist).
5. Transfer the pan with the eggs to the oven and broil 4 to 5 inches from the heat (or bake in the preheated oven for 1 to 3 minutes), until the top is set and lightly browned. Top with the green onions. Cut into wedges and serve hot, directly out of the pan.

Eggs with Cabbage and Prosciutto

Prep time: 5 minutes | Cook time: 10 minutes | Serves 1

1 tablespoon coconut oil or avocado oil
2 cups medium head cabbage, sliced
2 slices prosciutto, ham, or bacon
2 large eggs
½ teaspoon fine Himalayan salt

1. Heat an 8-inch skillet or griddle over medium heat. When it's hot, melt the oil in the skillet, swirling it around to grease the entire surface.
2. Add the cabbage, distributing it evenly over the whole skillet in one even layer. Let it cook undisturbed for about 5 minutes, until the bottom of the cabbage browns. Move the cabbage to one side of the skillet, forming a little mound.
3. Put the prosciutto slices on the other side of the skillet and cook for 2 to 3 minutes, until crispy, flipping once. Then push the prosciutto to the side, snuggled up against the cabbage.
4. Crack the eggs into the remaining space in the skillet and sprinkle everything with the salt. Let the eggs cook for 2 to 3 minutes, until the whites are no longer translucent and the edges are crispy. If the eggs look done except for little pools of raw white near the yolk, use a spatula to gently distribute the loose egg white over the cooked egg parts until they too are cooked.
5. Serve right away. You can even eat it right out of the skillet! If you have leftovers, store them covered in the fridge for up to 3 days.

Deviled Eggs with Smoked Paprika

Prep time: 10 minutes | Cook time: 12 minutes | Serves 12

12 large eggs
½ cup whole30- and paleo-compliant mayonnaise
1½ tablespoons Dijon mustard
Kosher salt, to taste
¼ cup capers packed in brine, drained, for garnish
¼ cup loosely packed fresh dill, finely chopped
1 teaspoon smoked paprika, for garnish

1. Fill a large bowl with ice and water and set it nearby.
2. Bring a large pot of water to a boil over high heat. Using a slotted spoon, slowly lower the eggs into the water, being careful not to crack them on the bottom of the pot. Cook the eggs for exactly 12 minutes for hard yolks and whites. Transfer the eggs to the ice bath and let cool for at least 5 minutes.
3. Peel the eggs and slice them in half lengthwise. Gently separate the yolks from the whites and place them in separate medium bowls. Set the whites aside.
4. Transfer the yolks from the bowl to a fine-mesh strainer and use a spoon to gently push them through back into the bowl. Add the mayonnaise and mustard, season with salt, and mix until completely smooth.
5. Arrange the egg whites cut-side up on a platter. Transfer the yolk mixture to a piping bag fitted with a wide star tip and pipe about 1 tablespoon of the mixture into each of the egg whites. (If you don't have a piping bag, transfer the yolk mixture to a zip-top plastic bag and cut a small bit of one corner off.)
6. Garnish the deviled eggs with the capers and dill. Dust each with a pinch of the paprika and serve.

Baked Sausage Scotch Eggs

Prep time: 15 minutes | Cook time: 24 minutes | Serves 6

2 teaspoons extra-virgin olive oil
¼ cup minced yellow onion
2 pounds (907 g) 85% lean ground turkey, chicken, or beef
½ cup minced apple
¼ cup finely chopped fresh sage
1 teaspoon dried marjoram leaves, crushed
1 teaspoon coarse salt
½ teaspoon black pepper
¼ teaspoon ground cinnamon
¼ teaspoon red pepper flakes (optional)
⅛ teaspoon ground ginger
12 large hard-cooked eggs, peeled
Avocado oil, clarified butter or ghee (optional)
Whole30-compliant coarse-grain mustard, for serving

1. Preheat the oven to 350°F (180°C). Line a large rimmed baking pan with parchment paper.
2. In a small skillet, heat the olive oil over medium heat. Add the onion and cook until tender, 4 to 5 minutes. Transfer the onion to a large bowl. Add the turkey, apple, sage, marjoram, salt, black pepper, cinnamon, red pepper flakes (if using), and ginger. Gently mix until well combined.
3. Divide the meat mixture into 12 equal portions. Form each portion into a ¼-inch-thick patty. For each Scotch egg, place the egg in the middle of the patty; enclose the egg in the meat, rolling to smooth the surface and seal any seams. Arrange the eggs on the pan at least 1 inch apart. Bake until the sausage is cooked through and lightly browned, 20 to 25 minutes.
4. Let cool completely. Store in an airtight container in a cooler or refrigerator until serving time.

Classic Shakshuka

Prep time: 10 minutes | Cook time: 25 minutes | Serves 2

2 tablespoons extra-virgin olive oil
½ cup chopped onion
1 cup chopped red bell pepper
4 cloves garlic, minced
1 (28-ounce / 794-g) can Whole30-compliant fire-roasted crushed tomatoes
1 to 2 tablespoons Whole30-compliant harissa
1 teaspoon ground cumin
½ teaspoon salt
6 large eggs
Black pepper, to taste
3 tablespoons chopped fresh parsley

1. Heat the oil in a large skillet over medium heat. Add the onion and cook, stirring, until slightly wilted, about 2 minutes. Add the bell pepper and garlic and cook, stirring, until the onion and pepper are tender, 4 to 5 minutes more. Add the tomatoes, harissa, cumin, and salt; bring to a boil. Reduce the heat to low and simmer, stirring occasionally, until the sauce has thickened, 10 to 15 minutes.
2. Use the back of a spoon to make six depressions in the sauce. Crack one egg into a small bowl and carefully slide the egg into one depression in the sauce. Repeat with the remaining eggs. Cook, covered, until the egg whites are completely cooked and the yolks begin to thicken but are not hard, 6 to 8 minutes. Remove from the heat. Season with black pepper and sprinkle with the parsley before serving.

Egg Florentine Cups

Prep time: 10 minutes | Cook time: 30 minutes | Serves 6

1 tablespoon ghee, plus more for greasing
1 shallot, finely chopped
½ red bell pepper, diced
Kosher salt and freshly ground black pepper, to taste
3 cups loosely packed baby spinach, finely chopped
11 large eggs
½ cup full-fat coconut milk
4 ounces (113 g) no-sugar-added smoked salmon, thinly sliced into ribbons

1. Preheat the oven to 325ºF (163ºC). Grease a 12-cup muffin tin with ghee and set it on a rimmed baking sheet to catch any spills.
2. In a large nonstick skillet, melt the ghee over medium heat. Add the shallot and bell pepper, season with a pinch each of salt and black pepper, and cook, stirring, until the vegetables are slightly softened, about 3 minutes. Add the spinach and cook, stirring, until wilted, about 2 minutes. Taste and adjust the salt and pepper as desired. Remove the pan from the heat.
3. In a large bowl, whisk together the eggs and coconut milk until thoroughly combined and smooth.
4. Using a spoon, distribute the vegetable mixture evenly among the prepared muffin cups. Divide the sliced salmon evenly over the vegetables, then ladle the egg mixture over the top. Bake until a toothpick or cake tester inserted into the center of an egg cup comes out clean, about 25 minutes.
5. Serve immediately, or let cool, transfer to an airtight container, and store in the refrigerator for up to 4 days.

Bistro Curly Endive and Egg Salad

Prep time: 10 minutes | Cook time: 20 minutes | Serves 2

4 cups packed curly endive
1½ tablespoons extra-virgin olive oil
1 tablespoon apple cider vinegar
1 teaspoon Whole30-compliant Dijon mustard
¼ teaspoon minced garlic
Salt and black pepper, to taste
4 slices Whole30-compliant bacon, cut into ¼-inch pieces
2 teaspoons white vinegar
4 large eggs

1. Wash and dry the endive. Place in a shallow salad bowl and chill until needed.
2. Combine the oil, apple cider vinegar, mustard, and garlic in a small jar with a lid. Season with salt and pepper. Cover and shake vigorously to combine. Set aside.
3. Cook the bacon in a small amount of water in a small skillet over medium-high heat for 5 minutes. Drain the bacon and dry the skillet. Return the bacon to the dry skillet and cook over medium heat until browned and crisp.
4. Meanwhile, fill a wide saucepan with 3 inches of water. Add the white vinegar and 1 teaspoon salt. Bring to a boil over high heat. Crack each egg into a separate small bowl or cup. Gently pour each egg into the boiling water. Remove the pan from the heat, cover, and let sit until the whites are firm but the yolks are still runny, about 4 minutes. Remove the poached eggs from the skillet with a slotted spoon and place on a paper towel-lined plate to drain.
5. Drizzle the endive with the vinaigrette, tossing to coat well. Divide the endive between two plates. Top each with two poached eggs and sprinkle with the bacon. Season with pepper and serve immediately.

Charred Tomatillo Salsa Over Omelet

Prep time: 10 minutes | Cook time: 45 minutes | Serves 2

Charred Tomatillo Salsa:
- 3 cloves garlic, unpeeled
- 4 tomatillos, husked, rinsed, and dried
- 1 medium poblano chile, stemmed, seeded, and quartered
- ½ small onion, cut into thin wedges
- 2 tablespoons snipped fresh cilantro
- 1 tablespoon fresh lime juice
- ½ teaspoon coarse salt
- ¼ teaspoon ground cumin

Omelet:
- 4 teaspoons extra-virgin olive oil
- 2 green onions, thinly sliced
- ½ cup thin bite-size strips green bell pepper
- 6 large eggs
- 2 tablespoons water
- ¼ teaspoon coarse salt
- ¼ teaspoon black pepper
- 1 cup coarsely chopped baby spinach

1. Make the salsa: Wrap the garlic in aluminum foil. Place the packet on a rack in the lower third of the oven. Adjust top oven rack to 4 or 5 inches from the broiler. Preheat the broiler. Line a baking pan with foil and combine the tomatillos, poblano, and onion on the pan. Place the pan on the top oven rack and broil for 8 to 10 minutes, turning the tomatillos once or twice, until the tomatillos and poblano skins are charred. Place the pan on a wire rack. Bring the foil up and around vegetables to fully enclose them. Let stand until cool. Change the oven setting to 400ºF (205ºC). Roast the garlic for 10 minutes more, then set on a wire rack to cool. Using a sharp knife, peel the skin off the cooled poblano quarters. Peel the cooled garlic. In a food processor, combine the poblano, tomatillos, onion, and garlic. Pulse until finely chopped. Transfer to a medium bowl. Stir in the cilantro, lime, juice, salt, and cumin.
2. Make the omelet: Heat 2 teaspoons of the olive oil in an 8-inch ceramic nonstick skillet with flared sides over medium heat. Add the green onions, reserving some of the green tops for garnish, and the bell pepper and cook, stirring occasionally, until the pepper is crisp-tender, 3 to 5 minutes. Transfer the bell pepper mixture to a small bowl.
3. Meanwhile, in a 2-cup glass measure, beat the eggs, water, salt, and black pepper until well combined. In the same skillet, heat 1 teaspoon of the olive oil over medium heat. Add half the egg mixture to the skillet. Cook and stir the eggs, pushing the cooked portion toward the center with a spatula and allowing the uncooked egg to flow under, until the eggs are set and have formed an even layer in the skillet. Spoon half the bell pepper mixture and half the spinach over one side of the egg. Fold the opposite side over the filling. Transfer the omelet to a serving plate and keep warm. Repeat with the remaining olive oil, egg mixture, bell pepper mixture, and spinach to make a second omelet.
4. Spoon ¼ cup of the charred tomatillo salsa over each omelet. Top with the reserved green onion.

Smoky Shrimp Omelet with Arugula

Prep time: 10 minutes | Cook time: 7 minutes | Serves 2

- 6 large eggs
- 1½ teaspoons fine Himalayan salt, divided
- 1 teaspoon ground black pepper
- 1 teaspoon liquid smoke
- ¼ cup garlic confit, with oil
- ¾- to 1-pound (340- to 454-g) large shrimp, peeled and deveined
- 2 teaspoons avocado oil, divided
- 1 cup arugula

1. Place the eggs, ½ teaspoon of the salt, the pepper, and the liquid smoke in a large mixing bowl. Whisk until frothy, then set aside.
2. Heat a 6-inch skillet over medium heat. When it's hot, place the confit in the skillet, quickly followed by the shrimp. Add the remaining teaspoon of salt and sauté for 2 to 3 minutes, until the shrimp are pink and beginning to coil. Then transfer everything from the skillet to a plate. Don't clean the pan.
3. In the same skillet, quickly add 1 teaspoon of the avocado oil, swirl it around, and pour in half of the whisked eggs. Once the bottom is no longer translucent, add 6 shrimp and half of the garlic. Cover the skillet with a tight-fitting lid and cook for 4 to 5 minutes.
4. Remove the lid and pick up the skillet to swirl the contents around for 30 seconds. There will be a thin layer of egg still fluid on the top, and moving it around like this will spread that layer out over the top of the omelet so it will finish cooking while leaving the omelet slightly moist. (If you like a dry omelet, you can pop it under the broiler for 1 to 2 minutes.)
5. Run a spatula along the edge of the omelet and slide it onto a plate. Put the skillet back on the stove and use the remaining ingredients to make the second omelet in the same way, starting with adding the remaining teaspoon of avocado oil.
6. Top each omelet with ½ cup arugula and serve right away. (I do not recommend making this to serve later as reheating will brown the eggs and overcook the shrimp.)

Bacon and Kale Frittata

Prep time: 10 minutes | Cook time: 40 minutes | Serves 4

4 slices bacon, thinly sliced
8 large eggs
¼ cup full-fat coconut milk
¼ cup finely chopped kale stems
Kosher salt and freshly ground black pepper, to taste
½ red bell pepper, diced
1 shallot, diced
1 large Roma (plum) tomato, thinly sliced

1. Preheat the oven to 325ºF (163ºC).
2. Place the bacon slices in a 10-inch oven-safe nonstick or cast-iron skillet and set it over medium heat. Cook, turning the bacon once or twice, until golden brown and slightly crispy, about 6 minutes. Transfer to paper towels to drain excess grease and set aside. Pour off all but 2 tablespoons of the rendered bacon fat in the skillet.
3. In a medium bowl, whisk together the eggs and coconut milk until thoroughly combined and smooth. Set aside.
4. Return the skillet to medium heat, add the kale stems, and season with salt and black pepper. Cook, stirring, until slightly softened, 3 to 4 minutes. Add the bell pepper and shallot and cook, stirring, for 2 minutes more, until softened. Pour the egg mixture into the pan and add the bacon. Gently stir to evenly distribute the ingredients.
5. Top with the tomato slices and transfer the pan to the oven. Cook for 20 to 25 minutes, until a toothpick or cake tester inserted into the center comes out clean. Serve immediately.

Persian Herby Frittata

Prep time: 15 minutes | Cook time: 16 minutes | Makes 1 (8-inch) frittata

4 tablespoons avocado oil or olive oil, divided
1 large onion, diced
2 cloves garlic, minced
1 green onion, white part only, minced
6 large eggs
1 teaspoon baking powder
1 teaspoon dried dill weed
1 teaspoon turmeric powder
½ teaspoon fine Himalayan salt
½ teaspoon ginger powder
1 cup minced fresh cilantro
1 cup minced fresh parsley
½ cup minced fresh basil

1. Heat an 8-inch skillet over medium or medium-low heat. If your stove runs hot, adjust the temperature; you don't want the bottom of the frittata to burn. When the skillet is hot, pour in 2 tablespoons of the avocado oil. Add the onions, garlic, and green onions and cook, stirring often, for 8 minutes, or until tender, translucent, and aromatic. Remove the onion mix from the skillet and set aside to cool. Put the skillet back on the stove over medium heat.
2. In a large bowl, whisk together the eggs, baking powder, seasonings, and fresh herbs. Add the cooled onion mix.
3. Turn on the broiler and set an oven rack just below it.
4. Drizzle the remaining 2 tablespoons of avocado oil into the skillet and pour in the egg mixture. Cover with a tight-fitting lid. Cook for 7 minutes, or until the edges of the frittata begin to separate from the skillet and the frittata is almost set but still wet in the center. Then remove the lid and place the skillet under the broiler for 1 to 2 minutes. Watch it carefully; you only need to broil it until the center is just set.
5. Remove the frittata from the oven. Run a spatula around the edge of the frittata and carefully shake it out of the skillet and onto a cutting board. Cut into four pieces, serve, and share.
6. Once the frittata has cooled to room temperature, you can store it in an airtight container in the refrigerator for up to 5 days. Enjoy the leftovers cold or gently warmed up in a 300ºF (150ºC) oven for 5 minutes.

Scrambled Egg with Salmon

Prep time: 5 minutes | Cook time: 10 minutes | Serves 3 or 4

8 large eggs
2 tablespoons ghee or grass-fed butter
4 ounces (113 g) no-sugar-added smoked salmon, thinly sliced into ribbons
2 tablespoons finely chopped fresh chives
Freshly ground black pepper, to taste

1. In a medium bowl, whisk the eggs vigorously until smooth.
2. In an 8-inch nonstick skillet, melt the ghee over medium-low heat, about 1 minute. Pour in the eggs and, using a spatula, gently drag the eggs from the outer edges of the pan toward the center. Cook, repeating this motion, until the eggs are only slightly runny, about 2 minutes. Add the salmon and cook, continuing to drag the eggs toward the center, until the eggs are cooked to the desired consistency, about 1 minute more.
3. Garnish with the chives, season with pepper, and serve immediately.

Sweet Potato Stacks with Hot Sauce

Prep time: 5 minutes | Cook time: 20 minutes | Serves 2

2 tablespoons extra-virgin olive oil
1 medium sweet potato, peeled and cut into eight ½-inch-thick rounds
¼ teaspoon salt
¼ teaspoon black pepper
2 teaspoons white vinegar
4 large eggs
1 clove garlic, minced
4 cups baby spinach
4 slices Whole30-compliant bacon, cooked until crisp
Whole30-compliant hot sauce, for serving

1. Heat 1 tablespoon of the olive oil in a large skillet over medium heat. Add the sweet potato rounds in a single layer and cook until fork-tender and browned on both sides, 3 to 5 minutes per side. Remove the sweet potatoes from the skillet and sprinkle with ⅛ teaspoon of the salt and ⅛ teaspoon of the pepper.
2. Meanwhile, fill a wide saucepan with 3 inches of water. Add the vinegar and bring to a boil over high heat. Crack each egg into a separate small bowl. Gently slide each egg into the boiling water. Remove the pan from the heat, cover, and let sit for 3 minutes for very soft yolks or 5 minutes for firm yolks. Remove the cooked eggs from the pan with a slotted spoon and place on a paper towel-lined plate to drain.
3. Heat the remaining 1 tablespoon oil in the large skillet over medium heat. Add the garlic and cook, stirring, until fragrant, about 30 seconds. Stir in the spinach and cook, stirring, until wilted, about 1 minute. Stir in the remaining ⅛ teaspoon salt and ⅛ teaspoon pepper.
4. On each plate, top four of the cooked sweet potato rounds with spinach, bacon, and two poached eggs. Serve with hot sauce for drizzling.

Baby Spinach and Tomato Frittata

Prep time: 10 minutes | Cook time: 10 to 15 minutes | Serves 2

6 large eggs, beaten
¼ teaspoon salt
¼ teaspoon black pepper
2 tablespoons cooking fat
½ onion, diced
1 cup diced seeded tomato (plus a few slices for topping the frittata)
1 (about 9-ounce / 255-g) bag baby spinach, roughly chopped
Grated zest and juice of ¼ lemon

1. Set the oven to broil.
2. In a mixing bowl, whisk the eggs with the salt and pepper.
3. Heat a large oven-safe skillet over medium heat. Add the cooking fat to the pan and swirl to coat the bottom. When the fat is hot, add the onion and tomato and cook, stirring, until softened, 2 to 3 minutes. Add the spinach and let it wilt for 30 seconds. Add the eggs and fold them into the vegetables with a rubber spatula. Cook, without stirring to let the eggs set on the bottom and sides of the pan, until the eggs are firm and still appear wet, 3 to 4 minutes. Lay a few tomato slices on top. Drizzle the lemon juice and sprinkle the lemon zest over the top.
4. Transfer the pan with the eggs to the oven and broil 4 to 6 inches from the heat (or bake in the preheated oven) for 3 to 5 minutes, until the top is golden brown. Cut into slices and serve hot out of the pan.

Soft-Boiled Scotch Eggs

Prep time: 10 minutes | Cook time: 33 minutes | Makes 8 eggs

6 cups water
8 large eggs
10 pork sausag, uncooked
2 tablespoons avocado oil
2 tablespoons shelled hemp seeds (aka hemp hearts) (optional)
1 teaspoon fine Himalayan salt

1. Preheat the oven to 400°F (205°C).
2. Bring the water to a rapid boil in a large pot. Gently place the eggs in the water and cook for 8 minutes.
3. Meanwhile, form the sausage mix into eight ¼-inch-thick, 4-inch-diameter patties. Place them on a sheet of parchment paper or a cutting board and set aside.
4. When the eggs are done, drain the hot water from the pot, leaving the eggs in it, then fill the pot with cold water and ice. Let the eggs chill in the ice bath for 2 minutes, then immediately peel them under the cold water.
5. Wrap the eggs: Place a pork patty in one hand. Using your other hand, place an egg in the center of the patty. Close your hand holding the pork around the egg and use your other hand to pinch the sausage closed. Gently shape the Scotch egg with both hands until it's smooth and even. Place the egg on a sheet pan, seam side down. Repeat with the remaining eggs and pork patties.
6. Brush or spray the eggs with the oil. Sprinkle with the hemp seeds (if using) and salt. Bake for 25 minutes.
7. Remove from the oven and dig in! Or you can let the eggs cool and store in an airtight container in the refrigerator for up to 5 days. I eat the leftovers cold, with a smear of homemade mayo on top.

Butternut Squash Frittata

Prep time: 10 minutes | Cook time: 15 minutes | Serves 2

1 cup firmly packed fresh basil leaves
¼ cup pine nuts or chopped walnuts, toasted
3 cloves garlic, chopped
1 tablespoon nutritional yeast (optional)
¼ teaspoon coarse salt
¼ teaspoon black pepper
4 tablespoons extra-virgin olive oil
1 small red or green bell pepper, cut into thin bite-size strips
¼ cup very thinly sliced onion
6 large eggs
⅓ cup thawed frozen puréed butternut squash

1. Preheat the oven to 375°F (190°C).
2. In a food processor, combine the basil, nuts, garlic, nutritional yeast (if using), ⅛ teaspoon of the salt, and ⅛ teaspoon of the black pepper. Cover and pulse until very finely chopped. With the food processor running, pour 3 tablespoons of the oil through the feed tube, processing until well combined and nearly smooth.
3. Heat the remaining 1 tablespoon oil in an oven-safe 6-inch nonstick skillet with flared sides over medium heat. Add the bell pepper and onion and cook, stirring occasionally, until the vegetables are tender, about 5 minutes. Meanwhile, in a medium bowl, whisk together the eggs, squash, remaining ⅛ teaspoon salt, and remaining ⅛ teaspoon black pepper.
4. Reduce the heat under the skillet to medium-low. Add the egg mixture and cook, without stirring, until the eggs begin to set. Cook, stirring, for 1 minute more. Remove the skillet from the heat. Spoon half the pesto in mounds onto the egg mixture; fold gently to partially mix the pesto into the egg. Spread the egg mixture into an even layer.
5. Transfer to the oven and bake for 6 to 9 minutes, until completely set. Let sit for 5 minutes before serving. Cut into four wedges. Divide the wedges between two serving plates. Top evenly with the remaining pesto.

Bacon, Spinach, and Tomato Breakfast Salad

Prep time: 10 minutes | Cook time: 15 minutes | Serves 2

6 cups baby spinach (about 6 ounces / 170 g)
1 ripe avocado, halved, pitted, peeled, and sliced
½ cup grape or cherry tomatoes, halved
4 slices Whole30-compliant bacon
1 small shallot, finely chopped
3 tablespoons extra-virgin olive oil
2 tablespoons red wine vinegar
¼ teaspoon dry mustard
⅛ teaspoon black pepper
2 teaspoons white vinegar
1 teaspoon salt
4 large eggs
Sliced green onions (optional)

1. Divide the spinach, avocado, and tomatoes between two serving bowls.
2. Cook the bacon until browned and crisp in a large skillet over medium heat. Drain the bacon on paper towels, reserving 3 tablespoons of the drippings in the skillet. Crumble the bacon and set aside.
3. Cook the shallot in the reserved bacon drippings over medium heat, stirring frequently, until tender, about 3 minutes. Remove from the heat; whisk in the oil, red wine vinegar, dry mustard, and pepper.
4. Meanwhile, fill a wide saucepan with 3 inches of water. Add the white vinegar and salt and bring to a boil over high heat. Crack each egg into a separate small bowl. Gently slide each egg into the boiling water. Remove the pan from the heat, cover, and let sit for 3 minutes for very soft yolks or 5 minutes for firm yolks. Remove the cooked eggs from the pan with a slotted spoon and place on a paper towel-lined plate to drain.
5. Top each bowl of the spinach mixture with two poached eggs and divide the crumbled bacon and the dressing evenly between them. If desired, sprinkle with green onions.

Fried Eggs with Veggie

Prep time: 10 minutes | Cook time: 15 minutes | Serves 2

6 tablespoons extra-virgin olive oil
2 cups sliced fresh mushrooms
12 ounces (340 g) fresh green beans, trimmed and cut into 2-inch pieces
1 sprig fresh thyme
1 clove garlic, minced
1 teaspoon salt
4 cups arugula
6 large eggs
½ teaspoon grated lemon zest
1 tablespoon fresh lemon juice
2 tablespoons finely chopped shallot
Black pepper, to taste

1. Heat 2 tablespoons of the olive oil in a large nonstick skillet over high heat. Add the mushrooms and cook, stirring occasionally, until just beginning to brown, about 3 minutes. Reduce the heat to medium and stir in the green beans, thyme, garlic, and ½ teaspoon of the salt. Cook, stirring frequently, for 2 minutes. Cover and cook, stirring once or twice, until the beans are crisp-tender, about 5 minutes. Remove and discard the thyme.
2. Spread the arugula on a large platter or in a large shallow bowl. Top with the hot vegetables. Let stand until the arugula wilts, about 5 minutes.
3. Meanwhile, wipe out the skillet. Heat 2 tablespoons of the oil in the skillet over medium-high heat. Fry the eggs in the hot oil until the whites are set and the yolks are cooked to your desired doneness, flipping the eggs if desired.
4. In a small bowl, whisk together the lemon zest and juice, the remaining 2 tablespoons oil, and the shallot.
5. Toss together the wilted arugula and vegetables. Drizzle with the dressing and top with the fried eggs. Sprinkle with the remaining ½ teaspoon salt and black pepper to taste.

Scrambled Eggs Breakfast Tacos

Prep time: 15 minutes | Cook time: 15 minutes | Serves 4

Sausage:
¼ cup apple cider
1 teaspoon kosher salt
1 teaspoon ground chipotle chile pepper
1 teaspoon dried sage, crushed, or 1 tablespoon finely chopped fresh sage
½ teaspoon dried thyme, crushed
½ teaspoon black pepper
½ teaspoon garlic powder
½ teaspoon onion powder
1 pound (454 g) ground pork

Eggs:
1 tablespoon clarified butter or ghee
8 large eggs
Kosher salt and black pepper, to taste
12 butterhead lettuce leaves
Whole30-compliant pico de gallo or hot sauce
Chopped avocado (optional)
Fresh cilantro leaves (optional)

1. Make the sausage: In a large bowl, combine the apple cider, salt, chipotle, sage, thyme, black pepper, garlic powder, and onion powder. Add the ground pork and use your hands to thoroughly mix in the seasonings.
2. In a large skillet, cook the sausage over medium-high heat until browned, using a wooden spoon to break up the meat into small pieces as it cooks. Use a slotted spoon to transfer the sausage to a bowl. Pour off any fat remaining in the skillet and wipe out the skillet.
3. Make the eggs: Set the skillet in which you cooked the sausage over medium heat and add the butter. In a medium bowl, whisk the eggs just until the yolks are broken. Pour the eggs into the skillet. Cook, stirring often, until they reach the desired doneness. Season with salt and black pepper.
4. Divide the sausage and eggs among the lettuce leaves. Top with pico de gallo and, if desired, avocado and cilantro.

Chapter 2 Breakfasts

Green Vegetable and Fruit Smoothie

Prep time: 10 minutes | Cook time: 0 minutes | Makes 2 (12-ounce) smoothies

- 1 cup chopped peeled cucumber (about 1 medium)
- 1 cup unsweetened nondairy milk of your choice
- 2 or 3 green kale leaves, stemmed
- 1 cup baby spinach
- 1 cup frozen cubed mango
- 1 banana, peeled
- 3 tablespoons hemp hearts
- 1 teaspoon culinary-grade matcha

1. Combine all the ingredients in a (preferably high-speed) blender. Blend until smooth.

Summer in A Glass

Prep time: 10 minutes | Cook time: 0 minutes | Makes 2 (14-ounce) smoothies

- 2 cups unsweetened soy milk or other nondairy milk
- ½ cup fresh or frozen cubed mango
- 1 orange, peeled and seeded
- ½ yellow bell pepper, chopped
- 1 (1-inch) piece fresh turmeric, peeled
- 3 tablespoons hemp seeds
- Ice, for serving (optional)

1. Combine all the ingredients except the ice (if using) in a (preferably high-speed) blender. Blend until smooth. Serve over ice or chilled.

Southern Fall Smoothie

Prep time: 10 minutes | Cook time: 10 minutes | Makes 2 (10-ounce) smoothies

- ½ cup 1-inch cubes peeled sweet potato
- 2 cups unsweetened soy milk or other nondairy milk
- 3 dates, pitted, or 2 tablespoons date paste (see here)
- ¼ teaspoon pure almond extract
- ¼ teaspoon freshly grated nutmeg
- Ice, for serving (optional)

1. Steam the sweet potato in a covered steamer basket over gently simmering water until tender, 10 to 15 minutes.
2. Transfer the sweet potato to a (preferably high-speed) blender. Add the remaining ingredients except the ice (if using) and blend until smooth. Serve over ice or chilled.

Sausage with Eggs and Home Fries

Prep time: 10 minutes | Cook time: 27 minutes | Serves 2

- 3 tablespoons cooking fat
- ¼ cup finely diced white onion
- ½ pound (227 g) ground meat (pork, chicken, turkey)
- ¼ teaspoon dried sage
- ¼ teaspoon salt
- ⅛ teaspoon black pepper
- ⅛ teaspoon garlic powder
- 1 sweet potato, peeled and cut into large dice
- ½ bell pepper, (any color), seeded, ribs removed, and diced
- 4 large eggs, cracked into a bowl

1. Preheat the oven to 350ºF (180ºC). Line a baking sheet with parchment paper.
2. To make the sausage, heat 1 tablespoon of the cooking fat in a large heavy skillet over medium-high heat. When the fat is hot, add the onion and cook, stirring, for until softened, about 2 minutes.
3. Transfer the onion to a mixing bowl and add the ground meat, sage, salt, pepper, and garlic powder. Form the mixture into 4 equal patties and set the sausage aside.
4. To make the home fries, return the same skillet to the stove and heat over medium-high heat. Melt 1 tablespoon of the cooking fat and swirl to coat the bottom of the pan. When the fat is hot, add the sweet potato and cook, stirring occasionally so all sides make contact with the hot pan, for 4 minutes. Add the bell pepper and cook, stirring, until softened, 2 to 3 minutes. Spread the home fries mixture evenly onto the prepared baking sheet. Bake for 5 minutes.
5. Meanwhile, to cook the sausage, return the same skillet to the stove and heat over medium heat. Add the sausage patties and cook until browned, about 2 minutes on each side.
6. Add the sausage to the home fries on the baking sheet. Return to the oven and bake for 5 to 7 minutes, until the sausage is no longer pink in the middle and the home fries are fork-tender.
7. Meanwhile, to cook the eggs, add the remaining 1 tablespoon cooking fat to the same skillet and melt over medium heat. Slide all 4 eggs gently into the pan and let them cook slowly, yolk-side up, until the yolks are cooked but still bright in color, 5 to 8 minutes.
8. Arrange the sausage patties and home fries on 2 plates. With a spatula, carefully remove the eggs from the pan and either lay them over the home fries or place on the side.

Mango and Pistachio Millet with Raspberry

Prep time: 10 minutes | Cook time: 22 minutes | Serves 6

2½ cups unsweetened soy milk or other nondairy milk, plus more if needed
1 cup unsweetened coconut milk
1 cup dry millet
3 tablespoons minced dried apricots
½ teaspoon pure vanilla extract
¼ cup unsalted pistachios, toasted
1½ cups fresh or frozen cubed mango
¼ cup fresh or frozen raspberries

1. In a medium saucepan, combine the soy milk and the coconut milk. Bring to a boil over medium heat. Stir in the millet with a wooden spoon. Reduce the heat to medium-low and simmer, stirring occasionally, until the millet is creamy and tender, 20 to 25 minutes.
2. Add the apricots, vanilla, half the pistachios, and half the mango, reduce the heat to low, and cook for 2 to 3 minutes more. Add a splash of soy milk if needed to keep the millet creamy. Remove from the heat.
3. Serve the millet topped with the raspberries, remaining pistachios, and remaining mango.

Southwest Egg Breakfast Bowls

Prep time: 10 minutes | Cook time: 16 minutes | Serves 4

2 tablespoons coconut oil
1 (12- to 14-ounce / 340- to 397-g) package Whole30-compliant smoked kielbasa or Polish beef sausage, thinly sliced crosswise
1 medium sweet potato, peeled, halved lengthwise, and thinly sliced crosswise
1 small green bell pepper, cut into strips
1 (16-ounce / 454-g) package cauliflower crumbles, or 4 cups raw cauliflower rice
2 green onions, thinly sliced
1 tablespoon clarified butter or ghee
4 large eggs
¼ teaspoon salt
⅛ to ¼ teaspoon black pepper
¾ cup Whole30-compliant salsa

1. Heat 1 tablespoon of the coconut oil in a large skillet over medium heat. Add the kielbasa and sweet potato, cover, and cook, stirring occasionally, for 5 minutes. Uncover and cook, stirring occasionally, until the potato is tender and the kielbasa is browned, about 5 minutes.
2. Meanwhile, heat the remaining 1 tablespoon coconut oil in a large nonstick skillet over medium heat. Add the bell pepper and cook, stirring occasionally, for 4 minutes. Add the cauliflower crumbles and green onions and cook, stirring occasionally, until the pepper is just tender and the cauliflower is heated through, 4 to 6 minutes more.
3. Spoon the sausage and potatoes and the cauliflower into shallow bowls. Cover with foil to keep warm.
4. Heat the butter in the nonstick skillet over medium heat. Break the eggs into the skillet and sprinkle with the salt and black pepper. Reduce the heat to medium-low. Cook the eggs until the whites are completely set and the yolks start to thicken, 2 to 3 minutes. Carefully turn the eggs over. Cook until the yolks are to desired doneness, 1 to 1½ minutes more.
5. Uncover the bowls and place an egg on top. Spoon the salsa on top and serve.

Fingerling Potatoes with Spring Asparagus

Prep time: 10 minutes | Cook time: 20 minutes | Serves 4

1 tablespoon plus 1½ teaspoons kosher salt
1 pound (454 g) fingerling potatoes
1 pound (454 g) asparagus
2 tablespoons clarified butter
¼ cup sliced shallots
½ teaspoon freshly ground black pepper
4 large eggs, poached

1. In a medium pot, bring 2 quarts water and 1 tablespoon of the salt to a boil over high heat. Add the potatoes. Cover and cook until they're just cooked through, about 10 minutes. Drain the potatoes and let cool. Cut the potatoes in half lengthwise and set aside.
2. Cut the woody ends off the asparagus, peel the rough layer off the ends of the stalks, and cut the stalks into thirds. Set aside.
3. In a large sauté pan, melt the clarified butter over medium heat, tilting the pan to coat the bottom. Arrange the potatoes cut-side down in the pan, sprinkle with ¾ teaspoon of the salt, and cook for 2 minutes. Add the shallots, asparagus, remaining ¾ teaspoon salt, and the pepper and cook for 2 minutes more. Gently toss the vegetables together, cover, and cook for 2 minutes more. Uncover, toss again, cover, and cook for 2 minutes more. Repeat until vegetables are tender, 4 to 6 minutes more.
4. Serve on a large platter or individual plates, with the poached eggs on top.

Cherry and Banana Cocoa Smoothie

Prep time: 10 minutes | Cook time: 0 minutes | Makes 2 (14-ounce) smoothies

3 cups unsweetened soy milk or other nondairy milk
¾ cup fresh or frozen pitted cherries
1 banana, peeled
2 dates, pitted
5 kale leaves, stemmed
¼ cup unsweetened raw or toasted cocoa powder
½ teaspoon pure vanilla extract
Ice, for serving (optional)

1. Combine all the ingredients except the ice (if using) in a (preferably high-speed) blender. Blend until smooth. Serve over ice or chilled.

Potato Croutons

Prep time: 5 minutes | Cook time: 40 minutes | Serves 4

1 tablespoon plus ½ teaspoon kosher salt
1½ pounds (680 g) fingerling potatoes
2 tablespoons plus 1 teaspoon of extra-virgin olive oil
1 teaspoon chopped fresh rosemary
1 teaspoon chopped fresh thyme
½ teaspoon freshly ground black pepper

1. Preheat the oven to 400ºF (205ºC).
2. Fill a medium pot with 2 quarts water, add 1 tablespoon of the salt, and bring to a boil over high heat. Add the potatoes and cook for 10 minutes. Drain and let cool, then cut the potatoes into cubes about the size of croutons.
3. In a medium bowl, stir together the olive oil, rosemary, thyme, remaining ½ teaspoon salt, and the pepper. Add the potatoes and toss to coat evenly. Transfer to a baking sheet. Roast for 15 minutes, or until beginning to brown. Remove from the oven, flip the potatoes over, and roast for 15 minutes more, or until well browned and crisped.

Poached Pear

Prep time: 5 minutes | Cook time: 25 minutes | Serves 8

1 cup unfiltered apple juice
½ teaspoon ground cinnamon
¼ teaspoon kosher salt
8 ripe but firm Bartlett pears, peeled, halved, and cored

1. In a medium bowl, combine ¼ cup water, the apple juice, cinnamon, and salt and stir well, until the cinnamon is thoroughly incorporated.
2. Arrange the pears cut side down in a single layer in a large skillet or wide pot with a lid. Put the pan on the stovetop. Evenly pour the apple juice mixture over the pears. Bring the liquid to a boil over high heat, then reduce the heat to medium, cover, and cook for 15 minutes.
3. Reduce the heat to medium-low, uncover, and simmer to reduce and thicken the sauce, about 10 minutes more. Serve pears with the liquid spooned over the top.

Hearty Pacific Northwest Mushroom Hash

Prep time: 15 minutes | Cook time: 16 minutes | Serves 4

1 large yam or sweet potato, scrubbed and cut into bite-size pieces
2 large Yukon Gold potatoes, scrubbed and cut into bite-size pieces
¼ cup Marsala wine
½ cup finely chopped leeks
8 ounces (227 g) golden chanterelle mushrooms, chopped if large
8 ounces (227 g) oyster or maitake mushrooms, chopped if large
3 garlic cloves, minced
Leaves from 2 sprigs rosemary
Pinch of sea salt
1½ teaspoons cracked black pepper
¼ cup low-sodium vegetable broth
2 tablespoons smoked paprika
4 large eggs, poached, for serving (optional)

1. Preheat the oven to 350ºF (180ºC). Line a baking sheet with parchment paper.
2. Arrange the yams and potatoes in a single layer on the prepared pan. Roast until the potatoes are barely tender but not completely soft, 8 to 10 minutes. Remove from the oven, drizzle with the wine, and shake the pan to coat the potatoes. Return the pan to the oven and roast until the potatoes are fork-tender, 4 to 6 minutes more.
3. Heat a large sauté pan over medium-high heat. When hot, add the leeks and dry sauté, stirring often, until they begin to stick to the pan and lightly brown, 1 to 2 minutes. Stir in the chanterelles, oyster mushrooms, garlic, rosemary, salt, and pepper and cook, stirring often, until the mushrooms begin to stick, 3 to 4 minutes. Add the broth and stir to deglaze the pan. Cook until the liquid has evaporated and the mushrooms are very tender. Stir in the yams, potatoes, and paprika.
4. If you eat eggs, serve each portion of hash topped with a poached egg.

Chia Seeds Pudding

Prep time: 10 minutes | Cook time: 0 minutes | Serves 4

1 cup bone broth
1 cup full-fat coconut milk
1 cup water
¼ cup cocoa powder
¼ cup steamed and then frozen cauliflower florets
¼ cup granulated erythritol, or 20 drops liquid stevia
3 tablespoons chia seeds
Pinch of fine Himalayan salt
Fresh blackberries, for garnish (optional)

1. Place all of the ingredients in a high-powered blender. Blend on high until the chia seeds are pulverized and the mix is completely smooth and thick.
2. Pour the mixture into four 6-ounce jars with lids, cover, and refrigerate for at least 4 hours to thicken. Garnish with blackberries before serving, if desired. Store in the refrigerator for up to 1 week.

Potato, Sausage and Bacon Breakfast Bites

Prep time: 10 minutes | Cook time: 30 minutes | Serves 4

2 slices Whole30-compliant bacon, chopped
4 ounces (113 g) ground turkey
⅓ cup chopped red or green bell pepper
¼ cup chopped onion
1⅓ cups coarsely shredded Yukon Gold potatoes (about 10 ounces)
½ teaspoon dried sage
¼ teaspoon dried thyme
¼ teaspoon garlic powder
¼ teaspoon salt
⅛ teaspoon black pepper
5 large eggs, beaten

1. Preheat the oven to 375ºF (190ºC). Lightly grease eight 2½-inch muffin cups.
2. In a large skillet, partially cook the bacon over medium heat, stirring occasionally, about 5 minutes. Add the turkey, bell pepper, and onion. Cook, stirring occasionally, until the turkey is cooked through and the bacon is crisp, 5 to 7 minutes. Transfer to a large bowl.
3. Add the potatoes, sage, thyme, garlic powder, salt, and pepper to the meat; stir to combine. Spoon the filling into the muffin cups. Pour the eggs over the filling until the cups are full.
4. Bake for about 20 minutes, until a knife inserted in the center comes out clean. Run the knife around the edges of the muffin cups to release the muffins. Serve warm.

Skillet Potatoes with Herbs

Prep time: 5 minutes | Cook time: 12 minutes | Serves 8

3 tablespoons extra-virgin olive oil
4 medium Yukon Gold potatoes, diced
1 medium yellow onion, diced
¾ teaspoon coarse salt
½ teaspoon black pepper
Fresh thyme leaves or chopped fresh cilantro or parsley (optional)

1. Heat the olive oil in a large heavy skillet over medium-high heat. Add the potatoes and onion. Cook, stirring occasionally, until tender and browned, about 10 minutes. If the potatoes are browned but not tender, cover, reduce the heat to medium, and cook an additional 2 to 3 minutes. Sprinkle with salt and pepper. Top with herbs, if desired.

Spinach and Arugula Breakfast Hash

Prep time: 10 minutes | Cook time: 15 minutes | Serves 8

3 tablespoons extra-virgin olive oil
4 large Yukon Gold potatoes, diced
1 medium yellow onion, diced
½ teaspoon salt
¼ teaspoon black pepper
2 cloves garlic, minced
1 (5-ounce / 142-g) container spinach and arugula salad blend
8 large eggs

1. In a large nonstick pan, heat the olive oil over medium-high heat. Add the potatoes and onion; sprinkle with the salt and pepper. Cook, stirring frequently, until the potatoes are tender and browned, 8 to 9 minutes. Add the garlic and salad greens; stir to combine. Cover and cook until the greens wilt, 2 to 3 minutes.
2. Make 8 indentations in the hash, and carefully break an egg into each indentation. Cover and cook just until the egg whites are set, 5 to 6 minutes. Season to taste.

Chapter 3 Beef

Beef Brisket with Celery Root Slaw

Prep time: 20 minutes | Cook time: 5 hours | Serves 6

For the Brisket:
- 1 sweet onion, sliced
- 1 (3- to 4-pound / 1.4- to 1.8-kg) beef brisket or arm roast
- ½ cup Whole30-compliant pomegranate juice
- 1 can (8-ounce / 227-g) Whole30-compliant tomato sauce
- 1 tablespoon chili powder
- 1 teaspoon grated orange zest
- ½ teaspoon chipotle powder
- ½ teaspoon celery seeds
- ½ teaspoon salt

For the Slaw:
- ⅓ cup Whole30-compliant mayonnaise
- 2 tablespoons fresh orange juice
- ½ teaspoon celery seeds
- ½ teaspoon salt
- ½ teaspoon black pepper
- 1 large celery root, peeled and coarsely shredded
- 2 carrots, peeled and shredded
- Sliced green onions (optional)

Make the Brisket
1. Place the onions and brisket in a 6-quart slow cooker. In a medium bowl, combine the pomegranate juice, tomato sauce, chili powder, orange zest, chipotle powder, celery seeds, and salt. Pour the pomegranate mixture over the brisket and onions. Cover and cook on low for 10 to 12 hours or on high for 5 to 6 hours, or until the brisket is tender.

Make the Slaw
1. In a medium bowl, combine the mayonnaise, orange juice, celery seeds, salt, and pepper. Add the celery root and carrots; toss to combine. Cover and chill for 1 to 4 hours.
2. Remove the roast from the cooker; reserve the cooking liquid. Cover the brisket with foil and let it rest for 10 minutes. Thinly slice the brisket and serve with the cooking liquid and the slaw. If desired, top the slaw with green onions.

Beef Short Ribs with Cauliflower Rice

Prep time: 20 minutes | Cook time: 3½ hours | Serves 4 to 6

For the Short Ribs:
- 2 teaspoons dried oregano, crushed
- 2 teaspoons fennel seeds, crushed
- ½ to 1 teaspoon red pepper flakes
- 1 teaspoon salt
- 12 bone-in beef short ribs
- 2 tablespoons extra-virgin olive oil (optional)
- 1 onion, chopped
- 1 bulb fennel, trimmed and chopped
- 1 green bell pepper, chopped
- ½ cup sliced pickled pepperoncini peppers
- 4 cloves garlic, minced
- 1 can (14½-ounce / 411-g) Whole30-compliant diced tomatoes

For the Cauliflower Rice:
- 2 (12-ounce / 340-g) packages frozen riced cauliflower
- 1 tablespoon extra-virgin olive oil
- ½ teaspoon dried oregano, crushed
- ½ teaspoon garlic powder
- Salt and black pepper, to taste
- ½ cup fresh basil leaves, torn
- ¼ cup sliced Whole30-compliant black or green olives

Make the Short Ribs
1. In a small bowl, combine the oregano, fennel seeds, red pepper flakes, and salt; rub onto the short ribs. If desired, in a large skillet, heat the olive oil and cook the short ribs on all sides until browned, about 10 minutes. In a 6-quart slow cooker, combine the onion, chopped fennel, bell pepper, pepperoncini peppers, and garlic. Add the short ribs; top with the tomatoes.
2. Cover and cook on low for 7 to 8 hours or on high for 3½ to 4 hours, or until the short ribs are tender. Remove the ribs from the cooker. Skim the fat from the cooking liquid.

Make the Cauliflower Rice
1. Cook the cauliflower rice according to the package directions; drain well. Stir in the olive oil, oregano, and garlic powder. Season to taste with salt and pepper.
2. Serve the short ribs and cooking liquid (not strained) over the cauliflower rice. Top with fresh basil and olives.

Citrus Beef Short Ribs

Prep time: 10 minutes | Cook time: 4 hours | Serves 4

1 medium onion, chopped
1 tablespoon grated orange zest, plus extra for sprinkling
½ cup fresh orange juice
2 tablespoons Whole30-compliant tomato paste
1 teaspoon chipotle powder
2 cloves garlic, minced
1 teaspoon salt
12 bone-in beef short ribs
1 package (12-ounce / 340-g) riced cauliflower and sweet potato, prepared according to package directions

1. In a 6-quart slow cooker, stir together the onion, orange zest, orange juice, tomato paste, chipotle powder, garlic, and salt. Place the ribs in the slow cooker; add the orange juice mixture and toss to coat.
2. Cover and cook on low for 8 to 9 hours or on high for 4 to 4½ hours.
3. Transfer the ribs to a serving platter. Skim the fat from the cooking liquid. Serve the ribs on the riced cauliflower and sweet potato, drizzled with the cooking liquid and topped with additional orange zest.

Beef Short Ribs with Vegetable and Parsley

Prep time: 15 minutes | Cook time: 4 hours | Serves 4

2 tablespoons dried sage
2 tablespoons dried oregano
2 teaspoons garlic powder
1 teaspoon salt
1 teaspoon coarse black pepper
8 to 12 bone-in beef short ribs
3 medium carrots, peeled and sliced diagonally ½ inch thick
2 medium yellow onions, coarsely chopped
4 cloves garlic, crushed
1 cup Whole30-compliant tomato juice
1 package (12-ounce / 340-g) frozen riced cauliflower and sweet potato
Grated zest and juice of 1 lemon
¼ cup chopped fresh parsley
2 teaspoons Whole30-compliant capers, drained
2 teaspoons extra-virgin olive oil
Fresh thyme sprigs

1. In a small bowl, combine the sage, oregano, garlic powder, salt, and pepper. Rub the ribs with the spice mixture. Place the carrots, onions, garlic, and tomato juice in a 6-quart slow cooker. Add the ribs.
2. Cover and cook on low for 8 hours or on high for 4 hours. Use a slotted spoon to transfer the beef and vegetables to a platter; cover to keep warm.
3. Transfer the cooking liquid to a medium saucepan. Skim the fat. Bring the sauce to a boil over medium heat. Reduce the heat and simmer until reduced by half, about 10 minutes.
4. Meanwhile, for the pilaf, prepare the riced cauliflower and sweet potatoes according to the package directions. Stir in the lemon zest and juice, parsley, capers, and olive oil.
5. Drizzle the sauce over the ribs and vegetables and top with fresh thyme. Serve on top of the pilaf.

Picadillo-Style Beef Chuck Roast

Prep time: 15 minutes | Cook time: 1¼ hours | Serves 6

2 tablespoons extra-virgin olive oil
1 medium yellow onion, finely chopped
1 medium red bell pepper, finely chopped
4 cloves garlic, minced
1 (2-to 2½-pound / 907- to 1135-g) boneless beef chuck roast, cut into 3 or 4 pieces
1 can (8-ounce / 227-g) Whole30-compliant tomato sauce
1 tablespoon red wine vinegar
2 teaspoons ground cumin
2 teaspoons dried oregano
1 teaspoon salt
¼ teaspoon black pepper
6 medium Yukon Gold potatoes, quartered
½ cup quartered pitted Whole30-compliant manzanilla olives or other green olives
⅓ cup unsulfured golden raisins
¼ cup Whole30-compliant capers, drained

1. On a 6-quart Instant Pot, select Sauté and adjust to Normal/Medium. Add the olive oil. When it's hot, add the onion, bell pepper, and garlic and cook, stirring occasionally, until softened, 3 to 5 minutes. Add the beef and cook until browned, about 5 minutes. Press Cancel. Add the tomato sauce, vinegar, cumin, oregano, salt, and pepper; stir to combine. Lock the lid in place.
2. Select Manual and cook on high pressure for 50 minutes. Use quick release.
3. Add the potatoes, olives, raisins, and capers. Lock the lid in place. Select Manual and cook on high pressure for 8 minutes. Use quick release.
4. Use a slotted spoon to remove the potatoes, vegetables, and beef. Use two forks to shred the beef. Serve the beef and vegetables over the potatoes.

Churrasco with Chimichurri

Prep time: 5 minutes | Cook time: 16 minutes | Serves 4

1 pound (454 g) skirt steak
1 teaspoon fine Himalayan salt
1 pound (454 g) asparagus
1 tablespoon avocado oil
½ cup versatile chimichurri

1. Heat a large cast-iron skillet over medium heat until it's really hot, about 10 minutes.
2. Meanwhile, score the meat, making shallow cuts on the underside in a crisscross pattern. Skirt steak usually comes in foot-long strips; cut the strip into three or four pieces that fit in the skillet. Sprinkle the meat with the salt.
3. When the skillet is hot, fit as many strips of steak as you can in the skillet without overcrowding it—you may need to cook them in two batches. Sear the steak for 4 minutes on each side, or until well browned with charred bits. The meat will be crispy on the outside and medium on the inside. For medium-well steak, cook for another minute on each side.
4. When there's enough space in the skillet—usually when you're on the last batch of steak strips—throw the asparagus in there, too. Drizzle with the oil and cook for 4 minutes, turning once.
5. Serve with chimichurri spooned over everything. Store leftovers in an airtight container in the fridge for up to 4 days. To reheat, sear in a hot skillet for 2 minutes on each side.

Fajita Beef Skillet Over the Cauliflower

Prep time: 15 minutes | Cook time: 10 minutes | Serves 4

1 pound (454 g) ground beef
1 tablespoon extra-virgin olive oil
1 small red onion, coarsely chopped
1 small red bell pepper, coarsely chopped
1 small yellow bell pepper, coarsely chopped
2 cloves garlic, minced
½ teaspoon salt
2 teaspoons chili powder
¼ teaspoon ground cumin
⅛ teaspoon cayenne pepper
1 tablespoon fresh lime juice
2 tablespoons chopped fresh cilantro
1 (16-ounce / 454-g) package cauliflower crumbles, or 4 cups raw cauliflower rice
Diced avocado and/or diced fresh tomato (optional)
Lime wedges

1. In a large skillet, cook the beef over medium-high heat, breaking it up with a wooden spoon, until browned, about 5 minutes. Drain off any fat and transfer the beef to a bowl.
2. Heat the olive oil in the same skillet over medium heat. Add the onion, bell peppers, garlic, and salt and cook, stirring occasionally, until the vegetables are crisp-tender, 4 to 6 minutes. Stir in the beef, chili powder, cumin, and cayenne and heat through for about 1 minute. Stir in the lime juice. Remove the skillet from the heat and stir in the cilantro.
3. Meanwhile, prepare the cauliflower crumbles according to the package directions.
4. Spoon the beef and vegetables over the cauliflower and top with avocado and/or tomato if desired; serve with lime wedges.

Meat Loaf with Sweet-Sour Glaze

Prep time: 15 minutes | Cook time: 1 hour | Serves 6 to 8

For the Glaze:
1 cup ketchup
¼ cup brown sugar
3 tablespoons apple cider vinegar
½ teaspoon hot sauce

For the Meat Loaf:
1 pound (454 g) ground beef
½ pound (227 g) ground veal
½ pound (227 g) ground pork
2 large eggs
1 cup finely chopped yellow onion
¾ cup gluten-free white bread crumbs
¾ cup chopped fresh parsley
¼ cup chopped fresh chives
2 tablespoons chopped fresh basil
1½ teaspoons kosher salt
½ teaspoon freshly ground black pepper
8 slices bacon

1. Preheat the oven to 350ºF (180ºC).
2. For the glaze: In a small bowl, stir together the ketchup, brown sugar, vinegar, and hot sauce until completely incorporated. Set aside (I always make double for dipping).
3. For the meat loaf: In a large bowl using your hands, mix together the beef, veal, pork, eggs, onion, bread crumbs, parsley, chives, basil, salt, and pepper. Form the mixture into an 8 × 6-inch loaf on a baking sheet. Cover the loaf with the bacon slices, laying them horizontally over the loaf, slightly overlapping, and tucking the ends underneath.
4. Bake for 45 minutes. Remove the meat loaf from the oven and brush on half the glaze. Return the pan to the oven and bake the meat loaf for about 15 minutes more, or until an instant-read thermometer inserted into the center reads 160ºF (71ºC). Remove from the oven, tent with foil, and allow to rest for 15 minutes before slicing and serving.
5. Serve with the remaining glaze on the side.

Slow Cooked Beef Short Ribs

Prep time: 10 minutes | Cook time: 8 hours | Serves 8

3 teaspoons salt
2 teaspoons black pepper
3 pounds (1.4kg) beef short ribs, trimmed
4 to 6 tablespoons cooking fat
1 onion, quartered
6 cloves garlic, peeled
4 sprigs fresh thyme
2 cups apple cider

1. Mix 2 teaspoons of the salt and all the pepper in a small bowl and use to season the short ribs evenly on both sides.
2. In an oven-safe heavy pot or Dutch oven, melt 4 tablespoons of the cooking fat over medium-high heat. When the fat is hot, sear the short ribs until each side is golden brown, about 1 minute on each side. (You'll likely have to do this in batches, adding another tablespoon of cooking fat to each new batch.)
3. Transfer all the ribs to a slow cooker. Add the onion, garlic, thyme, apple cider, and 8 cups of water and cook on low for 8 hours. When done, the short ribs should be fork-tender.
4. Transfer the short ribs to a bowl and shred, discarding the bones and excess fat. Ladle the cooking liquid, onion, and garlic into a food processor or blender, removing the thyme stems, and blend on low until thoroughly mixed. Transfer the blended sauce to a medium saucepot and bring to a simmer over medium heat. Cook until thickened, about 5 minutes. Season the sauce with the remaining 1 teaspoon salt.
5. Transfer the shredded short ribs to a serving bowl, toss with the sauce, and reserve. (You'll be using all of it to stuff the peppers for your tapas plate.)

Sirloin with Beans

Prep time: 15 minutes | Cook time: 2½ hours | Serves 6 to 8

2 tablespoons extra-virgin olive oil
1 large yellow onion, chopped
1 garlic clove, pressed
1½ pounds (680 g) ground sirloin
1½ tablespoons chili powder
1 tablespoon kosher salt
1 bay leaf
1 teaspoon chipotle chile powder (optional)
1 teaspoon garlic salt
¼ teaspoon dried oregano
¼ teaspoon cayenne pepper
5 cups fire-roasted crushed tomatoes
1 cup high-quality jarred marinara sauce
2 (15-ounce / 425-g) cans pinto, chili, or other beans, drained and rinsed
1 tablespoon balsamic vinegar

1. In a large Dutch oven, heat the olive oil over medium-high heat. Add the onion and garlic and cook, stirring, until translucent, about 5 minutes. Add the ground beef and cook, stirring and breaking up any lumps, until thoroughly cooked, about 10 minutes. Add the chili powder, salt, bay leaf, chipotle chile powder, if desired, garlic salt, oregano, and cayenne and cook, stirring, for 2 minutes.
2. In a food processor, working in batches if necessary, blend the tomatoes and marinara together. Add this mixture and the beans to the Dutch oven, then add 1 cup water and stir to combine well. Bring to a boil, then reduce the heat to medium-low and cook at a low simmer, uncovered, stirring occasionally, for 30 minutes. Reduce the heat to low, cover, and cook for 1½ hours more.
3. Stir in the vinegar, remove the bay leaf, and serve.

Beef and Sweet Potato Chili

Prep time: 20 minutes | Cook time: 25 minutes | Serves 4

1 tablespoon olive oil
1 pound (454 g) ground beef, bison, or lamb
2 cups chopped onion
1 medium serrano chile, seeded and finely chopped
3 cloves garlic, minced
1 (28-ounce / 794-g) can Whole30-compliant fire-roasted diced tomatoes, undrained
1 cup beef bone broth or Whole30-compliant beef broth
1 large sweet potato, peeled and cut into ¾-inch chunks (about 2 cups)
1 cup chopped red bell pepper
2 tablespoons chili powder
½ teaspoon ground chipotle chile pepper
½ teaspoon salt, plus more as needed
Chopped fresh cilantro (optional)
Sliced green onions (optional)

1. Heat the olive oil in a large pot over medium-high heat. Add the ground beef, onion, serrano chile, and garlic and cook, stirring frequently and breaking up the meat with a wooden spoon, until the meat is browned, about 5 minutes.
2. Stir in the tomatoes with their juices, broth, sweet potato, bell pepper, chili powder, chipotle, and salt and bring to a boil. Reduce the heat to low, cover, and simmer, stirring occasionally, until the sweet potato is tender, 20 to 25 minutes. If desired, season with additional salt. Serve the chili topped with cilantro and green onions, if desired.

Fall seven times, stand up eight.

Slow-Cooked Shawarma

Prep time: 15 minutes | Cook time: 8 hours | Serves 5 or 6

1 tablespoon fine Himalayan salt
1 tablespoon ground black pepper
1 tablespoon ground cumin
1 teaspoon ground cardamom
½ teaspoon ground nutmeg
3 pounds (1.4kg) boneless chuck short rib or shoulder
¼ cup coconut vinegar or red wine vinegar
3 tablespoons avocado oil
5 cloves garlic, peeled
1 large onion, quartered
1 lemon, quartered
1 navel orange, quartered

1. In a small bowl, mix together the salt, pepper, cumin, cardamom, and nutmeg. Rub the spice mixture all over the meat.
2. Place the meat in a large bowl and drizzle the vinegar and oil all over it. Add the garlic, onion, and citrus. Toss to combine, squeezing some juice out of the fruit. Cover and set in the refrigerator to marinate overnight.
3. When you're ready to cook, put everything in the slow cooker, meat on the bottom, citrus and onion quarters on top. Cook on low for 8 hours.
4. Discard the large pieces of citrus. Use two forks to shred the beef. If you like crispy beef, you can spread it on a sheet pan and broil it for 5 minutes to get delicious crispy tips. Divide the shredded beef among five or six plates, spoon the delicious slow cooker sauce over the meat, and serve.
5. Store leftovers in an airtight container in the fridge for up to 5 days or in the freezer for up to 30 days. To thaw and reheat, place in a preheated 400ºF (205ºC) oven for 10 to 20 minutes.

Hot Beef Arm Roast

Prep time: 30 minutes | Cook time: 8 hours | Serves 6

1 beef arm roast (2½ to 3 pounds / 1.1 to 1.4 kg)
6 cloves garlic, peeled
½ teaspoon dried rosemary
1 teaspoon salt
¼ teaspoon black pepper
2 pounds (907 g) russet potatoes, peeled and cut into 2-inch chunks
1 (8-ounce / 227-g) package button mushrooms, halved
1 medium yellow onion, sliced
2 tablespoons tapioca flour
¼ teaspoon garlic powder
2 tablespoons clarified butter or ghee

1. Cut three slits each into the top and bottom of the roast. Insert a garlic clove into each slit. In a small bowl, combine the rosemary, salt, and pepper. Sprinkle on both sides of roast. Place the roast in a slow cooker with ¼ cup water. Add the potatoes, mushrooms, and onion.
2. Cover and cook on low for 8 to 10 hours or on high for 4 to 5 hours. Transfer the beef to a cutting board or platter. Cover and keep warm. Transfer the potatoes to a large bowl.
3. Turn the slow cooker to high if using the low setting. In a small bowl, stir together the tapioca flour and 2 tablespoons water. Pour into the slow cooker. Cook, stirring occasionally, until the gravy has thickened, about 5 minutes.
4. Meanwhile, sprinkle the potatoes with the garlic powder; add the butter. Use a potato masher or fork to mash the potatoes to your desired consistency.
5. Serve the roast over the mashed potatoes, with gravy ladled over the top.

Mici with Mustard Dipping

Prep time: 5 minutes | Cook time: 8 minutes | Serves 4 or 5

2 pounds (907 g) lean ground beef
1 pound (454 g) ground pork
½ cup carbonated mineral water
4 garlic cloves, minced
1 tablespoon kosher salt, plus more for seasoning
2 teaspoons baking soda
1 teaspoon dried oregano
1 teaspoon freshly ground black pepper
¼ cup Dijon mustard, for serving

1. In a large bowl, combine the ground beef, ground pork, carbonated water, garlic, salt, baking soda, oregano, and pepper. Use your hands to thoroughly mix until the mixture is tacky and well combined. Test the seasoning by frying a tablespoon of the mixture in a dry nonstick skillet over medium-high heat. Taste the cooked portion and season the raw mixture with salt as needed. Cover the bowl with plastic wrap and refrigerate for at least 6 hours or up to overnight.
2. Line a baking sheet with parchment paper. Using your hands, form small, log-shaped kebabs approximately 3½ inches long and 1 inch thick, placing them on the baking sheet as you form them.
3. Heat a grill to medium-high (a charcoal grill is ideal, though gas is fine, too) or heat a cast-iron grill pan over medium-high heat. Grill the mici until browned and cooked through, 3 to 4 minutes per side.
4. Serve immediately, with toothpicks for picking up the mici and mustard for dipping.

Cuban Beef and Bell Peppers

Prep time: 10 minutes | Cook time: 8 hours | Serves 4

3 cloves garlic, minced
2 teaspoons dried oregano
1 teaspoon ground cumin
1 teaspoon salt
½ teaspoon black pepper
1 boneless beef chuck roast (2 pounds (907 g) / 907 g)
2 large red bell peppers, seeded, cored, and sliced
2 medium yellow onions, cut into 6 wedges each
¼ cup orange juice
¼ cup lime juice
1 avocado, halved, pitted, peeled, and sliced

1. In a small bowl, combine the garlic, oregano, cumin, salt, and black pepper. Rub the spice mixture onto both sides of the roast.
2. In a slow cooker, layer the peppers and onions. Pour the juices over the vegetables. Place the roast on the vegetables. Cover and cook on low for 8 to 10 hours or on high for 4 to 5 hours.
3. Using a slotted spoon, transfer the meat to a cutting board. Using a slotted spoon, remove the peppers and onions and set aside. Strain the cooking liquid and set aside. Use two forks to shred the meat; return to the slow cooker. Stir in the onions, peppers, and ½ cup of the cooking liquid. Serve the meat and vegetables with the avocado.

Beef Arm with Mushrooms and Snow Peas

Prep time: 25 minutes | Cook time: 7 hours | Serves 4

1 large sweet onion, halved and cut lengthwise into thin wedges
1 green bell pepper, thinly sliced lengthwise
1 boneless beef arm roast (2½ to 3 pounds / 1.1 to 1.4 kg), trimmed
Salt and black pepper, to taste
3 tablespoons coconut aminos
4 cloves garlic, minced
2 tablespoons grated fresh ginger
1 teaspoon olive oil
2 cups snow peas, trimmed
8 ounces (227 g) shiitake mushrooms, stemmed and sliced
1 bunch green onions, white and green parts, cut into 1-inch pieces

1. In a slow cooker, combine the onion and bell pepper. Season the beef with salt and pepper and add to the slow cooker. In a small bowl, combine the coconut aminos, garlic, ginger, and olive oil. Drizzle over the beef.
2. Cover and cook on low for 7 to 8 hours or on high for 3½ to 4 hours, or until tender. Remove the roast from the cooker. Cover with foil to keep warm.
3. Turn the slow cooker to high if using the low setting. Stir the snow peas, mushrooms, and green onions into the slow cooker. Cover and cook until the snow peas are crisp-tender and mushrooms are softened, 10 to 20 minutes. Slice or shred the beef and serve with the vegetables and mushrooms.

Sirloin, Zucchini, and Mushroom Stir-Fry

Prep time: 20 minutes | Cook time: 15 minutes | Serves 2 to 4

2 top sirloin medallions (about 8 ounces / 227 g total), sliced very thinly against the grain
2 tablespoons avocado oil
1 cup thinly sliced cremini or white button mushrooms
½ yellow onion, sliced
Kosher salt, to taste
1 zucchini, sliced into half-moons
1 jalapeño, seeded and thinly sliced (optional)
2 garlic cloves, thinly sliced
1 cup bean sprouts
¼ cup coconut aminos
½ teaspoon fish sauce
2 scallions, white and light green parts only, sliced into 2-inch pieces
1 tablespoon olive oil
1 tablespoon sesame seeds, for garnish

1. Pat the beef very dry with paper towels and set aside on a plate.
2. Heat a large stainless-steel sauté pan over medium heat for 5 minutes. Increase the heat to high, pour in the avocado oil, and heat until shimmering. Working in batches, add the beef and cook until browned, about 4 minutes, being careful not to overcrowd the pan. Transfer the cooked beef to a bowl and repeat to brown the remaining beef. You may notice that the beef bubbles and releases excess moisture as it browns; simply cook until it evaporates.
3. Reduce the heat to medium and add the mushrooms and onion. Season with salt and cook, stirring regularly to avoid burning, until softened, 3 to 4 minutes. Add the zucchini and jalapeño (if using) and cook, stirring, for 2 minutes. Add the garlic and cook, stirring, for 1 minute. Add the bean sprouts, coconut aminos, and fish sauce and cook, stirring occasionally, until the sauce has reduced by half, about 5 minutes.
4. Remove the pan from the heat. Return the beef to the pan and add the scallions and olive oil. Toss everything to coat. Garnish with the sesame seeds and serve immediately.

Beef Brisket Braised with Potatoes

Prep time: 20 minutes | Cook time: 10 hours | Serves 6

- 1 tablespoon Whole30-compliant coarse-grain mustard
- 3 cloves garlic, minced
- 1 teaspoon caraway seeds, crushed
- ½ teaspoon coarse salt
- ¼ teaspoon black pepper
- 2 to 2½ pounds (907 g to 1.1 kg) beef brisket, trimmed
- 1 to 1¼ pounds (454 to 567 g) 2- to 3-inch Yukon gold potatoes, scrubbed and halved
- 1 medium onion, cut into thin wedges
- 1 small head cabbage, cored and cut into 8 wedges
- 2 tablespoons cider vinegar
- 1 tablespoon clarified butter or ghee
- 1½ teaspoons snipped fresh dill

1. In a small bowl, combine the mustard, garlic, caraway seeds, salt, and pepper. Spread all over brisket. Place the potatoes, onion, and ½ cup water in a slow cooker. Lay the brisket on top of the vegetables. Cover and cook on low for 10 to 11 hours or on high for 5 to 5½ hours.
2. Turn the slow cooker to high if using the low setting. Add the cabbage to the slow cooker. Cover and cook until tender, about 30 minutes.
3. Transfer the brisket and vegetables to a serving platter. Skim the fat from the cooking juices; add the vinegar, butter, and dill. Whisk until well combined. Drizzle the liquid over the beef and vegetables and serve.

Asian Beef and Zucchini Noddles Soup

Prep time: 15 minutes | Cook time: 10 minutes | Serves 4

- 2 tablespoons coconut oil
- 1 small onion, halved and thinly sliced
- 6 ounces (170 g) fresh shiitake mushrooms, stemmed and sliced
- 2 cloves garlic, minced
- 2 teaspoons minced fresh ginger
- 5 cups beef bone broth or Whole30-compliant beef broth
- 2 tablespoons coconut aminos
- 2 teaspoons Red Boat fish sauce
- 1 teaspoon salt
- 2 medium zucchini
- 12 ounces (340 g) boneless beef sirloin steak, thinly sliced across the grain

Toppings:
- Fresh Thai basil leaves
- Fresh cilantro leaves
- Sliced green onion
- Sliced jalapeño
- Lime wedges

1. In a large pot, heat the coconut oil over medium heat. Add the onion and cook, stirring, until softened, about 2 minutes. Add the mushrooms and cook, stirring, for about 3 minutes. Add the garlic and ginger and cook, stirring, until fragrant, about 30 seconds. Add the broth, coconut aminos, fish sauce, and salt. Bring to a boil; reduce the heat to medium-low and simmer, uncovered, for 5 minutes.
2. Meanwhile, use a spiral slicer or julienne peeler to cut the zucchini lengthwise into long, thin strands (or use a regular vegetable peeler to cut the zucchini lengthwise into thin ribbons). Add the zucchini noodles to the simmering soup and cook until just tender, about 2 minutes. Add the sliced steak and simmer until just cooked, 30 to 60 seconds. Ladle the soup into bowls and serve with the toppings of your choice.

Russian Beef Stew Meat

Prep time: 25 minutes | Cook time: 3 hours | Serves 4

- 2 tablespoons avocado oil
- 2 pounds (907 g) beef stew meat, such as chuck, cut into 2-inch pieces
- 3 yellow onions (about 1 pound (454 g) / 454 g), diced
- 4 small carrots (about 10 ounces / 283 g total), cut into rounds
- 2 teaspoons kosher salt, plus more as needed
- 1 tablespoon freshly ground black pepper, plus more as needed
- 3 garlic cloves, coarsely chopped
- 1 pound (454 g) yellow potatoes (about 4), peeled and cut into 3-inch-long wedges

1. In a Dutch oven or heavy-bottomed pot, heat the avocado oil over medium-high heat. Add the beef and cook, stirring regularly, until browned on all sides and all the moisture has evaporated, about 15 minutes. Add the onions, carrots, salt, and pepper and cook, stirring and scraping up any browned bits from the bottom of the pan, until the vegetables have started to caramelize, 8 to 10 minutes. Add the garlic and cook, stirring, for 1 minute.
2. Add enough water to barely cover the meat and bring the liquid to a simmer. Reduce the heat to medium-low, cover, and cook, stirring occasionally, until the beef is soft, 1½ to 2 hours. If at any point the liquid evaporates enough that the meat is exposed, add water as needed to just barely cover the beef.
3. Add the potatoes and enough water to cover the contents of the pot. Cook until the potatoes are soft, 25 to 30 minutes. Taste and adjust the seasoning. Let cool for 5 minutes before serving.

Borscht

Prep time: 25 minutes | Cook time: 3 hours | Serves 8 to 10

2 pounds (907 g) cross-cut beef short ribs, cut into pieces between the bones
3 bay leaves
Kosher salt, to taste
1 teaspoon whole black peppercorns
2 tablespoons avocado oil
1½ pounds (680 g) beets, grated
3 carrots, grated
1 yellow onion, coarsely chopped
1 (6-ounce / 170-g) can tomato paste
2 pounds (907 g) white potatoes, peeled and cut into 2-inch cubes
1 large parsnip, peeled and diced
1 small green cabbage, thinly sliced
Juice of 1 lemon, plus more if needed
Freshly ground black pepper, to taste
¼ cup loosely packed fresh dill leaves, coarsely chopped
¼ cup loosely packed fresh parsley leaves, coarsely chopped

1. In a very large stockpot or Dutch oven, combine the ribs, bay leaves, 2 tablespoons salt, and the peppercorns. Add enough water to cover the ribs and bring to a boil over high heat. Reduce the heat to maintain a steady simmer, cover, and cook, skimming off any foam that rises to the surface, until the meat is falling off the bone, 1½ to 2 hours.
2. While the ribs cook, in a 4-quart stockpot, heat the avocado oil over medium heat. Add the beets, carrots, and onion and season with a pinch of salt. Cook, stirring often, until the vegetables are tender, about 12 minutes. Add the tomato paste and cook, stirring to coat the vegetables, until thickened, about 3 minutes. Remove from the heat and set aside.
3. When the ribs are tender and the meat is falling off the bone, add the potatoes and parsnip to the pot and cook until fork-tender, about 25 minutes. Reduce the heat to low, stir in the beet-carrot mixture, and cook until the broth has turned red, about 10 minutes. Add the cabbage and lemon juice and cook until the cabbage is slightly softened, about 10 minutes.
4. Taste the borscht and season with salt, pepper, or lemon juice as desired (it should taste sweet and sour). Remove from the heat and stir in the dill and parsley. Let the soup stand for 10 minutes before serving.

Catalina Beef Tacos

Prep time: 10 minutes | Cook time: 1½ hours | Serves 4 to 6

1⅔ cups chicken stock
1 dried ancho chile
1 dried New Mexico chile
1 tablespoon avocado oil
2 pounds (907 g) ground beef (80 to 85% lean ground beef is preferred but leaner ground beef will work as well)
1 yellow onion, diced
¾ teaspoon kosher salt, plus more as needed
5 garlic cloves, finely chopped
1 tablespoon granulated onion
1 teaspoon hot paprika
1 teaspoon ground cumin
1 teaspoon dried oregano, preferably Mexican

1. In a small saucepan, combine the stock, ancho chile, and New Mexico chile. Bring to a boil over high heat, remove from the heat, and cover with a lid. Let the chiles soak until soft, about 15 minutes. Stem and seed the chiles and transfer the flesh to a high-speed blender. Add the stock and blend on high until very smooth. Set aside.
2. In a large sauté pan or Dutch oven, heat the avocado oil over medium-high heat. Working in batches, add the ground beef and cook, breaking up the meat with a wooden spoon as it cooks, until browned, about 12 minutes. Use a slotted spoon to transfer the browned meat to a bowl and repeat to brown the remaining meat.
3. Discard all but 2 tablespoons of the fat from the pan. Return the pan to medium heat and add the onion and ¼ teaspoon of the salt. Cook, scraping up any browned bits from the bottom of the pan, until the onion is soft and translucent, 3 to 4 minutes. Add the garlic and cook, stirring, for 1 minute. Add the granulated onion, paprika, cumin, oregano, and remaining ½ teaspoon salt and cook, stirring, for 1 minute more.
4. Add the beef and the puréed chile mixture to the pan and toss to coat. Bring the mixture to a simmer, reduce the heat to low, cover, and cook, stirring occasionally, for at least 30 minutes or up to 1½ hours for a more concentrated flavor. Taste and adjust the salt before serving.

Beef Stroganoff with Coconut Sour Cream

Prep time: 15 minutes | Cook time: 15 minutes | Serves 2

Coconut Sour Cream:
1 (13½-ounce / 383-g) can full-fat coconut milk, unshaken and refrigerated overnight
Juice of 1 lemon, plus more if needed

Stroganoff:
2 tablespoons avocado oil
½ pound (227 g) beef steak (such as top sirloin medallions, top sirloin, flank, flat iron, or even tenderloin), cut into thin strips
1 tablespoon ghee
1 cup thinly sliced cremini or white button mushrooms
Kosher salt, to taste
1 shallot, thinly sliced
3 garlic cloves, thinly sliced
½ cup chicken stock
1 tablespoon whole-grain or Dijon mustard
Freshly ground black pepper, to taste
2 tablespoons finely chopped fresh dill, plus more for garnish

1. Make the coconut sour cream: Without shaking the can, carefully open it and spoon the solidified white cream into a medium bowl (save the coconut water left in the can, if you'd like). Add the lemon juice to the coconut cream and whisk until smooth and creamy. Taste and add more lemon juice, if desired. Cover the bowl with plastic wrap and refrigerate until ready to use. (The coconut sour cream will keep in the refrigerator for up to 5 days.)
2. Make the stroganoff: In a large stainless-steel or cast-iron skillet, heat the avocado oil over high heat. Add the steak and cook, undisturbed, until browned on the first side, 2 to 3 minutes. Flip the steak slices and cook for 1 minute, until lightly browned. Transfer the browned steak to a bowl.
3. Reduce the heat to medium and add the ghee to the pan. When it has melted, add the mushrooms and season with salt. Cook, stirring, until the mushrooms have browned and any moisture they release has evaporated, 4 to 5 minutes. Add the shallot and garlic and cook, scraping up any browned bits from the bottom of the pan, for 2 to 3 minutes. Pour in the stock and stir, scraping up any stubborn browned bits, and cook until the stock has reduced by one-quarter, about 1 minute.
4. Add 1 cup of the coconut sour cream (reserve the rest for another use), the mustard, and a pinch of pepper and stir to combine. Gently simmer the sauce for 2 to 3 minutes, reducing the heat if needed to maintain a simmer. Taste and adjust the seasoning as desired. Return the beef to the pan and toss to coat with the sauce. Remove the pan from the heat, sprinkle in the dill, and toss once more to combine. Garnish with more dill and serve immediately.

Basil Sirloin Medallions with Veggie

Prep time: 20 minutes | Cook time: 15 minutes | Serves 2

¼ cup coconut aminos
2 garlic cloves, finely chopped
1 teaspoon grated fresh ginger
1 teaspoon arrowroot starch
½ teaspoon fish sauce
1 to 2 tablespoons coconut oil
2 top sirloin medallions (8 ounces / 227 g total), thinly sliced against the grain
2 carrots, thinly sliced on an angle
2 celery stalks, thinly sliced on an angle
2 scallions, white and green parts separated and thinly sliced on an angle
½ cup raw unsalted cashews
1 fresh Thai bird's-eye chile, finely chopped
1 cup loosely packed fresh basil leaves, coarsely chopped if large
Cauliflower rice or steamed jasmine rice, for serving

1. In a mason jar, combine the coconut aminos, garlic, ginger, arrowroot starch, and fish sauce. Seal the jar tightly and shake vigorously until the sauce is completely smooth. Set aside.
2. In a large wok or cast-iron skillet, melt the coconut oil over high heat. Add the beef and cook, undisturbed, until browned on the bottom, 2 to 3 minutes. Add the carrots, celery, scallion whites, cashews, and Thai chile and cook, stirring frequently, until the vegetables have softened slightly but retain some crunch, 4 to 5 minutes. Pour in the coconut aminos sauce and toss to coat. Cook until the sauce has reduced by one-quarter, about 4 minutes. If you find that the sauce is drying out too quickly, add 1 to 2 tablespoons water as needed.
3. Remove the pan from the heat and sprinkle in the basil and the scallion greens. Toss to combine and serve immediately over cauliflower rice.

Beef Short Ribs with Two Mushrooms

Prep time: 30 minutes | Cook time: 2 hours | Serves 2

3 tablespoons extra-virgin olive oil
1 cup chopped carrots
½ cup thinly sliced celery
½ cup chopped onion
4 to 6 bone-in beef short ribs (1 to 1¼ pounds / 454 to 567 g total)
1 cup beef bone broth or Whole30-compliant beef broth
¾ teaspoon salt
Black pepper, to taste
¼ cup dried porcini mushrooms
Boiling water
1 cup sliced cremini mushrooms
1 clove garlic, minced
2 teaspoons coconut aminos
1 teaspoon Whole30-compliant coarse-grain mustard

1. Preheat the oven to 325°F (163°C).
2. Heat 1 tablespoon of the olive oil in a 3- to 4-quart brazier or oven-safe skillet over medium heat. Add the carrots, celery, and onion to the hot oil and cook, stirring occasionally, for 5 minutes. Use a slotted spoon to transfer the vegetables to a bowl. Add the short ribs to the pan. Brown the ribs, turning to brown all sides evenly. Spoon the vegetables around the ribs in the pan. Add ½ cup of the broth. Sprinkle the meat and vegetables with ½ teaspoon of the salt and pepper to taste. Bring to a boil. Cover the pan with the lid, transfer to the oven, and cook for 2 to 2½ hours, until the meat is very tender.
3. Place the dried mushrooms in a small bowl and add just enough boiling water to cover them. Let stand for 10 minutes. Drain the mushrooms in a fine-mesh sieve set over a bowl to catch the soaking liquid; set the liquid aside. Rinse the mushrooms well and chop them.
4. In a medium saucepan, heat the remaining 2 tablespoons oil over medium heat. Add the porcini and cremini mushrooms and cook, stirring occasionally, until tender and lightly browned, 6 to 8 minutes. Add the garlic and cook, stirring, for 1 minute more.
5. In a small bowl, whisk together the coconut aminos and mustard. Add the mustard mixture to the pan with the mushrooms. Stir in the remaining ½ cup broth and the mushroom soaking liquid. Bring to a boil. Reduce the heat to medium-low and simmer, uncovered, until the liquid has reduced slightly, 3 to 5 minutes. Add the remaining ¼ teaspoon salt and pepper to taste.
6. Transfer the ribs to a serving platter. Use a slotted spoon to transfer the vegetables to the pan with the mushrooms. Skim the fat off the top of the cooking juices in the brazier. Add the cooking juices to the mushroom mixture and bring just to a boil. Spoon the vegetables and sauce over the ribs to serve.

Grilled Beef Skirt

Prep time: 10 minutes | Cook time: 10 minutes | Serves 2

2 tablespoons fresh lime juice
2 tablespoons finely chopped onion
1 tablespoon plus 2 teaspoons extra-virgin olive oil
2 teaspoons finely chopped fresh ginger
3 cloves garlic, minced
½ teaspoon coarse salt
¼ teaspoon black pepper
1 (12-ounce / 340-g) beef skirt or scored flank steak
16 cherry tomatoes
1 cup fresh cilantro leaves
½ cup fresh parsley leaves
2 tablespoons fresh oregano leaves
¼ cup avocado oil or extra-virgin olive oil
2 teaspoons red wine vinegar
¼ teaspoon red pepper flakes
Lettuce leaves, for serving (optional)

1. In a shallow dish, combine the lime juice, onion, 1 tablespoon of the olive oil, the ginger, one-third of the garlic, ⅛ teaspoon of the salt, and ⅛ teaspoon of the black pepper. Add the steak and turn to coat. Cover and marinate in the refrigerator for 1 to 4 hours, turning the meat occasionally.
2. If using wooden skewers, soak them in water to cover for 30 minutes to 1 hour to prevent them from burning.
3. In a medium bowl, combine the tomatoes, remaining 2 teaspoons olive oil, ⅛ teaspoon of the salt, and remaining ⅛ teaspoon black pepper. Toss to coat. Thread the tomatoes evenly on two 10- to 12-inch skewers, leaving ¼ inch of space between the tomatoes.
4. Preheat a grill to medium heat. Remove the steak from the marinade and discard the marinade. Grill the steak over direct heat until the internal temperature reaches 145 to 150°F (63 to 66°C), 10 to 12 minutes for skirt steak or 15 to 17 minutes for flank steak. Grill the tomatoes for 4 to 6 minutes, or until softened and browned. Remove the steak and tomatoes from the grill. Cover the steak with aluminum foil and let rest for 5 minutes.
5. Meanwhile, in a food processor or blender, combine the cilantro, parsley, avocado oil, oregano, vinegar, remaining ⅛ teaspoon salt, the red pepper flakes, and remaining garlic. Process or blend until the mixture is well combined and finely chopped, but not completely smooth.
6. Thinly slice the steak across the grain. Serve on plates with the tomatoes. Spoon the cilantro sauce evenly over all. If desired, serve with lettuce leaves to make lettuce wraps. (Use any leftover cilantro sauce on your morning eggs.)

Fall seven times, stand up eight.

Mushroom Stuffed Sirloin Roulade

Prep time: 25 minutes | Cook time: 25 minutes | Serves 4

- 5 tablespoons extra-virgin olive oil
- 8 ounces (227 g) cremini mushrooms, finely chopped
- 1 cup finely chopped red onion
- ½ cup finely chopped red bell pepper
- 4 cloves garlic, minced
- 1 tablespoon chopped fresh oregano
- ¾ cup chopped fresh basil
- 1 tablespoon almond flour
- 1 teaspoon grated lemon zest
- 1 teaspoon salt
- 1 pound (454 g) green beans, trimmed
- ½ teaspoon red pepper flakes
- 1 beef sirloin or round steak (1¼ to 1½ pounds / 567 to 680 g)
- 2 tablespoons Whole30-compliant tomato paste
- 1 cup beef bone broth or Whole30-compliant beef broth

1. Preheat the oven to 400°F (205°C).
2. Heat 1 tablespoon of the olive oil in a large skillet over medium-high heat. Add the mushrooms and cook, stirring occasionally, until lightly browned, about 3 minutes. Add ½ cup of the onion and the bell pepper. Cook, stirring occasionally, until the onion is tender, 3 minutes. Add half the garlic and the oregano. Cook, stirring, for 1 minute more. Remove from the heat and stir in ½ cup of the basil, the almond flour, lemon zest, and ½ teaspoon of the salt. Transfer the mushroom mixture to a bowl and set aside to cool slightly. Rinse and dry the skillet.
3. Trim away any excess fat from the edges of the steak. Place the steak on a work surface. With the notched edge of a meat mallet, pound the steak to about ¼ inch thick. Spread the mushroom mixture over the steak to within ½ inch of the edges. Starting on a long side, roll up the meat and tie it with 100% cotton kitchen string.
4. In a medium bowl, combine the green beans, 2 tablespoons of the oil, the remaining garlic, and the remaining ½ teaspoon salt and toss. Spread the beans evenly on a large baking sheet. Roast for 18 to 20 minutes, until the beans are lightly browned and crisp-tender.
5. In the same skillet, heat the remaining 2 tablespoons olive oil over medium-high heat. Sear the meat in the hot oil and cook, turning occasionally, to sear evenly on all sides. Remove the meat from the skillet. Add the remaining ½ cup onion to the skillet. Cook, stirring, until softened, about 5 minutes. Stir in the tomato paste, then whisk in the broth. Bring the broth to a boil. Return the meat to the skillet and spoon some of the sauce over the meat. Cover and reduce the heat to medium-low. Simmer gently, turning once, until the internal temperature of the roulade is 160°F (71°C), 8 to 10 minutes. Sprinkle with the remaining ¼ cup basil.
6. Transfer the roulade to a cutting board and let rest for 5 to 10 minutes. Remove the string and cut into ½-inch-thick slices. Serve the meat and sauce with the green beans.

Beef Hamburger Soup

Prep time: 20 minutes | Cook time: 1 hour | Serves 6 to 8

- 1 tablespoon extra-virgin olive oil
- 1 pound (454 g) lean ground beef
- 3 celery stalks, diced (about 1½ cups)
- 3 carrots, diced (about 1½ cups)
- 1 red onion, diced
- 1 red bell pepper, diced
- Kosher salt, to taste
- 4 garlic cloves, finely chopped
- 4 cups beef stock
- 1 (28-ounce / 794-g) can crushed tomatoes
- 3 yellow potatoes, peeled, if desired, and cubed
- 2 bay leaves
- 1 tablespoon fresh thyme leaves
- ½ teaspoon freshly ground black pepper, plus more as needed
- 2 cups frozen chopped green beans
- ½ cup thinly sliced dill pickles, for garnish

1. In a large Dutch oven or heavy-bottomed stockpot, heat the olive oil over medium-high heat. Working in batches, add the ground beef and cook, breaking up the meat with a wooden spoon as it cooks, until browned, 10 to 12 minutes. Using a slotted spoon, transfer the beef to a bowl and repeat to brown the remaining beef.
2. Discard all but 2 tablespoons of the rendered fat from the pot. Return the pot to medium heat and add the celery, carrots, onion, and bell pepper. Season with salt. Cook the vegetables for 2 to 3 minutes, using a wooden spoon to scrape up any browned bits from the bottom of the pot. Add the garlic and cook, stirring, for 1 minute.
3. Return the browned beef back to the pot and add the stock, crushed tomatoes, potatoes, bay leaves, thyme, pepper, and 2 cups water. Bring to a boil over high heat, then reduce the heat to medium-low, cover, and cook at a steady simmer, stirring occasionally to prevent burning, for 30 minutes. Add the green beans and cook until they are warmed through, 2 to 3 minutes. Taste and adjust the seasoning.
4. For best results, let the soup cool in the pot for about 30 minutes before serving. Ladle into individual bowls, top with slices of dill pickle, and serve.

Pineapple Beef Steak Kabobs

Prep time: 25 minutes | Cook time: 10 minutes | Serves 4

2 pounds (907 g) lean beef steak (sirloin, flank, strip), cut into 1-inch pieces
¼ cup unsweetened pineapple juice
3 tablespoons coconut aminos
2 tablespoons fresh lemon juice
1 serrano chile pepper, seeded and thinly sliced
2 teaspoons grated fresh ginger
1 clove garlic, minced
¼ teaspoon salt
¼ teaspoon black pepper
1 small pineapple, peeled, cored, and cut into 1½-inch chunks
2 bell peppers, seeded and cut into 1½-inch pieces
1 onion, cut into 8 wedges

1. Place the steak in a resealable plastic bag or nonreactive bowl with a lid and add the pineapple juice, coconut aminos, lemon juice, serrano chile, ginger, garlic, salt, and black pepper. Toss the steak to coat thoroughly with the marinade. Seal the bag or cover the bowl and marinate the steak in the refrigerator for 1 to 24 hours.
2. If using wooden skewers, soak them in water for 30 minutes to 1 hour to prevent them from burning.
3. Remove the steak from the refrigerator 30 minutes before cooking. Preheat a grill to medium heat.
4. Drain the steak, reserving the marinade. Prepare the kabobs by threading the steak, pineapple, bell peppers, and onion onto the skewers, leaving a ¼-inch space between each piece. Brush the kabobs with the marinade.
5. Grill the kabobs over direct heat, brushing them with the marinade and turning them once or twice, for 8 to 12 minutes, until the vegetables are tender and steak is cooked to the desired doneness. Discard any remaining marinade.

Tender Beef Pot Roast

Prep time: 15 minutes | Cook time: 6 to 8 hours | Serves 2

1½ pounds (680 g) beef roast (chuck, boneless short ribs, brisket, top round, rump)
1 teaspoon salt
½ teaspoon black pepper
1 onion, sliced
3 carrots, unpeeled and cut into 2-inch pieces
3 stalks celery, cut into 1-inch pieces
1 small butternut squash, peeled and large-diced
2 cloves garlic
2 sprigs thyme
2 cups beef broth or water

1. Set your slow cooker to low heat, and season your roast with the salt and pepper.
2. Add the beef roast, onions, carrots, celery, butternut squash, garlic, and thyme sprigs to the slow cooker. Top with the broth or water (or enough to cover the roast halfway) and leave the roast to cook for 6 to 8 hours. The roast should be fork-tender when done.
3. Remove the roast, transfer to a large plate or serving dish, and cover with foil. Allow the meat to rest for 15 minutes before serving.
4. Remove the thyme springs from the broth and discard. Slice the roast against the grain. Divide the meat and vegetables on individual plates, and ladle broth over the top.

Stuffed Bell Peppers with Beef

Prep time: 20 minutes | Cook time: 30 minutes | Serves 2

4 red, yellow, or orange bell peppers (preferably round in shape)
3 tablespoons cooking fat
¼ cup finely chopped onion
2 cloves garlic, minced (or 1 teaspoon garlic powder)
4 kale leaves, stems removed, leaves finely chopped
1 pound (454 g) ground meat (beef, lamb, bison)
2 tablespoons tomato paste
¼ teaspoon cumin
¼ teaspoon chili powder
½ teaspoon salt
¼ teaspoon black pepper
1 cup finely chopped peeled winter squash (butternut, acorn, etc.)

1. Preheat the oven to 350°F (180°C). Line a deep baking dish with parchment paper.
2. With a paring knife, slice around the top of each bell pepper and gently pull up on the stem. Discard the seeded core. Place the peppers in the prepared dish. Bake for 10 minutes, until softened. Set aside.
3. Meanwhile, melt the cooking fat in a large skillet over medium heat and swirl to coat the bottom. When the fat is hot, add the onion and cook, stirring with a wooden spoon, until translucent, 2 to 3 minutes. Add the garlic and continue to cook until aromatic, about 1 minute. Add the kale and cook for 1 minute, stirring. Add the ground meat and cook, breaking up the meat with a spatula or wooden spoon and stirring it into the vegetables, for 2 to 3 minutes. Stir in the tomato paste, cumin, chili powder, salt, and pepper. Cook until the meat is mostly browned, 7 to 9 minutes. Stir in the squash and cook until the squash is slightly softened, 2 to 3 minutes.
4. Divide the meat and squash mixture evenly among the softened bell peppers. Return to the oven and bake for 10 minutes, until the peppers look wrinkly and the beef is slightly browned on top.

Fall seven times, stand up eight. -Chapter 3 Beef

Thai-Style Beef Curry with Green Beans

Prep time: 25 minutes | Cook time: 7 hours | Serves 4

1 tablespoon coconut oil, plus more as needed
2 pounds (907 g) charcoal steak, cut into 1-inch cubes
1 teaspoon coarse salt
½ teaspoon black pepper
1 yellow onion, sliced
3 cloves garlic, minced
1 (14-ounce / 397-g) can full-fat coconut milk
3 tablespoons Whole30-compliant Thai red curry paste
2 teaspoons Red Boat fish sauce
1 pound (454 g) fresh green beans, trimmed

1. Heat the coconut oil in a heavy skillet over medium-high heat. Season the steak with the salt and pepper. Add the beef to the skillet and cook, stirring occasionally, until browned on all sides, about 5 minutes. Place the meat in a slow cooker.
2. Cook the onion in the same skillet, adding additional coconut oil if needed. Cook, stirring, until the onion is soft, 4 to 5 minutes. Add the garlic and cook, stirring, until fragrant, about 30 seconds. Add the coconut milk and curry paste, stirring to scrape up any brown bits from the bottom of the skillet. Stir in the fish sauce. Transfer to the slow cooker.
3. Cover and cook on low for 7 to 8 hours or on high for 3½ to 4 hours. Add the green beans and cook on high for 30 minutes more, until the beans are crisp-tender.

Braised Beef Brisket

Prep time: 15 minutes | Cook time: 4 hours | Serves 2

1 tablespoon salt
1 teaspoon black pepper
1½ pounds (680 g) beef brisket, trimmed
3 tablespoons cooking fat
½ medium onion, peeled and quartered
4 cloves garlic, peeled
2 sprigs fresh thyme
5 cups beef bone broth or water

1. Preheat the oven to 350ºF (180ºC).
2. Mix the salt and pepper in a small bowl and use to season the brisket evenly on both sides.
3. In a Dutch oven or deep flameproof roasting pan, melt the cooking fat over medium-high heat, coating the bottom of the pan. When the fat is hot, add the brisket and sear until golden brown, about 2 minutes on each side. Remove the brisket from the pan.
4. Reduce the heat to medium under the same pan and add the onion. Cook, scraping the bottom of the pot with a wooden spoon to prevent burning, until the onion is softened, 2 to 3 minutes. Add the garlic and cook until aromatic, about 1 minute. Add the thyme, broth or water, and brisket, increase the heat to medium-high, and bring to a boil.
5. Cover the pot, transfer to the oven, and bake, turning the meat after each hour, for 3½ to 4 hours, until the brisket is fork tender.
6. Transfer the brisket to a bowl and shred or slice thin, discarding the excess fat. Discard the thyme stems.
7. Ladle the cooking liquid, onions, and garlic from the pan into a food processor or blender. Blend the sauce completely. Place the pan back on the stovetop, return the sauce to the pan, and bring to a simmer over medium-high heat. Simmer until the sauce coats the back of a wooden spoon, about 5 minutes.
8. Serve the brisket warm with the sauce.

Beef Steaks with Garlic-Shallot Purée

Prep time: 15 minutes | Cook time: 25 minutes | Serves 2

2 steaks (5 ounces / 142 g each) for grilling (sirloin, strip, rib eye, tenderloin)
1 teaspoon salt
1 teaspoon black pepper
2 cloves garlic, peeled
1 shallot, peeled
2 tablespoons extra-virgin olive oil
1 avocado, split lengthwise, pitted, and peeled

1. Remove the steaks from the refrigerator 30 minutes before cooking. Preheat a grill to high heat and the oven to 350ºF (180ºC). Line a baking sheet with foil.
2. Mix the salt and pepper in a small bowl and use two-thirds of the mixture to season the steaks.
3. Toss the garlic and shallot in 1 tablespoon of the olive oil and arrange on the prepared baking sheet. Season evenly with the remaining salt and pepper. Roast in the oven for 25 minutes, until the cloves are soft throughout. Transfer the garlic and shallots to a food processor, add the remaining 1 tablespoon olive oil, and purée. Transfer the purée to a dish, cover with foil to keep warm, and set aside.
4. Lay the steaks on the hot grill and sear for 2 to 3 minutes. The steaks should pull off easily when they are seared. Turn the steaks over and sear the other side, 1 to 2 minutes, or to desired doneness. Let the steaks rest for 5 to 10 minutes.
5. Meanwhile, sear the avocado halves pitted side down on the grill until lightly browned, 3 to 4 minutes.
6. Arrange the avocado and steaks on plates and top the steaks with the warm garlic and shallot purée.

Steak Fajita Bowls with Veggie

Prep time: 20 minutes | Cook time: 10 minutes | Serves 4

Beef:
- 1 pound (454 g) flank steak or skirt steak, thinly sliced
- 1 teaspoon paprika
- ½ teaspoon salt
- ½ teaspoon dried oregano
- ½ teaspoon garlic powder
- ½ teaspoon ground cumin
- ¼ teaspoon black pepper
- ⅛ teaspoon cayenne pepper
- 1 tablespoon extra-virgin olive oil

Vegetables:
- 1 tablespoon extra-virgin olive oil
- 2 small red, green, and/or yellow bell peppers, cut into ½-inch strips
- 1 small red onion, halved and cut into ¼-inch slices
- 1 clove garlic, minced
- 1 (12-ounce / 340-g) package frozen riced cauliflower or 4 cups raw riced cauliflower
- ¼ teaspoon salt
- ⅛ teaspoon black pepper
- 1 cup Whole30-compliant guacamole
- ½ cup Whole30-compliant salsa
- ¼ cup chopped fresh cilantro (optional)
- Lime wedges (optional)

1. Make the beef: Place the beef in a medium bowl. In a small bowl, combine the paprika, salt, oregano, garlic powder, cumin, black pepper, and cayenne. Sprinkle the spice mixture over the beef and toss to coat. Let stand while cooking the vegetables.
2. Make the vegetables: In a large skillet, heat 1 table-spoon olive oil over medium heat. Add the bell peppers and onion. Cook, stirring frequently, until the vegetables are crisp-tender, 7 to 8 minutes. Stir in the garlic. Transfer the vegetables to a serving dish; cover to keep warm.
3. Meanwhile, prepare the cauliflower rice according to the package directions. Add the salt and pepper; stir to combine. Cover to keep warm.
4. In the same large skillet, heat 1 tablespoon olive oil over medium heat; add the beef. Cook, stirring frequently, 3 to 4 minutes or to desired doneness.
5. Spoon the cauliflower into four shallow serving bowls. Top with the vegetables, beef, guacamole, and salsa. If desired, sprinkle with cilantro and serve with lime wedges.

Mongolian Beef and Mixed Greens

Prep time: 12 minutes | Cook time: 8 minutes | Serves 4

- 2 tablespoons coconut aminos
- 1 tablespoon Red Boat fish sauce
- 2 teaspoons olive oil
- 1 pound (454 g) beef sirloin tips, skirt steak, or boneless short ribs, thinly sliced
- 1 piece (3 inches) fresh ginger, peeled and cut into matchsticks
- 2 fresh red chile peppers, seeded and cut into matchsticks or thinly sliced (optional)
- 3 cloves garlic, minced
- 3 green onions, cut into 3-inch lengths, white and green parts separated
- 4 tablespoons clarified butter, ghee, or coconut oil
- 1 (5-ounce / 142-g) container mixed greens

1. Combine the coconut aminos, fish sauce, and olive oil in a large bowl. Add the beef and turn to coat. Cover the bowl and marinate in the refrigerator for 15 to 20 minutes.
2. Meanwhile, in a small bowl, combine the ginger, chile peppers, garlic, and white parts of the green onions.
3. In a large skillet, melt 1 tablespoon of the butter over medium heat. Add the beef and marinade to the skillet and cook, tossing with tongs occasionally, until no longer pink, 4 to 5 minutes. Transfer the meat and sauce to a bowl.
4. In the same skillet, heat the remaining 3 tablespoons butter. Add the ginger mixture and cook over medium heat, stirring, until fragrant, 1 to 2 minutes. Add the meat and green parts of green onions to the skillet; toss to combine.
5. Serve the beef and sauce over the mixed greens.

Indian Masala Steak Stir-Fry

Prep time: 15 minutes | Cook time: 10 minutes | Serves 4

- 1 tablespoon Whole30-compliant garam masala
- ½ teaspoon garlic salt
- 2 tablespoons coconut oil
- 1 medium onion, cut into thin wedges
- 2 large yellow and/or red bell peppers, cut into strips
- 1½ pounds (680 g) strip steak, flank steak, or skirt steak, cut into strips
- 2 teaspoons minced fresh ginger
- Fresh cilantro, for serving

1. In a small bowl, stir together 3 tablespoons water, the garam masala, and garlic salt; set aside.
2. Heat 1 tablespoon of the oil in a large skillet over medium-high heat. Add the onion and cook, stirring, for 1 minute. Add the bell pepper and cook, stirring, until beginning to soften but still crisp, about 3 minutes. Transfer the onion and pepper to a plate and cover to keep warm.
3. In the same skillet, heat the remaining 1 tablespoon oil over medium-high heat. Add the meat and ginger and cook, stirring, until meat is desired doneness 1 to 2 minutes. Stir in the onion and pepper and heat through, about 1 minute. Garnish with the cilantro and serve.

Black Pepper Beef and Coleslaw Stir-Fry

Prep time: 10 minutes | Cook time: 6 hours | Serves 4

1½ pounds (680 g) beef stir-fry strips
2 cups thinly sliced onions
5 cloves garlic, minced
1 tablespoon minced fresh ginger
½ cup Whole30-compliant beef broth or beef bone broth
2 teaspoons Red Boat fish sauce
1 teaspoon black pepper
1 (14-ounce / 397-g) bag packaged coleslaw mix (shredded cabbage and carrots)
½ teaspoon grated lime zest
1 tablespoon lime juice
Chopped fresh cilantro and/or basil (optional)

1. Combine the beef, onions, garlic, ginger, broth, fish sauce, and ½ teaspoon of the black pepper in a slow cooker. Cover and cook on low for 6 to 7 hours or on high for 3 to 4 hours.
2. Just before serving, stir in the remaining ½ teaspoon black pepper, the coleslaw mix, and the lime zest and juice. Top each serving with cilantro and/or basil, if desired.

Sirloin Steak and Broccoli Stir-Fry

Prep time: 15 minutes | Cook time: 15 minutes | Serves 4

2 tablespoons coconut aminos
1 tablespoon minced fresh ginger
4 cloves garlic, minced
¼ teaspoon salt
1 pound (454 g) boneless top sirloin steak, trimmed and cut against the grain into ⅛-inch slices
4 tablespoons olive oil
3 cups small broccoli florets
1 medium red onion, quartered and thinly sliced
1 cup packaged shredded carrots, or 2 medium carrots, shredded
1 cup low-sodium Whole30-compliant beef broth or beef bone broth
2 teaspoons arrowroot
¼ to ½ teaspoon red pepper flakes
6 cups packaged shredded green cabbage
1 tablespoon sesame seeds, toasted

1. In a medium bowl, combine the coconut aminos, ginger, garlic, and salt. Add the beef and mix well. Let the beef stand at room temperature while cooking the vegetables.
2. In a large skillet, heat 1 tablespoon of the olive oil over medium-high heat. Add the broccoli, onion, and carrots. Cook, stirring, until the vegetables are crisp-tender, about 3 minutes. Transfer the vegetables to a bowl and set aside.
3. Add 1 tablespoon olive oil to the skillet. Add half the beef and cook, stirring, until slightly pink in the center, 2 to 3 minutes. Add to the bowl with the vegetables. Add 1 tablespoon olive oil to the skillet and cook the remaining beef, stirring, until slightly pink in center, 2 to 3 minutes. Return the vegetables and cooked beef to the skillet.
4. In a small bowl, whisk together the broth, arrowroot, and pepper flakes until smooth. Push the meat and vegetables to the edges of the skillet. Pour the broth mixture into the center. Cook over medium-high heat, stirring, until thickened, 1 to 2 minutes. Stir the meat and vegetables into the sauce. Transfer the stir-fry to a large serving bowl and cover to keep warm. Carefully wipe out the skillet with paper towels.
5. Add the remaining 1 tablespoon olive oil to the skillet and heat over medium-high heat. Add the cabbage and cook, stirring, until bright green and wilted, 1 to 2 minutes. Spoon the stir-fry over the cabbage, sprinkle with the sesame seeds, and serve.

Balsamic Chuck Roast and Veggies

Prep time: 30 minutes | Cook time: 5½ hours | Serves 4

1 tablespoon coconut oil
1½ to 2 pounds (907 g) (680 to 907 g) boneless chuck roast or bottom round, cut into 1½-inch cubes
Salt and black pepper, to taste
1 pound (454 g) large carrots, peeled and cut into 1-inch pieces
1 pound (454 g) parsnips, peeled and cut into ½-inch pieces
1 pound (454 g) small red potatoes, halved
1 medium onion, chopped
1 clove garlic, minced
2 cups Whole30-compliant beef broth or beef bone broth
¼ cup balsamic vinegar
2 teaspoons Whole30-compliant dried Italian seasoning
Chopped fresh parsley (optional)

1. Heat the coconut oil in a large heavy skillet over medium-high heat. Season the beef lightly with salt and pepper. Add the beef to the skillet and cook, stirring occasionally, until browned on all sides, about 5 minutes. Place the beef in a slow cooker with the carrots, parsnips, and potatoes.
2. Add the onion to the same skillet and add additional coconut oil if needed. Cook, stirring frequently, until the onion is soft, 4 to 5 minutes. Add the garlic and cook, stirring, until fragrant, about 30 seconds. Add the broth, vinegar, and Italian seasoning and stir to scrape up any brown bits on the bottom of the skillet. Transfer to the slow cooker.
3. Cover and cook on low for 5½ to 6 hours or on high for 3 hours. Top servings with parsley, if desired.

Seared Sirloin Steak with Asparagus

Prep time: 10 minutes | Cook time: 40 minutes | Serves 4

1 pound (454 g) asparagus
1 pound (454 g) sirloin steak
2 teaspoons kosher salt
½ teaspoon freshly ground black pepper
5 tablespoons plus 2 teaspoons extra-virgin olive oil
1 pound (454 g) brown mushrooms, trimmed and quartered lengthwise
2 teaspoons coconut aminos

1. Preheat the oven to 400°F (205°C).
2. Cut off the woody stems of the asparagus. Peel the rough ends and, with your knife at a 45-degree angle to the cutting board, cut each stalk into thirds. Set aside.
3. Thoroughly season the steak with 1 teaspoon of the salt and the pepper.
4. Heat a large oven-safe skillet (I use heavy-duty cast iron) over high heat. Add 2 tablespoons of the olive oil, being sure to coat the bottom of the pan. Reduce the heat to medium-high and add the steak to the skillet. Cook until well browned on the first side, about 3 minutes. Flip and brown the other side for 1 minute. Transfer the skillet to the oven and cook the steak until medium-rare, about 4 minutes (or 3 to 4 minutes longer, if you prefer medium). Remove the skillet from the oven and transfer the steak to a wooden board, reserving the juice from the skillet. Partially tent the steak with aluminum foil and let rest for 15 minutes.
5. Return the skillet to medium-high heat. Add half the mushrooms, season with ⅛ teaspoon of the salt, and add 1 tablespoon of the olive oil, if needed. Cook, stirring, for 2 minutes, then cover and cook until they have released liquid and look shiny, about 2 minutes more. Transfer the mushrooms, along with all the juices from the skillet, to a bowl and set aside. Add 1 tablespoon of the olive oil, the remaining mushrooms, and ⅛ teaspoon of the salt to the pan and cook the same way as the first batch.
6. In the same skillet, heat 1 tablespoon plus 2 teaspoons of the olive oil over medium heat. Add the asparagus and ½ teaspoon of the salt and cook for 4 minutes, stirring once halfway through. Stir again, cover, and cook for 2 minutes more. Stir again and cook, uncovered, until the asparagus is soft and cooked through, about 4 minutes more.
7. Turn off the heat and add the steak jus, mushrooms and all their juices, and the coconut aminos to the skillet with the asparagus. Stir to combine well.
8. Cut the steak into ¼-inch-thick slices and serve on top of the mushrooms and asparagus.

Pan-Seared Beef Rib-Eye with Arugula

Prep time: 5 minutes | Cook time: 15 minutes | Serves 4

1 (1½- to 2-pound / 680- to 907-g) bone-in rib-eye steak
2 tablespoons ghee or lard, divided
2 teaspoons fine Himalayan salt
5 cloves garlic, peeled
3 sprigs fresh oregano, thyme, or sage
2 cups fresh arugula

1. Set the rib-eye out to come to room temperature about 30 minutes before you begin cooking.
2. Place a large cast-iron skillet in the oven and preheat the oven to 425°F (220°C).
3. While the oven heats, brush the steak with 1 tablespoon of the ghee and sprinkle it with the salt.
4. When the oven has come to temperature, remove the skillet and set it on the stovetop over medium heat. Place the steak in the skillet and sear for 2 minutes. Flip the steak with tongs and top it with the garlic and herbs. Sear for 2 minutes on the other side, then place the skillet with the steak in the oven for 8 to 10 minutes, depending on the thickness of the steak and the desired doneness.
5. Remove the skillet from the oven and return it to the stovetop over medium heat. Move the herbs and garlic to the side of the pan and dollop the remaining tablespoon of ghee over them.
6. Carefully tilt the skillet so the fat pools with the garlic and herbs. Using a small spoon, repeatedly pour this pooled fat over the steak as it cooks for 2 minutes.
7. Remove the steak from the skillet and set it on a cutting board to rest for 5 minutes. When ready to serve, run a sharp knife along the inside of the bone to separate the meat, then slice the steak against the grain in very thin slices.
8. Divide the steak slices among four plates. Add ½ cup arugula to each plate and spoon the pan sauce all over the arugula. Enjoy!
9. It's a shame to eat meat this good as leftovers—it's just not the same. But if you have extra, cut it up into small pieces and store in an airtight container in the fridge for up to 4 days. Reheat in a hot skillet. Rib-eye is fatty, so it will be nice and crispy; toss it with eggs or greens for a beef hash.

Traditional Picadillo

Prep time: 20 minutes | Cook time: 1 hour | Serves 6 to 8

- 1 tablespoon avocado oil
- 2 pounds (907 g) lean ground beef
- 1 large yellow onion, thinly sliced
- 1 red bell pepper, diced
- 5 garlic cloves, finely chopped
- 2 teaspoons smoked Spanish paprika
- 2 teaspoons ancho chile powder
- 1 teaspoon ground cumin
- 1 teaspoon dried oregano
- 1 teaspoon kosher salt, plus more as needed
- 1 teaspoon freshly ground black pepper, plus more as needed
- 1½ cups chicken stock
- 1½ cups sliced pitted green olives, such as Manzanilla
- ¼ cup no-sugar-added dark raisins (optional)
- 2 bay leaves

1. In a large Dutch oven or heavy-bottomed pot, heat the avocado oil over medium-high heat. Working in batches, add the ground beef and cook, breaking it up with your spoon as it cooks, until browned, about 12 minutes. Transfer the beef to a bowl and repeat to cook the remaining meat.
2. Discard all but 2 tablespoons of the rendered fat from the pot and set it over medium heat. Add the onion and bell pepper and cook, stirring, until the onion is slightly caramelized, 8 to 10 minutes. Add the garlic and cook, stirring, until fragrant, about 1 minute. Add the paprika, ancho chile powder, cumin, oregano, salt, and black pepper. Stir, letting the spices warm and toast, for 1 minute. Add the stock and stir, using your spoon to scrape up any browned bits from the bottom of the pot.
3. Return the beef to the pot and add the olives, raisins (if using), and bay leaves. Increase the heat to medium-high and bring the sauce to a simmer. Reduce the heat to low, cover, and cook, stirring occasionally to prevent burning, until the beef is tender, at least 30 minutes or up to 1 hour for a more intensely flavored finished product. Taste and season with additional salt and pepper as desired. Discard the bay leaves. Let stand 10 minutes before serving.

Herb Beef Eye of Round Roast

Prep time: 5 minutes | Cook time: 3 hours | Serves 6

- 1 (2½-pound / 1.1-kg) beef eye of round roast
- 3 tablespoons extra-virgin olive oil
- 2 teaspoons kosher salt
- 1 teaspoon freshly ground black pepper
- 1 teaspoon chopped fresh rosemary
- ½ teaspoon dried oregano
- 5 garlic cloves, smashed and unpeeled
- 1 cup chicken stock

1. Preheat the oven to 500ºF (260ºC).
2. Put the beef in a roasting pan. Thoroughly coat with the olive oil, rolling it around to completely cover. Season the beef with the salt, pepper, rosemary, and oregano. Remove the beef from the pan and set aside.
3. Set a roasting rack securely in the pan and spread the unpeeled garlic cloves over the bottom of the pan. Pour ½ cup of the stock into the pan, then put the beef on the rack.
4. Transfer to the oven and reduce the oven temperature to 475ºF (245ºC). Roast for 12½ minutes if you prefer medium-rare, or about 16 minutes for medium. (In case your roast is not exactly 2½ pounds (1.1 kg), the calculation is 5 minutes per pound for medium-rare and closer to 6½ minutes per pound for medium.) Turn off the oven and leave the beef in the (turned-off) oven to slowly cook for 2½ hours more.
5. Remove the beef from the oven and transfer it to a cutting board to rest for 30 minutes.
6. Set the roasting pan on the stovetop over low heat. Add the remaining ½ cup stock and stir, scraping up all the caramelized bits from the bottom of the pan. Transfer the liquid to a small saucepan and set aside.
7. Slice as much of the beef as needed for serving. Pour any juices from the cutting board into the saucepan, stir, and warm the jus over medium heat.
8. Pour the jus over the sliced meat and serve. To keep it juicy, store the leftover piece of beef whole, not sliced.

Pepperoncini-Flavour Skirt Steak

Prep time: 15 minutes | Cook time: 45 minutes | Serves 4

- 1¼ pounds (567 g) skirt steak, thinly sliced across the grain into 3-inch pieces
- 4 tablespoons coconut oil, plus 1 teaspoon melted
- 2 teaspoons arrowroot starch
- 1½ teaspoons kosher salt
- ½ teaspoon freshly ground black pepper
- ¼ cup finely chopped shallots
- 1½ cups thinly sliced yellow bell peppers
- ½ cup thinly sliced scallions
- 2 Thai chiles, seeded and sliced into thin rounds
- 1 cup quartered green beans, blanched
- ½ cup stemmed and thinly sliced jarred pepperoncini
- 1 tablespoon pressed garlic
- 2 tablespoons coconut aminos
- 2 tablespoons brine from the jar of pepperoncini
- 1 cup fresh basil leaves

1. In a medium bowl, combine the steak, 1 teaspoon melted coconut oil, the arrowroot, 1 teaspoon of the salt, and the black pepper. Toss to coat thoroughly. Set aside for 5 minutes.
2. Heat a large sauté pan over high heat. When hot, reduce to medium-high and melt 1 tablespoon of the coconut oil in the pan. Add half the steak and cook until seared, about 2 minutes. Flip and cook until browned, about 30 seconds. Transfer the steak to a large plate and set aside. Carefully wipe out the pan with a paper towel, then add 1 tablespoon of the coconut oil and repeat with the remaining steak. Set aside with the other cooked steak.
3. Wipe out the pan and return it to medium-high heat. Melt the remaining 2 tablespoons coconut oil in the pan. When the oil is hot, reduce the heat to medium, add the shallots, and cook, stirring, until beginning to brown, about 30 seconds. Add the bell peppers, scallions, Thai chiles, and remaining ½ teaspoon salt and cook, stirring, until the bell peppers begin to soften, about 1 minute. Add the green beans and cook, stirring well, until warmed through, about 1 minute more. Add the pepperoncini and garlic and cook, stirring, for 30 seconds.
4. Return the beef to the pan, along with any juices collected on the plate, and add the coconut aminos and the pepperoncini brine. Stir to combine, then reduce the heat to medium-low. Add the basil, stir again, and turn off the heat. Serve.

Steak au Poivre with Green Peppercorn Sauce

Prep time: 15 minutes | Cook time: 14 minutes | Serves 2

- 2 (10- to 12-ounce / 283- to 340-g) filets mignons (or substitute your favorite cut such as bavette, rib eye, skirt, porterhouse, flat iron, or New York strip), at least 1½ inches thick
- Kosher salt, to taste
- 3 tablespoons avocado oil
- 1 shallot, finely chopped
- ¼ cup full-fat coconut milk
- ½ cup chicken stock
- 1 tablespoon green peppercorns in brine, drained
- 1 teaspoon loosely packed fresh thyme leaves, finely chopped
- Freshly ground black pepper, to taste
- 1 tablespoon ghee

1. Pat the steaks dry with paper towels and liberally season all sides with salt. Place on a rimmed baking sheet and set aside for 1 hour at room temperature.
2. When ready to cook the steaks, heat a large cast-iron skillet over medium heat for 5 minutes. Increase the heat to medium-high and pour in 2 tablespoons of the avocado oil. Heat until oil is shimmering and carefully place the steaks in the skillet. Cook, flipping the steaks every 60 seconds, until the internal temperature registers 130°F (54°C) to 135°F (57°C) on an instant-read thermometer, about 8 minutes. Remove the steaks from the pan and transfer them to a wire rack to rest for 10 minutes.
3. While the steaks rest, wipe the skillet clean with a paper towel, then place it over medium heat. Pour in the remaining 1 tablespoon avocado oil, then add the shallot. Cook, stirring, until softened, 1 to 2 minutes. Stir in the coconut milk and cook, stirring occasionally, until the liquid has reduced by about half, about 2 minutes.
4. Add the stock, green peppercorns, thyme, and a pinch of black pepper. Cook until the sauce has reduced again by half, about 4 minutes. Fold in the ghee and stir until it has melted. Taste the sauce and season with salt and pepper as desired.
5. Slice the steaks against the grain and arrange them on a serving platter. Spoon the green peppercorn sauce over the top and serve.

Ritzy Short Rib Ragù

Prep time: 10 minutes | Cook time: 3½ hours | Serves 6 to 8

2 pounds (907 g) English-cut bone-in beef short ribs
Kosher salt, to taste
1 tablespoon avocado oil
3 celery stalks, diced
2 carrots, diced
1 yellow onion, diced
12 garlic cloves, smashed and peeled
2 (24-ounce / 680-g) cans or jars tomato puree
6 sprigs thyme
2 bay leaves
Freshly ground black pepper, to taste
Handful of fresh basil leaves, torn

1. Heat a Dutch oven or electric pressure cooker over medium-high heat for 5 minutes. Pat the short ribs very dry with paper towels and generously season them on all sides with salt. Increase the heat to medium-high and pour in the avocado oil. Heat the oil until shimmering, add the short ribs in batches, and cook until browned, 3 to 4 minutes on each side. Transfer the browned meat to a bowl and set aside.
2. Reduce the heat to medium and add the celery, carrots, and onion to the pot. Season with a pinch of salt. Cook, stirring and scraping up all the browned bits from the bottom of the pot, until the vegetables are softened, 10 to 12 minutes. Stir in the garlic and cook, stirring, for 1 minute.
3. Return the browned meat to the pot and add the tomato puree, thyme, and bay leaves. Season with ½ teaspoon each of salt and pepper, stir to combine, and bring the sauce to a simmer. Reduce the heat to low, cover, and cook until the meat is fall-apart tender, 2½ to 3 hours. If using a pressure cooker, lock on the lid and cook on HIGH pressure for 1½ hours. If the ragù has reduced too much or becomes clumpy, simply add a little bit of stock to thin it out. It should coat the back of a spoon.
4. Transfer the meat to a bowl and shred it with two forks. Discard the bones, thyme sprigs, and bay leaves. If you're using a pressure cooker, you may want to reduce the sauce briefly over medium-low heat with the pot uncovered, depending on your tastes and the consistency of the sauce.
5. Return the shredded meat to the pot and stir in the basil. Taste and adjust the seasoning as desired. Serve immediately.

West African Suya Stir-Fry

Prep time: 15 minutes | Cook time: 25 minutes | Serves 4

2 tablespoons raw pumpkin seeds
2 tablespoons whole flax seeds or flaxseed meal
2 tablespoons avocado oil, lard, or unsalted butter
1 medium onion, sliced
3 cloves garlic, minced
1 pound (454 g) tri-tip or sirloin steak
1½ teaspoons fine Himalayan salt, divided
1 teaspoon garlic powder
1 teaspoon ginger powder
1 teaspoon ground black pepper
¼ teaspoon ground cloves
½ cup bone broth
2 tablespoons coconut aminos
½ teaspoon liquid smoke (optional)
½ pound (227 g) fresh green beans, trimmed and halved

1. Place the seeds in a coffee grinder, blender, or mortar and pestle and grind to a coarse crumble. Set aside.
2. Heat a large skillet over medium heat. When it's hot, add the avocado oil, onions, and garlic. Sauté, stirring occasionally, until tender, about 8 minutes.
3. Meanwhile, cut the beef into ½-inch pieces and place in a bowl with ¾ teaspoon of the salt, the garlic power, ginger powder, pepper, ground cloves, and ground seeds. Toss to combine and coat the beef.
4. When the onion is tender, add the beef and all of the seedy seasoning mix to the skillet. Sauté, stirring often, until the meat is browned, about 8 minutes. As you stir, a lot of the seasoning will begin to stick to the bottom of the skillet; that's okay.
5. Stir in the broth, coconut aminos, and liquid smoke (if using) and bring to a quick simmer. Use a spoon or spatula to gently scrape all the seasonings off of the bottom of the skillet and stir them in.
6. Add the green beans to the skillet and sauté, stirring often, for another 4 to 5 minutes. Sprinkle in the remaining ¾ teaspoon of salt.
7. Stir well and serve! Store leftovers in an airtight container in the fridge for up to 5 days. Reheat in a skillet over medium heat for 5 minutes or in the microwave on high for 1 to 2 minutes.

Bacon-Wrapped Beef Meatloaf

Prep time: 10 minutes | Cook time: 50 minutes | Serves 6

- 1½ pounds (680 g) ground beef (85% lean)
- ½ large red onion, minced
- 4 cloves garlic, minced
- 2 teaspoons dry mustard
- 2 teaspoons garlic powder
- 1½ teaspoons fine Himalayan salt
- 1 teaspoon ground black pepper
- 1 teaspoon onion powder
- 2 tablespoons avocado oil
- 2 tablespoons flaxseed meal
- 2 tablespoons red wine vinegar
- ½ pound (227 g) bacon (7 or 8 slices)

1. Preheat the oven to 400ºF (205ºC). Line a sheet pan with parchment paper.
2. Place the ground beef, onions, garlic, dry mustard, garlic powder, salt, pepper, and onion powder in a large bowl and mix thoroughly to combine.
3. Add the avocado oil, flaxseed meal, and vinegar and mix again until thoroughly combined.
4. On one side of the sheet pan, shape the meat mixture into a loaf about 8 inches long and 3 to 4 inches tall. Lay the bacon slices in the center of the sheet pan and line them up so the sides overlap by ¼ inch. Lay the meatloaf in the center of the bacon. Bring the bacon slices up, wrapping them around the meatloaf and creating a seam at the top. Make sure to wrap tightly. Quickly flip the meatloaf over so the bacon seam is on the bottom. Fix the bacon slices if needed to make sure there are no gaps.
5. Bake the meatloaf for 50 minutes, or until the bacon is browned and crispy. Remove from the oven and let cool for 10 minutes.
6. Cut the meatloaf into slices the same width as the bacon slices. Serve right away.
7. Store leftovers in an airtight container in the fridge for up to a week. Reheat the slices in a skillet over medium heat until warm.

Hawaii Lazy Moco

Prep time: 10 minutes | Cook time: 15 minutes | Serves 4

- 4 cups riced cauliflower
- 2 tablespoons bacon fat, lard, or ghee, divided
- 2 teaspoons fine Himalayan salt, divided
- 1 pound (454 g) ground beef (85% lean)

For the Gravy:
- 3 tablespoons ghee or lard
- 2 tablespoons coconut flour
- 1 cup bone broth
- 1 tablespoon coconut vinegar
- 3 sprigs fresh thyme or rosemary
- ½ teaspoon fine Himalayan salt
- ½ teaspoon ground black pepper
- 4 large eggs

1. Preheat the oven to 425ºF (220ºC).
2. Spread the cauliflower on a sheet pan so that it takes up about three-quarters of it. Drizzle 1 tablespoon of the bacon fat over the cauliflower and sprinkle with 1 teaspoon of the salt.
3. Form the beef into four patties about ¼ inch thick and make an indentation in the center of each patty. Coat the patties with the remaining tablespoon of fat and sprinkle with the remaining teaspoon of salt. Line them up next to the riced cauliflower in the empty space on the sheet pan. Place in the oven and roast for 15 minutes.
4. Meanwhile, make the gravy: Melt the ghee in a small saucepan over medium-high heat. Whisk in the coconut flour and keep whisking until the flour is browned and smells toasty, almost like popcorn. This will take only a few minutes. Then pour in the broth and vinegar and stir until the mixture is smooth and fluid. Add the thyme sprigs, salt, and pepper and bring to a boil. Reduce the gravy for 5 to 8 minutes, whisking occasionally, until it becomes thick. When it's ready, it will coat a back of a spoon. Remove the gravy from the heat and discard the thyme sprigs.
5. When the patties have about 5 minutes left to cook, heat a large skillet over medium heat. When it's hot, lightly grease the skillet, then crack in the eggs. Cook, undisturbed, until the whites are cooked through. Remove from the heat. Use the edge of the spatula to separate the eggs.
6. Assemble four plates, each with a cup of riced cauliflower topped with a burger patty, a generous amount of gravy over the patty, and a fried egg. Enjoy!
7. Store leftovers in an airtight container in the fridge for up to 5 days. To reheat, place in a skillet over medium heat, and fry the egg to order.

Fall seven times, stand up eight.

Chapter 4 Pork

Balsamic and Herb Pork Tenderloin

Prep time: 10 minutes | Cook time: 2 hours | Serves 4

2 teaspoons smoked salt or regular salt
1 teaspoon cracked black pepper
½ teaspoon garlic powder
½ teaspoon dried rosemary, crushed
½ teaspoon dried thyme
2 pounds (907 g) Whole30-compliant pork tenderloin, trimmed
¼ cup balsamic vinegar
2 tablespoons coconut aminos
2 medium yellow onions, cut into 6 wedges, root partially attached
2 fresh rosemary sprigs
12 ounces (340 g) Broccolini, trimmed

1. In a small bowl, combine the salt, pepper, garlic powder, rosemary, and thyme. Rub the mixture on the pork.
2. In a 6-quart slow cooker, combine the vinegar and coconut aminos. Place the pork and onions in the slow cooker and top with the fresh rosemary. Cover and cook on high for 2 hours. Remove and discard the fresh rosemary. Add the Broccolini to the slow cooker. Cover and cook until wilted, 8 to 10 minutes.
3. Slice the pork and sprinkle with additional pepper. Serve with the onions and Broccolini.

Pork Tenderloin with Squash and Shallots

Prep time: 10 minutes | Cook time: 2½ hours | Serves 4

1 (1½-pound / 680-g) medium butternut squash, peeled, seeded, and cut into 1-inch cubes
2 medium shallots, coarsely chopped
½ cup apple cider
¾ teaspoon salt
½ teaspoon black pepper
1 teaspoon smoked paprika
1 teaspoon dried thyme
1½ pounds (680 g) Whole30-compliant pork tenderloin, trimmed
Fresh thyme (optional)

1. In a 4-quart slow cooker, combine the squash, shallots, cider, ¼ teaspoon of the salt, and ¼ teaspoon of the pepper. In a small bowl, stir together the paprika, dried thyme, and the remaining ½ teaspoon salt and ¼ teaspoon pepper; sprinkle over the pork. Add the pork to the slow cooker. Cover and cook on low for 5 to 6 hours or on high for 2½ to 3 hours.
2. Transfer the pork to a cutting board. Let rest for 5 minutes, then cut into ½-inch slices. Strain the cooking liquid. Drizzle servings of the pork and vegetables with some of the cooking liquid. If desired, sprinkle with additional pepper and fresh thyme and serve.

Garlicky Pork Butt Roast with Collards

Prep time: 10 minutes | Cook time: 2½ hours | Serves 6

3 pounds (1.4 kg) pork butt roast
1 tablespoon Whole30-compliant garlic pepper seasoning
8 cups chopped collard greens, tightly packed
3 slices Whole30-compliant bacon, chopped
½ large red onion, sliced
¼ cup chopped garlic
¼ teaspoon black pepper
1 tablespoon cider vinegar

1. Rub the pork roast on all sides with the garlic pepper seasoning. Place the seasoned roast in a 6-quart slow cooker with ¼ cup water. Add the collards, bacon, onion, and garlic. Sprinkle with the pepper.
2. Cook for 5 to 6 hours on low or 2½ to 3 hours on high, or until the pork falls apart easily with a fork. Transfer the pork to a platter or cutting board; tent with foil to rest 10 minutes.
3. Stir the vinegar into the collard greens. If the pork is wrapped in a string mesh, cut it apart carefully with kitchen shears. Slice the pork and serve with the collard greens.

Baby Back Ribs with Brussels Sprouts

Prep time: 10 minutes | Cook time: 3 hours | Serves 4

1 teaspoon salt
¼ teaspoon black pepper
1 teaspoon onion powder
3½ pounds baby back ribs, membrane removed, cut into 4 portions
1 (10-ounce / 283-g) bottle Whole30-compliant barbecue sauce
1 medium red onion, minced
4 cloves garlic, minced
¼ cup pitted dates, finely chopped
12 ounces (340 g) fresh Brussels sprouts

1. In a small bowl, combine the salt, pepper, and onion powder. Rub the ribs with the seasoning. Lay the ribs, bone sides down, in a 6-quart slow cooker. Pour the barbecue sauce over the ribs. Add the onion, garlic, and dates.
2. Cover and cook on low for 6 to 7 hours or on high for 3 to 3½ hours. Transfer the ribs to a platter, or to a large foil-lined baking sheet if broiling. Skim the fat from the cooking liquid. Spoon some of the cooking liquid over the ribs.
3. Meanwhile, prepare the frozen Brussels sprouts according to the package directions, or roast fresh sprouts.
4. Broil the ribs, if desired: Place an oven rack 4 inches from the broiler and preheat the broiler. Broil the ribs for 3 to 5 minutes, or until the sauce begins to bubble.
5. Serve the ribs with the Brussels sprouts alongside.

Pork Loin and Vegetable Yellow Curry

Prep time: 20 minutes | Cook time: 2½ hours | Serves 4

1 (14½-ounce / 411-g) can Whole30-compliant coconut milk
1½ teaspoons grated fresh ginger
1 teaspoon salt
1 teaspoon ground turmeric
1 teaspoon Whole30-compliant yellow curry powder
½ to 1 teaspoon Whole30-compliant garam masala
½ teaspoon ground cinnamon
½ teaspoon red pepper flakes
½ teaspoon garlic powder
1½ pounds (680 g) Whole30-compliant boneless pork loin, cut into 1-inch cubes
1 (10-ounce / 283-g) package shredded carrots
1 medium yellow onion, roughly chopped
1 (2-pound / 907-g) medium head cauliflower, cut into florets, or 4 cups purchased cauliflower florets
2 Roma (plum) tomatoes, cored and chopped
1 serrano chile pepper, seeded and minced (optional)
1 (12-ounce / 340-g) package frozen riced cauliflower and broccoli, prepared according to package directions, or 3 cups raw cauliflower and broccoli rice
Chopped fresh cilantro

1. In a small bowl, whisk together the coconut milk, ginger, salt, turmeric, curry powder, garam masala, cinnamon, red pepper flakes, and garlic powder until thoroughly combined.
2. In a 4-quart slow cooker, combine the pork, carrots, onion, cauliflower florets, tomatoes, and serrano pepper (if using). Add the coconut milk mixture and stir gently to combine.
3. Cover and cook on low for 5 hours or on high for 2½ hours. Serve the stew over the riced cauliflower and broccoli and top with chopped cilantro.

Teriyaki Pork Tenderloin

Prep time: minutes | Cook time: 2 hours | Serves 4

¼ cup pineapple juice
¼ cup coconut aminos
2 cloves garlic, minced
½ teaspoon ground ginger
Dash cayenne pepper
1½ pounds (680 g) Whole30-compliant pork tenderloin, trimmed
¼ teaspoon black pepper
1 cup chopped fresh pineapple
¼ cup sliced green onions
1 (12-ounce / 340-g) package frozen cauliflower rice, prepared according to package directions or 3 cups raw cauliflower rice

1. In a 3½- to 4-quart slow cooker, stir together the pineapple juice, coconut aminos, garlic, ginger, and cayenne. Sprinkle the pork with the pepper; add to the slow cooker and turn to coat.
2. Cover and cook on low for 4 to 5 hours or on high for 2 to 2½ hours.
3. Transfer the pork to a cutting board; strain the cooking liquid. Cut the pork into ½-inch slices. Drizzle the pork with some of the cooking liquid and top with the pineapple and green onions. Serve with the cauliflower rice.

Coriander-Crusted Pork Tenderloin

Prep time: 15 minutes | Cook time: 25 minutes | Serves 2

3 tablespoons plus 1 teaspoon Whole30-compliant Dijon mustard
1 Whole30-compliant pork tenderloin (1 to 1½ pounds / 454 to 680 g), trimmed
3 tablespoons coriander seeds, lightly crushed
1 tablespoon black peppercorns, lightly crushed
¾ teaspoon coarse salt
2 tablespoons extra-virgin olive oil
1 large shallot, thinly sliced
1 tart-sweet apple (such as Pink Lady), cored and thinly sliced
½ teaspoon dried thyme leaves, crushed
½ cup unfiltered apple cider
1 tablespoon cider vinegar
⅛ teaspoon black pepper

1. Preheat the oven to 400ºF (205ºC).
2. Spread 3 tablespoons of the mustard over the tenderloin. Evenly press the coriander seeds and peppercorns onto the tenderloin. Season with ½ teaspoon salt.
3. In an extra-large ovenproof skillet, heat 1 tablespoon olive oil over medium-high heat. Add the tenderloin, top side down, and brown on all sides, 8 to 10 minutes. (If the mustard-and-seed crust falls off in places, use a spoon to press it onto the top of the tenderloin after you turn it.)
4. Transfer the skillet to the oven. Roast for 10 to 15 minutes, until the tenderloin is 145ºF (63ºC). Carefully remove the skillet from the oven; transfer the tenderloin to a cutting board. Tent with foil and let rest for 5 minutes.
5. Meanwhile, in a medium skillet, heat the remaining 1 tablespoon olive oil over medium heat. Add the shallot, apple, and thyme. Cook, stirring frequently, until the shallot and apple are crisp-tender, 4 to 5 minutes. Add the cider and simmer until reduced by half, about 3 minutes. Whisk in the vinegar and remaining 1 teaspoon mustard. Season with the remaining ¼ teaspoon salt and the pepper.
6. To serve, slice the tenderloin into medallions. Arrange 3 medallions on each of two plates. Top with a generous ⅓ cup of the apple compote. (You will probably have some leftover pork and compote.)

Cabbage and Pork Sausage Casserole

Prep time: 6 minutes | Cook time: 3 hours | Serves 6 to 8

4 cups water
1 large head savoy or napa cabbage
10 pork sausage, uncooked
2 tablespoons butter, ghee, or avocado oil
½ teaspoon fine Himalayan salt (optional; omit if using salted butter)
Leaves from 2 sprigs fresh thyme (optional)

1. Bring the water to a simmer in a large oven-safe sauté pan (no more than 12 inches across) with a tight-fitting lid.
2. While the water heats, fill a large bowl with ice water, then core the cabbage and gently pull apart the leaves without tearing them.
3. Put half of the cabbage leaves in the simmering water, cover, and blanch for 1 minute. Use tongs to quickly remove the leaves and transfer them to the bowl of ice water. Repeat with the remaining leaves.
4. Remove the cabbage leaves from the ice water and pat them dry. I like to lay them on clean kitchen towels. This allows me to choose my leaves carefully for the casserole. Save six to eight of the biggest leaves for the top layer.
5. Preheat the oven to 300ºF (150ºC).
6. Pour the water out of the pan, dry the pan, and lightly grease it. Place a thin layer of cabbage leaves on the bottom.
7. Spread one-third of the sausage over the cabbage leaves in a thin, even layer, making sure to spread it all the way to the sides of the pan. Add another layer of cabbage leaves, dot the leaves with some butter, sprinkle with a pinch of salt (if using), and add another layer of sausage. Repeat again: one more layer of cabbage leaves and one more layer of sausage.
8. Top the final sausage layer with the cabbage leaves that you set aside for the top, making the thickest layer of cabbage yet. Dot the leaves with butter and cover the pan with the lid.
9. Place the pan in the oven and bake the casserole for 2½ hours. Uncover and bake for another 30 minutes. Remove from the oven and sprinkle with the thyme leaves (if using). Use a large spoon to serve this soft casserole.
10. Serve warm, hearty meal any time of the year.
11. Store in an airtight container in the fridge for up to 5 days. Reheat in a preheated 350ºF (180ºC) oven, uncovered, for 10 to 20 minutes.

Pork with White BBQ Sauce and Collard Greens

Prep time: minutes | Cook time: 1 hour | Serves 4

For the Ribs:
1½ teaspoons salt
1 teaspoon black pepper
1 teaspoon garlic powder
1 teaspoon onion powder
1 (4-pound / 1.8-kg) rack pork spareribs or baby back ribs, membrane removed and cut into 4 portions
¼ cup cider vinegar

For the Sauce:
½ cup Whole30-compliant avocado mayonnaise
2 tablespoons cider vinegar
½ teaspoon Whole30-compliant hot sauce
½ teaspoon coconut aminos
¼ teaspoon onion powder
¼ teaspoon garlic powder
⅛ teaspoon salt
⅛ teaspoon black pepper

For the Collard Greens:
2 tablespoons extra-virgin olive oil
2 cloves garlic, minced
1 (1-pound / 454-g) bag cleaned and chopped collard greens or 2 bunches collard greens, stemmed and chopped
1 tablespoon cider vinegar
½ teaspoon salt
¼ teaspoon red pepper flakes

Make the Ribs

1. In a small bowl, combine the salt, pepper, garlic powder, and onion powder. Sprinkle over the ribs. In a 6-quart Instant Pot, combine 1 cup water and the vinegar. Add the rack and place the ribs on the rack. Lock the lid in place.
2. Select Manual and cook on high pressure for 20 minutes. Use natural pressure for 10 minutes, then quick release the remaining pressure. Remove the rack and discard the cooking liquid.

Make the Sauce

1. Meanwhile, in a small bowl, whisk together the mayonnaise, vinegar, hot sauce, coconut aminos, onion powder, garlic powder, salt, and pepper.
2. Preheat the broiler. Place the ribs on a foil-lined large rimmed baking sheet, meaty sides up. Spoon the sauce on the ribs. Broil until bubbly and starting to brown, about 3 minutes.
3. Make the Collard Greens
4. On the Instant Pot, select Sauté and adjust to Normal/Medium. Add the olive oil. When it's hot, add the garlic and cook, stirring, for 30 seconds. Add the collard greens. Use tongs to toss the greens with the oil and garlic. Press Cancel. Add 1 cup of water to the pot. Lock the lid in place.
5. Select Manual and cook on high pressure for 3 minutes. Use quick release. Drain and discard the liquid. Use tongs to transfer the collard greens to a bowl. Toss with the vinegar, salt, and red pepper flakes. Serve the ribs with the collard greens.

Herb Pork Loin and Spiced Cauliflower

Prep time: 15 minutes | Cook time: 2 hours | Serves 8

1 (3-pound / 1.4-kg) Whole30-compliant boneless pork loin or sirloin roast
¼ cup chopped fresh parsley
1 tablespoon chopped fresh oregano
1 tablespoon fresh thyme leaves
2 cloves garlic, minced
2 teaspoons grated lemon zest
½ teaspoon salt
½ teaspoon black pepper
1 (28-ounce / 794-g) can Whole30-compliant whole tomatoes, undrained, cut up
1 tablespoon fresh lemon juice
1 tablespoon dried oregano, crushed
2 teaspoons ground ancho chile powder
1 teaspoon ground allspice
6 cups small cauliflower florets
2 tablespoons chopped fresh parsley

1. Make a lengthwise cut down the center of the pork, cutting to within 1 inch of the other side. Butterfly it open. In a small bowl, combine the parsley, oregano, thyme, garlic, lemon zest, salt, and pepper. Spread the herb mixture over the pork. Fold the pork back together and tie in three or four places with kitchen string. Place in a 6-quart slow cooker.
2. In a medium bowl, combine the tomatoes, lemon juice, oregano, ancho chile, and allspice. Pour over the pork.
3. Cover and cook on low for 4½ to 5½ hours or on high for 2 to 2½ hours. Turn the slow cooker to high if using the low setting. Stir in the cauliflower. Cover and cook for 15 to 20 minutes, or until the cauliflower is tender. Stir in the parsley.
4. Transfer the roast to a cutting board; cut the strings. Let the roast rest for 5 minutes before slicing. Serve the pork with the cauliflower and sauce.

Korean-Style Pot Roast with Jicama Salad

Prep time: 20 minutes | Cook time: 4 hours | Serves 4

For the Pot Roast:
1 teaspoon onion powder
2 teaspoons coarse ground black pepper
1 (2-pound / 907-g) chuck roast, trimmed
Grated zest and juice of 1 orange
¼ cup coconut aminos
2 tablespoons Whole30-compliant fish sauce
2 tablespoons rice wine vinegar
4 cloves garlic, crushed
1 piece (½ inch) fresh ginger, peeled and thinly sliced
1 jalapeño, seeded and halved
2 teaspoons red pepper flakes

For the Jicama Salad:
¾ pound (340.2-g) jicama, peeled and cut into matchsticks
½ orange bell pepper, finely diced
¼ cup slivered red onion
1 small orange, segmented
¼ cup fresh lime juice
1 tablespoon extra-virgin olive oil
1 small jalapeño, seeded and minced

Make the Pot Roast
1. In a small bowl, combine the onion powder and pepper. Rub the roast on all sides with the spice mixture. In a 6-quart slow cooker, combine the orange juice and zest, coconut aminos, fish sauce, vinegar, garlic, ginger, jalapeño, and red pepper flakes. Add the roast and turn to coat.
2. Cover and cook on low for 8 to 10 hours or on high for 4 to 5 hours.

Make the Jicama Salad
1. Meanwhile, in a medium bowl, combine the jicama, bell pepper, onion, and orange segments. Drizzle with the lime juice and olive oil; toss to combine. Sprinkle with the jalapeño.
2. Remove the roast from the slow cooker. Use two forks to shred the meat. Drizzle with some of the cooking juices and serve with the jicama salad.

Pork Sausage

Prep time: 10 minutes | Cook time: 15 minutes | Makes 10 patties

2 pounds (907 g) ground pork
2 ribs celery, minced
4 cloves garlic, minced
2 teaspoons Dijon mustard
2 teaspoons fine Himalayan salt
1 teaspoon dried thyme leaves
1 teaspoon ground black pepper
¼ teaspoon ginger powder
¼ teaspoon ground cinnamon
Pinch of ground nutmeg

1. Place all of the ingredients in a large bowl and mix thoroughly with your hands.
2. Heat a large cast-iron skillet over medium heat. While it heats, shape the pork mixture into patties, about ¼ cup per patty.
3. When the skillet is hot, place four or five patties in the pan, without crowding the pan. Cook the patties for 6 minutes per side, or until the internal temperature reaches 165ºF (74ºC). Repeat with the remaining patties.
4. This sausage stores well side by side in an airtight container in the refrigerator for up to 5 days or in the freezer for up to 30 days. To reheat, place in a preheated 350ºF (180ºC) oven for 8 to 10 minutes.

Walnut-Crusted Pork Tenderloin with Greens

Prep time: 10 minutes | Cook time: 30 minutes | Serves 2

- 1 pound (454 g) pork tenderloin
- 2 tablespoons mustard powder
- 1 tablespoon paprika
- 1 tablespoon onion powder
- 1 tablespoon garlic powder
- 1½ teaspoons salt
- 1½ teaspoons black pepper
- ½ cup chopped walnuts
- 3 cups salad greens
- ½ cup balsamic vinaigrette

1. Remove the pork from the refrigerator approximately 30 minutes before cooking.
2. Preheat the oven to 375ºF (190ºC).
3. If necessary, trim the pork tenderloin, removing the tough outer skin. (This is generally not necessary on boneless cuts of pork loin, but see the tip below for details.) Pat the tenderloin dry with a paper towel. Mix the mustard powder, paprika, onion powder, garlic powder, salt, and pepper in a small bowl. Rub the pork evenly with the spice mixture.
4. In a food processor or by hand, pulse or chop the walnuts until finely chopped. Coat the pork evenly with three quarters of the chopped walnuts. Place the tenderloin in a baking pan and roast for 25 to 30 minutes, until the internal temperature reaches 145ºF (63ºC). Let the pork rest for 10 minutes.
5. Slice the tenderloin into ½-inch-thick medallions. Place the salad greens on plates, top with the pork slices, sprinkle the remaining chopped walnuts, and drizzle with the balsamic vinaigrette.

Pork Loin with Potato and Fruit Smash

Prep time: 10 minutes | Cook time: 3 hours | Serves 6

- 2½ pounds (1.1 kg) Whole30-compliant pork loin
- 1 teaspoon dried thyme
- ½ teaspoon Whole30-compliant garlic and herb seasoning
- ¼ teaspoon black pepper
- 1½ pounds (680 g) sweet potatoes, peeled and cut into 2-inch chunks
- 2 cooking apples, such as Fuji, peeled, cored, and quartered
- 2 cooking pears, such as Bartlett, peeled, cored, and quartered
- 1 teaspoon ground cinnamon
- ½ teaspoon salt
- ½ cup fresh or frozen cranberries
- 1 tablespoon cider vinegar

1. Place the pork in a 6-quart slow cooker and add ¼ cup water. In a small bowl, stir together the thyme, seasoning blend, and pepper. Rub the spice mixture over the pork.
2. In a large bowl, combine the sweet potatoes, apples, and pears. Sprinkle with the cinnamon and salt and toss to combine. Add to the cooker and top with the cranberries.
3. Cover and cook for 6 hours on low or for 3 hours on high.
4. Use a slotted spoon to transfer the sweet potatoes, apples, pears, and cranberries to a large bowl. Use a potato masher or fork to mash to desired consistency. Stir in the vinegar.
5. Slice the pork and serve with the smash.

Pork Loin Back Ribs with Mole Verde

Prep time: 15 minutes | Cook time: 2¼ hours | Serves 4

- ½ cup roasted pepitas, plus more for serving
- 1 (28-ounce / 794-g) can tomatillos, undrained
- 1 medium white onion, coarsely chopped
- ½ cup packed coarsely chopped fresh cilantro, plus more for serving
- 1 jalapeño, seeded (if desired) and roughly chopped
- 3 cloves garlic, minced
- ¾ teaspoon salt
- 2½ pounds (1.1 kg) pork loin back ribs, membrane removed, cut into 4 portions
- ¼ teaspoon black pepper
- 1 tablespoon fresh lime juice
- 1 (12-ounce / 340-g) package frozen riced butternut squash

1. Make the mole verde: In a spice grinder, process the pepitas in batches until finely ground. Transfer to a food processor or blender. Add the tomatillos, onion, cilantro, jalapeño, garlic, and ¼ teaspoon of the salt. Cover and process until smooth.
2. Lightly season the ribs with the remaining ½ teaspoon salt and the pepper. Place in a 4-quart slow cooker. Pour the mole verde over the ribs.
3. Cover and cook on low for 4½ to 5 hours or on high for 2¼ to 2½ hours. Remove the ribs from the cooker.
4. Adjust an oven rack to 4 inches below the broiler. Preheat the broiler. Place the ribs, meaty sides up, in a large baking pan. Broil until browned, about 4 minutes. Cover to keep warm.
5. Skim the fat from the mole verde sauce and transfer to a medium saucepan. Bring to a boil. Reduce the heat and simmer, stirring occasionally, until slightly thickened, about 10 minutes. Stir in the lime juice.
6. Meanwhile, prepare the butternut squash according to the package directions.
7. Serve the mole verde sauce with the ribs and butternut squash. Top with additional roasted pepitas and cilantro.

Pork Char Siu with Vegetable Medley

Prep time: 25 minutes | Cook time: 40 minutes | Serves 4

For the Pork Char Siu:
- 2 tablespoons toasted sesame oil
- 2 pounds (907 g) Whole30-compliant pork tenderloin, cut into 4-inch pieces
- 2 teaspoons salt
- 1 cup minced white onion
- 8 cloves garlic, minced
- 1 tablespoon Whole30-compliant tomato paste
- 1 tablespoon Whole30-compliant five-spice powder
- 1 cup pineapple juice
- ½ cup apple juice concentrate
- ¼ cup coconut aminos
- 1 tablespoon Whole30-compliant fish sauce
- 1 tablespoon red wine vinegar

For the Vegetable Medley:
- 1 tablespoon toasted sesame oil
- 1 tablespoon minced garlic
- 1 piece (1 inch) fresh ginger, peeled and minced
- 2 green onions, sliced
- 1 cup shredded cabbage
- 1 cup broccoli florets
- 4 cups cauliflower florets
- 2 tablespoons coconut aminos
- ½ teaspoon salt
- 2 large eggs, lightly beaten

1. Make the char siu: On a 6-quart Instant Pot, select Sauté and adjust to Normal/Medium. Add the sesame oil to the pot. When it's hot, add the pork and salt. Cook, stirring occasionally, until browned on all sides, about 5 minutes. Transfer the pork to a medium bowl; set aside. Add the onion and garlic to the pot. Cook, stirring occasionally, until lightly golden, about 5 minutes. Add the tomato paste and five-spice powder. Cook, stirring, for 1 minute. Press Cancel. Add the pineapple juice, apple juice concentrate, coconut aminos, fish sauce, and vinegar. Return the pork to the pot.
2. Lock the lid in place. Select Manual and cook on high pressure for 15 minutes. Use quick release. Transfer the pork to a platter; cover to keep warm.
3. On the Instant Pot, select Sauté and adjust to Normal/Medium. Bring the sauce to a simmer. Cook, stirring occasionally, until the sauce is reduced by half, 15 to 20 minutes.
4. Make the vegetable medley: Meanwhile, heat the sesame oil in an extra-large skillet over medium-high heat. Add the garlic, ginger, and green onions. Cook, stirring, until the garlic is lightly browned, about 30 seconds. Add the cabbage, broccoli, and cauliflower and cook, stirring, for 8 to 10 minutes. Add the coconut aminos, salt, and 2 tablespoons water. When the water has evaporated, move the vegetables to one side of the pan. Add the eggs to the empty side and cook, stirring frequently, to scramble the eggs, 1 to 2 minutes. Stir the eggs into the vegetables.
5. Serve the sauce over the pork with the vegetable medley alongside.

Cider-Brined Roasted Pork Tenderloin

Prep time: 30 minutes | Cook time: 15 minutes | Serves 3

Pork:
- 2 cups apple cider
- 3 tablespoons salt
- 2 bay leaves
- 2 cloves garlic, crushed
- 2 teaspoons caraway seeds
- 1 teaspoon black peppercorns
- 1 pork tenderloin (1¼ to 1½ pounds / 567 to 680 g)

Slaw:
- ¼ cup apple cider
- 2 tablespoons extra-virgin olive oil
- 1 tablespoon apple cider vinegar
- 1 teaspoon caraway seeds
- 1 teaspoon Whole30-compliant coarse-grain mustard
- ¼ teaspoon salt
- 1 (16-ounce / 454-g) jar Whole30-compliant sauerkraut, drained well
- 1 red or green bell pepper, seeded and finely chopped
- 1 large carrot, coarsely shredded
- ½ small sweet onion, finely chopped
- 1 stalk celery, finely chopped
- 1 tablespoon extra-virgin olive oil
- Black pepper, to taste

1. Make the pork: In a small saucepan, combine the apple cider, salt, bay leaves, garlic, caraway, and peppercorns. Bring to a boil, stirring to dissolve the salt. Remove from the heat and let stand for 15 minutes. Stir in ½ cup ice cubes. Let stand until completely cool.
2. Trim the pork tenderloin, removing any tough silver skin. Place in a resealable plastic bag and pour in the cooled brine. Squeeze any air from the bag and seal. Place the bag in a dish and refrigerate for 6 to 8 hours.
3. Make the slaw: In a medium bowl, whisk together the apple cider, olive oil, vinegar, caraway, mustard, and salt. Add the sauerkraut, bell pepper, carrot, onion, and celery; toss to coat. Cover and chill for at least 2 hours before serving.
4. Preheat the oven to 425ºF (220ºC). Remove the pork from the brine and pat it dry with paper towels (discard the brine). Rub the pork with the olive oil and sprinkle with black pepper. Heat a large oven-safe skillet over medium-high heat. Sear the pork on all sides until lightly browned. Transfer the skillet to the oven and roast the tenderloin for 15 to 20 minutes or until the internal temperature is 145ºF (63ºC). Let rest for 10 minutes.
5. Thinly slice the pork and serve it over or alongside the slaw.

Pork Chops with Sweet Potato Colcannon

Prep time: 15 minutes | Cook time: 25 minutes | Serves 4

- 1 large sweet potato, peeled and roughly chopped
- 2 tablespoons clarified butter or ghee
- 1 bunch Swiss chard, stalks removed, roughly chopped
- 1 leek, finely sliced
- ½ teaspoon salt
- ½ teaspoon black pepper
- 4 (1-inch-thick) boneless pork loin chops

1. Fill a large saucepan with salted water and bring to a boil. Add the sweet potato, reduce the heat to a simmer, and cook until softened, 6 to 8 minutes. Drain the water and heat the potato in the saucepan for 1 minute to remove excess moisture. Transfer to a bowl and cover to keep warm.
2. In the same saucepan, heat 1 tablespoons of the butter over low heat. Add the chard, leek, ¼ teaspoon of the salt, and ¼ teaspoon of the black pepper. Cook, stirring, until the leek and chard are softened, 6 to 8 minutes. Remove from the heat and keep warm.
3. Meanwhile, in a large skillet, heat the remaining 1 tablespoon butter over high heat. Lightly season the pork chops with the remaining ¼ teaspoon salt and ¼ teaspoon black pepper. Add the chops to the skillet and cook until the internal temperature is 145ºF (63ºC), 3 to 4 minutes on each side.
4. Combine the leeks, Swiss chard, and sweet potato. Serve with the pork chops.

Pork Tenderloin and Bell Pepper Stir-Fry

Prep time: 15 minutes | Cook time: 10 minutes | Serves 2

- 2 tablespoons coconut aminos
- 2 tablespoons apple cider
- 1 tablespoon rice vinegar
- 2 cloves garlic, minced
- 2 teaspoons minced fresh ginger
- ⅛ teaspoon red pepper flakes
- 2 tablespoons coconut oil
- 12 ounces (340 g) pork tenderloin, cut into thin, bite-size strips
- 1 small red bell pepper, cut into bite-size strips
- 1 (8-ounce / 227-g) bag fresh sugar snap peas
- 2 green onions, sliced on the bias, white and green parts separated
- 2 teaspoons sesame seeds, toasted

1. In a small bowl, mix the coconut aminos, cider, vinegar, garlic, ginger, and pepper flakes; set aside.
2. Heat 1 tablespoon of the coconut oil in a large skillet or wok over medium-high heat. Add the pork and cook, stirring, until no longer pink, 2 to 3 minutes. Remove the pork from the skillet.
3. In the same skillet, heat the remaining 1 tablespoon coconut oil over medium-high heat. Add the bell pepper, snap peas, and white parts of the green onions. Cook, stirring, until the vegetables are crisp-tender, 3 to 5 minutes. Stir in the coconut aminos mixture. Cook, stirring, for 1 minute more. Return the pork to the skillet and heat through.
4. Serve the stir-fry topped with the remaining green onions and the sesame seeds.

Spaghetti Squash with Pork Arrabbiata Sauce

Prep time: 15 minutes | Cook time: 25 minutes | Serves 4

- 1 (2-pound / 907-g) spaghetti squash
- 1 pound (454 g) ground pork
- 3 ounces (85 g) pancetta, chopped
- 1 medium onion, chopped
- 3 cups coarsely chopped seeded Roma (plum) tomatoes
- ½ cup drained Whole30-compliant roasted red peppers, chopped
- 4 cloves garlic, minced
- 2 teaspoons dried Italian seasoning
- ½ teaspoon salt
- ½ teaspoon red pepper flakes
- ½ teaspoon fennel seeds, finely crushed (optional)
- ¼ cup chopped fresh basil
- 1 tablespoon extra-virgin olive oil

1. Cut the squash lengthwise in half. Scrape out the seeds and strings. Place the squash halves, cut sides down, in a 2-quart rectangular microwave-safe baking dish. Add ½ cup water to the dish. Microwave, uncovered, on high until the squash is tender, 14 to 16 minutes. Let the squash stand until cool enough to handle.
2. Meanwhile, in a large skillet, cook the ground pork, pancetta, and onion over medium-high heat, stirring, until the pork is no longer pink. Drain off the fat. Add the tomatoes, roasted peppers, garlic, Italian seasoning, salt, crushed pepper, and fennel seeds (if using). Cover and cook over medium heat, stirring occasionally, until the tomatoes are softened, 4 to 5 minutes. Uncover and continue to cook, stirring and mashing with a spatula, until the mixture is saucy and well combined, 3 to 4 minutes more. Remove from the heat. Stir in the basil.
3. Use a fork to scrape the squash flesh into a medium bowl. Drizzle with the olive oil and season lightly with salt. Toss gently to coat. Spoon the arrabbiata sauce over the squash and serve.

Pork Loin Chops with Zucchini Noodles

Prep time: 15 minutes | Cook time: 15 minutes | Serves 4

4 (¾-inch-thick) boneless pork loin chops
1 large egg
1 cup almond flour
½ teaspoon salt
½ teaspoon black pepper
3 tablespoons clarified butter or ghee
2 (11-ounce / 311.8-g) packages zucchini noodles; or 3 medium zucchini, spiralized, long noodles snipped if desired
¾ cup Whole30-compliant chicken broth or chicken bone broth
6 green onions, cut into 1-inch pieces
¼ cup chopped fresh parsley
Grated zest and juice of 1 lemon
1 tablespoon capers

1. Preheat the oven to 200ºF (93ºC).
2. Place each chop between two pieces of plastic wrap. Use the flat side of a meat mallet to flatten the chops to ¼-inch thickness. Combine the flour, salt, and pepper in another shallow dish. Dip each chop into the egg, turning to coat. Allow the excess to drip off, then dip into the flour mixture, turning to coat.
3. Melt 2 tablespoons of the butter in an extra-large skillet over medium-high heat. Add the pork and cook until browned and cooked through, 3 to 4 minutes per side. Transfer the pork to a platter and keep warm in the oven.
4. Melt the remaining 1 tablespoon of butter in the skillet. Add the spiralized zucchini and cook, stirring, until crisp-tender, about 3 minutes. Transfer the noodles to the platter and cover to keep warm.
5. Add the broth to the skillet and bring to a boil. Add the green onions and cook, stirring, until the broth is reduced slightly, about 2 minutes. Stir in the parsley, lemon zest and juice, and capers. Drizzle the sauce over the pork and noodles.

Baby Back Ribs with Spiced Rub

Prep time: 10 minutes | Cook time: 1¼ hours | Serves 2

For the Rub:
2 tablespoons dried oregano
1 teaspoon mustard powder
1 teaspoon onion powder
1 teaspoon garlic powder
1 tablespoon paprika
½ teaspoon cumin
1 teaspoon salt
1 teaspoon black pepper

For the Pork:
2 pounds (907 g) baby back ribs
1 cup chicken broth or water
2 cups BBQ sauce

1. Make the rub: Mix the oregano, mustard powder, onion powder, garlic powder, paprika, cumin, salt, and pepper in a small bowl. Set the ribs flesh-side up on a large piece of foil and coat evenly with the rub. Marinate in the refrigerator for 3 to 24 hours (the longer the better).
2. Preheat the oven to 300ºF (150ºC).
3. Place the ribs in a casserole or glass baking dish. Pour the chicken broth or water into the dish and cover with foil. Bake for 1 hour, or until the meat pulls back from the rib bones.
4. Preheat a grill to medium heat 350ºF (180ºC). Place the ribs directly over the heat and grill until nicely charred, 6 to 8 minutes on each side. If you don't have a grill, increase the oven temperature to 475ºF (245ºC) and cook the ribs for 10 minutes on each side.
5. Remove the ribs from the grill or oven and immediately baste generously with the BBQ sauce. Serve with the remaining sauce.

Bavarian Pot Rump Roast

Prep time: 10 minutes | Cook time: 2½ hours | Serves 8 to 10

2 tablespoons extra-virgin olive oil or oil of your choice
1 (5-pound / 2.3-kg) rump roast
⅔ cup coarsely chopped onion
1 bay leaf
1 (8-ounce / 227-g) can crushed tomatoes
2 tablespoons sugar
2 tablespoons red wine vinegar
1 tablespoon ground cinnamon
2 teaspoons kosher salt
1 teaspoon ground ginger
1 (12-ounce / 340-g) bottle or can of ale or beer of your choice

1. Preheat the oven to 350ºF (180ºC).
2. In a Dutch oven, heat the olive oil over medium heat. Put the roast in the Dutch oven and brown it evenly on all sides, about 10 minutes total. Remove the roast from the pan and set aside. Discard the grease in the pot.
3. Return the roast to the Dutch oven, add the onion and bay leaf, and set aside.
4. In a food processor or blender, combine 1½ cups water, the crushed tomatoes, sugar, vinegar, cinnamon, salt, and ginger and process until thoroughly combined. Pour the mixture over the roast in the Dutch oven, then pour the beer over the roast.
5. Cover the Dutch oven and bake until the meat is cooked to your preferred doneness, 2 to 2½ hours. Remove the meat from the pot. Allow the meat to rest for 30 minutes. Carve the roast, then return the sliced meat to the sauce from the pot.

Pork Shoulder with Pear Sauce

Prep time: 15 minutes | Cook time: 3½ hours | Serves 8

- 4 garlic cloves
- ¼ cup packed fresh flat-leaf parsley
- 6 fresh sage leaves
- 1½ tablespoons kosher salt
- 2 teaspoons ground allspice
- 1½ teaspoons freshly ground black pepper
- 1 teaspoon ground cinnamon
- 1 teaspoon freshly grated nutmeg
- 1 teaspoon ground coriander
- ½ teaspoon ground cloves
- 1 (5-pound / 2.3-kg) boneless pork shoulder, with fat cap intact

For the Pear Sauce:
- 2 garlic cloves, chopped
- ½ teaspoon kosher salt
- 5 ripe green pears, peeled, cored, and cut into ½-inch cubes
- 2 tablespoons fresh lemon juice
- ½ teaspoon ground white pepper
- 2 tablespoons extra-virgin olive oil

1. On a cutting board, use the side of a chef's knife to mash the chopped garlic. When it starts to become juicy, add the salt and mash it with the garlic until combined and broken down into a paste.
2. In a medium saucepan over medium heat, stir together the pears and ½ cup water. Once hot, cover, reduce the heat to medium-low, and simmer until the pears are very soft, about 15 minutes.
3. Transfer the mixture to a food processor or blender and process until smooth. Return the pureed pears to the saucepan and simmer over medium heat, stirring frequently, until the sauce has reduced to about 1 cup; the time will vary, but this can take up to 20 minutes.
4. Transfer the sauce back to the food processor or blender. Add the garlic paste, lemon juice, and white pepper and pulse to combine. With the motor running, slowly add the olive oil in a thin, consistent stream and process until the sauce is emulsified. Serve spooned over the slices of pork roast.
5. In a food processor, combine the garlic, parsley, sage, salt, allspice, pepper, cinnamon, nutmeg, coriander, and cloves and pulse until the mixture is broken down to a granular paste.
6. With a paring knife, make crosshatch cuts in the meat, about 2 inches deep, at 2-inch intervals. Press the spice paste into each cut; if any remains, spread it over the surface of the meat. Wrap the meat in plastic wrap, set it on a baking sheet, and refrigerate overnight or for up to 2 days, if you have the time.
7. When ready to cook the pork, preheat the oven to 350ºF (180ºC). Remove the pork from the refrigerator and let it come to room temperature.
8. Transfer the pork to a large baking dish with sides. Bake for 3 hours, or until the internal temperature is 180ºF (82ºC). Remove the pork and deglaze the pan with 1 cup water. Set aside.
9. Slice the pork and serve on a platter, topped with deglazed juices and pear sauce.

Traditional Caldo Verde

Prep time: 10 minutes | Cook time: 32 minutes | Serves 6

- 2 tablespoons extra-virgin olive oil
- 1 large white onion, sliced or coarsely chopped
- Kosher salt, to taste
- 3 garlic cloves, smashed and peeled
- 1 tablespoon smoked Spanish paprika
- 1 teaspoon cayenne pepper (optional)
- 4 cups chicken stock
- 3 Japanese yams or yellow potatoes, peeled and cut into 2-inch cubes
- ½ pound (227 g) cured (Spanish) chorizo, sliced into thin discs
- 1 large bunch collard greens, leaves stemmed and sliced into thin ribbons

1. In a large Dutch oven or heavy-bottomed pot, heat the olive oil over medium-high heat. Add the onion and season with salt. Cook, stirring, until the onion is soft and translucent, 10 to 12 minutes. Add the garlic and cook, stirring, until tender and fragrant but not browned, 1 to 2 minutes. Add the paprika and cayenne (if using) and cook, stirring continuously to avoid burning the spices, for just 1 minute.
2. Stir in the stock, yams, and 4 cups water. Increase the heat to high and bring the liquid to a gentle boil. Cover the pot with the lid ajar and cook until the yams are fork-tender, 10 to 12 minutes.
3. Remove the pot from the heat and, using an immersion blender, blend the soup directly in the pot until smooth. (Alternatively, let the soup cool briefly, then carefully ladle it into a blender and blend until smooth; return the blended soup to the pot.) Increase the heat to maintain a simmer and add the chorizo and collards. Cook until the chorizo is softened slightly and the collards have significantly wilted and reduced in volume, about 10 minutes.
4. Taste and adjust the seasoning. Ladle into individual bowls and serve.

Pork and Veggie Stuffed Cabbage

Prep time: 15 minutes | Cook time: 2¼ hours | Serves 6

2 large heads white cabbage, cored
1 (28-ounce / 794-g) can whole tomatoes, crushed
1 (14-ounce / 397-g) can tomato sauce
1½ cups chicken stock
3½ teaspoons kosher salt
1½ teaspoons freshly ground black pepper
1 teaspoon granulated garlic
½ teaspoon dried oregano
¼ teaspoon cayenne pepper
2 tablespoons extra-virgin olive oil
2 tablespoons clarified butter
4 cups chopped brown mushrooms (½-inch pieces)
1 cup chopped yellow onion
3 tablespoons minced seeded red Fresno pepper
2 cups chopped zucchini (¾-inch pieces)
½ cup chopped yellow squash (¾-inch pieces)
2 pounds (907 g) ground pork
1 large egg, beaten

1. Fill a large pot three-quarters full of water and bring to a boil. Put the whole cabbage core-side down in the boiling water and cook for 4 minutes. Flip it to the other side and cook for 2 minutes more, making sure not to overcook it. Using a sharp paring knife, gently remove the outside leaves and stack them carefully on a platter. If some don't look quite wilted enough, note that the leaves will continue to cook when stacked hot like this. Continue boiling and flipping the cabbage, removing the soft outer leaves. As you remove the leaves, any remaining core will begin to stick out; cut it off.
2. Repeat until you have removed most of the cabbage leaves. At a certain point toward the center, they are really small and not helpful for rolling, but they can be used later to line the baking dish. Set the leaves aside to cool. Once cool, use a knife to gently remove the rib from the center of each leaf, taking care not to puncture or tear the leaves.
3. Preheat the oven to 350ºF (180ºC).
4. In a blender, combine the crushed tomatoes, tomato sauce, and chicken stock, blending thoroughly. Transfer the mixture to a large pot and bring to a boil over medium-high heat. Add 1 teaspoon of the salt, ½ teaspoon of the black pepper, ½ teaspoon of the granulated garlic, the oregano, and the cayenne and stir to combine thoroughly. Set aside.
5. In a large skillet, combine the olive oil and clarified butter and heat over high heat, stirring to combine. Add the mushrooms and onion to the pan and cook, stirring frequently, for 2 minutes. Reduce the heat to medium and cook, stirring, until the mushrooms and onion are golden in color, 3 to 4 minutes more. Stir in the Fresno peppers and cook for 1 minute. Add the zucchini, squash, 1 teaspoon of the salt, and ½ teaspoon of the black pepper and cook, stirring frequently, until the zucchini and squash are just crisp-tender, about 2 minutes more. Set aside to cool.
6. In a medium bowl, combine the pork, the remaining 1½ teaspoons salt, ½ teaspoon black pepper, and ½ teaspoon granulated garlic, and the egg and mix thoroughly with your hands (or a spoon). Add the mushroom mixture to the bowl and mix well.
7. Layer the bottom of an 11 × 14-inch ceramic baking dish with some of the small or not-so-perfect cabbage leaves to help keep the stuffed cabbage from burning. Start filling the best of the leaves: Take a large cabbage leaf and scoop ⅓ cup of the filling into the center. Fold the sides over and roll up from the bottom. Put the stuffed cabbage, seam-side down, in the baking dish. Continue stuffing the cabbage leaves, placing them side-by-side in the baking dish, pressed gently but snugly together, until the dish is full.
8. Rewarm the tomato sauce and spoon it over the cabbage rolls. Cover the dish with aluminum foil. Using the point of a sharp paring knife, make very small "X" marks in the foil above each stuffed cabbage to allow ventilation as they bake. Bake for 2 hours, or until a fork goes into the cabbage easily. Serve.

Pork Loin Chops with Watermelon Salad

Prep time: 15 minutes | Cook time: 10 minutes | Serves 4

Pork Chops:
2 teaspoons chili powder
½ teaspoon salt
¼ teaspoon black pepper
2 tablespoons extra-virgin olive oil
2 teaspoons fresh lime juice
4 boneless pork loin chops (6 ounces / 170 g each), cut 1 inch thick

Salad:
4 cups chopped seedless watermelon, chilled
¼ cup thinly sliced red onion
2 tablespoons chopped fresh cilantro
1 tablespoon extra-virgin olive oil
1 tablespoon fresh lime juice
¼ teaspoon salt
⅛ teaspoon black pepper
Lime wedges and chopped fresh cilantro, for serving (optional)

1. Make the pork chops: Preheat a grill to medium heat.
2. In a small bowl, combine the chili powder, salt, and pepper. Whisk in the olive oil and lime juice. Brush both sides of the pork chops with the oil mixture. Grill the chops, turning once, until the internal temperature is 145°F (63°C), 7 to 9 minutes. Let the chops rest for 3 to 5 minutes.
3. Make the salad: In a medium bowl, combine the watermelon, onion, and cilantro. Drizzle with the olive oil and lime juice. Sprinkle with the salt and pepper; toss gently to coat.
4. Serve the grilled pork chops with the watermelon salad. If desired, serve with lime wedges and sprinkle with additional cilantro.

Potato, Pork Sausage, and Kale Soup

Prep time: 10 minutes | Cook time: 30 minutes | Serves 4

1 pound (454 g) ground pork
2 teaspoons Italian seasoning, crushed
½ teaspoon salt, plus more as needed
½ teaspoon smoked paprika
¼ teaspoon fennel seeds
¼ teaspoon black pepper, plus more as needed
⅛ teaspoon red pepper flakes
1 tablespoon extra-virgin olive oil
½ cup chopped onion
3 cloves garlic, minced
4 cups chicken bone broth or Whole30-compliant chicken broth
1 (14½-ounce / 411-g) can diced tomatoes, undrained
1 pound (454 g) red potatoes, cut into ¾-inch chunks
4 cups chopped fresh kale or Swiss chard leaves
2 teaspoons chopped fresh thyme leaves

1. In a large bowl, combine the ground pork, Italian seasoning, salt, paprika, fennel seeds, black pepper, and red pepper flakes; mix well.
2. Heat the olive oil in a large pot over medium heat. Add the pork mixture, the onion, and the garlic. Cook, stirring frequently, until the meat is browned.
3. Stir in the broth, tomatoes with their juices, and potatoes. Bring to a boil. Reduce the heat to low, cover, and simmer, stirring occasionally, until the potatoes are just tender, 15 to 20 minutes. Add the kale and thyme and cook, uncovered, until the kale is tender, 5 minutes more. Season with additional salt and black pepper and serve.

Pork Patties with Ginger Sauce

Prep time: 15 minutes | Cook time: 20 minutes | Makes 8 patties

2 pounds (907 g) ground pork
2 cloves garlic, minced
2 green onions, minced, plus more for garnish
2 ribs celery, minced
1 tablespoon coconut aminos
1 tablespoon sesame oil
1 teaspoon fine Himalayan salt
1 teaspoon ground black pepper
3 large eggs
1 tablespoon coconut flour
1 tablespoon unflavored grass-fed beef gelatin
1 tablespoon cooking fat, plus more if needed
Sesame seeds, for garnish
½ cup ginger sauce, for serving

1. In a large bowl, crumble the ground pork. Add the garlic, green onions, celery, coconut aminos, sesame oil, salt, and pepper and mix thoroughly with your hands.
2. Add the eggs and mix with your hands until well combined. Add the coconut flour and gelatin and mix until the meat mixture feels like a sticky dough.
3. Heat a large cast-iron skillet over medium heat.
4. While the pan heats, shape the pork mixture into eight large patties. Place the cooking fat in the hot skillet. Add three or four patties at a time and sear for 5 minutes per side, or until the centers feel firm, like the palm of your hand, and both sides are browned. Repeat with the remaining pork patties, adding more cooking fat to the skillet as needed between batches.
5. Garnish the patties with sesame seeds and more green onion slices and serve with the sauce on the side.
6. Store leftover patties in an airtight container, stacked or standing up in rows. Reheat in a preheated 350°F (180°C) oven for 5 to 10 minutes.

Mojo Pork Shoulder

Prep time: 10 minutes | Cook time: 8 hours | Serves 8 to 10

½ cup fresh orange juice
½ cup fresh lime juice
¼ cup extra-virgin olive oil
4 garlic cloves, coarsely chopped
1 tablespoon ground coriander
1 teaspoon dried oregano
1 (3- to 4-pound / 1.4- to 1.8-kg) bone-in pork shoulder
Kosher salt and freshly ground black pepper, to taste
¼ cup loosely packed fresh cilantro leaves, finely chopped
8 fresh mint leaves, finely chopped

1. In a blender or food processor, combine the orange juice, lime juice, olive oil, garlic, coriander, and oregano and blend until completely smooth.
2. Using a fork, poke the pork shoulder all over. Liberally season all sides of the meat with salt and pepper. Put the pork in a large zip-top plastic bag set on a rimmed baking sheet (to catch any juices). Pour in the marinade. Massage the pork to coat with the marinade, squeeze as much air out of the bag as possible, and seal the bag. Refrigerate the pork overnight.
3. Transfer the pork and all of the marinade to a slow cooker. Cover and cook on Low for 6 to 8 hours or on High for 3 to 4 hours, until the meat is falling off the bone.
4. Transfer the pork to a bowl and let cool for 10 to 15 minutes, then use two forks to shred the meat.
5. If desired, set the oven to broil. Transfer the shredded pork to an oven-safe dish and broil in the top third of the oven for 3 to 4 minutes, until crispy.
6. Transfer all of the rendered juices from the slow cooker or roasting pan to a bowl. Let the juices sit, undisturbed, for 5 minutes so the fat rises to the top. Using a spoon, remove as much fat from the surface of the liquid as possible.
7. Stir the cilantro and mint into the rendered juices and serve as a sauce for the pork.

Rosemary Pork with Red Potatoes

Prep time: 20 minutes | Cook time: 10 minutes | Serves 2

3 tablespoons extra-virgin olive oil
1 tablespoon Whole30-compliant whole-grain mustard
2 cloves garlic, minced
1 teaspoon chopped fresh rosemary
¼ teaspoon salt
¼ teaspoon black pepper
8 small red potatoes, quartered
1 small red onion, cut into 8 wedges
2 bone-in pork chops, cut ½ to ¾ inch thick

1. Preheat the oven to 425ºF (220ºC).
2. In a small bowl, stir together 1 tablespoon of the olive oil, the mustard, garlic, rosemary, salt, and pepper. In a medium bowl, toss the potatoes and onion with half of the mustard mixture. Brush the remaining mustard mixture on both sides of the chops.
3. Heat 1 tablespoon of the olive oil in a large cast-iron or heavy ovenproof skillet over medium-high heat. Add the chops to the skillet and cook, turning once, until browned, about 2 minutes. Transfer the chops to a plate and cover to keep warm.
4. Heat the remaining 1 tablespoon olive oil in the same skillet over medium heat. Add the potatoes and onion and cook, stirring occasionally, until browned, about 5 minutes.
5. Arrange the chops in with the potatoes and onions. Transfer the skillet to the oven and bake until the internal temperature of the chops is 145ºF (63ºC) and the potatoes are tender, 10 to 15 minutes.

Pork Shoulder Curry with Asparagus

Prep time: 15 minutes | Cook time: 7 hours | Serves 4 to 6

1½ to 2 pounds (907 g) (680 to 907 g) boneless pork shoulder, cut into 2-inch cubes
3 medium red, yellow, and/or green bell peppers, sliced, or 3 cups frozen sliced bell peppers, thawed slightly
1 medium onion, cut into ½-inch wedges
1 cup Whole30-compliant chicken broth or chicken bone broth
¼ cup Whole30-compliant green curry paste
1 pound (454 g) asparagus, cut into 1- to 2-inch pieces
1 (14-ounce / 397-g) can full-fat Whole30-compliant coconut milk
1 cup sliced fresh basil leaves
1 (12-ounce / 340-g) bag frozen riced cauliflower, cooked according to package directions; or 3 cups cauliflower rice, cooked (optional)
Lime wedges (optional)

1. Combine the pork, bell peppers, onion, broth, and curry paste in a slow cooker. Cover and cook on low for 7 to 8 hours or on high for 3½ to 4 hours.
2. Turn the slow cooker to high if using the low setting. Stir in the asparagus. Cover and cook until the asparagus is crisp-tender, 15 to 20 minutes. Stir in the coconut milk and basil. Serve the stew over the cauliflower rice and with lime wedges, if desired.

Basil Pork Tenderloin and Cauliflower Curry

Prep time: 10 minutes | Cook time: 25 minutes | Serves 4

2 teaspoons coconut oil
2 tablespoons Whole30-compliant green curry paste
1 pound (454 g) pork tenderloin, sliced into bite-size strips
1 small onion, chopped
1 Thai chile, seeded and finely chopped (optional)
3 cups bite-size cauliflower florets
¾ cup diced orange bell pepper
1 cup full-fat coconut milk
¾ cup chicken bone broth or Whole30-compliant chicken broth
1½ teaspoons Red Boat fish sauce or coconut aminos
4 fresh basil leaves (preferably Thai basil), rolled and sliced crosswise into thin ribbons
Lime wedges, for serving

1. Heat the coconut oil in a large nonstick skillet over medium-high heat. Add the curry paste and cook, stirring, for 1 minute. Add the pork and cook, stirring occasionally, until no longer pink, 3 to 5 minutes. Transfer the pork to a bowl and cover to keep warm.
2. Add the onion and the chile (if using) to the same skillet and cook over medium-high heat, stirring occasionally, until tender, 3 to 4 minutes. Add the cauliflower and bell pepper and cook, stirring occasionally, for 2 minutes more. Stir in the coconut milk and broth. Bring to a simmer. Cover and simmer for 8 minutes. Stir in the pork and fish sauce and cook, uncovered, until the pork is heated through, about 2 minutes. Garnish with the sliced basil and serve with lime wedges.

Pork Chops with Parsnip Purée

Prep time: 10 minutes | Cook time: 25 minutes | Serves 4

Parsnip Purée:
4 cups chicken stock
2 pounds (907 g) parsnips, peeled and cut into ¼-inch-thick rounds
2 tablespoons clarified butter
1 teaspoon granulated garlic

Pork and Greens:
8 thin-cut boneless pork chops (about 1½ pounds / 680 g)
1 teaspoon kosher salt
½ teaspoon freshly ground black pepper
3 tablespoons extra-virgin olive oil
6 cups greens of your choice (such as spinach, Swiss chard, or kale), rinsed and dried
Chopped fresh parsley, for garnish

1. For the parsnip purée: In a medium pot, bring the stock to a boil over high heat. Add the parsnips, partially cover the pot, and cook until tender, about 20 minutes. Drain the parsnips, reserving ½ cup of the stock, and return both to the pot.
2. Using an immersion blender, purée the parsnips with the reserved broth until smooth. Add the clarified butter and the granulated garlic and stir until well combined.
3. For the pork and greens: Season the pork chops on both sides with the salt and pepper.
4. In a large sauté pan, heat the olive oil over medium-high heat. Working in batches if necessary, add the pork chops and cook until well browned on the edges, 3½ to 4½ minutes on the first side. Then flip and cook until done, about 1 minute more. If needed to brown evenly, use a bacon presser to flatten the pork chops in the pan. Transfer the pork chops to a large plate and set aside. Repeat with the remaining pork chops.
5. Add the greens to the pan and cook over medium heat, stirring, until just wilted, 1 to 2 minutes, depending on the greens you've chosen.
6. Serve the pork chops on top of the parsnip purée with the greens alongside, and top with any pork drippings from the plate, if you're lucky enough to have them.

Pork Shoulder with Butternut Squash

Prep time: 10 minutes | Cook time: 3 hours | Serves 2

2 teaspoons paprika
1 teaspoon chili powder
1 teaspoon garlic powder
1 teaspoon onion powder
1 teaspoon salt
½ teaspoon black pepper
½ lime, juiced
1½ pounds (680 g) pork shoulder (boneless)
1 butternut squash, 1-inch diced
1 bunch kale, stems removed, leaves chopped
1 cup diced tomatoes

1. Preheat the oven to 300ºF (150ºC).
2. Mix the paprika, chili powder, garlic powder, onion powder, salt, and pepper in a small bowl. Add the lime juice and stir. Place the pork in a Dutch oven or deep roasting pan and coat all sides of the pork with the spice mixture. Add 1 cup of water and cover tightly with a lid or aluminum foil. Cook in the oven, turning the pork shoulder in the pan every 45 minutes.
3. After 2 hours and 15 minutes, add the butternut squash and ½ cup of water to the Dutch oven or pan. Cook for 30 more minutes, then add the kale and tomatoes. Place back in the oven for 15 minutes more.
4. Remove the pan from the oven and leave covered until you are ready to serve. With tongs or a slotted spoon, arrange the vegetables on plates, then break the pork apart into generous chunks and place over the vegetables. Spoon the braising liquid from the pan over the pork.

Pork Sausage Potato Hash

Prep time: 20 minutes | Cook time: 20 minutes | Serves 4

- ¼ cup fresh blood orange juice or orange juice
- 1 tablespoon sweet paprika
- 1 tablespoon chopped fresh parsley
- 2 teaspoons fennel seeds, lightly crushed
- 1 teaspoon dried oregano, crushed
- 1 teaspoon kosher salt
- ½ teaspoon black pepper
- 1 pound (454 g) ground pork
- 1½ cups chopped onion
- 1 cup chopped red or yellow bell pepper
- 1 pound (454 g) Yukon Gold potatoes, peeled, if desired, and diced
- ⅓ cup beef bone broth or Whole30-compliant beef broth
- 4 cups fresh baby spinach

1. In a large bowl, combine the orange juice, paprika, parsley, fennel seeds, oregano, salt, and black pepper. Add the pork and mix with your hands until thoroughly combined.
2. Cook the meat mixture in a large skillet over medium-high heat until browned, breaking it up into small pieces with a wooden spoon as it cooks. Add the onion and bell pepper and cook, stirring frequently, until the vegetables are just tender, about 5 minutes.
3. Stir in the potatoes. Cook, stirring, for 2 minutes. Add the broth and bring to a boil. Reduce the heat to medium-low, cover, and simmer, stirring occasionally, until the potatoes are very tender, 15 to 20 minutes. Gently stir in the spinach. Remove the skillet from the heat and let stand until the spinach is wilted, 4 to 5 minutes.

Pork Chops with Spiced Applesauce

Prep time: 5 minutes | Cook time: 20 minutes | Serves 2

- 1 teaspoon salt
- 1 teaspoon black pepper
- 2 bone-in pork chops (about 1 pound (454 g) / 454 g total)
- 3 tablespoons cooking fat
- 1 onion, sliced
- 2 apples, peeled, cored and diced
- ½ cup apple cider
- ½ teaspoon ground ginger
- ½ teaspoon allspice
- 1 pinch nutmeg
- 2 generous handfuls frisée

1. Preheat the oven to 350°F (180°C).
2. Mix the salt and pepper in a small bowl and use to season both sides of the pork chops.
3. Melt 2 tablespoons of the cooking fat in a large skillet over medium-high heat. When the fat is hot, add the pork chops and sear until you see a golden brown crust, 2 to 3 minutes. Turn and sear the other side for 2 minutes.
4. Transfer the pork chops to a baking dish and roast in the oven until the internal temperature reaches 140°F (60°C), 10 to 15 minutes, depending on thickness.
5. While the pork is roasting, combine the remaining 1 tablespoon fat and the onion in the same skillet. Cook over medium heat until the onion is translucent, 2 to 3 minutes. Add the apple, apple cider, ginger, allspice, and nutmeg. Cook (while scraping all the tasty bits off the bottom with a wooden spoon), until the apples soften, about 5 minutes.
6. Transfer the applesauce to a food processor or blender and blend until smooth.
7. Place the frisée on plates. Top with the pork and serve with the applesauce.

Pork Scaloppini with Cremini Mushrooms

Prep time: 10 minutes | Cook time: 15 minutes | Serves 2

- 2 thick, boneless center-cut pork chops (4 to 6 ounces / 113 to 170 g each)
- Salt and black pepper, to taste
- 2 tablespoons clarified butter or ghee
- 1 tablespoon extra-virgin olive oil
- 8 ounces (227 g) cremini mushrooms, sliced
- 1 clove garlic, minced
- ⅔ cup Whole30-compliant coconut milk
- 1 tablespoon chopped fresh tarragon

1. Cut each pork chop in half horizontally to make a total of four thin pieces. Place each between two sheets of plastic wrap and use the flat side of a meat mallet to flatten to an ⅛-inch thickness. (Your butcher can do this for you.) Season both sides of the chops with ¼ teaspoon salt and ¼ teaspoon pepper.
2. Heat the butter in a heavy large skillet over medium-high heat. As soon as the butter begins to smoke, carefully add the chops to the pan. Cook, turning once, until browned, 2 to 4 minutes. Transfer the chops to a serving platter and cover with foil to keep warm.
3. Add the olive oil to the same skillet and reduce the heat to medium. Add the mushrooms, ⅛ teaspoon salt, and ⅛ teaspoon pepper and cook, stirring frequently, until the mushrooms are tender and browned, 4 to 5 minutes longer. Add the garlic and cook for 1 minute. Add the coconut milk and scrape up any browned bits on the bottom of the skillet. Bring to a boil, reduce the heat, and simmer, 3 minutes longer. Stir in the tarragon. Spoon the sauce over the chops and serve.

Spice-Crusted Roast Pork Tenderloin

Prep time: 15 minutes | Cook time: 25 minutes | Serves 2 or 3

Vinaigrette:
- ¼ cup extra-virgin olive oil
- 2 tablespoons apple cider vinegar
- 1 tablespoon fresh orange juice
- 1 teaspoon fresh lime juice
- 1 clove garlic, minced
- Salt and black pepper, to taste

Pork:
- 1 cup fresh orange juice
- ¼ cup fresh lime juice
- 1¾ teaspoons ground cumin
- 1 teaspoon salt
- 1 teaspoon smoked paprika
- ½ teaspoon dried oregano, crushed
- 2 cloves garlic, minced
- 1 pork tenderloin (1 to 1¼ pounds / 454 to 567 g)
- 2 teaspoons orange zest
- ½ teaspoon black pepper
- 1 tablespoon extra-virgin olive oil

Salad:
- 1 tablespoon extra-virgin olive oil
- 3 rings fresh pineapple (1 inch thick)
- 2 bunches watercress, thick stems removed, or 3 cups baby arugula
- ½ ripe avocado, peeled and cubed
- Red onion slivers

1. Make the vinaigrette: In a small bowl, whisk together the olive oil, vinegar, orange juice, lime juice, and garlic. Season with salt and pepper. Cover and refrigerate until ready to serve.
2. Make the pork: In a resealable plastic bag or nonreactive bowl with a lid, combine the orange juice, lime juice, ¾ teaspoon of the cumin, ½ teaspoon of the salt, the paprika, oregano, and garlic. Add the pork to the bag or bowl and turn the meat to coat it with the marinade. Seal the bag or cover the bowl and marinate in the refrigerator, turning occasionally, for 2 hours.
3. Preheat the oven to 425ºF (220ºC). Remove the pork from the marinade and pat it dry with paper towels (discard the marinade).
4. In a small bowl, combine the orange zest, the remaining ½ teaspoon salt, remaining 1 teaspoon cumin, and the pepper. Rub the mixture over the pork with your fingers.
5. Heat the olive oil in a large oven-safe skillet over medium-high heat. Add the pork and sear on both sides, about 10 minutes. Transfer the skillet to the oven and roast for 15 minutes, until the internal temperature is 145ºF (63ºC). Transfer the pork to a cutting board and let rest for 5 minutes before slicing.
6. Make the salad: In a ceramic nonstick skillet, heat the olive oil over medium heat. Add the pineapple rings and cook, turning once, until caramelized, 5 to 8 minutes. Let the pineapple cool slightly and then cut it into bite-size pieces. Place the watercress in a medium bowl and toss with half the vinaigrette. Arrange the watercress on a platter and top with the pineapple and avocado. Drizzle with the remaining vinaigrette and sprinkle with red onion.
7. Serve the pork with the salad.

Pork Shoulder Lettuce Wraps with Salsa

Prep time: 30 minutes | Cook time: 8 hours | Serves 4

Pork:
- 1 large sweet onion, cut into thin wedges
- 1 tablespoon chili powder
- 2 teaspoons ground cumin
- 2 teaspoons salt
- 1 teaspoon garlic powder
- Pinch of cayenne pepper
- 2 pounds (907 g) boneless pork shoulder
- 1 tablespoon extra-virgin olive oil
- 1 cup chicken bone broth or Whole30-compliant chicken broth

Salsa:
- 1 ripe medium peach, peeled, pitted, and chopped
- ¼ cup roughly chopped fresh cilantro
- 2 tablespoons finely chopped shallot
- ½ to 1 small jalapeño, seeded and finely chopped
- 1 tablespoon fresh lime juice
- Pinch of salt
- 8 to 12 large butterhead or Bibb lettuce leaves

1. Make the pork: Place the onion wedges in a slow cooker. In a large bowl, combine the chili powder, cumin, salt, garlic powder, and cayenne. Trim the fat from the pork shoulder. Cut the pork into 2-inch pieces and add to the spice mixture. Toss gently to coat.
2. Heat the olive oil in a large skillet over medium-high heat. Cook the pork, in two batches, in the hot oil until browned on all sides. Using a slotted spoon, transfer the pork to the slow cooker. Pour the broth over the pork. Cover and cook on low for 8 to 10 hours or on high for 4 to 5 hours.
3. Make the salsa: Meanwhile, in a medium bowl, combine the peach, cilantro, shallot, jalapeño, lime juice, and salt. Cover and chill for up to 2 hours.
4. To serve: Use a slotted spoon to transfer the pork to a cutting board and use two forks to shred the pork. Place the shredded pork in a bowl. Remove the onion from the cooking liquid and add to the pork. Skim off the fat from the cooking liquid. Add enough cooking liquid to the pork mixture to moisten. Spoon the shredded pork into the center of the lettuce leaves. Top with the salsa.

Pork Carnitas

Prep time: 15 minutes | Cook time: 2½ hours | Serves 2

1½ tablespoons salt
1 teaspoon black pepper
2 pounds (907 g) pork butt, cut into 4-inch cubes
2 tablespoons cooking fat
½ medium onion, roughly chopped
3 cloves garlic, minced
½ teaspoon chili powder
¼ teaspoon ground cinnamon
¼ cup sliced (½-inch pieces) green onions
Juice of ½ lime

1. Preheat the oven to 350ºF (180ºC).
2. Mix 1 tablespoon of the salt and all of the pepper in a bowl. Use to season the pork butt evenly.
3. In a heavy pot or Dutch oven over medium heat, melt the cooking fat, swirling to coat the bottom of the pan. When the fat is hot, add the pork (be sure not to overcrowd) and brown all sides, 3 to 4 minutes per side. Remove the pork from the pot and set aside.
4. In the same pot, reduce the heat to medium-low, add the onion, and cook, stirring, until translucent, 4 to 5 minutes. Add the garlic and cook, stirring vigorously to prevent burning, until aromatic, about 1 minute. Add 1 cup of water, the chili powder, and cinnamon. Increase the heat to medium high, return the pork to the pot, and bring to a boil.
5. Cover the pot with a lid or tightly wrapped foil. Transfer to the oven and bake for 2 ½ hours, turning the meat after each hour. The pork should be fork-tender when done.
6. Transfer the pork to a bowl and shred with a fork or two, discarding any excess fat. Incorporate the cooking liquid from the pot, then add the green onions and lime juice. Season with the remaining ½ tablespoon salt.

Green Chile Pork Shoulder

Prep time: 20 minutes | Cook time: 2½ hours | Serves 6

2 tablespoons coconut oil or extra-virgin olive oil
3 to 3½ pounds (1.4 to 1.6 kg) boneless pork shoulder, trimmed
1 teaspoon salt
½ teaspoon black pepper
1 medium yellow onion, chopped
1 (16-ounce / 454-g) jar Whole30-compliant salsa verde
2 poblano chile peppers, seeded and chopped
1 jalapeño, seeded and chopped (optional)
2 cloves garlic, minced
1 tablespoon Whole30-compliant chili powder
2 teaspoons ground cumin
1 teaspoon dried oregano, crushed
1 teaspoon ground coriander

1. Preheat the oven to 325ºF (163ºC).
2. In a large Dutch oven over medium-high heat, heat the oil. Rub the pork with salt and pepper on all sides. Add the pork and cook until all sides are browned, about 3 minutes per side. Remove the pork. Add the onion and bring to a simmer, scraping the browned bits with a wooden spoon. Add the salsa verde, poblanos, jalapeño (if using), garlic, chili powder, cumin, oregano, and coriander. Mix together.
3. Return the pork to the Dutch oven; cover and place in the oven. Bake until the meat is very tender and the internal temperature is 145ºF (63ºC), 2½ to 3 hours. Transfer the meat to a cutting board. Use two forks to pull the meat apart into large shreds and place the shreds in a serving bowl. Skim the fat from the cooking liquid. Drizzle about 2 cups cooking liquid over the meat to moisten. Discard the remaining cooking liquid.

Cider Pulled Pork Butt

Prep time: 10 minutes | Cook time: 6 hours | Serves 6 to 8

Rub:
1 tablespoon salt
1½ teaspoons smoked paprika
1½ teaspoons garlic powder
½ teaspoon chili powder
½ teaspoon ground ginger
½ teaspoon black pepper

Pork:
4 pounds (1.8 kg) boneless pork butt
1 large sweet onion, sliced
1½ cups unsweetened, unfiltered apple cider

1. Make the rub: Combine all the seasonings in a small bowl. Sprinkle the rub over the pork and rub it in with your fingers.
2. Arrange the onion slices on the bottom of a slow cooker. If necessary, cut the pork to fit in the cooker then place on top of the onions. Add the apple cider. Cover and cook on low for 8 to 10 hours or on high for 6 to 7 hours.
3. Carefully transfer the meat to a large platter and allow it to rest for a few minutes. Strain the cooking liquid through a fine-mesh strainer into a large bowl. Place 1 cup of the liquid back into the slow cooker; discard the remaining liquid and the onion.
4. Using two forks, shred the meat. Return the meat to the slow cooker and toss with the cooking liquid. Season to taste with additional salt and pepper, if desired.

One pound at a time. -Chapter 4 Pork

Chili Verde Pork Tenderloin

Prep time: 25 minutes | Cook time: 50 minutes | Serves 10

Verde Sauce:
- 2 jalapeños
- 6 tomatillos, husks removed and chopped (about 2 cups)
- 1 (16-ounce / 454-g) can roasted green chilies
- ¼ cup fresh cilantro leaves, plus more for garnish

Chili Base:
- 1 tablespoon extra-virgin olive oil or avocado oil
- 2 pounds (907 g) Whole30-compliant pork tenderloin, cut into ½-inch cubes
- 4 cloves garlic, minced
- 1 medium yellow onion, chopped
- 1 pound (454 g) Yukon Gold potatoes, chopped
- 1 green bell pepper, chopped
- 1 tablespoon ground cumin
- ½ teaspoon salt
- 1½ teaspoons Whole30-compliant chili powder
- 1 teaspoon black pepper
- 1 teaspoon dried oregano
- 6 cups Whole30-compliant chicken broth
- ¾ cup Whole30-compliant coconut milk

1. Adjust the oven racks so one is about 6 inches from the broiler heat. Preheat the broiler. Line a small baking pan with foil.
2. Make the verde sauce: Cut the jalapeños in half; remove the seeds, if desired. Place the jalapeños, cut sides down, on the baking pan. Broil until charred, about 4 minutes.
3. Place the jalapeños, tomatillos, green chilies, and cilantro in a blender. Cover and pulse until combined yet chunky.
4. Make the chili base: In a large pot over medium-high heat, heat the olive oil. Add the pork and cook until opaque, 5 to 7 minutes. Add the garlic, onion, potatoes, bell pepper, cumin, salt (if desired), chili powder, black pepper, and oregano. Cook, stirring, until the vegetables begin to soften, 6 to 7 minutes.
5. Add the verde sauce and chicken broth to the pork mixture. Turn the heat to medium-high and bring to a gentle boil for 5 minutes. Turn the heat to low and simmer until the pork is cooked through and the potatoes are tender, about 30 minutes. Stir in the coconut milk.
6. Top servings with cilantro.

Pork Sausage with Sweet Potatoes

Prep time: 25 minutes | Cook time: 25 minutes | Serves 2

Sausage:
- 1 pound (454 g) ground pork
- ¼ teaspoon ground sage
- ¼ teaspoon garlic powder
- ¼ teaspoon dried thyme
- ¼ teaspoon onion powder
- ⅛ teaspoon cayenne pepper
- ⅛ teaspoon nutmeg
- 1 teaspoon salt
- ⅛ teaspoon black pepper
- Grated zest of 1 lemon

Sweet Potatoes:
- 2 medium sweet potatoes, peeled and cut into large dice
- 4 tablespoon ghee or clarified butter
- ½ cup full-fat coconut milk
- 1 onion, thinly sliced
- ¼ teaspoon salt
- ¼ teaspoon black pepper

1. Preheat the oven to 350°F (180°C). Bring 4 cups of water to a boil in a medium pot over medium-high heat. Line a baking sheet with parchment paper.
2. Prepare the sausage: In a large mixing bowl, mix all the sausage ingredients. Form into 8 equal patties. Place on a plate and chill in the freezer for 10 to 15 minutes while starting the sweet potato mash.
3. Cook the sweet potatoes in the boiling water until fork tender, 10 to 15 minutes. Drain and return the potatoes to the pot. Add 1 tablespoon of the ghee and coconut milk. Using a potato masher, immersion blender, or large kitchen fork, mash and mix the sweet potatoes with the ghee and the coconut milk. Cover the pot to keep warm and set aside.
4. Remove the sausage from the freezer and place on the parchment paper-lined baking sheet. Bake the sausage patties in the oven for 12 to 15 minutes, until the internal temperature reaches 145°F (63°C), and no pink remains in the middle of the patty.
5. Meanwhile, heat the remaining 3 tablespoons of ghee in a large skillet over medium heat, swirling to coat the bottom of the pan. When the ghee is hot, add the onion and cook for 15 minutes, turning them periodically as they begin to brown and caramelize. (Do not rush this step, the browner the color, the more concentrated the flavor will be.)
6. Transfer the mashed sweet potatoes to a bowl or serving dish and top with the caramelized onions. Season with salt and pepper and stir to combine. Serve with the sausage patties.

Pork Chops with Mashers and Pesto

Prep time: 25 minutes | Cook time: 20 minutes | Serves 4

Pesto:
½ cup extra-virgin olive oil
1 bunch curly kale, stemmed
½ cup unsalted roasted pepitas (pumpkin seeds)
1 tablespoon lemon juice
1 tablespoon Whole30-compliant prepared horseradish
1 teaspoon grated lemon zest
½ teaspoon coarse salt

Mashers:
2 pounds (907 g) Yukon Gold potatoes, peeled, if desired, and quartered
1 pound (454 g) parsnips, peeled and cut into 2-inch pieces
¼ cup clarified butter or ghee
½ cup chicken bone broth or Whole30-compliant chicken broth
½ teaspoon coarse salt
½ teaspoon black pepper

Chops:
4 bone-in pork loin chops (6 to 8 ounces / 170 to 227 g each), cut ½ to 1 inch thick
Coarse salt and black pepper, to taste
Finely chopped fresh chives

1. Make the pesto: In a food processor, combine the olive oil, kale, pepitas, lemon juice, horseradish, lemon zest, and salt. Process until smooth. Refrigerate until ready to serve.
2. Make the mashers: Place the potatoes and parsnips in a large saucepan or Dutch oven. Add cold water to cover and bring to a boil. Reduce the heat to low and simmer until tender, 20 to 25 minutes. Drain and return the vegetables to the hot saucepan. In a small saucepan, heat the butter and broth over medium-low heat until hot. Add the hot broth mixture to the vegetables. Add the salt and pepper. Mash with a potato masher until smooth.
3. Make the chops: While the potatoes are cooking, preheat a grill to high. Lightly season the chops with salt and pepper. Sear the chops on the grill over direct heat until a crust forms, 1 to 2 minutes per side. Reduce the grill temperature to medium or move the chops to indirect heat. Close the grill lid and cook until the internal temperature of the chops is 145°F (63°C), about 5 minutes. Let the chops rest for 3 to 5 minutes.
4. Sprinkle the potato-parsnip mashers with chives and serve alongside the pork chops, topped with the pesto.

Apple-Pork Chops and Spinach

Prep time: 20 minutes | Cook time: 15 minutes | Serves 2

2 tart red apples, cored and sliced
3 tablespoons extra-virgin olive oil
2 bone-in pork chops (about 8 ounces / 227 g each)
¼ teaspoon salt
¼ teaspoon black pepper
2 tablespoons finely chopped shallot
½ cup chicken bone broth or Whole30-compliant chicken broth
¼ cup apple cider
1 teaspoon Whole30-compliant whole-grain mustard
4 cups packed fresh spinach

1. Preheat the oven to 425°F (220°C).
2. Toss the apple slices with 1 tablespoon of the olive oil in a bowl. Spread the apple slices in a single layer on a rimmed baking sheet. Bake for 10 minutes.
3. Meanwhile, heat 1 tablespoon of the oil in a medium skillet over medium heat. Pat the pork chops dry with paper towels and sprinkle both sides with the salt and pepper. Add the pork chops to the hot skillet. Cook until browned, about 2 minutes per side. Transfer the chops to the baking sheet with the apples and roast for 10 to 15 minutes, until the internal temperature of the chops is at least 145°F (63°C) and the apples are tender.
4. Combine the remaining 1 tablespoon oil and the shallot in the same skillet used to brown the pork chops. Cook over medium heat until the shallot is translucent, 2 to 3 minutes. Add the broth, apple cider, and mustard. Bring to a boil, stirring to scrape up any brown bits from the bottom of the skillet. Reduce the heat and simmer, uncovered, until reduced by half, 3 to 4 minutes. Stir in the spinach and cook, stirring, until wilted, about 30 seconds.
5. Using a slotted spoon, divide the wilted spinach between two plates. Top with the pork chops and apples. Serve with the remaining pan sauce, if desired.

Tarragon Grilled Pork Chops

Prep time: 20 minutes | Cook time: 10 minutes | Serves 2

- 2 tablespoons extra-virgin olive oil
- 2 tablespoons Whole30-compliant coarse-grain mustard
- ¼ teaspoon black pepper
- 1 tablespoon chopped fresh tarragon
- 2 bone-in pork rib chops, cut ¾ inch thick
- 1 large zucchini
- 12 to 14 cherry tomatoes
- 1 tablespoon fresh lemon juice
- Pinch of salt

1. In a small bowl, stir together the olive oil, mustard, tarragon, and pepper. Spoon half the marinade into a second small bowl.
2. Brush half the marinade over both sides of the chops. Place the chops on a plate and cover with plastic wrap. Marinate in the refrigerator for 30 minutes to 1 hour.
3. If using wooden skewers, soak them in water for 30 minutes to 1 hour to prevent them from burning.
4. Preheat a grill to high.
5. Use a vegetable peeler or mandoline to slice the zucchini lengthwise into long, thin strips (you should have 12 strips). Thread the zucchini strips accordion-style on the skewers, placing the tomatoes between the zucchini. Stir the lemon juice and salt into the reserved marinade. Drizzle or brush the marinade over the kabobs.
6. Grill the chops over direct heat until they are seared on both sides and easily come off the grill, 4 to 6 minutes. Reduce the grill temperature to medium (or move the chops to indirect heat). Grill until the internal temperature is 145°F (63°C), 3 to 5 minutes. Let the chops rest for 3 to 5 minutes.
7. Grill the kabobs over direct heat, turning occasionally, until the zucchini is just tender and starting to brown, 3 to 4 minutes.
8. Serve the chops with the kabobs.

Dried Apricot Stuffed Pork Chops

Prep time: 25 minutes | Cook time: 15 minutes | Serves 2

- 2 teaspoons clarified butter or ghee
- ½ cup finely chopped celery
- 1 shallot, minced
- 6 unsulfured dried apricots, chopped
- 1 tablespoon chicken bone broth or Whole30-compliant chicken broth
- ⅛ teaspoon salt, plus more as needed
- ⅛ teaspoon red pepper flakes
- 2 teaspoons finely chopped fresh parsley
- 2 boneless pork chops, ¾ inch thick
- Black pepper, to taste
- 1 tablespoon extra-virgin olive oil

1. Preheat the oven to 350°F (180°C).
2. Melt the butter over medium heat in a small skillet. Add the celery and shallot and cook, stirring until the celery is crisp-tender, 3 minutes. Add the apricots and broth and cook, until the apricots are softened, about 1 minute. Season with the salt and red pepper flakes. Stir in the parsley. Remove the skillet from the heat.
3. Make a pocket in each chop with a small sharp knife, cutting almost through to the opposite side. Spoon the apricot mixture into the pockets, pressing lightly to close the opening as much as possible. Season the chops lightly with additional salt and black pepper.
4. Heat the olive oil over high heat in an oven-safe skillet. Sear the chops in the hot oil until browned, about 2 minutes per side. Transfer the skillet to the oven and bake for about 15 minutes or until the chops are cooked through and their internal temperature is 145°F (63°C). Let the chops rest for 5 minutes. Serve.

Chapter 5 Lamb

Marinated Lamb Leg

Prep time: 10 minutes | Cook time: 2 hours | Serves 4

½ cup extra-virgin olive oil
Grated zest and juice of 1 lemon
1 tablespoon fresh rosemary
1 tablespoon fresh thyme
1 teaspoon salt
½ teaspoon black pepper
1 (6- to 8-pound / 2.7- to 3.6-kg) bone-in leg of lamb

1. Combine the olive oil, lemon zest and juice, rosemary, thyme, salt, and pepper in a large nonreactive mixing bowl and whisk until blended. Pat the lamb dry with a paper towel, place in the bowl with the marinade, and turn to coat all of the meat. Cover with aluminum foil and refrigerate for 8 hours, turning the lamb and basting after 4 hours. (If you don't have a turkey baster, just use a large spoon to pour the marinade over the lamb a few times.)
2. Preheat the oven to 400ºF (205ºC). Place the marinated lamb in a large roasting pan and roast uncovered for 30 minutes. Reduce the oven temperature to 325ºF (163ºC) and continue roasting for 90 minutes to 2 hours, until the internal temperature is 135ºF (57ºC) (for medium rare) or 140ºF (60ºC) (for medium). Cooking times will vary depending on the size of your lamb and your oven, so begin checking the temperature with a meat thermometer at the 90-minute mark, and continue to check every 10 minutes thereafter.
3. Remove the lamb from the oven and allow it to rest for 10 minutes before carving as described in the menu introduction.

Tahini Lamb with Almonds and Parsley

Prep time: 10 minutes | Cook time: 30 minutes | Serves 3 or 4

1½ pounds (680 g) ground lamb (you can substitute ground beef, if you like)
1 large yellow onion, finely chopped
4 garlic cloves, finely chopped
¼ cup loosely packed fresh parsley leaves, finely chopped, plus more for garnish
2 teaspoons kosher salt
1½ teaspoons ground coriander
1 teaspoon Aleppo pepper or red pepper flakes
½ teaspoon ground cumin
½ teaspoon freshly ground black pepper
½ cup tahini
¼ cup unsalted slivered almonds, toasted, for garnish

1. In a large bowl, combine the lamb, onion, garlic, parsley, salt, coriander, Aleppo pepper, cumin, and black pepper. Mix with your hands until just combined. Cover and refrigerate for at least 6 hours or up to overnight.
2. Preheat the oven to 425ºF (220ºC).
3. Divide the mixture between two 8-inch pie dishes and flatten it into an even layer using your hands. Roast, uncovered, for 8 to 10 minutes, until the meat is cooked through. Pour the tahini over the top and return the pans to the oven. Roast for 3 minutes more.
4. Garnish with parsley leaves and the toasted almonds and serve immediately.

Curried Lamb and Potatoes

Prep time: minutes | Cook time: 2 hours | Serves 6 to 8

2 pounds (907 g) lamb stew meat, cut into 2-inch cubes
Kosher salt, to taste
2 tablespoons coconut oil
1 large yellow onion, sliced
4 garlic cloves, coarsely chopped
1 tablespoon curry powder
1 (14-ounce / 397-g) can full-fat coconut milk
2 pounds (907 g) Yukon Gold potatoes, peeled and quartered
2 bay leaves
1 fresh red chile, such as Anaheim or finger, thinly sliced
¼ cup fresh cilantro leaves, for garnish

1. Pat the lamb dry with paper towels and liberally season all sides with salt.
2. In a large Dutch oven, melt the coconut oil over medium-low heat. Add the lamb and brown on all sides, 12 to 15 minutes total; work in batches if needed so as not to crowd the pan. Transfer the browned meat to a bowl and set aside.
3. Add the onion, garlic, and a pinch of salt to the pot. Cook, scraping up any browned bits from the bottom of the pot, until the onion is slightly soft, 4 to 5 minutes. Add the curry powder, stir to coat the onion, and cook for another minute.
4. Add about half the coconut milk and again scrape up any browned bits from the bottom of the pot. Once you can see that there are no more stuck-on brown bits, add the remaining coconut milk, the browned lamb, potatoes, bay leaves, and chile. Pour in enough water to nearly cover the meat and potatoes. Stir everything to combine. Bring to a boil, then reduce the heat to low, cover, and cook until the lamb is tender, about 1½ hours. Taste and adjust the seasoning as desired.
5. Ladle into individual serving bowls, garnish with the cilantro leaves, and serve.

You will never win if you never begin.

Garlic-Roasted Leg of Lamb Roast

Prep time: 10 minutes | Cook time: 1⅓ hours | Serves 6

- 1 (3- to 4-pound / 1.4- to 1.8-kg) boneless leg of lamb roast
- 4 to 5 cloves garlic, peeled and cut into slivers
- 2 tablespoons fresh lemon juice
- 2 tablespoons extra-virgin olive oil
- 1½ teaspoons dried rosemary
- ½ teaspoon salt
- ½ teaspoon black pepper

1. Let the roast stand at room temperature for 30 minutes before you begin cooking.
2. Preheat the oven to 450ºF (235ºC). Line a large rimmed baking pan with parchment paper.
3. Using a sharp paring knife, make small holes ¼- to ½-inch deep and about 1 inch apart all over the fat side of the roast. Insert the garlic slivers into each cut.
4. In a small bowl, whisk together the lemon juice and oil. Drizzle over the lamb and massage to coat. Sprinkle with rosemary, salt, and pepper.
5. Place the roast on the baking pan and roast for 10 minutes. Turn the heat down to 325ºF (163ºC) and roast for an additional 1 hour and 10 minutes, or until 135ºF (57ºC) (medium-rare) or 145ºF (63ºC) (medium) when tested with a meat thermometer at the thickest part of the roast.
6. Transfer the lamb to a cutting board and tent with foil; let rest for at least 10 minutes. Slice and transfer to a serving platter.

Lamb Loaves with Cauliflower and Apricots

Prep time: 15 minutes | Cook time: 45 minutes | Serves 4

- 12 unsulphured dried apricots, finely chopped
- 6 cups bite-sized cauliflower florets
- 2 tablespoons olive oil
- 2 teaspoons salt
- 1 large egg, lightly beaten
- ⅓ cup chopped green onion
- 2 tablespoons chopped fresh cilantro
- 2 ¼ teaspoons chili powder
- 1½ pounds (680 g) lean ground lamb or lean ground beef
- 1 tablespoon balsamic vinegar

1. Preheat the oven to 375ºF (190ºC). Line a rimmed baking pan with parchment paper.
2. Place the apricots in a small saucepan and add enough water to cover. Bring to a boil. Remove from the heat and let stand while preparing the cauliflower.
3. In a large bowl, toss together the cauliflower, olive oil, and ½ teaspoon of the salt. Arrange on one end of the pan and bake for 10 minutes. Remove from the oven and stir.
4. Meanwhile, using the same bowl, stir together the egg, green onion, cilantro, chili powder, and remaining 1½ teaspoons salt. Drain the apricots well. Add the drained apricots and lamb to the egg mixture and gently mix well. Divide the lamb mixture into four equal portions. Shape each portion into a 4 × 2-inch loaf. Place the loaves on the other end of the pan. Bake, stirring the cauliflower once, until the cauliflower is tender and the internal temperature of the meat loaves is 160ºF (71ºC), 30 to 35 minutes.
5. Drizzle the lamb loaves with the balsamic vinegar and serve with the cauliflower.

Green Curry Lamb Stew Meat

Prep time: 15 minutes | Cook time: minutes | Serves 6 to 8

For the Sauce
- 1 (14-ounce / 397-g) can Whole30 compliant coconut milk
- ½ cup chopped fresh cilantro
- 4 garlic cloves
- 1 (½-inch) piece fresh ginger
- 1 serrano or Thai chile pepper, stemmed
- 1 tablespoon freshly squeezed lime juice
- 1 teaspoon sea salt

For the Stew
- 2 pounds (907 g) lamb stew meat
- 1 small sweet onion, cut into half-moons
- ¼ pound green beans, cut into 3-inch pieces
- 1 medium zucchini, chopped
- 1 yellow bell pepper, chopped
- 6 to 8 cremini mushrooms, quartered
- 1 handful fresh Thai basil leaves

Make the Sauce
1. Place all the ingredients into a blender and blend on high until smooth. Pour the sauce into a 3- or 4-quart slow cooker.
2. Assemble the Stew
3. Add the lamb stew meat and onion to the sauce in the slow cooker, cover, and cook on low for 5 hours or on high for 2½ hours.
4. Add the remaining vegetables, stir, and continue to cook for another 1 to 1½ hours on low; or an additional 30 minutes on high. You may want to add the green beans first because they take longer to cook than the other vegetables; let them cook for about 10 minutes, then add remaining vegetables.
5. If you don't have a slow cooker, simmer the sauce, meat, and onions in a covered pot on the stovetop on the lowest heat for 1½ to 2 hours. Then add the remaining vegetables and continue to simmer until tender, about 20 minutes more.

Pomegranate Braised Lamb Shanks with Almonds

Prep time: 10 minutes | Cook time: 2¾ hours, | Serves

- 4 (8-ounce / 227-g) lamb shanks
- 3 tablespoons avocado oil
- 1 tablespoon kosher salt
- 1 tablespoon ground coriander
- 2 teaspoons ground cumin
- ½ teaspoon ground cinnamon
- 2 cups beef stock
- 2 tablespoons no-sugar-added pomegranate molasses
- 1 tablespoon arrowroot starch
- ¼ cup unsalted slivered almonds, toasted, for garnish
- 2 tablespoons finely chopped fresh parsley leaves, for garnish

1. Drizzle the lamb shanks with 1 tablespoon of the avocado oil and season all sides with the salt, coriander, cumin, and cinnamon. Cover and set aside at room temperature for 1 hour or refrigerate for up to 24 hours. If you refrigerate the lamb, let it come to room temperature for 1 hour before cooking.
2. Heat a large Dutch oven over medium heat for at least 5 minutes. Increase the heat to medium-high and add the remaining 2 tablespoons avocado oil, heating until it shimmers. Add the lamb shanks in batches and brown on all sides, 12 to 15 minutes total. Pour in the stock and use a wooden spoon to scrape up any browned bits from the bottom of the pot. Stir in the pomegranate molasses and bring the liquid to a steady simmer. Reduce the heat to low, cover, and cook until the lamb is falling off the bone, 1½ to 2 hours.
3. Carefully transfer the lamb to a plate and set aside. Pour the cooking juices into a bowl. Let it sit for 5 minutes and then use a large spoon or ladle to skim off as much fat as possible. Return the juices to the pan and bring to a simmer over medium heat. Cook until the sauce has reduced by about half, 15 to 20 minutes.
4. In a small bowl, whisk the arrowroot starch with 1 tablespoon cold water until the arrowroot has dissolved. Pour the arrowroot mixture into the sauce and stir until the sauce has thickened, about 2 minutes. Return the lamb shanks to the pot and stir to coat with the sauce. Cook until warmed through, about 3 minutes.
5. Arrange the lamb shanks on a serving platter. Spoon over the remaining sauce and garnish with the almonds and parsley.

Lamb Chops and Potatoes with Pesto

Prep time: 10 minutes | Cook time: 25 minutes | Serves 2

Chops:
- 4 lamb loin or rib chops (about 1 pound (454 g) / 454 g)
- 1 clove garlic, halved
- 2 teaspoons snipped fresh thyme
- Coarse salt and black pepper, to taste

Potatoes:
- 6 fingerling potatoes
- Coarse salt, to taste
- 1 tablespoon extra-virgin olive oil
- Black pepper, to taste

Pesto:
- 2 cups packed arugula
- ½ cup almonds, toasted
- ½ cup walnut oil or extra-virgin olive oil
- 1 teaspoon grated lemon zest
- 1 tablespoon fresh lemon juice
- 1 clove garlic, minced
- ¼ teaspoon coarse salt
- ⅛ teaspoon cayenne pepper

1. Preheat a grill to medium heat.
2. Make the chops: Trim the fat from the chops. Rub both sides of the chops with the garlic. Lightly season the chops with the thyme and salt and black pepper to taste, rubbing in the seasoning with your fingers. Let stand at room temperature while you prepare the potatoes and pesto.
3. Make the potatoes: Put the potatoes in a large saucepan with enough water to cover. Lightly salt the water. Bring to a boil and cook until the potatoes can be pierced with the tip of a knife but are not completely tender, 9 to 10 minutes. Drain. When cool enough to handle, cut the potatoes in half lengthwise and toss with the olive oil and salt and black pepper to taste.
4. Make the pesto: In a food processor, combine the arugula, almonds, walnut oil, lemon zest and juice, garlic, salt, and cayenne. Process until smooth.
5. Grease the grill rack. Place the chops and potatoes on the greased rack over direct heat. Cover and grill the chops, turning once, for 12 to 14 minutes for medium-rare (145°F / 63°C) or 15 to 17 minutes for medium (160°F / 71°C). Grill the potatoes, turning once, for 10 minutes, or until they are tender and have grill marks.
6. Serve the lamb chops with the pesto and grilled potatoes.

Tunisian-Style Lamb and Squash Stew

Prep time: 30 minutes | Cook time: 7 hours | Serves 6

1½ pounds (680 g) ground lamb or ground beef
1 to 2 tablespoons harissa
1 teaspoon ground cumin
1 teaspoon ground coriander
½ teaspoon ground ginger
½ teaspoon ground turmeric
¼ teaspoon cayenne pepper
¼ teaspoon ground cinnamon
1 medium butternut squash (about 1½ pounds / 680 g), peeled, seeded, and cut into 1-inch cubes
1 medium green bell pepper, coarsely chopped
1 medium yellow onion, chopped
3 cloves garlic, minced
3 cups Whole30-compliant beef broth
1 (14½-ounce / 411-g) can Whole30-compliant fire-roasted diced tomatoes, undrained
⅓ cup unsulfured golden raisins
⅓ cup chopped fresh parsley
⅓ cup pine nuts, toasted
Lemon wedges, for serving

1. In a large skillet over medium heat, cook the lamb, breaking it up with a wooden spoon, until browned, about 5 minutes. Drain off the fat. Add the harissa, cumin, coriander, ginger, turmeric, cayenne, and cinnamon and stir until combined. Transfer the meat to a slow cooker. Stir in the squash, bell pepper, onion, and garlic. Pour the broth over all.
2. Cover and cook on low for 7 to 8 hours or on high for 3½ to 4 hours. Turn the slow cooker to high if using the low setting. Stir the tomatoes and raisins into the stew. Cover and cook for 10 minutes.
3. Serve, topped with the parsley and pine nuts and accompanied by lemon wedges.

Gyro-Inspired Skillet Sausages

Prep time: 10 minutes | Cook time: 30 minutes | Makes 12 sausages

1 pound (454 g) ground lamb
1 pound (454 g) ground beef (85% lean)
1 tablespoon dried oregano
2 teaspoons fine Himalayan salt
2 teaspoons ground black pepper
1 teaspoon ground cumin
1 small onion, roughly chopped
½ cup chopped fresh parsley or cilantro
2 large eggs
2 tablespoons coconut flour
1 tablespoon cooking fat, or more if needed

1. In a large bowl, mix together the ground beef and lamb using your hands. Add the oregano, salt, pepper, and cumin and mix thoroughly. Set aside.
2. Place the onions, parsley, and eggs in a food processor or blender. Pulse until the parsley and onion are finely minced and almost pureed. Add this to the meat mixture along with the coconut flour. Mix thoroughly.
3. Heat a large cast-iron skillet over medium heat. While it heats, shape the sausages: Take about ¼ cup of the meat mixture and roll it into a cylindrical shape no more than 2 inches in diameter and 3 inches long. Repeat with the rest of the meat mixture.
4. When the sausages are ready and the skillet is hot, heat the cooking fat in the skillet. Add four sausages, or as many as will fit without crowding the pan, and cook for 15 minutes, using tongs to gently turn the sausages every 3 to 5 minutes so they brown on all sides. When they have a nice dark crust on all sides, transfer them to a paper towel–lined plate.
5. Repeat with the next two batches of sausages, adding more cooking fat as needed between batches. There might be quite a bit of splatter, so use a splatter screen if you have one to avoid a mess.
6. Store leftovers in an airtight container in the fridge for up to 4 days. To reheat, bake in a preheated 350°F (180°C) oven for 5 minutes.

Chapter 6 Fish and Seafood

Shrimp Gumbo with Cauliflower

Prep time: 15 minutes | Cook time: 2 hours | Serves 4

1 pound (454 g) fresh or frozen peeled and deveined medium shrimp
2 Whole30-compliant chicken and apple sausage links or 6 ounces Whole30-compliant andouille sausage, coarsely chopped
1 cup fresh or frozen sliced okra
½ cup diced green bell pepper
½ cup diced onion
½ cup diced celery
1 (14½-ounce / 411-g) can Whole30-compliant whole tomatoes, drained and cut-up
1 bay leaf
¾ teaspoon Whole30-compliant Cajun seasoning
¼ teaspoon salt
¼ teaspoon black pepper
½ teaspoon filé powder
1 (16-ounce / 454-g) package cauliflower crumbles, prepared according to package directions or 3 cups raw cauliflower rice
Chopped fresh flat-leaf parsley
Whole30-compliant hot sauce (optional)

1. Thaw the shrimp, if frozen. In a 6-quart slow cooker, combine the shrimp, sausage, okra, bell pepper, onion, celery, tomatoes, bay leaf, Cajun seasoning, salt, and pepper.
2. Cover and cook on low for 4 hours or on high for 2 hours, or just until the shrimp is opaque and the vegetables are cooked through. Turn the slow cooker to high if using the low setting. Stir in the filé powder. Cook, stirring, until slightly thickened, about 3 minutes.
3. Discard the bay leaf. Serve the gumbo over the cauliflower, and sprinkle with parsley. If desired, pass hot sauce at the table.

Shrimp with Vinaigrette and Salad

Prep time: 15 minutes | Cook time: 1 hour | Serves 4

For the Shrimp:
¼ cup pickling spice
1 pound (454 g) peeled and deveined jumbo shrimp
For the Vinaigrette:
¾ cup sliced peaches, fresh or thawed frozen
¼ cup avocado oil
3 tablespoons white wine vinegar
1 teaspoon harissa paste
¼ teaspoon salt
For the Salad:
6 cups shredded Napa cabbage
1 cup chopped tomatoes
½ cup thinly sliced cucumber
¼ cup sliced green onions
¼ cup almond slices, toasted
1 (8-ounce / 227-g) bottle clam juice
½ teaspoon salt
¼ teaspoon black pepper

Make the Shrimp
1. Place the pickling spice on a 6 x 6-inch piece of cheesecloth. Fold up the edges, tie with cotton kitchen string, and place in a 4-quart slow cooker. Add the shrimp, clam juice, salt, and pepper. Cover and cook for 2 hours on low or 1 hour on high, or until the shrimp are pink and opaque. Transfer to a large plate with a slotted spoon; cover and chill for 30 minutes. Discard the cooking liquid and spice bag.
2. Make the Vinaigrette
3. In a food processor or blender, combine the peaches, avocado oil, vinegar, harissa, and salt. Cover and process or blend until smooth. If the vinaigrette is thick, add water, 1 teaspoon at a time. Cover and refrigerate until serving.

Make the Salad
1. Divide the cabbage among four serving plates. Top with the tomatoes, cucumber, and chilled shrimp. Drizzle with the vinaigrette and sprinkle with green onion and almond slices.

Balsamic-Glazed Salmon and Sweet Potatoes

Prep time: 10 minutes | Cook time: 2 hours | Serves 6

2 pounds (907 g) sweet potatoes, peeled and cut into 1-inch pieces
1 medium red onion, cut into thin wedges
3 tablespoons balsamic vinegar
2 teaspoons Whole30-compliant coarse-grain mustard
1 teaspoon salt
1½ pounds (680 g) fresh or frozen salmon fillet, thawed if frozen, skin removed
½ teaspoon dried thyme
½ teaspoon ground coriander
¼ teaspoon ground ginger
¼ teaspoon black pepper

1. In a 6-quart slow cooker, combine the sweet potatoes, onion, ⅓ cup water, the vinegar, mustard, and ½ teaspoon of the salt. Toss to coat and spread in an even layer. Cover and cook on low for 4 to 5 hours or on high for 2 to 2½ hours, or just until the potatoes are tender.
2. Rinse the salmon with cold water; pat dry with paper towels. Cut the salmon crosswise in half. In a small bowl, combine the remaining ½ teaspoon salt, the thyme, coriander, ginger, and pepper. Sprinkle evenly over the salmon.
3. Turn the slow cooker to high if using the low setting. Gently stir the potato mixture. Lay the salmon pieces on the potatoes. Cover and cook on high until the salmon flakes easily when tested with a fork, about 25 minutes.
4. Transfer the salmon to a cutting board; cut into 6 portions. Serve the salmon and potatoes drizzled with some of the cooking liquid.

Shrimp and Vegetable with Lemon Sauce

Prep time: 10 minutes | Cook time: 15 minutes | Serves 4

- 1 tablespoon olive oil
- 1 medium zucchini, trimmed, halved lengthwise, and cut into half-moons
- 1 medium red bell pepper, cut into thin strips
- 1 pound (454 g) peeled and deveined extra-large shrimp
- 3 cloves garlic, minced
- ¼ cup clarified butter or ghee
- ¼ cup fresh lemon juice
- ½ teaspoon salt
- ¼ teaspoon black pepper
- 1 (16-ounce / 454-g) package cauliflower crumbles, or 4 cups raw cauliflower rice
- ¼ cup chopped fresh parsley (optional)

1. Heat the olive oil in a large skillet over medium-high heat. Add the zucchini and pepper strips and cook, stirring occasionally, for 3 minutes. Add the shrimp and garlic and cook, turning the shrimp and stirring vegetables once, until the shrimp are opaque, 5 to 6 minutes. Transfer the shrimp mixture to a bowl and cover to keep warm.
2. To make the lemon pan sauce, reduce the heat to medium and melt the butter in the skillet. Add the lemon juice, salt, and black pepper, bring to a boil, and whisk until smooth.
3. Meanwhile, cook the cauliflower crumbles according to the package directions.
4. Spoon the shrimp and vegetables over the cauliflower. Drizzle with the lemon sauce, sprinkle with parsley if desired, and serve.

Green-Chile Squash with Seeds-Crusted Fish

Prep time: 15 minutes | Cook time: 2½ hours | Serves 4

For the Green-Chile Squash:
- 4 cups diced butternut squash
- 2 poblano peppers, seeded and chopped
- 1 jalapeño, seeded and finely chopped
- 2 cloves garlic, minced
- 1 teaspoon ground cumin
- ½ teaspoon garlic powder
- ¾ teaspoon salt
- ½ teaspoon black pepper
- 2 tablespoons extra-virgin olive oil

For the Fish:
- 2 tablespoons extra-virgin olive oil
- 2 teaspoons sesame seeds
- 1½ teaspoons cumin seeds
- 1 teaspoon brown or yellow mustard seeds
- ¾ teaspoon salt
- ½ teaspoon black pepper
- 4 (5- to 6-ounce / 142- to 170-g) cod, salmon, or halibut fillets

Make the Green-Chile Squash
1. In a 5- to 6-quart slow cooker, combine the squash, poblanos, jalapeño, garlic, cumin, garlic powder, salt, and pepper. Drizzle with the olive oil and toss to coat. Cover and cook on low for 4 to 6 hours or on high for 2 to 3 hours, or until the squash is just tender.

Make the Fish
1. In a small bowl, combine the olive oil, sesame seeds, cumin seeds, mustard seeds, salt, and pepper. Rub the seed paste on the fish. Place the fish in the cooker on top of the squash mixture. Turn the slow cooker to high if using the low setting. Cover and cook for 30 to 35 minutes, or until the fish flakes easily with a fork.
2. Use a slotted spoon to serve the fish with the chiles and squash.

Zucchini-Wrapped Cod Fillet with Brussels Sprouts

Prep time: 10 minutes | Cook time: 20 minutes | Serves 4

- 4 (6-ounce / 170-g) cod fillets
- ¾ teaspoon coarse salt
- ¾ teaspoon black pepper
- 2 to 3 small zucchini, ends trimmed
- 3 tablespoons extra-virgin olive oil or avocado oil
- 1 lemon, cut into 8 slices
- 1 teaspoon fresh thyme leaves
- 4 cups Brussels sprouts, trimmed and halved

1. Preheat the oven to 400ºF (205ºC). Line a rimmed baking pan with parchment paper.
2. Rinse the cod and pat dry. Sprinkle with ½ teaspoon of the salt and ½ teaspoon of the black pepper.
3. Slice the zucchini into 1/16-inch-thick long ribbons using a vegetable peeler or mandoline, turning the zucchini to avoid the seeds. Wrap the ribbons around the fillets, overlapping slightly, and tuck each end under the fillet. Place on half of the baking pan and drizzle with 1 tablespoon of the olive oil. Place two lemon slices on top of each fillet and sprinkle with the thyme.
4. In a medium bowl, drizzle the Brussels sprouts with the remaining 2 tablespoons olive oil and sprinkle with the remaining ¼ teaspoon salt and ¼ teaspoon black pepper. Toss to coat. Place the Brussels sprouts, cut sides down, on the other half of the pan.
5. Roast for 15 to 20 minutes, until the fish just barely starts to flake when pulled apart with a fork and the Brussels sprouts are browned.

Sheet Pan Shrimp with Roasted Broccoli

Prep time: 10 minutes | Cook time: 35 minutes | Serves 2

4 cups broccoli florets
2 teaspoons toasted sesame oil
⅛ teaspoon salt
⅛ teaspoon red pepper flakes
1 lemon, thinly sliced, seeds removed
12 ounces (340 g) peeled and deveined extra-large shrimp
2 cloves garlic, minced
2 tablespoons clarified butter or ghee, melted
1 tablespoon coconut aminos

1. Preheat the oven to 400ºF (205ºC). Line a large rimmed baking pan with parchment paper.
2. In a large bowl, toss together the broccoli, sesame oil, salt, and pepper flakes. Spread the broccoli and lemon slices on half of the pan. Roast for 20 to 25 minutes, until the broccoli begins to brown. Stir the broccoli and turn the lemon slices over.
3. Meanwhile, in the same large bowl, toss together the shrimp, garlic, butter, and coconut aminos.
4. Add the shrimp in single layer to the other half of the pan. Roast the broccoli, lemon slices, and shrimp for 8 to 12 minutes, until the shrimp are opaque.

Shrimp and Vegetable Sauce over Squash

Prep time: 20 minutes | Cook time: 3½ hours | Serves 6

1½ pounds (680 g) Roma (plum) tomatoes, peeled (if desired) and chopped
1 medium red bell pepper, coarsely chopped
1 cup sliced cremini or button mushrooms
1 cup chopped peeled eggplant
⅓ cup Whole30-compliant tomato paste
6 cloves garlic, minced
2 teaspoons dried oregano
1½ teaspoons coarse salt
¼ to ½ teaspoon red pepper flakes
1½ pounds (680 g) fresh or thawed frozen peeled and deveined extra-jumbo shrimp
½ cup chopped fresh basil
1 (2½-pound / 1.1-kg) spaghetti squash
2 tablespoons extra-virgin olive oil
¼ teaspoon black pepper
½ cup chopped Whole30-compliant Kalamata olives
⅓ cup pine nuts, toasted if desired

1. In a 4-quart slow cooker, stir together the tomatoes, bell pepper, mushrooms, eggplant, tomato paste, garlic, oregano, 1 teaspoon of the salt, and the red pepper flakes.
2. Cover and cook on low for 6 to 7 hours or on high for 3 to 3½ hours.
3. Turn the slow cooker to high if using the low setting. Add the shrimp. Cover and cook for 30 minutes, or until the shrimp are pink and opaque. Stir in ¼ cup of the basil.
4. Meanwhile, cut the squash lengthwise in half and scrape out the seeds and strings. Place the squash halves, cut sides down, in a 2-quart rectangular microwave-safe baking dish and add ½ cup water. Microwave on high, uncovered, until the squash is tender, 14 to 16 minutes. Let the squash stand until cool enough to handle. Use a fork to scrape the flesh into a medium bowl. Drizzle with the olive oil and sprinkle with the remaining ½ teaspoon salt and the black pepper.
5. Serve the shrimp and vegetable sauce over the squash. Sprinkle with olives, pine nuts, and remaining ¼ cup basil.

Mediterranean Calamari with Veggie

Prep time: 15 minutes | Cook time: minutes | Serves 2

¾ pound (340.2-g) calamari, with tentacles, if possible
3 tablespoons extra-virgin olive oil
1 shallot, thinly sliced
1 garlic clove, finely chopped
2 tablespoons sliced sun-dried tomatoes packed in oil, drained
1 tablespoon capers
packed in brine, drained
Pinch of red pepper flakes
Pinch of dried oregano
Kosher salt and freshly ground black pepper, to taste
1 tablespoon balsamic vinegar
1 tablespoon fresh parsley leaves, for garnish
2 or 3 lemon wedges, for garnish

1. Pat the calamari dry with a paper towel. Using the tip of a very sharp knife, gently score one side of each calamari in a crosshatch pattern. Set aside.
2. Put the olive oil, shallot, and garlic in a large stainless-steel or nonstick skillet. Cook over medium-high heat, stirring, until the shallot is soft and translucent, 2 to 3 minutes. Add the calamari (including the tentacles, if using) and cook, tossing regularly, for about 2 minutes. Add the sun-dried tomatoes, capers, red pepper flakes, oregano, and a pinch each of salt and black pepper and cook until the calamari are slightly firm, 1 to 2 minutes. Add the vinegar and cook, stirring and scraping up any browned bits from the bottom of the pan, until the liquid has slightly reduced, about 2 minutes. Taste and season with more salt and black pepper, if desired.
3. Lay the calamari in a serving bowl, scored-side up. Spoon the pan sauce and any tentacles over the top and garnish with the parsley. Serve with the lemon wedges for spritzing. Enjoy immediately.

Pink Shrimp and Tomatoes with Pesto

Prep time: 5 minutes | Cook time: 10 minutes | Serves 4

2 tablespoons cooking fat
¼ onion, finely chopped
1 clove garlic, minced
¾ pound (340.2-g) raw shrimp, peeled and deveined
2 cups cherry or grape tomatoes, cut in half
1 cup pesto

1. Heat the cooking fat in a large skillet over medium heat. When the fat is hot, add the onion and cook, stirring, for 2 minutes. Add the garlic and cook until aromatic, about 1 minute. Add the shrimp and toss to coat with the onion and garlic. Let the shrimp cook for about 1 minute, then add the tomatoes. Add ¼ cup water, cover, and cook until the shrimp are bright pink and in the shape of a "C" and the tomatoes are tender and starting to wrinkle, 4 to 6 minutes.
2. Transfer the contents of the pan to a serving dish, and toss with the pesto.

Sea Scallops and Veggie with Aioli

Prep time: 15 minutes | Cook time: 25 minutes | Serves 4

1 teaspoon ground coriander
¾ teaspoon black pepper
⅛ teaspoon ground nutmeg
1 pound (454 g) fresh or thawed frozen sea scallops
3 tablespoons extra-virgin olive oil
12 ounces (340 g) small round red potatoes, quartered
2 medium parsnips, peeled and cut crosswise into ½-inch-thick slices
1 medium shallot, cut into wedges
1 teaspoon coarse salt
1 medium zucchini or yellow summer squash, cut into 1½-inch pieces
½ cup Whole30-compliant avocado mayonnaise
2 tablespoons fresh lemon juice
1 small clove garlic, minced
Pinch saffron threads, crushed (optional)
Dash coarse salt
½ cup fresh basil leaves

1. In a small bowl, combine the coriander, ¼ teaspoon of the pepper, and the nutmeg. Sprinkle the seasoning on the scallops.
2. On a 6-quart Instant Pot, select Sauté and adjust to Normal/Medium. Add 1 tablespoon of the olive oil to the pot. When it's hot, add half the scallops and cook, turning once, just until browned, 2 to 3 minutes. Transfer the scallops to a plate; cover to keep warm. Repeat with 1 tablespoon of the oil and the remaining scallops.
3. In a large bowl, combine the potatoes, parsnips, and shallot. Drizzle with the remaining 1 tablespoon oil and sprinkle with the salt and remaining ½ teaspoon pepper. Toss to coat.
4. Add ¾ cup water to the pot. Place the rack in the bottom of the pot. Add the potato mixture to the rack. Lock the lid in place.
5. Select Manual and cook on high pressure for 9 minutes. Use quick release. Arrange the scallops and zucchini in an even layer on the potato mixture. Lock the lid in place.
6. Select Manual and cook on high pressure for 1 minute. Use quick release.
7. In a small bowl, stir together the mayonnaise, lemon juice, garlic, saffron (if using), and the dash salt.
8. Sprinkle the scallops and vegetables with the basil and serve with the aioli.

Shrimp on Cauliflower Grits with Bacon

Prep time: 15 minutes | Cook time: 15 minutes | Serves 4

2 slices Whole30-compliant bacon, chopped
For the Cauliflower Grits:
2 (12-ounce / 340-g) bags frozen riced cauliflower, or 6 cups raw cauliflower rice (below)
¼ cup clarified butter or ghee
2 teaspoons minced garlic
½ teaspoon salt
½ teaspoon black pepper
½ cup Whole30-compliant unsweetened almond milk
For the Shrimp:
1 tablespoon clarified butter or ghee
1½ pounds (680 g) peeled and deveined medium shrimp
2 teaspoons minced garlic
½ cup sliced green onions
2 tablespoons fresh lemon juice
2 tablespoons chopped fresh parsley

1. In a large skillet, cook the bacon over medium heat until crisp. Transfer to paper towels and set aside. Reserve 1 tablespoon of the drippings in the skillet.

Make the Cauliflower Grits

2. While the bacon is cooking, place the riced cauliflower in a large microwave-safe bowl. Cover and cook on high for 5 to 6 minutes or until hot. Let stand 1 minute. Add the butter, garlic, salt, black pepper, and almond milk. Using an immersion blender, blend until fairly smooth. Cover and keep warm while cooking the shrimp.

Make the Shrimp

1. Add the butter to the skillet with the bacon drippings. Add the shrimp and cook over medium-high heat, stirring, for 1 minute. Add the garlic and green onions. Cook, stirring, until the shrimp are opaque, about 3 minutes more. Stir in the lemon juice.
2. Serve the shrimp on the grits, sprinkled with the bacon and parsley.

Dijon Salmon with Cashews

Prep time: 10 minutes | Cook time: 30 minutes | Serves 4

¼ cup coconut aminos
2 garlic cloves, finely chopped
1 tablespoon Dijon mustard
1 tablespoon toasted sesame oil
1½ teaspoons grated fresh ginger
1 (2-pound/ 907-g) side of salmon, scaled and boned
¼ cup raw unsalted cashews, coarsely chopped
2 scallions, white and light green parts only, thinly sliced

1. In a medium bowl, combine the coconut aminos, garlic, mustard, sesame oil, and ginger and whisk until smooth. Place the salmon in a zip-top plastic bag, add the marinade, and massage to coat. Seal the bag and refrigerate for 1 to 4 hours.
2. Meanwhile, in a dry skillet, toast the cashews over medium heat until golden brown, about 5 minutes. Set aside.
3. Position racks near the top and bottom of the oven and preheat to 375°F (190°C).
4. Remove the salmon from the marinade, letting any excess drip off. Discard the remaining marinade. Place the salmon skin-side down in a roasting pan or rimmed baking sheet. Transfer the salmon to the bottom rack of the oven and cook until the thickest part registers 115°F (46°C) on an instant-read thermometer for medium-rare, about 20 minutes.
5. Set the oven to broil.
6. Transfer the salmon to the top rack of the oven. Cook until the top of the salmon is golden brown and it reads 125°F (52°C) internally, about 5 minutes more.
7. Garnish with the toasted cashews and the scallions. Serve immediately.

Cod Fillet with Spinach Cream Sauce

Prep time: 10 minutes | Cook time: 13 minutes | Serves 2

2 (8-ounce / 227-g) or 4 (4-ounce / 113-g) cod fillets, about 1 inch thick
1 tablespoon all-purpose blackening spice
1 tablespoon extra-virgin olive oil
½ red bell pepper, diced
1 shallot, diced
2 garlic cloves, finely chopped
1 cup full-fat coconut milk
2 tablespoons fresh lemon juice, plus more if needed
2 cups packed baby spinach
¼ cup loosely packed fresh parsley leaves, finely chopped
Kosher salt, to taste

1. Pat the cod fillets dry with a paper towel. Lightly season both sides of each fillet with the spice.
2. In a large nonstick skillet, heat the olive oil over medium-high heat. Gently lay the fish in the hot oil and cook until the fish is medium-rare and the center of each fillet reads 110°F (43°C) on an instant-read thermometer, about 2½ minutes per side. Transfer the cod to a plate or baking sheet, tent with aluminum foil, and set aside.
3. Discard all but 1½ tablespoons of the oil from the skillet. Return the skillet to medium-high heat, add the bell pepper and shallot, and cook, stirring, until they begin to soften, about 2 minutes. Add the garlic and cook, stirring, for 1 minute. Stir in the coconut milk and lemon juice and cook, stirring regularly, until the sauce has reduced by one-quarter, about 4 minutes. Add the spinach and parsley and cook, stirring occasionally, until the spinach has just wilted, 1 to 2 minutes. Taste the sauce and adjust the seasoning with salt and more lemon juice, as desired. Return the cod fillets to the sauce to gently warm through, then serve.

Salmon Fillet with Lemon-Basil Pesto

Prep time: 15 minutes | Cook time: 15 minutes | Serves 4

For the Lemon-Basil Pesto:
2 cups packed fresh basil leaves
½ cup extra virgin olive oil
⅓ cup roasted, salted cashews
3 garlic cloves
2 tablespoons pine nuts
2 tablespoons fresh lemon juice
Kosher salt and freshly ground black pepper, to taste

For the Salmon:
¼ cup gluten-free panko breadcrumbs (optional; I use Ian's brand) (omit for Whole30, paleo, grain-free)
1 tablespoon extra virgin olive oil (optional)
4 (6- to 8-ounce / 170- to 227-g) salmon fillets
Kosher salt and freshly ground black pepper, to taste

1. Preheat the oven to 375°F (190°C) and line a large baking sheet with parchment paper.
2. make the pesto In a blender or food processor, combine the basil, olive oil, cashews, garlic, pine nuts, and lemon juice and blend until smooth. Taste and add salt and pepper to your taste. Blend once more and set aside.
3. make the salmon If you're making the panko crust, toss together the breadcrumbs with the olive oil in a medium bowl until well combined. Set aside.
4. Arrange the salmon on the prepared baking sheet and spread 3 to 4 tablespoons of the pesto over the top of each fillet. Sprinkle evenly with the breadcrumbs, if using, and add a pinch each of salt and pepper. Bake for 15 to 20 minutes, until the salmon flakes easily with a fork.

Paprika Salmon

Prep time: 10 minutes | Cook time: 15 minutes | Serves 4

- 2 tablespoons cane sugar
- 1 tablespoon paprika
- 1 tablespoon chili powder
- 1 teaspoon kosher salt
- 2 teaspoons unsweetened cocoa powder
- 1 teaspoon dry mustard
- 1 teaspoon freshly ground black pepper
- ¼ teaspoon cayenne pepper
- 4 (6-ounce / 170-g) pieces salmon
- 3 tablespoons extra-virgin olive oil

1. Heat a grill to medium-high.
2. In small bowl, stir together the sugar, paprika, chili powder, salt, cocoa powder, mustard, black pepper, and cayenne until combined thoroughly. Reserve 3 tablespoons for this recipe and set the rest aside for another use.
3. Using a pastry brush, brush the salmon with the oil to thoroughly coat all sides. Sprinkle the 3 tablespoons of spice blend evenly over the salmon, using about 2 teaspoons per piece and coating them well. Let rest for 5 minutes.
4. Put the fillets on the grill and cook until just cooked through, about 3 minutes each side, or until done to your liking. Serve with Green Beans Almondine.

Salmon Fillet with Mustard-Dill Cream Sauce

Prep time: 10 minutes | Cook time: 10 minutes | Serves 2

- 2 (8-ounce / 227-g) skinless salmon fillets, about 1 inch thick
- 1 teaspoon sweet Spanish paprika
- Kosher salt and freshly ground black pepper, to taste
- 1 tablespoon extra-virgin olive oil
- 2 garlic cloves, finely chopped
- 1 cup full-fat coconut milk
- 2 tablespoons fresh lemon juice, plus more if needed
- 1 tablespoon Dijon mustard
- 1 tablespoon capers packed in brine, drained
- ¼ cup loosely packed fresh dill, finely chopped

1. Pat the salmon fillets dry with paper towels. Lightly season both sides with the paprika and salt and pepper.
2. In a large nonstick skillet, heat the olive oil over medium-high heat. Gently lay the fish in the hot oil and cook until the fish is medium-rare and the center of each fillet reads 110°F (43°C) on an instant-read thermometer, about 2½ minutes per side. Transfer the salmon to a plate or baking sheet, tent with aluminum foil, and set aside.
3. Discard all but 1½ tablespoons of the fat from the skillet. Return the skillet to medium-high heat, add the garlic, and cook, stirring, for 30 seconds. Stir in the coconut milk, lemon juice, mustard, and capers. Cook, stirring regularly, for 4 minutes. Remove the skillet from the heat and stir in the dill. Taste the sauce and adjust the seasoning with more pepper and lemon juice, if desired. Return the salmon to the sauce to gently warm it, then serve.

Toasted Coconut Salmon Fillet

Prep time: 10 minutes | Cook time: 7 minutes | Serves 4 to 6

- 1 (1½-pound / 680-g) salmon fillet
- 1 teaspoon fine Himalayan salt
- 1 tablespoon nutritional yeast
- ¼ cup coconut butter
- 1 teaspoon grated lemon zest
- 1 teaspoon dried thyme leaves
- 1 green onion, sliced, for garnish

1. Preheat the oven to 400°F (205°C).
2. Lay the salmon skin side down on a sheet pan. Run your fingers along the length of the fish to check for pin bones. They will be difficult to see but easy to feel. If they are present, use kitchen tweezers or pliers to pull them out.
3. Sprinkle the fillet evenly with the salt. Let it sit at room temperature while the oven preheats.
4. When the oven is ready to go, sprinkle the nutritional yeast evenly over the fillet, then spread the coconut butter over it, leaving clumps of it here and there. Sprinkle the lemon zest and then the thyme over the fillet, as evenly as possible.
5. Roast the salmon on the middle rack of the oven for 5 minutes, then set the oven to broil. Broil for 2 to 3 minutes, until the clumps of coconut butter are browned and the fish is cooked through. If you're making king salmon, which tends to be much larger, it may need to cook longer. A good indicator that the salmon is ready is that the meat flakes easily. Test this at 1-minute intervals until the thickest part of the fish easily flakes when pierced with a fork.
6. Remove the salmon from the oven. Let it rest for a few minutes, then garnish the fillet with the green onion slices. Slice the fillet into as many portions as you need and lift the pieces off of the skin with a spatula to serve.
7. Store leftovers in an airtight container in the fridge for up to 4 days. To reheat, flake and sauté the salmon in a skillet over medium heat for 4 minutes.

Ceviche with Avocado

Prep time: 10 minutes | Cook time: 0 minutes | Serves 6

1 pound (454 g) fresh wild-caught white fish
8 lemons, halved
5 limes, halved
1 cup minced red onions
½ cup minced fresh cilantro
1 teaspoon fine Himalayan salt
1 teaspoon ground black pepper
1 teaspoon peeled and minced fresh ginger
3 cloves garlic, minced
½ medium Hass avocado, peeled, pitted, and diced

1. Cut the fish into ½-inch cubes and place in a large glass or ceramic mixing bowl. Put a fine-mesh sieve over the bowl and squeeze all of the lemons and limes over the fish, using the sieve to catch the seeds.
2. Flatten the fish so it is submerged in the citrus juice. Place the squeezed lemon and lime halves cut side down on top of the fish. Cover and set in the fridge for 40 minutes.
3. While the fish marinates, in a small bowl, mix the onions, cilantro, salt, pepper, ginger, and garlic.
4. Remove the fish from the fridge and add the onion mix to the bowl. Use a wooden spoon to combine.
5. Just before serving, add the diced avocado. Enjoy right away or store in a covered glass container in the fridge until the following day.

Sole Fillet with Olives, Pistachios, and Tarragon

Prep time: 20 minutes | Cook time: 1 hour | Serves 4

For the Fish:
8 (3- to 4-ounce / 85- to 113-g) sole fillets, thawed if frozen
4 teaspoons extra-virgin olive oil
½ teaspoon salt
¼ teaspoon black pepper

For the Relish:
1 cup Whole30-compliant Castelvetrano olives or other green olives, pitted and sliced lengthwise into quarters
¼ cup finely chopped salted toasted pistachios
2 tablespoons extra-virgin olive oil
1 tablespoon grated lemon zest
1 tablespoon chopped fresh tarragon
1 clove garlic, minced

For the Vinaigrette:
3 tablespoons extra-virgin olive oil
1 tablespoon fresh lemon juice or cider vinegar
1 teaspoon Whole30-compliant Dijon mustard
⅛ teaspoon salt
⅛ teaspoon black pepper
1 (5-ounce / 142-g) package mixed salad greens
1 small fennel bulb, thinly sliced

Make the Fish
1. Cut four 15-inch squares of parchment paper. Place 2 fillets, stacked on top of each other, on each of the four squares. Drizzle each stack with 1 teaspoon of the olive oil and season with the salt and pepper. Bring up two opposite edges of the paper and fold several times over the fish. Fold in the ends. Place the packets in a 6-quart slow cooker.
2. Cover and cook on low for 2 to 2¼ hours or on high for 1 to 1½ hours, or until the fish just starts to flake with a fork.

Make the Relish
1. In a small bowl, combine the olives, pistachios, olive oil, lemon zest, tarragon, and garlic; set aside.
2. Make the Vinaigrette
3. In a small jar, combine the olive oil, lemon juice, mustard, salt, and pepper; shake until well combined.
4. In a large bowl, combine the greens and fennel; drizzle with the vinaigrette and toss to coat.
5. Serve the fish on the salad, spooning the relish on top of the fish.

Salmon and Blueberry Salad in Avocado Boats

Prep time: 10 minutes | Cook time: 0 minutes | Serves 2

1 medium Hass avocado
¼ cup blueberries
¼ cup sliced radishes
2 tablespoons minced fresh parsley
1 (6-ounce / 170-g) can wild-caught salmon
3 tablespoons Whole30-compliant mayonnaise
Pinch of fine Himalayan salt
½ teaspoon ground black pepper
Squeeze of lemon (optional)
¼ cup pickled red onion, for serving

1. Cut the avocado in half and remove the pit. Cut a ¼-inch grid pattern into each avocado half with a paring knife. Use a spoon to scoop out a few squares of avocado where the pit used to be and surrounding that area. You want to make space for the salad.
2. Place the scooped-out avocado in a small bowl. Add the blueberries, sliced radishes, and parsley. Drain the salmon and use a fork to flake it into the bowl.
3. Add the mayo, salt, and pepper. Mix until well combined. Then spoon half of the mixture into one avocado boat and the rest into the second. Give them a squeeze of lemon (if desired) and serve with pickled onions on the side.

Seared Scallops with Bacon and Spinach

Prep time: 15 minutes | Cook time: 25 minutes | Serves 2

For the Spinach:
- 4 slices bacon, diced
- 1 small onion, diced
- 1 sprig fresh rosemary
- ¼ teaspoon ground nutmeg
- ½ pound (227 g) baby spinach

For the Scallops:
- 1 tablespoon lard
- 8 jumbo scallops
- 1 teaspoon fine Himalayan salt
- ½ teaspoon turmeric
- 2 tablespoons coconut aminos
- 2 tablespoons bone broth
- 2 tablespoons bone broth
- 1 tablespoon nutritional yeast
- 2 teaspoons granulated garlic
- ¼ teaspoon fine Himalayan salt powder

1. Cook the spinach: Place the bacon in a large skillet over medium heat. Let it cook undisturbed until it begins to sizzle, about 3 minutes. Add the onions, rosemary, and nutmeg. Cook, stirring occasionally, for about 15 minutes, until the bacon is crispy and the onions are translucent. Remove the rosemary sprig. Transfer half of the bacon-and-onion mixture to a dish and set aside to use later as a garnish.
2. Add the spinach to the skillet a fistful at a time, letting each fistful wilt before adding more. Mix in the broth, nutritional yeast, granulated garlic, and salt. Bring to a simmer and cook, stirring continuously, for 2 minutes.
3. Transfer the spinach mixture to a large bowl, cover, and set aside, but keep it close to the stove so it stays warm.
4. Cook the scallops: Wipe the skillet with a paper towel and set it back on the burner over medium heat. Let it heat for a minute or two, then add the lard. While the lard heats, lay the scallops on a cutting board and pat them dry with a paper towel or clean kitchen towel. Rub the salt and turmeric all over the scallops.
5. Once the lard is hot—it should be a little bubbly but not smoking—add the scallops to the skillet, making sure not to crowd them. Let them sear undisturbed for 2 minutes, then use a very thin spatula to carefully scrape them up and flip them over, revealing a beautiful golden crust. Sear undisturbed for another 2 minutes, then add the coconut aminos to the skillet. Swirl the pan to get the coconut aminos all over the scallops, then use the spatula to remove the scallops from the skillet and set them on two serving plates.
6. Add the broth to the skillet and bring it to a quick simmer. Use a spatula to deglaze the pan, lifting up any flavor left behind and any aminos that have caramelized on the bottom. Pour this pan sauce over the scallops.
7. Serve right away with the spinach on the side. Garnish with the reserved bacon and onions. Enjoy!
8. I don't recommend eating leftover scallops, as reheating them can make them rubbery. Store leftover spinach and bacon in the fridge for up to 3 days.

Citrus Cod with Spinach

Prep time: 5 minutes | Cook time: 25 minutes | Serves 4

- 2½ teaspoons kosher salt, plus a pinch
- 1 teaspoon freshly ground black pepper
- 1 teaspoon finely grated lemon zest
- 4 (6-ounce / 170-g) pieces cod
- ½ cup almond meal, for dusting
- ¼ cup extra-virgin olive oil
- 1 cup quartered grape or cherry tomatoes
- ¼ cup clarified butter
- 1 tablespoon fresh lemon juice
- 1 tablespoon fresh orange juice
- 1 tablespoon coconut aminos
- 1 tablespoon Whole30-compliant capers
- 2 tablespoons chicken stock
- 2 cups chopped spinach

1. Preheat the oven to 200°F (93°C).
2. In a small bowl, stir together the salt, black pepper, and lemon zest. Set aside.
3. Pat the cod dry with a paper towel. Sprinkle each piece thoroughly with the spice blend, then dust them on all sides with the almond meal.
4. In a large sauté pan, heat the olive oil over medium-high heat. Add the cod to the pan, then immediately reduce the heat to medium. Cook the cod until golden and just cooked through, about 3 minutes per side, or a bit longer for thicker pieces. Transfer the fish to a baking sheet and put it in the oven to keep warm.
5. Wipe out the pan and set it over medium heat. Combine the tomatoes, clarified butter, lemon juice, orange juice, coconut aminos, capers, and a pinch of salt in the pan, stir, and bring to a boil. Reduce the heat to medium and simmer until the tomatoes begin to soften, about 1 minute. Add the spinach and the stock and cook, stirring to combine well, until the spinach has wilted, about 1 minute.
6. Remove the fish from the oven. Use some of the spinach and the tomatoes from the sauce as a base on each serving plate. Then put the cod pieces on the spinach and tomatoes and top with the sauce to serve.

Pan-Seared Cod Fillet

Prep time: 10 minutes | Cook time: 28 minutes | Serves 4

4 (6-ounce / 170-g) boneless, skinless cod fillets
1 teaspoon fine Himalayan salt
3 tablespoons ghee or bacon fat
2 sprigs fresh parsley
1 green onion, sliced
1 tablespoon garlic confit
Lime or lemon halves, for garnish (optional)

1. Pat the fish fillets dry and rub the salt all over them.
2. Heat a large cast-iron skillet over medium heat until it's very hot, rotating the pan halfway every few minutes. Drip water on it to check the temperature; when the droplets dance, it's ready.
3. Melt the ghee in the skillet. Add the fish fillets, being careful not to crowd the pan—cook two fillets at a time if you have to. Sear the fish for 4 to 6 minutes. When the edges of the fish begin to look opaque white and you can see that it is golden underneath, use a thin spatula to flip the fish.
4. Place the parsley, green onion slices, and garlic confit around the fish. Cook for 3 to 4 minutes, until the fish is tender and flakes easily with a fork.
5. Transfer the fish to a serving platter. Spoon the ghee mixture over the fish. Garnish with lime halves, if desired. Let it rest for 3 to 5 minutes before serving.
6. I'm not a fan of leftover fish. Cook as many fillets as you have people to feed to avoid having leftovers. If they can't be avoided, store leftovers in an airtight container in the fridge for up to 3 days.

Light Tuna Lettuce Wraps

Prep time: 10 minutes | Cook time: 0 minutes | Serves 6

3 tablespoons coconut aminos
1 tablespoon toasted sesame oil
1 piece (¾ inch) fresh ginger, peeled and finely chopped
2 teaspoons rice vinegar
½ teaspoon red pepper flakes
3 (5-ounce / 142-g) pouches light tuna
2 green onions, green tops only, finely chopped
2 tablespoons chopped fresh cilantro
12 small Bibb lettuce leaves
2 teaspoons sesame seeds, toasted (optional)

1. In a medium bowl, whisk together the coconut aminos, sesame oil, ginger, vinegar, and red pepper flakes. Add the tuna, green onion tops, and cilantro. Stir until combined.
2. To serve, arrange the lettuce leaves on a large serving platter. Divide the tuna mixture among the leaves. Sprinkle with sesame seeds, if desired.

Shrimp with Mashed Potatoes

Prep time: 15 minutes | Cook time: 50 minutes | Serves 4

1 tablespoon plus 3½ teaspoons kosher salt
2 pounds (907 g) small white potatoes
7 tablespoons clarified butter
¾ cup chicken stock
1 to 2 teaspoons red pepper flakes
1 tablespoon coarsely ground black pepper
1 tablespoon extra-virgin olive oil
¼ cup plus 2 tablespoons chopped shallots
2 pounds (907 g) cherry tomatoes, halved
1 (8-ounce / 227-g) jar Whole30-compliant clam juice
1 pound (454 g) rock shrimp or small wild-caught shrimp, peeled and deveined (if possible)
Chopped fresh parsley, for garnish (optional)

1. Preheat the oven to 175ºF (79ºC).
2. Fill a medium pot with water, add 1 tablespoon of the salt, and bring to a boil over high heat. Add the potatoes and boil until soft, about 20 minutes. Drain the potatoes and transfer them to a large bowl.
3. Add 1½ teaspoons of the salt and 3 tablespoons of the clarified butter to the bowl with the potatoes and smash and mix using a potato masher. Add the stock and stir to combine. Cover the potatoes and transfer to the oven to keep warm.
4. Heat a large sauté pan over medium heat. Dry-roast the red pepper flakes in the pan for just a few seconds, then add the black pepper and dry-roast it for a few seconds, or until fragrant. Add the olive oil and 1 tablespoon of the clarified butter and cook, stirring, until the butter has melted and combined with the oil and spices. Add the shallots and 1 teaspoon of the salt. Stir to combine and cook, stirring, until the shallots are translucent, 1 to 2 minutes. Add the tomatoes and clam juice and stir to combine. Cook for 10 minutes, then reduce the heat to medium-low and simmer until the tomatoes break down to form a luscious sauce, 15 to 20 minutes, depending on how firm your tomatoes are.
5. Add the remaining 3 tablespoons clarified butter and stir to combine. Add the shrimp and remaining 1 teaspoon salt and cook, stirring occasionally, until the shrimp are just cooked through, about 3 minutes.
6. Spoon the potatoes onto a plate. Top with the shrimp and tomato sauce and serve garnished with parsley, if desired.

You are your only limit.

Sweet and Sour Red Snapper

Prep time: 10 minutes | Cook time: 20 minutes | Serves 4

4 (6-ounce / 170-g) red snapper fillets
1 teaspoon kosher salt
½ teaspoon freshly ground black pepper
½ teaspoon ground coriander
½ teaspoon ground ginger
¼ cup extra-virgin olive oil
3 medium carrots, finely julienned
6 garlic cloves, pressed
½ cup fresh orange juice
1 tablespoon red curry paste
2 tablespoons puréed mango
2 tablespoons coconut aminos
2 tablespoons fresh lemon juice
1 tablespoon fresh lime juice

1. Preheat the oven to warm.
2. Season each piece of fish with the salt and black pepper. Then season with the coriander and ginger.
3. In a large sauté pan, heat the olive oil over high heat. When the oil is warm, reduce the heat to medium. Add the fish to the pan, skin-side down, and cook until just cooked through, turning once, about 6 minutes total (or longer, if your fillets are on the thicker side). Transfer the fish to an oven-safe plate and keep warm in the oven.
4. In the same pan, cook the carrots and garlic over medium-high heat, stirring and scraping the bottom of the pan to loosen the fish bits, until brown and caramelized, about 3 minutes. Reduce the heat to medium.
5. In a medium bowl, stir together the orange juice and red curry paste. Add the mixture to the pan and stir. Add the mango purée, coconut aminos, lemon juice, and lime juice and cook, stirring to combine well, until thoroughly warmed.
6. To serve, scoop some of the carrots out of the sauce to use as the base on your plate. Put the fish on top of the carrots and spoon the sauce over.

Pan-Seared Sea Scallops with Orange Sauce

Prep time: 5 minutes | Cook time: 20 minutes | Serves 4

1 pound (454 g) large sea scallops
⅛ teaspoon plus ¼ teaspoon kosher salt
⅛ teaspoon freshly ground black pepper
6 tablespoons clarified butter
1 teaspoon finely grated orange zest
3 tablespoons fresh orange juice
1 teaspoon finely chopped garlic
1 tablespoon minced fresh tarragon leaves

1. Rinse the scallops in cold water, then place between two towels and let dry for 10 minutes. When the scallops are completely dry, season them with ⅛ teaspoon of the salt and the pepper. Set aside.
2. In a small saucepan, melt 5 tablespoons of the clarified butter over medium-low heat. Add the garlic and stir, cooking for 1 minute until fragrant. Add the orange zest, orange juice, tarragon, and remaining ¼ teaspoon salt and stir to combine. Remove from the heat and set aside.
3. In a medium cast-iron pan, melt the remaining 1 tablespoon clarified butter over high heat. Reduce the heat to medium-high and add the scallops to the pan. Cook until lightly browned on the bottom, about 2½ minutes. Flip to the other side and cook until just cooked through, about 1½ minutes more. Transfer the scallops to a serving dish and set aside.
4. Pour the mixture from the small saucepan into the skillet. Warm the sauce over low heat, stirring and scraping up any caramelized bits from the bottom of the pan, for 30 seconds, then pour the sauce over the scallops.
5. Serve immediately.

Pineapple Salmon Fillet

Prep time: 5 minutes | Cook time: 15 minutes | Serves 4

2 tablespoons clarified butter or ghee
4 pineapple rings, halved
1 teaspoon minced fresh ginger
½ teaspoon black or white sesame seeds
4 skin-on salmon fillets (5 to 6 ounces / 142 to 170 g each)
½ teaspoon salt
¼ teaspoon black pepper
1 tablespoon coconut oil
Chopped green onion (optional)

1. In a large nonstick skillet, heat the butter over medium-high heat. Add the pineapple, ginger, and sesame seeds and cook, turning once, until the pineapple is golden, 6 to 8 minutes. Transfer to a plate and cover to keep warm. Carefully wipe out the skillet.
2. Sprinkle the salmon with the salt and pepper. Heat the same pan over medium heat until very hot. Add the coconut oil and heat until you see ripples across the surface. Place the salmon in the skillet, skin side down. Cook, without touching, until the salmon has cooked about three-fourths of the way up the fillets, 4 to 5 minutes. Using a spatula, carefully turn the salmon over. Cook until the salmon just barely starts to flake when pulled apart with two forks, 2 to 3 minutes longer.
3. Serve the salmon with the caramelized pineapple and drizzle any pan juices over the top. If desired, top with green onion.

Shrimp and Fish Cakes with Snap Peas

Prep time: 15 minutes | Cook time: 20 minutes | Serves 4

- 1 pound (454 g) shrimp, peeled and deveined
- ½ pound (227 g) white-fleshed fish, such as cod, haddock, or halibut
- ¾ cup finely chopped green beans
- ¾ cup thinly sliced scallions
- ¾ cup diced carrots
- Juice from 3 tablespoons grated fresh ginger
- 3 tablespoons finely chopped lemongrass
- 1 large egg, beaten
- 1½ tablespoons coconut aminos
- ½ teaspoon ground white pepper
- 1½ teaspoons kosher salt
- 2 tablespoons extra-virgin olive oil
- 2 cups sugar snap peas, blanched

1. In a food processor, combine the shrimp and fish and pulse for just 3 seconds, making sure to keep them somewhat chunky so the fish cakes hold together when cooked. Transfer the mixture to a medium bowl.
2. Add the greens beans, scallions, carrots, ginger juice, lemongrass, egg, coconut aminos, white pepper, and salt and mix to combine well with the seafood. Using a food scale, make 3-inch patties weighing 3 ounces / 85 g each. Set aside.
3. In a large stainless steel skillet, heat the olive oil over medium to medium-low heat. Working in batches if needed, add the fish patties to the hot oil and fry until a golden brown crust forms on the bottom, about 4 minutes. Gently flip the patties and fry for 1 minute, then cover the pan and cook the patties until the shrimp is cooked through in the middle, about 3 minutes more. Remove from the heat and set aside.
4. For each serving, put some of the sugar snap peas in a bowl and top with 2 fish cakes.

Cassava-Crusted Calamari

Prep time: 10 minutes | Cook time: 20 minutes | Serves 4

- 1 pound (454 g) calamari, cut into ½-inch rounds
- 1 teaspoon kosher salt
- ½ teaspoon freshly ground black pepper
- ½ teaspoon cayenne pepper
- 4 large eggs, beaten
- 2 cups cassava flour
- 1 cup coconut oil

1. Preheat the oven to 200ºF (93ºC). Line a baking sheet with parchment.
2. Put the calamari in a medium bowl, sprinkle with the salt, black pepper, and cayenne, and toss thoroughly to coat.
3. Put the beaten eggs in a shallow bowl and the cassava flour in a second shallow bowl. Working in batches and using your left hand for the cassava flour and your right hand for the egg, put 3 or 4 calamari pieces into the egg mixture. Stick your right index finger into the center of the calamari tubes and spin them around to thoroughly coat the inside as well as outside with egg. Pick up the pieces and allow the excess egg to drip off, then put them in the flour and, using your dry hand, sprinkle the flour over the calamari to coat. Stick your left index finger in the center of the calamari tubes and spin them around to ensure they are completely coated inside and out. Shake off any excess flour and set the coated pieces aside on a plate. Repeat to coat the remaining calamari.
4. In a large sauté pan, melt ½ cup of the coconut oil over medium-high heat. When the oil is hot, working in batches, add the coated calamari to the pan and fry until golden and crispy, about 1 minute, then flip and fry on the second side for 1 minute. Use a slotted spoon to transfer the calamari to the prepared baking sheet and keep warm in the oven. Repeat until you have cooked half the calamari, then carefully discard the used cooking oil. Add the remaining ½ cup coconut oil to the pan, heat it over medium-high heat, and cook the remaining calamari (in batches, as needed). Serve.

Asian Shrimp and Zucchini Noodles

Prep time: 25 minutes | Cook time: 10 minutes | Serves 4

- ¼ cup rice vinegar
- 3 tablespoons coconut aminos
- 3 cloves garlic, minced
- 1 tablespoon minced fresh ginger
- ¼ teaspoon salt
- 1½ tablespoons olive oil
- 1 large yellow onion, slivered
- 1½ pounds (680 g) peeled and deveined medium shrimp
- 3 medium red and/or green bell peppers, cut into matchsticks
- 2 (10.7-ounce / 303-g) packages zucchini noodles; or 3 medium zucchini, spiralized, long noodles snipped if desired
- 3 green onions, sliced

1. In a small bowl, mix together the vinegar, coconut aminos, garlic, ginger, and salt.
2. Heat the olive oil in an extra-large skillet or wok over medium-high heat. Add the onion and cook, stirring, until it just starts to become tender, about 2 minutes. Stir in the vinegar mixture and cook until slightly reduced, about 1 minute. Add the shrimp, bell pepper, and zucchini noodles. Cook, stirring, until the shrimp are opaque and the vegetables are crisp-tender, 5 to 8 minutes. Top with the green onions and serve.

You are your only limit.

Shrimp with Pine Nuts

Prep time: 15 minutes | Cook time: 5 minutes | Serves 2

12 ounces (340 g) shrimp (medium or jumbo size), peeled and deveined, tails removed
Extra-virgin olive oil, for brushing
⅛ teaspoon coarse salt
⅛ teaspoon black pepper
⅓ cup pine nuts, chopped
2 cloves garlic, minced
1 teaspoon grated lemon zest
2 tablespoons snipped fresh parsley
Lemon wedges, for serving

1. Preheat the broiler to high. Line a large rimmed baking sheet with aluminum foil.
2. Rinse the shrimp and pat them dry with paper towels. Use a sharp knife to split the shrimp horizontally, cutting almost through to the opposite sides, but leaving the shrimp halves attached.
3. Open the shrimp so they lay flat. Arrange the shrimp, flat sides down, on the prepared baking sheet and brush lightly with olive oil. Sprinkle with the salt and pepper.
4. In a small bowl, combine the pine nuts, garlic, lemon zest, and 1 tablespoon olive oil.
5. Broil the shrimp, 4 to 5 inches from the heat, until almost completely opaque, 4 to 5 minutes for jumbo shrimp or 2 to 3 minutes for medium shrimp. Carefully flip each shrimp. Spoon the pine nut mixture evenly on the shrimp. Broil for 1 minute more.
6. To serve, divide the shrimp between two serving plates. Sprinkle with the parsley and serve with lemon wedges for squeezing over the shrimp.

Fish Fillet en Papillote

Prep time: 15 minutes | Cook time: 15 minutes | Serves 2

1 cup chopped seeded tomato
1 small shallot, thinly sliced
2 cloves garlic, minced
2 tablespoons extra-virgin olive oil
1½ teaspoons herbes de Provence
¼ teaspoon salt
2 halibut or cod fillets (5 to 6 ounces / 142 to 170 g each)
⅛ teaspoon black pepper
8 Kalamata or oil-cured black olives, pitted and halved
1 tablespoon chopped fresh parsley
Lemon wedges, for serving

1. Preheat the oven to 425°F (220°C).
2. Combine the tomato, shallot, garlic, 1 tablespoon of the olive oil, herbes de Provence, and ⅛ teaspoon of the salt in a medium bowl; mix well.
3. Cut two 12 × 15-inch squares of parchment paper. Rinse the fish and pat dry with paper towels. Place a fillet on each piece of parchment about 4 inches from the edge of the shorter sides. Sprinkle the fish with the remaining ⅛ teaspoon salt and the pepper. Spoon the tomato mixture on top of the fish and drizzle with the remaining 1 tablespoon olive oil.
4. Working with one packet at a time, fold the parchment over the fish, making the edges of the parchment even with each other. Starting at the bottom of the fold, tightly crimp the edges of the parchment to seal, making a half-moon-shaped packet.
5. Arrange the packets on a large baking sheet. Bake for about 12 minutes, until the fish just barely starts to flake when pulled apart with a fork (carefully open the packets to check doneness).
6. To serve, place each packet on a dinner plate; carefully open the packets. Top with the olives and parsley. Serve with lemon wedges.

Mussels and Squash in Spicy Tomato Sauce

Prep time: 20 minutes | Cook time: 10 minutes | Serves 4

2 tablespoons extra-virgin olive oil
4 medium shallots, finely chopped
4 cloves garlic, minced
1 (28-ounce / 794-g) can Whole30-compliant diced tomatoes
½ to 1 teaspoon red pepper flakes
½ teaspoon salt
½ teaspoon black pepper
2 pounds (907 g) mussels, scrubbed and debearded
2 medium yellow summer squash, trimmed and shaved into ribbons
2 tablespoons fresh lemon juice
½ cup chopped fresh basil

1. Heat 1 tablespoon of the olive oil in an extra-large skillet over medium heat. Add the shallots and garlic and cook, stirring, just until softened, about 2 minutes. Add the tomatoes, pepper flakes, salt, and pepper and bring to a boil. Add the mussels. Cover and cook until the mussels are just starting to open, 3 to 4 minutes.
2. Stir in the squash ribbons. Continue to cook, stirring occasionally, until the mussels have opened and the squash is crisp-tender, 1 to 2 minutes. Discard any mussels that do not open. Drizzle the lemon juice and remaining 1 tablespoon olive oil over the mussels and squash, top with the basil, and serve.

Lemon Dill Salmon Fillet

Prep time: 10 minutes | Cook time: 1 hour | Serves 4

4 salmon fillets (4 to 6 ounces / 113 to 170 g each), skin removed
½ teaspoon salt
½ teaspoon black pepper
2 Meyer lemons or regular lemons, sliced and seeded, plus additional lemon wedges for serving
1 tablespoon chopped fresh dill, plus more for serving
1 cup diced English cucumber
1 medium red bell pepper, diced
2 teaspoons cider vinegar
1 garlic clove, minced

1. Line a slow cooker with parchment paper. Sprinkle the salmon with the salt and pepper and place on the parchment. Top with the lemon slices and dill.
2. Cover and cook on high for 1 hour.
3. Meanwhile, in a small bowl, combine the cucumber, bell pepper, vinegar, and garlic. Cover and refrigerate until serving.
4. Remove the salmon from the slow cooker; discard the lemon slices. Top the salmon with the cucumber salad and additional chopped dill and serve with lemon wedges.

Scallops with Ginger-Blueberry Sauce

Prep time: 10 minutes | Cook time: 10 to 15 minutes | Serves 2

Ginger-Blueberry Sauce:
1 cup fresh or frozen blueberries
1½ teaspoons finely chopped fresh ginger
¼ teaspoon salt

Scallops:
¾ pound (340 g) sea scallops, patted dry
½ teaspoon salt
½ teaspoon black pepper
3 tablespoons cooking fat

1. Make the ginger-blueberry sauce: Defrost your blueberries (if necessary), then combine with 1 cup of water in a small saucepan over medium-high heat. Let the mixture reach a boil, then add the ginger and salt. Reduce the heat to medium and cook for 5 minutes, letting the blueberries burst and release their juice and the ginger steep.
2. The sauce can be left chunky, but it looks prettier if you blend it in a food processor or with an immersion blender to a smooth consistency. Just return it to the pan after blending to keep warm.
3. Make the scallops: Season both sides evenly with the salt and pepper. Heat the cooking fat in a large skillet over medium-high heat. When the fat is hot, add the scallops in a single layer (you may need to cook them in batches). Cook until the scallops begin to pull away from pan and brown, 2 to 3 minutes. Using kitchen tongs, turn the scallops and repeat the searing on the other side, for another 2 minutes.
4. Transfer the scallops to a serving dish or individual plates. Top with ¼ to ½ cup of the blueberry sauce. Serve warm or at room temperature.

Ginger Snapper Fillet with Shiitake Mushrooms

Prep time: 10 minutes | Cook time: 15 minutes | Serves 2

1½ teaspoons olive oil
1¼ cups sliced shiitake mushroom caps (3 to 4 ounces / 85 to 113 g)
2½ teaspoons grated lemon zest
Salt and black pepper, to taste
1 cup chicken bone broth, Whole30-compliant chicken broth, or water
2 teaspoons coconut aminos
2 red snapper fillets (6 ounces / 170 g each)
1 tablespoon thinly sliced fresh ginger
2 teaspoons avocado oil
1 clove garlic
½ teaspoon black or white sesame seeds
4 cups sliced bok choy
Lemon wedges, for serving
Fresh chives, snipped (optional)

1. Heat 1 teaspoon of the olive oil in a large skillet over medium heat. Add 1 cup of the mushrooms and cook, stirring, until tender, 3 to 4 minutes. Stir in ½ teaspoon of the lemon zest. Season with salt and pepper. Remove the mushroom mixture from the pan and keep warm.
2. Combine the remaining ¼ cup mushrooms, the broth, remaining 2 teaspoons lemon zest, the coconut aminos, and ¼ teaspoon of the olive oil in the same skillet. Bring to a boil. Reduce the heat to keep the liquid at a low simmer. Carefully add the fish. Sprinkle the fish lightly with salt and place the ginger slices on top. Cover and cook until the fish barely starts to flake when pulled apart with a fork, 4 to 5 minutes. Remove the fish from the skillet and cover to keep warm. Discard the poaching liquid and wipe out the skillet with a paper towel.
3. Heat the avocado oil in the skillet over medium heat. Add the garlic and sesame seeds and cook, stirring, for 1 minute. Stir in the bok choy and cook, covered, stirring occasionally, until the stems are crisp-tender and the leaves are wilted, 3 to 5 minutes. Remove the skillet from the heat and lightly season the bok choy with salt; drizzle with the remaining ¼ teaspoon olive oil.
4. Spoon the bok choy onto two dinner plates. Top each with a fish fillet and spoon sautéed mushrooms onto the fish. Serve with lemon wedges and sprinkle with chives, if desired.

Mexican-Style Tuna Boats

Prep time: 10 minutes | Cook time: 0 minutes | Serves 2

1 avocado, pitted and peeled
2 (5-ounce / 142-g) cans tuna, drained
3 green onions, thinly sliced
Juice of 1½ limes
½ jalapeño, minced
1 tablespoon minced fresh cilantro
½ teaspoon chili powder
½ teaspoon salt
⅛ teaspoon black pepper
1 head endive, separated into leaves

1. In a medium sized bowl, mash the avocado with a fork, leaving it slightly chunky. Add the tuna to the bowl, flaking it apart with a fork, and mix to combine with the avocado. Add the onions, juice of 1 lime, jalapeño, cilantro, chili powder, salt, and pepper and mix well.
2. Spoon the tuna mixture into the endive leaves. Sprinkle a dusting of chili powder. Squeeze the juice from the remaining ½ lime over the top and serve.

Lobster Mac Skillet

Prep time: 15 minutes | Cook time: 22 minutes | Serves 4

For the Sauce:
1½ tablespoons cooking fat
½ red onion, diced
2 medium carrots, diced
5 cloves garlic, minced
1 cup bone broth
2 tablespoons nutritional yeast
1 tablespoon red wine vinegar
1 large egg
1½ tablespoons cooking fat
1 pound (454 g) broccoli, cut into florets
2 tablespoons coconut butter, divided
1 pound (454 g) precooked langostino tails
1 teaspoon Dijon mustard
1 teaspoon fine Himalayan salt
1 teaspoon ground black pepper
¼ teaspoon ground nutmeg
3 slices bacon, chopped
¼ cup pickled red onion

1. Preheat the oven to 400°F (205°C).
2. Make the sauce: Heat a large oven-safe skillet over medium heat. When it's hot, place the cooking fat in it, then add the onions, carrots, and garlic. Sauté until the onions are translucent, about 5 minutes. Add the broth, cover, and simmer for 5 minutes, or until the carrots are very tender. You should be able to mash them with a spoon.
3. Carefully transfer everything from the skillet to a blender or food processor. Add the nutritional yeast and vinegar and blend until smooth. Then, with the blender running on low, add the egg and blend until completely smooth. Set aside.
4. Put the skillet back on the stove over medium heat and add the 1½ tablespoons of fat. Add the broccoli florets and 1 tablespoon of the coconut butter, stir until well combined, and sauté for 2 minutes. Add the langostino tails, mustard, salt, pepper, and nutmeg. Sauté, stirring frequently, for 2 minutes.
5. Mix in the sauce. Top with the remaining tablespoon of coconut butter, the bacon, and the pickled onions. Set the skillet on the middle rack of the oven and bake for 8 to 10 minutes, until the bacon is crispy. Serve right away!
6. If there are leftovers (doubtful), store them in an airtight container in the fridge for up to 5 days. To reheat, sauté over high heat for 5 minutes.

Jamaican Jerk Salmon with Fruity Salsa

Prep time: 10 minutes | Cook time: 10 minutes | Serves 4

Salsa:
1 ripe mango, pitted, peeled, and chopped
1 ripe avocado, halved, pitted, peeled, and chopped
½ cup chopped red bell pepper
½ cup roughly chopped fresh cilantro leaves
1 small fresh jalapeño, seeded and finely chopped
1 tablespoon fresh lime juice
Salt, to taste

Fish:
1½ teaspoons dried thyme, crushed
½ teaspoon garlic powder
½ teaspoon salt
½ teaspoon ground allspice
¼ teaspoon cayenne pepper
¼ teaspoon ground cinnamon
4 skinless salmon fillets (6 to 8 ounces / 170 to 227 g each), about 1 inch thick
1 tablespoon extra-virgin olive oil
6 cups fresh baby spinach

1. Make the salsa: In a medium bowl, gently combine the mango, avocado, bell pepper, cilantro, jalapeño, and lime juice. Season with salt. Cover and refrigerate for up to 2 hours.
2. Make the fish: Grease the grill rack. Preheat the grill to medium heat. In a small bowl, combine the thyme, garlic powder, salt, allspice, cayenne, and cinnamon; set aside. Rinse the fish; pat dry with paper towels. Brush both sides of the fish with the olive oil. Sprinkle with the spice blend and rub it in with your fingers. Grill the fish over direct heat for 8 to 12 minutes, turning once, until it barely starts to flake when pulled apart with a fork.
3. To serve, divide the spinach leaves between two plates. Top with the grilled salmon and mango salsa.

Ahi Tuna with Tangy Fruit Salsa

Prep time: 15 minutes | Cook time: 5 minutes | Serves 2

Salsa:
- 1 mango, pitted, peeled, and diced
- 1 medium tomato, seeded and diced
- 2 green onions, minced
- 1 avocado, halved, pitted, peeled, and diced
- ¼ cup roughly chopped fresh cilantro
- ½ jalapeño, seeded and minced
- Juice of 1 lime
- ⅛ teaspoon salt
- ⅛ teaspoon black pepper

Tuna:
- 2 ahi tuna steaks (4 to 6 ounces / 113 to 170 g each), about 1 inch thick
- Avocado oil
- 1 teaspoon black sesame seeds
- 1 teaspoon white sesame seeds
- ¼ teaspoon salt
- ¼ teaspoon black pepper

1. Make the salsa: In a medium bowl, combine all the salsa ingredients and toss to mix.
2. Make the tuna: Brush both sides of the tuna with a small amount of avocado oil. Season both sides with the sesame seeds, salt, and black pepper.
3. Heat a large ceramic nonstick skillet or cast-iron skillet over medium-high heat. Add the tuna and sear for 2 minutes on one side. Turn the tuna over and sear the other side for 2 minutes, until browned and crusty on the outside and rare inside. Serve the salsa with the tuna steaks.

Citrus-Ginger Glazed Halibut Fillet

Prep time: 10 minutes | Cook time: 20 minutes | Serves 2

Glaze:
- ½ cup apple cider
- Grated zest and juice of 2 lemons
- Juice of 1 orange
- ½ tablespoon grated fresh ginger (or ½ teaspoon ground ginger)

Fish:
- 3 tablespoons cooking fat
- 2 halibut fillets (5 ounces / 142 g each)
- 1 teaspoon salt
- ½ teaspoon black pepper

1. Preheat the oven to 400ºF (205ºC).
2. For the glaze: Cook the apple cider in a small saucepan over medium-high heat until reduced to about 1 tablespoon, 4 to 6 minutes. Add the lemon juice, orange juice, and ginger and cook until reduced by half, 3 to 5 minutes. Remove the pan from the heat and add the lemon zest. Set aside.
3. For the fish: Heat 2 tablespoons of the cooking fat in a large skillet over high heat, swirling to coat the bottom of the pan. While the fat is heating, season the halibut with the salt and pepper. When the fat is hot, place the fish top-side-down in the pan and sear for 2 to 3 minutes. While the fish is searing, melt the remaining 1 tablespoon cooking fat (if necessary), line a baking sheet with parchment paper, and brush half of the fat on the paper.
4. Remove the halibut from the pan and transfer seared-side-up to the greased, lined baking sheet. Brush the remaining cooking fat over the top of the halibut. Bake in the oven for 10 to 12 minutes, until the flesh is just barely firm and flakes easily with a fork. Transfer the fish to a serving dish or individual plates and spoon the glaze over the top just before serving.

Harissa Salmon Fillets with Warm Salad

Prep time: 10 minutes | Cook time: 10 minutes | Serves 2

- 2 tablespoons Whole30-compliant harissa paste
- 2 teaspoons coriander seeds, crushed
- 2 teaspoons grated lemon zest
- 2 skin-on salmon fillets (6 to 8 ounces / 170 to 227 g each)
- 2 tablespoons extra-virgin olive oil
- 1 small yellow onion, cut into slivers
- 1 small red bell pepper, seeded and cut into matchsticks
- 1 small green bell pepper, seeded and cut into matchsticks
- 1 tablespoon fresh lemon juice
- 1 large ripe tomato, seeded and chopped
- 1 clove garlic, thinly sliced
- ¼ teaspoon sea salt, plus more as needed
- Black pepper, to taste
- ¼ cup snipped fresh cilantro

1. Preheat the oven to 450ºF (235ºC).
2. In a small bowl, mix together the harissa, coriander, and lemon zest. Place the salmon fillets, skin side down, in a shallow baking pan. Wearing plastic or rubber gloves, spoon the harissa mixture on top of the salmon and rub it in with your fingers. Let the salmon stand while you prepare the salad.
3. Heat the olive oil in a large skillet over medium heat. Add the onion and bell peppers and cook, stirring, for 5 minutes. Add the lemon juice, tomato, garlic, salt, and black pepper to taste and cook, stirring, until the tomato begins to soften, about 3 minutes. Remove the skillet from the heat and top with the cilantro. Let the salad stand while you roast the salmon.
4. Roast the salmon for 4 to 6 minutes per ½-inch thickness, until the fish just barely starts to flake when pulled apart with a fork. Season with salt. Serve the salmon with the warm salad.

Speedy Shrimp Scampi

Prep time: 10 minutes | Cook time: 10 minutes | Serves 2

2 tablespoons finely chopped garlic (about 3 large cloves)
1 tablespoon ghee
1 tablespoon extra-virgin olive oil
¾ pound (340 g) raw jumbo shrimp, peeled, tails on, and deveined
1 teaspoon red pepper flakes (optional)
⅓ cup chicken stock
1 tablespoon fresh lemon juice
Kosher salt and freshly ground black pepper, to taste
¼ cup loosely packed fresh parsley leaves, finely chopped

1. In a large stainless-steel or nonstick skillet, combine the garlic, ghee, and olive oil. Cook over medium-high heat, stirring, until the garlic is fragrant, about 2 minutes. Pat the shrimp very dry with a paper towel. Add them to the pan and cook, stirring, until slightly pink, about 2 minutes per side. Add the red pepper flakes (if using) and cook, stirring, for 1 minute.
2. Add the stock and lemon juice and cook until the liquid has reduced by about a quarter, about 2 minutes. Taste the sauce and season with salt and black pepper. Remove the pan from the heat and stir in the parsley. Serve immediately.

Cod Fillet in Tomato and Pepper Sauce

Prep time: 10 minutes | Cook time: 4 hours | Serves 4

2 medium yellow bell peppers, sliced
3 medium shallots, sliced
3 cloves garlic, minced
1 (14½-ounce / 411-g) can Whole30-compliant diced tomatoes
4 cod fillets (5 to 6 ounces / 142 to 170 g each)
¼ teaspoon salt
¼ teaspoon black pepper
1 tablespoon chopped fresh flat-leaf parsley
1 tablespoon Whole30-compliant capers, drained
1 teaspoon grated lemon zest
1 tablespoon extra-virgin olive oil

1. In a slow cooker, combine the bell peppers, shallots, garlic, and tomatoes. Cover and cook on low for 4 to 5 hours or on high for 2 to 2½ hours.
2. If on low, turn the slow cooker to the high setting. Place the fish fillets on the sauce. Sprinkle with the salt and pepper. Cover and cook just until the fish starts to flake with a fork, 30 to 40 minutes.
3. Top the cod with the parsley, capers, lemon zest, and olive oil, and serve.

Salmon with Cauliflower and Spinach Salad

Prep time: 30 minutes | Cook time: 15 minutes | Serves 4

Salad:
1 small head cauliflower, broken into large florets
2 tablespoons extra-virgin olive oil
2 cups baby spinach or kale (not packed)
1 cup grape tomatoes, halved
⅓ cup thinly sliced fresh basil leaves
⅓ cup sliced almonds, toasted

Vinaigrette:
⅓ cup extra-virgin olive oil
3 tablespoons champagne vinegar, white wine vinegar, or apple cider vinegar
1 tablespoon finely chopped shallots
1 teaspoon Whole30-compliant Dijon mustard
¼ teaspoon salt
¼ teaspoon black pepper

Fish:
4 skinless salmon fillets (6 to 8 ounces / 170 to 227 g each)
Extra-virgin olive oil
Salt and black pepper, to taste
2 tablespoons chopped fresh chives
Lemon wedges, for serving

1. Grease a grill rack and preheat the grill to medium heat.
2. Make the salad: In a food processor, pulse the cauliflower (in batches) until the pieces are the size of couscous. In a large skillet, cook the cauliflower couscous in the olive oil, stirring occasionally, until tender and just beginning to brown, about 5 minutes. Transfer to a large bowl. Add the spinach, tomatoes, basil, and almonds and toss to combine.
3. Make the vinaigrette: In a small bowl, whisk together the olive oil, vinegar, shallots, and mustard. Season with the salt and pepper. Drizzle the couscous salad with the vinaigrette and toss to coat.
4. Make the salmon: Brush the salmon with olive oil and season with salt and pepper. Close the grill lid and grill the salmon until it is nicely seared, crispy, and releases easily from the grill, about 6 minutes. Turn the salmon and grill until it barely starts to flake when pulled apart with a fork, about 2 minutes. Remove the salmon from the grill and let rest for 3 minutes.
5. Sprinkle the salmon with the chives and serve with the cauliflower couscous salad and lemon wedges.

Fish en Papillote

Prep time: 20 minutes | Cook time: 2 hours | Serves 4

1 pound (454 g) haricot verts or slender green beans, trimmed
2 red or yellow bell peppers, thinly sliced (3 cups)
1 small onion, thinly sliced (1 cup)
2 cloves garlic, minced
1 teaspoon smoked paprika
1½ teaspoons black pepper
1 teaspoon salt
2 tablespoons plus 2 teaspoons extra-virgin olive oil
4 cod or halibut fillets (5 to 6 ounces / 142 to 170 g each)

1. In a large bowl, combine the green beans, bell peppers, onion, garlic, smoked paprika, 1 teaspoon of the pepper, and ½ teaspoon of the salt. Drizzle with 2 tablespoons of the olive oil and toss to combine. Cut four 15-inch squares of parchment paper. Divide the vegetable mixture into 4 portions and place one in the center of each piece of parchment.
2. Lightly drizzle the fish with the remaining 2 teaspoons olive oil and season with the remaining ½ teaspoon each salt and pepper. Place the fillets over the vegetable mixture on the parchment. Bring up two opposite edges of paper and fold several times over the fish. Fold in the ends.
3. Place the packets in an oval slow cooker. Cover and cook on high for 2 to 3 hours, or until the fish flakes easily with a fork.

Basil Roasted Salmon Fillet with Broccoli

Prep time: 15 minutes | Cook time: 25 minutes | Serves 2

½ cup fresh basil leaves
½ cup fresh parsley leaves
6 tablespoons extra-virgin olive oil
1 tablespoon fresh lemon juice
1 teaspoon salt
1 teaspoon black pepper
½ teaspoon grated lemon zest
¼ cup almond flour
2 salmon fillets (6 ounces / 170 g each)
3 small heads broccoli with the stems attached (about 1 pound (454 g) / 454 g total)
½ cup sliced almonds, toasted

1. Preheat the oven to 400ºF (205ºC).
2. Combine the basil, parsley, 4 tablespoons of the oil, lemon juice, ½ teaspoon of the salt, ½ teaspoon of the pepper, and the lemon zest in a blender or food processor. Cover and pulse until smooth. Pour the herb mixture into a bowl and stir in the almond flour.
3. Place the salmon fillets in a large roasting pan or on a rimmed baking sheet. Pack the herb mixture on the top of each fillet.
4. Trim the broccoli stems to about 3 inches below the florets. Slice the broccoli heads lengthwise into 1-inch-thick slabs (two or three slabs per head), cutting from the bottom of the stems through the crown to preserve the shape of the broccoli. Brush both sides of each broccoli slice with the remaining 2 tablespoons olive oil and sprinkle with the remaining ½ teaspoon salt and ½ teaspoon pepper. Arrange the broccoli in a single layer in the pan around the salmon.
5. Roast the broccoli and salmon for 25 minutes, until the salmon just barely starts to flake when pulled apart with a fork and the broccoli is lightly browned, turning the broccoli once halfway through roasting. Sprinkle the broccoli with the toasted almonds before serving.

Thai-Style Red Curry Shrimp

Prep time: 20 minutes | Cook time: 15 minutes | Serves 4

1 tablespoon coconut oil
1 small onion, chopped
2 cloves garlic, minced
2 teaspoons minced fresh ginger
1 (14-ounce / 397-g) can Whole30-compliant coconut milk
2 tablespoons Whole30-compliant Thai red curry paste
1 tablespoon coconut aminos
1 pound (454 g) peeled and deveined large shrimp
4 cups fresh baby spinach
1 tablespoon fresh lime juice, plus lime wedges for serving
1 (16-ounce / 454-g) package cauliflower crumbles, or 4 cups raw cauliflower rice
Torn fresh basil, for serving
Lime wedges, for serving

1. In a large skillet, heat the oil over medium heat. Add the onion and cook, stirring occasionally, until tender, 3 to 4 minutes. Add the garlic and ginger and cook, stirring, until fragrant, about 1 minute. Stir in the coconut milk, curry paste, and coconut aminos. Bring to a boil, then reduce the heat and simmer for 5 minutes. Add the shrimp and cook, stirring occasionally, until opaque, about 5 minutes. Remove from the heat and stir in the spinach and lime juice.
2. Meanwhile, prepare the cauliflower crumbles according to the package directions. Serve the shrimp curry over the cauliflower rice. Top with the fresh basil and serve with lime wedges.

Fish and Vegetable Stir-Fry

Prep time: 15 minutes | Cook time: 10 minutes | Serves 2

Fish:
2 skinless cod or sea bass fillets, cut about ½ inch thick (5 to 6 ounces / 142 to 170 g each)
⅛ teaspoon coarse salt
⅛ teaspoon black pepper
¼ cup almond meal
¼ cup unsweetened flaked coconut
¼ cup finely chopped shallots
1 tablespoon coconut oil, melted

Vegetables:
1 tablespoon coconut oil
1 bunch fresh broccolini, trimmed, or 1 cup fresh broccoli florets
¾ cup halved and thinly sliced yellow summer squash
¼ cup sliced quartered onion
1 cup coarsely shredded napa cabbage
8 snow peas, trimmed and halved lengthwise
2 teaspoons minced fresh ginger
1 clove garlic, minced
1 tablespoon olive oil
1 tablespoon coconut aminos
1 tablespoon Whole30-compliant rice vinegar
2 teaspoons sesame seeds, toasted (optional)

1. Preheat the oven to 425ºF (220ºC).
2. Make the fish: Line a baking sheet with parchment paper. Rinse the fish; pat dry with paper towels. Place the fish on the prepared baking sheet. Sprinkle the fish with the salt and pepper. In a small bowl, combine the almond meal, flaked coconut, and shallots. Add the coconut oil to the coconut mixture and mix well. Spoon the coconut mixture evenly on top of the fish fillets.
3. Bake the fish for 8 to 11 minutes, until the topping is browned and the fish just barely starts to flake when pulled apart with a fork.
4. Make the vegetables: Heat the coconut oil in a wok or large nonstick skillet over medium heat. Add the broccolini; cover and cook for 2 minutes. Uncover and cook, stirring, for 2 minutes more. Add the squash and onion. Cook, stirring, until the vegetables are crisp-tender, 3 to 5 minutes. Add the cabbage, snow peas, ginger, and garlic. Cook, stirring, for 2 minutes. Add the olive oil, coconut aminos, and rice vinegar. Cook, stirring, for 1 minute.
5. Divide the vegetable stir-fry between two serving plates. Top with the fish. Sprinkle with sesame seeds, if desired.

Cod Fillet with Olive Relish and Pilaf

Prep time: 10 minutes | Cook time: 20 minutes | Serves 4

Relish:
½ cup pitted green olives
½ cup extra-virgin olive oil
1 shallot, minced
2 tablespoons fresh orange juice
2 teaspoons fresh thyme leaves
1 teaspoon ground ancho chile
½ teaspoon grated orange zest

Fish:
4 cod fillets (5 to 6 ounces / 142 to 170 g each)
2 tablespoons extra-virgin olive oil
½ teaspoon dried thyme
½ teaspoon salt
½ teaspoon black pepper

Pilaf:
1 head cauliflower, cut into florets
2 tablespoons olive oil
1 small poblano pepper, seeded and finely chopped
1 shallot, minced
½ teaspoon salt
½ teaspoon black pepper
¼ cup sliced almonds, toasted
2 tablespoons fresh lemon juice

1. For the relish: In a food processor, combine all the ingredients for the relish. Pulse until the mixture is very finely chopped and forms a loose paste. Transfer the olive relish to a bowl and set aside.
2. For the fish: Preheat the oven to 400ºF (205ºC). Arrange the fish on a rimmed baking sheet. Drizzle with the olive oil. Sprinkle with the dried thyme, salt, and black pepper. Roast for 20 minutes, until the fish just barely starts to flake when pulled apart with a fork.
3. For the pilaf: Place half the cauliflower in a food processor and pulse into a rice-like consistency, 15 to 20 pulses. Transfer to a bowl and repeat with the remaining cauliflower. In a large skillet, heat the olive oil over medium heat. Add the poblano and shallot and cook, stirring, until just tender, about 5 minutes. Add the cauliflower, salt, and black pepper. Cook, stirring frequently, until the cauliflower is just tender and beginning to brown, about 5 minutes. Stir in the almonds and lemon juice.
4. Serve the fish over the pilaf and top with the olive relish. Store leftover relish in an airtight container in the refrigerator for up to 3 days.

Chapter 7 Poultry

Stuffed Bell Peppers with Turkey

Prep time: 10 minutes | Cook time: 2½ hours | Serves 4

1 tablespoon extra-virgin olive oil	compliant taco seasoning
1½ pounds (680 g) ground turkey	¾ cup Whole30-compliant salsa
½ cup chopped onion	4 medium red or yellow bell peppers
3 cloves garlic, minced	Chopped fresh cilantro
1 tablespoon Whole30-	

1. In a large skillet, heat the oil over medium-high heat. Add the turkey, onion, garlic, and taco seasoning and cook, stirring with a wooden spoon to break up the meat, until browned. Stir in the salsa.
2. Place a small rack in a 5- to 6-quart slow cooker. Add ¼ cup water to the slow cooker. Cut a thin slice from the top of each pepper to remove the stem. Use a small, sharp knife to cut out the seeds and membranes, keeping the peppers intact. Set the peppers, cut sides up, on the rack in the cooker. Spoon the turkey mixture into the peppers. Cover and cook on low for 2½ to 3 hours, until the peppers are tender.
3. Carefully transfer the peppers to a serving platter. Discard the cooking liquid. Serve, topped with cilantro.

Chicken Tikka Masala with Cauliflower Rice

Prep time: 20 minutes | Cook time: 4 hours | Serves 6

2½ pounds (1.1 kg) boneless, skinless chicken thighs	1 piece (1 inch) fresh ginger, peeled and minced
2 teaspoons kosher salt	¼ teaspoon cayenne pepper (optional)
2 (13½-ounce / 382.7-g) cans Whole30-compliant coconut milk, refrigerated overnight	1 medium onion, chopped
	1 (28-ounce / 794-g) can Whole30-compliant crushed tomatoes
1 tablespoon turmeric	2 tablespoons Whole30-compliant tomato paste
2 teaspoons ground coriander	1 tablespoon fresh lemon juice
2 teaspoons Whole30-compliant curry powder	2 (12-ounce / 340-g) packages frozen riced cauliflower or 6 cups raw cauliflower rice
2 teaspoons ground cumin	¼ teaspoon salt
2 teaspoons Whole30-compliant garam masala	Chopped fresh parsley
5 large garlic cloves, crushed	

1. Sprinkle both sides of the chicken with the salt. Cut each piece of chicken in half, then into 1-inch strips. Set aside.
2. Open one of the cans of coconut milk carefully; the top part should be solid. Spoon the solid portion into a large bowl and add ½ cup of the liquid. Stir in the turmeric, coriander, curry powder, cumin, garam masala, garlic, ginger, and cayenne pepper (if using). Add the chicken to the marinade. If needed, add more of the liquid portion of the coconut milk to cover. Cover and refrigerate overnight.
3. Combine the onion, crushed tomatoes, tomato paste, and lemon juice in a 6-quart slow cooker. Add the chicken and marinade and stir.
4. Cover and cook on high for 4 hours.
5. For the coconut cream, open the second can of coconut milk and spoon the solid portion into a medium bowl. Add ½ cup of the liquid and stir until no lumps remain.
6. Prepare the riced cauliflower according to the package directions.
7. Use a slotted spoon to transfer the chicken to a bowl; cover to keep warm. Use an immersion blender to blend the cooking liquid in the slow cooker until smooth. Add ¾ cup of the coconut cream; blend well. (Or transfer the cooking liquid to a blender, add the coconut cream, and blend.) Add the salt.
8. Serve the chicken over the cauliflower rice. Top with the sauce and sprinkle with parsley.

Zucchini-Basil Chicken Thighs Hash

Prep time: 10 minutes | Cook time: 10 minutes | Serves 2

2 tablespoons coconut oil	boneless, skinless chicken thighs, diced
¼ cup finely chopped red onion	1 teaspoon dried oregano, crushed
2 green onions, thinly sliced	1 teaspoon salt
2 cloves garlic, minced	2 tablespoons balsamic vinegar
2 medium zucchini, trimmed and diced	¼ cup thinly sliced fresh basil
1¼ pounds (567 g)	

1. Melt the coconut oil in a large skillet over medium heat. Add the red onion, green onions, and garlic and cook, stirring, until tender and starting to brown, about 1 minute. Add the zucchini and cook, stirring occasionally, until softened and starting to brown, 4 to 5 minutes.
2. Add the chicken, oregano, and salt and cook, stirring occasionally, until the chicken is cooked through and starting to brown, 5 to 6 minutes. Gently stir in the vinegar and basil and serve.

Southwest Turkey Legs with Fruit Salad

Prep time: 15 minutes | Cook time: 3½ hours | Serves 4

For the Turkey Legs:
2 teaspoons salt
1 teaspoon black pepper
1 teaspoon cumin
1 teaspoon coriander
1 teaspoon cayenne
1 teaspoon onion powder
4 turkey legs

For the Fruit Salad:
2 cups assorted melon chunks, such as cantaloupe and honeydew
1 cup fresh pineapple chunks
2 oranges, peeled and sectioned
¼ cup fresh orange juice
2 tablespoons fresh lime juice
2 tablespoons extra-virgin olive oil
¼ teaspoon coriander
¼ cup chopped fresh mint

1. Cook the turkey legs: Pour 1 cup water into a 6-quart slow cooker and add a steamer basket. In a small bowl, combine the salt, pepper, cumin, coriander, cayenne, and onion powder. Rub the seasoning over the turkey legs. Tightly wrap each leg in a piece of aluminum foil about 12 x 12 inches. Place the legs on the steamer basket.
2. Cover and cook on low for 7 hours or on high for 3½ hours. Remove the turkey from the slow cooker; let cool for 10 minutes before removing the foil.
3. Make the fruit salad: Meanwhile, in a medium bowl, combine the melon, pineapple, and oranges. In a small bowl, combine the orange juice, lime juice, olive oil, and coriander. Add to the fruit and toss. Sprinkle with the mint.
4. Serve the turkey legs with the fruit salad.

Italian Turkey Meatballs with Marinara Sauce

Prep time: 20 minutes | Cook time: 3 hours | Serves 4

For the Meatballs:
1 (19-ounce / 538.6-g) package ground turkey breast
¼ cup minced onion
¼ cup minced mushrooms
1 tablespoon minced garlic
4 teaspoons tapioca flour
1 tablespoon Whole30-compliant Italian seasoning
½ teaspoon fennel seeds, crushed
¼ teaspoon red pepper flakes
¼ teaspoon sea salt
¼ teaspoon black pepper
1 large egg, lightly beaten

For the Sauce:
1 (28-ounce / 794-g) can Whole30-compliant crushed tomatoes
½ cup grated carrots
¼ cup grated onion
1 tablespoon minced garlic
1 tablespoon Whole30-compliant Italian seasoning
1 bay leaf

To Serve
2 (10½-ounce / 297.7-g) packages zucchini noodles or 3 medium zucchini, spiralized
2 tablespoons chopped fresh parsley

1. Make the meatballs: Preheat the oven to 400°F (205°C). In a large bowl, combine the turkey, minced onion, mushrooms, and garlic. In a small bowl, stir together the tapioca flour, Italian seasoning, fennel seeds, red pepper flakes, salt, and black pepper. Add the tapioca mixture and the egg to the turkey mixture and mix until thoroughly combined. Let sit 5 minutes. Shape into 16 meatballs. Place on a foil-lined baking pan and bake for 10 minutes.
2. Make the sauce: In a 6-quart slow cooker, combine 1 cup water with the tomatoes, carrots, grated onion, garlic, Italian seasoning, and bay leaf. Add the meatballs.
3. Cover and cook on low for 6 hours or on high for 3 hours. Discard the bay leaf.
4. Meanwhile, prepare the zucchini noodles according to the package directions. Divide the noodles among four serving bowls. Top each with four meatballs and sauce. Sprinkle with parsley and serve.

Instant Pot Turkey Chili with Avocado

Prep time: 10 minutes | Cook time: 13 minutes | Serves 4

1 tablespoon extra-virgin olive oil
1 (19-ounce / 538.6-g) package lean ground turkey
1 large yellow onion, chopped
2 cloves garlic, minced
1 teaspoon salt
1 (28-ounce / 794-g) can Whole30-compliant crushed tomatoes
1 medium yellow bell pepper, chopped
1 medium jalapeño, seeded and chopped
1 tablespoon chili powder
1 medium avocado, halved, pitted, peeled, and diced
2 tablespoons chopped fresh cilantro

1. On a 6-quart Instant Pot, select Sauté and adjust to Normal/Medium. Add the oil to the pot. When it's hot, add the turkey, onion, garlic, and salt. Cook, stirring occasionally with a wooden spoon to break up the meat, until browned, 8 to 10 minutes. Select Cancel.
2. Stir in ½ cup water, the tomatoes, bell pepper, jalapeño, and chili powder. Lock the lid in place. Select Manual and cook on high pressure for 5 minutes. Use quick release.

Top servings with the avocado and cilantro.

Skillet Buttered Chicken Thighs

Prep time: 15 minutes | Cook time: 17 minutes | Serves 4

1¼ pounds (567 g) boneless, skinless chicken thighs, cut into 1-inch pieces
1 tablespoon garam masala
½ teaspoon salt
⅛ teaspoon cayenne pepper
2 tablespoons clarified butter or ghee
1 medium onion, chopped
3 cloves garlic, minced
1 tablespoon minced fresh ginger
1 (14½-ounce / 411-g) can Whole30-compliant diced tomatoes, undrained
1 cup Whole30-compliant coconut milk
1 (12-ounce / 340-g) package frozen riced cauliflower and sweet potato
2 tablespoons chopped fresh cilantro

1. In a medium bowl, toss the chicken with the garam masala, salt, and cayenne. In an extra-large skillet, heat the butter over medium-high heat. Add the chicken and cook, stirring occasionally, until browned, 4 to 6 minutes. Stir in the onion and cook, stirring occasionally, until the onion is softened, 2 to 3 minutes. Add the garlic and ginger and cook, stirring, for 1 minute.
2. Stir in the diced tomatoes and juice and bring to a boil. Reduce the heat and simmer until the chicken is cooked through, 10 to 12 minutes longer. Stir in the coconut milk and heat through, about 1 minute.
3. Meanwhile, prepare the riced cauliflower and sweet potato according to package directions.
4. Spoon the butter chicken over the cooked cauliflower and sweet potato, top with the cilantro, and serve.

Patrick's Golden Chicken Fingers

Prep time: 10 minutes | Cook time: 6 minutes | Serves 4

2 large boneless, skinless chicken breasts
1 teaspoon kosher salt
¼ teaspoon freshly ground black pepper
2 large eggs
2 tablespoons milk
1 cup all-purpose flour
1 cup vegetable oil

1. Cut each chicken breast crosswise on an angle into 10 strips. Season the strips with the salt and pepper. Set aside.
2. Beat the eggs and milk together until the striations are gone, then pour them into a shallow, rimmed dish. Put the flour in a separate shallow, rimmed dish.
3. One by one, thoroughly cover each chicken strip in flour, then dredge in the egg, then remove and gently drop into the flour, covering thoroughly. Handling each chicken finger as minimally as possible, shake off any excess flour and set aside on a plate.
4. In a medium skillet, heat the vegetable oil over high heat until hot but not smoking (you can test the oil with a corner of a chicken strip—if it audibly sizzles, it's hot enough). Reduce the heat to medium-high. Working in batches, fry the chicken strips in the hot oil until golden brown, 2 to 3 minutes, flipping them halfway through. Transfer them to a tea towel–lined plate to drain. Repeat to cook the remaining chicken strips. Serve.

Chicken Breast with Ginger and Basil

Prep time: 10 minutes | Cook time: 11 minutes | Serves 2

2 (6-ounce / 170-g) boneless, skinless chicken breast halves
Coarse salt and black pepper, to taste
2 tablespoons coconut oil
1 tablespoon fresh lime juice
1 tablespoon minced fresh ginger
½ cup Whole30-compliant chicken broth or chicken bone broth
1 cup packaged shredded carrots, or 2 medium carrots, shredded
1 medium red onion, slivered
1 cup sliced sugar snap peas
¼ teaspoon crushed red pepper
2 tablespoons snipped fresh basil

1. Place the chicken breasts between two pieces of plastic wrap and use the flat side of a meat mallet to flatten them to a ¼-inch thickness. Lightly season both sides with salt and pepper.
2. Heat 1 tablespoon of the coconut oil in a large skillet over medium heat. Add the chicken and cook until golden, 3 to 4 minutes per side, adding more oil if needed. Remove the chicken from the skillet and cover to keep warm.
3. Add the lime juice, ginger, and broth to the skillet, scraping up any browned bits on the bottom of the skillet. Bring to a boil, reduce the heat, and simmer until the pan sauce is reduced to about ¼ cup, 1 to 2 minutes. Remove the skillet from the heat.
4. Meanwhile, heat the remaining 1 tablespoon coconut oil in a medium skillet over medium-high heat. Add the carrots, onion, snap peas, and crushed red pepper and cook, stirring, until crisp-tender, about 4 minutes.
5. Arrange the chicken and vegetables on serving plates and drizzle the pan juices over all. Sprinkle with the fresh basil and serve.

It is never too late.

Orange Chicken Breast with Cauliflower Rice

Prep time: 15 minutes | Cook time: 10 minutes | Serves 4

1 teaspoon grated orange zest	butter or ghee
¾ cup fresh orange juice	1½ pounds (680 g) boneless, skinless chicken breasts, cut into 1-inch pieces
1 tablespoon coconut aminos	
1 teaspoon rice vinegar	1 (12-ounce / 340-g) bag fresh broccoli, carrots, and snow peas stir-fry vegetables
2 cloves garlic, minced	
1 teaspoon minced fresh ginger	
¼ teaspoon salt	1 (16-ounce / 454-g) package cauliflower crumbles, or 4 cups raw cauliflower rice
1 teaspoon tapioca flour, or 2½ teaspoons arrowroot powder	
1 tablespoon clarified	2 green onions, sliced

1. In a small bowl, mix together the orange zest and juice, coconut aminos, rice vinegar, garlic, ginger, and salt. In another small bowl, whisk together 2 teaspoons cold water and the tapioca flour until smooth.
2. Heat the butter in a large skillet over medium-high heat. Add the chicken and cook, stirring, until fully cooked, 5 to 6 minutes. Transfer the chicken to a plate and cover to keep warm.
3. Stir the orange juice mixture into the same skillet and bring to a boil, stirring, over medium-high heat. Whisk in the tapioca flour mixture until smooth. Add the stir-fry vegetables and cook, stirring frequently, until the vegetables are crisp-tender and the sauce has thickened slightly, 4 to 6 minutes. Stir in the chicken and heat through, about 1 minute.
4. Meanwhile, prepare the cauliflower crumbles according to the package directions.
5. Spoon the chicken and vegetables over the cauliflower, sprinkle with green onions, and serve.

Chicken with Red Bell Pepper

Prep time: 15 minutes | Cook time: 20 minutes | Serves 4

2 tablespoons extra-virgin olive oil	1 (14½-ounce / 411-g) can Whole30-compliant diced tomatoes
1½ pounds (680 g) bone-in, skin-on chicken thighs	
1 teaspoon salt	½ cup Whole30-compliant chicken broth or chicken bone broth
½ teaspoon black pepper	
2 medium red bell peppers, chopped	¼ to ½ teaspoon red pepper flakes
1 medium onion, chopped	Sliced fresh basil leaves (optional)
2 cloves garlic, minced	

1. Heat 1 tablespoon of the olive oil in a large heavy skillet over medium-high heat. Season the chicken with ½ teaspoon of the salt and ¼ teaspoon of the pepper. Add the chicken and cook, turning once, until the skin is browned, about 5 minutes. Transfer to a plate and cover to keep warm.
2. In the same skillet, heat the remaining 1 tablespoon olive oil over medium heat. Add the bell peppers, onion, and garlic and cook, stirring frequently, until tender, 3 to 4 minutes. Stir in the tomatoes, broth, pepper flakes, and the remaining ½ teaspoon salt and ¼ teaspoon pepper. Cook until the mixture begins to thicken slightly, 5 to 7 minutes.
3. Return the chicken to the skillet. Cover and reduce the heat to low. Cook until the chicken is no longer pink and the internal temperature is 170ºF (77ºC), 12 to 15 minutes. Serve with basil, if desired.

Fresh Rosemary Whole Chicken

Prep time: 5 minutes | Cook time: 45 minutes | Serves 2 to 4

1 (2½- to 3-pound / 1.1- to 1.4-kg) whole chicken	Kosher salt and freshly ground black pepper, to taste
1 tablespoon coarsely chopped fresh rosemary	

1. Preheat the oven to 425ºF (220ºC). Line a 4-inch-deep roasting pan with parchment paper.
2. Pat the chicken very dry with paper towels. Using sharp kitchen shears or a sharp knife, cut along one side of the backbone, leaving the other side attached. Lay the chicken breast-side up on a cutting board and press down on the breastbone with your hands to flatten the chicken. Liberally season the chicken all over with the rosemary and salt and pepper. Transfer the chicken breast-side up to the prepared roasting pan.
3. Roast on the bottom rack of the oven for 40 to 45 minutes, until the thickest part of the thigh registers 165ºF (74ºC) on an instant-read thermometer. Use a turkey baster or large spoon to baste the chicken with the juices from the pan.
4. Set the oven to broil, but keep the chicken on the bottom rack (putting the parchment paper closer to the broiler could cause it to catch fire). Broil for 4 to 5 minutes, until the skin is golden brown and crispy.
5. Transfer the chicken to a grooved cutting board to catch any juices and let it rest for 5 to 10 minutes before carving and serving.

Turkey and Veggie Chili

Prep time: 10 minutes | Cook time: 20 minutes | Serves 4

1 tablespoon extra-virgin olive oil	2 teaspoons ground cumin
1 pound (454 g) ground turkey	½ teaspoon salt
2 cloves garlic, minced	1 (12-ounce / 340-g) package chopped butternut squash
1 (14-ounce / 397-g) package fresh or frozen diced carrots, celery, and onion blend	1 (28-ounce / 794-g) can Whole30-compliant fire-roasted diced tomatoes, undrained
2 tablespoons chili powder	

1. Toppings such as Whole30-compliant guacamole, chopped fresh cilantro, sliced green onions, finely chopped jalapeño, and/or lime wedges (optional)
2. Heat the olive oil in a large skillet over medium-high heat. Add the turkey and garlic and cook, breaking up the meat with a wooden spoon, until the turkey is browned, about 5 minutes. Add the carrot mixture, chili powder, cumin, and salt and cook, stirring occasionally, until the vegetables are tender, 5 minutes.
3. Add the squash and tomatoes and bring to a boil. Reduce the heat and simmer, stirring occasionally, until the squash is tender, 10 to 12 minutes. Serve with the toppings, if desired.

Cajun Chicken Wings

Prep time: 5 minutes | Cook time: 30 minutes | Serves 2

2 pounds (907 g) chicken wings	large matchsticks, for serving
1 tablespoon avocado oil	3 celery stalks, cut into large matchsticks, for serving
2 tablespoons cajun spice rub	
2 large carrots, cut into	

1. Preheat the oven to 425ºF (220ºC). Line a baking sheet with parchment paper.
2. Dry the chicken wings thoroughly with a paper towel. Place them in a large bowl, add the avocado oil, and toss to coat. Add the Cajun seasoning and toss to coat.
3. Arrange the wings in a single layer on the prepared baking sheet and bake on the bottom rack of the oven for 30 to 35 minutes, until the internal temperature registers 165ºF (74ºC) on an instant-read thermometer and the wings are crispy. Serve immediately with the carrot and celery sticks.

Chicken with Jerk Rub

Prep time: 5 minutes | Cook time: 35 minutes | Serves 4 to 8

8 chicken quarters	1 cup jerk rub
Kosher salt, to taste	

1. Preheat the oven to 425ºF (220ºC). Line a rimmed baking sheet with parchment paper.
2. Remove the chicken from the bag, letting any excess rub drip off (discard the bag). Place the chicken skin-side up on the prepared baking sheet and roast on the bottom rack for 35 to 40 minutes, until the thickest part of the thigh registers 165ºF (74ºC) on an instant-read thermometer. Check the chicken halfway through the cooking time; if you notice it is browning unevenly, rotate the baking sheet 180ºF (82ºC).
3. Let the chicken rest in the pan for 5 minutes before serving.

Hawaiian Chicken and Pineapple Burgers

Prep time: 10 minutes | Cook time: 12 minutes | Serves 8

2 pounds (907 g) ground chicken	almond flour
1¼ cup drained canned pineapple tidbits	1 tablespoon coconut oil
¼ cup coconut aminos	½ teaspoon salt
10 green onions, finely chopped	1 tablespoon extra-virgin olive oil
¼ cup plus 2 tablespoons	8 Bibb lettuce leaves
	½ cup Whole30-compliant mayonnaise

1. Preheat the oven to 200ºF (93ºC). Line a large rimmed baking pan with parchment paper.
2. In a large bowl, stir together the chicken, pineapple, coconut aminos, onions, almond flour, coconut oil, and salt. With wet hands, divide the mixture into 8 equal portions then shape into ¾-inch-thick patties. Place the patties on the baking pan. Place in the freezer for 15 minutes to firm up.
3. In a large nonstick skillet, heat the olive oil over medium-high heat. When the skillet is hot, add 4 patties. Cook, turning once halfway through, until browned and cooked through 165ºF (74ºC). Transfer to a platter; cover with foil and place in the oven to keep warm. Repeat with the remaining patties, adding more oil to the pan if necessary.
4. To serve, spread about 1 tablespoon mayonnaise on each lettuce leaf; top with the patties.

It is never too late. -Chapter 7 Poultry

Kung Pao Chicken Lettuce Cups

Prep time: 10 minutes | Cook time: 13 minutes | Serves 4

2 tablespoons avocado oil
1 pound (454 g) ground chicken
1 red bell pepper, diced
4 scallions, white and green parts separated and thinly sliced
¼ cup raw cashews
½ cup teriyaki sauce
Kosher salt, to taste
8 iceberg lettuce leaves, for serving

1. Heat a large cast-iron or carbon-steel wok or skillet over medium heat for 5 minutes. Increase the heat to high and pour in the avocado oil. Heat until shimmering, then add the ground chicken. Cook, stirring and breaking up the meat as it cooks, until the chicken is browned and all the moisture has evaporated, 4 to 5 minutes. Add the bell pepper, the scallion whites, and the cashews and cook, stirring, until the peppers have softened slightly, 2 to 3 minutes. Stir in the teriyaki sauce and toss to coat. Cook, stirring occasionally, until the sauce has reduced by about one-quarter, 2 to 3 minutes.
2. Sprinkle in the scallion greens and stir. Taste and season with salt as desired.
3. Transfer the chicken to a serving bowl and serve with the iceberg lettuce leaves on a plate alongside.

Whole Chicken with Steak Spice

Prep time: 5 minutes | Cook time: 43 minutes | Serves 4

1 (2½- to 3-pound / 1.1- to 1.4-kg) whole chicken
2 tablespoons extra-virgin olive oil or ghee
2 tablespoons montreal steak spice

1. Position a rack in the bottom third of the oven and preheat the oven to 400ºF (205ºC).
2. Pat the chicken very dry with paper towels and place it breast-side up on a rimmed baking sheet or in a roasting pan. Rub the chicken with the olive oil and season it with the Montreal steak spice. Roast on the bottom rack until the thickest part of the thigh registers 165ºF (74ºC) on an instant-read thermometer, 40 to 50 minutes. Baste the chicken with the rendered juices from the pan.
3. Set the oven to broil, but keep the chicken on the bottom rack (putting the parchment paper closer to the broiler could cause it to catch fire). Broil for 3 to 4 minutes, until the skin is golden brown and crispy.
4. Transfer the chicken to a grooved cutting board to catch any juices and let it rest for 10 minutes before carving and serving.

Chicken Meatballs with Tomato Cream Sauce

Prep time: 10 minutes | Cook time: 30 minutes | Serves 3 or 4

Meatballs:
2 pounds (907 g) ground chicken
1 large egg
¼ cup finely chopped fresh parsley leaves
2 tablespoons finely chopped sun-dried tomatoes packed in olive oil, drained
1 shallot, finely chopped
2 garlic cloves, finely chopped
2 teaspoons kosher salt
1 teaspoon dried basil
½ teaspoon freshly ground black pepper
2 tablespoons extra-virgin olive oil, plus more as needed

Sun-Dried Tomato Cream Sauce:
1 tablespoon extra-virgin olive oil
1 red bell pepper, diced
1 shallot, finely chopped
2 garlic cloves, finely chopped
1¼ cups full-fat coconut milk
2 tablespoons coarsely chopped sun-dried tomatoes packed in olive oil, drained
1 tablespoon Dijon mustard
Kosher salt and freshly ground black pepper, to taste

1. Make the meatballs: In a large bowl, combine the ground chicken, egg, parsley, sun-dried tomatoes, shallot, garlic, salt, basil, and pepper. Mix with your hands until well combined. Rub a small amount of olive oil on your hands and form the mixture into meatballs slightly larger than golf balls, setting them on a baking sheet as you roll them.
2. In a large sauté pan, heat the olive oil over medium-high heat. Add the meatballs to the pan and cook until browned on all sides and cooked through, about 15 minutes. Transfer the meatballs to a platter and set aside.
3. Make the sun-dried tomato cream sauce: Wipe the sauté pan clean with a paper towel, return the pan to medium-high heat, and pour in the olive oil. Add the bell pepper and shallot and cook, stirring, until slightly softened, 3 to 4 minutes. Add the garlic and cook, stirring, for 30 seconds. Add the coconut milk, sun-dried tomatoes, and mustard and season with salt and black pepper. Cook, stirring occasionally, until the sauce has reduced by at least a quarter, about 4 minutes. Taste and adjust the seasoning, if desired.
4. Remove the pan from the heat, add the meatballs to the sauce, and toss to coat. Let the meatballs sit until they have warmed through, about 3 minutes. Serve immediately.

Mustard Chicken Salad Lettuce Cups

Prep time: 15 minutes | Cook time: 0 minutes | Serves 15

- ¾ cup Whole30-compliant mayonnaise
- 1 tablespoon Whole30-compliant coarse-grain brown mustard
- 1 jalapeño, seeded and minced
- 1 piece (½ inch) fresh ginger, peeled and grated
- 1 teaspoon Whole30-compliant garam masala
- 1 teaspoon cumin seeds, toasted
- ½ teaspoon ground turmeric
- ½ teaspoon black pepper
- 3 cups diced cooked chicken
- 1 mango, pitted, peeled, and diced
- ½ small red onion, finely chopped
- ½ teaspoon salt
- 1 head Bibb lettuce, leaves separated (15 leaves)
- Chopped fresh cilantro or parsley

1. In a large bowl, whisk together the mayonnaise, mustard, jalapeño, ginger, garam masala, cumin seeds, turmeric, and black pepper. Add the chicken, mango, and red onion. Toss gently to combine. Season to taste with salt.
2. To serve, arrange the lettuce leaves on one or two large platters or trays. Spoon about ½ cup chicken salad into each leaf. Sprinkle with the cilantro or parsley.

Poultry Breast-Asparagus Roll-Ups

Prep time: 5 minutes | Cook time: 3 minutes | Serves 4

- 24 thin asparagus spears, trimmed and cut into 7-inch pieces
- 16 slices Whole30-compliant deli smoked chicken or turkey breast
- ½ cup olive tapenade
- 1 cup lightly packed baby spinach, stems removed
- ½ cup drained roasted red peppers, cut into ¼-inch slices

1. Place a steamer basket in a large, deep skillet; expand to almost flat. Add water to just below the bottom of the basket and bring to a boil. Add the asparagus. Cover and steam until crisp-tender, about 3 minutes. Place in ice water to cool. Drain.
2. Layer two slices of chicken to make eight stacks. Pat dry with paper towels. Spread about 1 tablespoon of the tapenade over each chicken stack. Top it with 3 to 4 spinach leaves. Pat the pepper slices dry with paper towels and place on the spinach. Lay 3 asparagus spears in the middle of each stack. Roll the chicken around the asparagus. Secure the rolls with toothpicks. Place the roll-ups in an airtight container. Chill for at least 2 hours before traveling.

Greek Whole Chicken and Potatoes

Prep time: 15 minutes | Cook time: 50 minutes | Serves 4

Lemon and Garlic Sauce:
- ½ cup fresh lemon juice
- ½ cup extra-virgin olive oil
- 2½ tablespoons red wine vinegar
- 1 garlic clove, pressed
- 1 teaspoon dried oregano
- ¾ teaspoon kosher salt
- ½ teaspoon Dijon mustard
- ¼ teaspoon freshly ground black pepper

Chicken:
- 1 (4-pound / 1.8-kg) whole chicken, cut in half
- 1 teaspoon kosher salt
- ½ teaspoon freshly ground black pepper
- 1½ teaspoons extra-virgin olive oil
- 4 Yukon Gold potatoes, sliced into ¼-inch-thick rounds
- 1 lemon, sliced into ¼-inch-thick rounds
- Chopped fresh parsley, for garnish

1. Adjust the oven rack to 6 inches below the broiler. Preheat the oven to broil. Line a large baking sheet with parchment paper.
2. For the sauce: In a large bowl, add the lemon juice and using a whisk, slowly add the olive oil. Then add the vinegar, garlic, oregano, salt, mustard, and black pepper, stirring well. Set aside.
3. For the chicken: Thoroughly season each chicken half with the salt and black pepper, then generously rub every crevice with the olive oil. Put the chicken skin-side down on the lined baking sheet and put the pan on the adjusted rack in the oven. Broil for 15 minutes, until beginning to turn golden.
4. Remove the baking sheet from the oven and flip the chicken over to the other side. Return to the oven and broil for 20 minutes more, or until cooked through, golden brown, and bubbling. Remove the pan from the oven and set the chicken aside. Once cool enough to handle, cut each half into 3 pieces: legs, thighs, and breasts with wings attached.
5. Arrange the sliced potatoes and lemons on the baking sheet. Return to the oven and cook for 10 to 12 minutes, or until the potatoes and lemons begin to brown. Remove the baking sheet from the oven, put the chicken on top of the potatoes and lemons, and pour ½ cup of the lemon and garlic sauce evenly over the top.
6. Return to the oven and broil until the chicken is further browned and crispy, about 5 minutes. Remove the chicken from the pan and drain off any excess liquid from the pan (so that the potatoes can cook to a crisp). Return the potatoes to the oven and broil until crisped and cooked through, 10 to 15 minutes more.
7. Serve the potatoes and lemons with the chicken and the remaining lemon and garlic sauce, either poured over the top or as a dipping sauce.

It is never too late. -Chapter 7 Poultry

Salsa Verde Chicken Breast

Prep time: 20 minutes | Cook time: 4 hours | Serves 4

1 to 1½ pounds (454 to 680 g) boneless, skinless chicken breast
¼ teaspoon ground cumin
¼ teaspoon sea salt
¼ teaspoon black pepper
2 cups quartered husked tomatillos (4 to 5)
2 poblano peppers, stems removed and quartered
½ cup diced onion
2 tablespoons sliced garlic
2 cups chopped fresh cilantro
Juice of ½ lime
½ teaspoon salt

1. Place the chicken breasts and ¼ cup water in a slow cooker. Sprinkle with the cumin, salt, and pepper. Add the tomatillos, poblano peppers, onion, and garlic.
2. Cover and cook on low for 4 hours or on high for 2 hours.
3. Transfer the chicken to a platter with a slotted spoon; cover and keep warm. Transfer the tomatillos, peppers, onion, and garlic to a blender or food processor. Add the cilantro, lime juice, and salt. Cover and blend or process until almost smooth. Chop or shred the chicken, stir into the sauce, and serve over cooked riced vegetables or veggie noodles.

Stir-Fried Chicken Breast and Bok Choy

Prep time: 15 minutes | Cook time: 10 minutes | Serves 4

1 pound (454 g) chicken breast stir-fry strips
¼ teaspoon salt
¼ teaspoon black pepper
2 tablespoons extra-virgin olive oil
1 tablespoon finely chopped fresh lemongrass
1 tablespoon minced fresh ginger
4 cloves garlic, minced
½ teaspoon red pepper flakes
4 heads baby bok choy, coarsely chopped
¼ cup roasted salted cashews, finely chopped
¼ cup chopped fresh cilantro

1. Season the chicken with the salt and black pepper. Heat 1 tablespoon of the olive oil in a large skillet over medium-high heat. Add the chicken and cook, stirring occasionally, until the chicken is almost cooked through, about 5 minutes.
2. Add the lemongrass, ginger, garlic, and pepper flakes to the skillet. Cook, stirring, for 1 minute. Add the remaining 1 tablespoon olive oil. Add the bok choy and cook, stirring, until beginning to soften but still crisp, 2 to 3 minutes. Remove the skillet from the heat. Top with the cashews and cilantro and serve.

Turkey Tenderloins with Pepper

Prep time: 15 minutes | Cook time: 35 minutes | Serves 4

1½ pounds (680 g) turkey tenderloins
½ teaspoon salt
½ teaspoon black pepper
2 tablespoons extra-virgin olive oil
4 cups sliced sweet mini peppers
1 serrano chile pepper, halved, seeded, and thinly sliced
1 medium onion, sliced
3 cloves garlic, minced
1 pint cherry or grape tomatoes
¼ cup balsamic vinegar
2 tablespoons torn fresh basil

1. Preheat the oven to 425°F (220°C).
2. Season the turkey with the salt and black pepper. Heat the oil in an ovenproof skillet over medium-high heat. Add the turkey and cook until browned, 2 to 3 minutes per side.
3. Remove the turkey from the skillet. Add the bell peppers, chile, onion, and garlic to the skillet and cook, stirring occasionally, until just softened, 3 to 5 minutes. Stir in the tomatoes and vinegar.
4. Return the turkey to the skillet and transfer to the oven. Roast until the turkey is cooked through, 25 to 30 minutes. Let the turkey rest 5 minutes then cut into slices. Top with the basil and serve.

Spanish Chicken Breast Cauliflower Skillet

Prep time: 20 minutes | Cook time: 20 minutes | Serves 4

4 slices Whole30-compliant bacon, chopped
1 pound (454 g) boneless, skinless chicken breasts or thighs, diced
1 medium onion, chopped
1 red bell pepper, chopped
4 cloves garlic, minced
1 (28-ounce / 794-g) can Whole30-compliant diced tomatoes
½ teaspoon black pepper
¼ teaspoon cayenne pepper
¼ teaspoon salt
4 cups cauliflower florets
½ cup pimento-stuffed Spanish olives, halved

1. In a large skillet, cook the bacon over medium-high heat until crisp, about 5 minutes. Transfer with a slotted spoon to paper towels to drain, leaving the bacon fat in the skillet.
2. Add the chicken to the skillet and cook, stirring, until opaque, 2 to 3 minutes. Stir in the onion, bell pepper, and garlic. Cook, stirring until the onions are softened, about 4 minutes. Add the tomatoes, black pepper, cayenne pepper, and salt. Bring to a boil and add the cauliflower. Cover and simmer until the cauliflower is just tender, about 5 minutes. Top with the bacon and olives and serve.

Whole30 Fauxsole Verde con Pollo

Prep time: 20 minutes | Cook time: 35 minutes | Serves 6 to 8

For the Salsa Verde:
- 1½ pounds (680 g) tomatillos, husked and washed well
- 1 jalapeño
- 1 poblano pepper
- 1 cubanelle pepper
- ¼ cup loosely packed fresh cilantro leaves
- 2 tablespoons fresh lime juice
- 1 teaspoon ground cumin
- 1 teaspoon ground coriander
- Kosher salt, to taste

For the Soup:
- 2 tablespoons extra-virgin olive oil
- 1 yellow onion, diced
- 5 or 6 garlic cloves, smashed and peeled
- Kosher salt, to taste
- 1½ pounds (680 g) boneless, skinless chicken thighs
- 3 white or yellow potatoes, peeled and cut into ¼-inch cubes
- 2 avocados, diced, for serving
- ½ red onion, thinly sliced, for serving
- Fresh cilantro leaves, for garnish

Make the Salsa Verde
1. Preheat the oven to 450ºF (235ºC). Line a baking sheet with parchment paper.
2. Place the tomatillos stem-side down on the prepared baking sheet, then arrange the jalapeño, poblano, and cubanelle peppers on the baking sheet as well. Roast for 25 to 30 minutes, until the tomatillos and peppers are slightly charred and begin to release their juices. Let cool for at least 5 minutes, then peel, stem, and seed the peppers and transfer the flesh to a blender or food processor and add the tomatillos.
3. Add the cilantro, lime juice, cumin, coriander, and salt to the blender and blend until smooth. Taste and season with salt as desired. Pour the salsa verde into a sealable container and set aside until ready to use. (The salsa will keep for up to 1 week in the refrigerator.)

Make the Soup
1. In a large Dutch oven or stockpot, heat the olive oil over medium heat. Add the onion, garlic, and a pinch of salt and cook, stirring occasionally, until the onion is soft and translucent, about 10 minutes. Add the chicken, potatoes, 2 cups of the salsa verde, and 10 cups of water to the pot. Bring to a low simmer and cook, skimming off and discarding any foam that rises to the surface, until the chicken registers 165ºF (74ºC) on an instant-read thermometer at the thickest part of a thigh, 12 to 14 minutes.
2. Transfer the chicken to a bowl and let cool, then shred the meat with your hands or two forks. Return the shredded chicken to the pot and stir. Let the soup rest for 10 to 15 minutes before serving.
3. Ladle the soup into individual serving bowls. Garnish with the avocado, red onion, and cilantro. Store any leftover salsa in the refrigerator or reserve for another use.

Piri Piri Whole Chicken

Prep time: 10 minutes | Cook time: 45 minutes | Serves 4

- 1 small yellow onion, halved
- ¼ cup extra-virgin olive oil
- ¼ cup red wine vinegar
- Juice of ½ lemon
- 4 garlic cloves, peeled
- 2 fresh red finger chiles (or Anaheim chiles, if not available)
- 1 (1-inch) piece fresh ginger, peeled
- 1 tablespoon kosher salt
- 1 teaspoon smoked paprika
- 1 teaspoon sweet paprika
- 1 teaspoon dried oregano
- ½ teaspoon cayenne pepper, plus more if desired
- 1 (2½- to 3-pound / 1.1- to 1.4-kg) whole chicken

1. In a blender, combine the onion, olive oil, vinegar, lemon juice, garlic, chiles, ginger, salt, smoked paprika, sweet paprika, oregano, cayenne, and ¼ cup water. Blend on high speed until smooth.
2. Dry the chicken with paper towels. Using sharp kitchen shears or a sharp knife, cut along one side of the backbone, leaving the other side attached. Lay the chicken breast-side up on a cutting board and press down on the breastbone with your hands to flatten the chicken. Put the chicken in a large zip-top plastic bag and pour in the marinade. Massage the marinade all over the chicken, then squeeze as much air out of the bag as possible and seal. Place it on a baking sheet with the chicken breast-side down and refrigerate for at least 4 hours or up to overnight.
3. Preheat the oven to 425ºF (220ºC). Line a 4-inch-deep roasting pan with parchment paper.
4. Remove the chicken from the marinade, letting any excess drip off (discard the bag). Place the chicken in the prepared roasting pan and roast on the bottom rack for 40 to 45 minutes, until the thickest part of the thigh registers 165ºF (74ºC) on an instant-read thermometer. Use a turkey baster or large spoon to baste the chicken with the rendered juices in the pan.
5. Set the oven to broil, but keep the chicken on the bottom rack (putting the parchment paper closer to the broiler could cause it to catch fire). Broil for 4 to 5 minutes, until the skin is golden brown and crispy.
6. Transfer the chicken to a grooved cutting board to catch any juices and let it rest for 5 to 10 minutes before carving and serving.

It is never too late. -Chapter 7 Poultry

Chicken with Sweet Potatoes and Mushrooms

Prep time: 30 minutes | Cook time: 6 hours | Serves 6

1 cup Whole30-compliant chicken broth
3 cloves garlic, minced
4 small sweet potatoes, scrubbed and halved lengthwise (about 1 pound (454 g) / 454 g total)
1 teaspoon dried thyme
¾ teaspoon salt
¾ teaspoon black pepper
12 small bone-in chicken thighs, skin removed
3 cups thinly sliced cremini mushrooms
½ cup chopped red onion
1 tablespoon coconut oil, melted
3 strips Whole30-compliant bacon, crisp-cooked and crumbled
Fresh thyme leaves (optional)

1. In a slow cooker, combine the chicken broth and garlic. Place the potatoes, cut sides down, in the cooker. In a small bowl, combine the dried thyme, ½ teaspoon of the salt, and ½ teaspoon of the pepper. Place half the chicken thighs, meaty sides up, on the potatoes. Sprinkle with half the thyme mixture. Repeat with remaining chicken and thyme mixture. Add the mushrooms and red onion to the cooker in an even layer.
2. Cover and cook on low for 6 to 7 hours or on high for 3 to 3½ hours. Remove the chicken and potatoes from the cooker. When cool enough to handle, remove the potato skins. Place the potato flesh in a medium bowl; add the coconut oil and the remaining ¼ teaspoon salt and ¼ teaspoon pepper. Using a potato masher, mash potatoes until smooth.
3. Serve the chicken and vegetables with the mashed potatoes and drizzle with the cooking liquid. Top the servings with bacon and, if desired, fresh thyme.

Green Chile Chicken Thigh Stew

Prep time: 25 minutes | Cook time: 6 hours | Serves 4

1½ pounds (680 g) baby red or gold potatoes
8 bone-in chicken thighs (about 2 pounds (907 g) / 907 g total), skin removed
1 (4-ounce / 113-g) can Whole30-compliant diced green chiles
½ cup Whole30-compliant chicken broth
2 medium tomatillos, husks removed and diced
3 cloves garlic, minced
2 teaspoons ground cumin
1 teaspoon ground coriander
1 teaspoon salt
½ teaspoon black pepper
Grated zest and juice of 1 lime
½ cup chopped fresh cilantro

1. Place the potatoes in a slow cooker. Arrange the chicken over the potatoes. In a medium bowl, combine the green chiles, broth, tomatillos, garlic, cumin, coriander, salt, and pepper. Pour over the chicken and potatoes in the cooker. Cover and cook on low for 6 hours or on high for 3 hours.
2. Drizzle the chicken and potatoes with the lime juice and sprinkle with the lime zest and cilantro.

Chicken with Kielbasa Stuffed Mushrooms

Prep time: 15 minutes | Cook time: 30 minutes | Serves 4

For the Chicken:
2 tablespoons finely diced drained oil-packed dried tomatoes
1 teaspoon extra-virgin olive oil
1 clove garlic, minced
1 teaspoon fresh thyme leaves
½ teaspoon coarse salt
¼ teaspoon black pepper
1¼ to 1½ pounds (567- to 680-g) bone-in chicken thighs

For the Mushrooms:
4 (¼-pound / 113.4-g total) medium portobello mushrooms
4 ounces (113 g) Whole30-compliant smoked kielbasa, diced
1 cup chopped fresh kale
2 tablespoons finely diced drained oil-packed dried tomatoes
1 tablespoon oil from oil-packed dried tomatoes
2 cloves garlic, minced

1. Preheat the oven to 425ºF (220ºC). Line a large rimmed baking pan with parchment paper.

Make the Chicken

2. In a small bowl, combine the dried tomatoes, olive oil, garlic, thyme, salt, and black pepper. For each thigh, run a finger under the skin to lift it off the meat, but leaving it attached along the sides. Spoon some of the thyme mixture under the skin. Place the thighs on one side of the pan. Roast for 5 minutes.

Make the Mushrooms

3. Meanwhile, remove the stems and gills from the mushrooms. Use a damp paper towel to wipe the mushrooms clean. Add the mushrooms, gill sides down, to the pan. Roast until the mushrooms are just tender, 15 to 18 minutes.
4. Meanwhile, in a medium bowl, combine the kielbasa, kale, tomatoes, tomato oil, and garlic. Turn the mushrooms over. Spoon the kielbasa filling into the mushrooms. Roast until the chicken is no longer pink and a thermometer inserted in the thigh registers 175ºF (79ºC) and the mushrooms are just tender, 10 to 15 minutes longer.

Mojo Roast Chicken Wings

Prep time: 5 minutes | Cook time: 30 minutes | Serves 4

½ cup fresh orange juice
¼ cup fresh lime juice
¼ cup extra-virgin olive oil
4 garlic cloves, peeled
1 jalapeño
1 teaspoon dried oregano
1 tablespoon ground coriander
3½ to 4 pounds (1.6 to 1.8 kg) chicken wings
Kosher salt and freshly ground black pepper, to taste
¼ cup loosely packed fresh cilantro leaves
8 fresh mint leaves

1. In a blender, combine the orange juice, lime juice, olive oil, garlic, jalapeño, oregano, and coriander. Blend on high speed until smooth.
2. Season both sides of the chicken wings with 3 teaspoons salt and ½ teaspoon pepper. Place the wings in a large zip-top plastic bag and pour in half the marinade. Massage the wings to coat with the marinade, then squeeze out as much air from the bag as possible and seal the bag. Set it on a rimmed baking sheet and refrigerate for at least 4 hours or up to overnight.
3. Add the cilantro and mint to the remaining marinade and blend until smooth. Taste and season with salt and pepper as desired. Transfer the mojo sauce to a jar, cover, and refrigerate until needed.
4. Position an oven rack in the lower third of the oven and preheat the oven to 425°F (220°C). Line a rimmed baking sheet with parchment paper.
5. Arrange the wings in a single layer on the prepared baking sheet (discard the marinade left in the bag) and roast for 30 to 35 minutes, until the wings are golden brown and register 165°F (74°C) on an instant-read thermometer.
6. Serve the wings with the mojo sauce alongside for dipping.

Tangy Chicken Skewers

Prep time: 10 minutes | Cook time: 20 minutes | Makes 4 skewers

2 pounds (907 g) boneless, skinless chicken thighs (about 8 thighs)
1 navel orange, halved
1 lemon, halved
1 large onion, quartered
3 tablespoons coconut aminos
1 tablespoon olive oil or avocado oil
2 teaspoons fine Himalayan salt
2 teaspoons ground cumin
1 teaspoon Dijon mustard
1 teaspoon dried thyme leaves
1 teaspoon ground black pepper

1. Cut the chicken thighs in half lengthwise and put them in a large bowl. Squeeze the orange halves into the bowl and throw them in; do the same thing with the lemon halves. Add the rest of the ingredients and mix thoroughly. Cover the bowl with plastic wrap and place it in the refrigerator to marinate for at least 2 hours.
2. Set the chicken out about 30 minutes before you thread it on the skewers; otherwise it will be uncomfortably cold to handle. If you're using bamboo or wooden skewers, use this time to soak the skewers in water.
3. Give the chicken mix a toss and remove the orange and lemon halves. Thread four pieces of chicken and one piece of onion onto each skewer.
4. Spray or brush the grill with cooking fat. Heat the grill to medium-high heat (between 350°F (180°C) and 400°F (205°C). Place the skewers on the hottest part of the grill. Cook for 20 minutes, turning every 5 minutes.
5. Remove the skewers from the grill and serve right away! If you're making extra, let the skewers cool to room temperature, use a fork to remove the pieces from the skewers, and store them in an airtight container for up to 5 days in the refrigerator.

Onion Chicken Meatballs

Prep time: 20 minutes | Cook time: 15 minutes | Serves 2

1 pound (454 g) ground chicken thigh
1 large egg, beaten
¼ onion, finely chopped
2 cloves garlic, minced
2 teaspoons minced fresh oregano, (or 1 teaspoon dried oregano)
1 teaspoon salt
½ teaspoon black pepper
2 tablespoons cooking fat, plus more if needed

1. Preheat the oven to 350°F (180°C). Line a baking sheet with parchment paper.
2. Thoroughly mix the chicken, egg, onion, garlic, oregano, salt, and pepper in a large bowl. Roll into 15 to 20 meatballs, each about the size of a golf ball.
3. Melt the cooking fat in a large skillet over medium-high heat. When the fat is hot, add the meatballs (depending on the size of your pan, you may have to do this in batches). Cook for about 30 seconds per side, turning to prevent burning, until browned all over, about 5 minutes. Reduce the heat and add more cooking fat if the pan begins to smoke.
4. Transfer the meatballs to the prepared baking sheet. Transfer to the oven to finish cooking for 8 to 10 minutes, until the internal temperature reaches 160°F (71°C). Let the meatballs rest for 5 minutes and serve.

It is never too late. -Chapter 7 Poultry

Turmeric Chicken

Prep time: 5 minutes | Cook time: 1 hour | Serves 4

1 tablespoon hot paprika
1 tablespoon ground coriander
1 tablespoon smoked paprika
1 tablespoon Aleppo pepper
1 tablespoon caraway seeds
1 tablespoon ground sumac
¼ cup grated fresh ginger
¼ cup grated fresh turmeric
12 bone-in, skin-on chicken thighs (about 3½ pounds / 1.6 kg total)
3 teaspoons kosher salt
1 cup full-fat unsweetened coconut milk, blended
⅓ cup extra-virgin olive oil
3 tablespoons fresh lime juice
6 garlic cloves, chopped
Chopped fresh parsley, for garnish

1. In a small bowl, stir together the hot paprika, coriander, smoked paprika, Aleppo pepper, caraway seeds, and sumac. Measure out 3 tablespoons of the spice blend for this recipe and set aside. Save the remainder for another day.
2. Squeeze the juice from the grated ginger into a bowl, discarding the pulp. Set aside. Do the same with the grated turmeric and set aside.
3. Arrange the chicken thighs in a shallow container and sprinkle with 1½ teaspoons of the salt. Set aside.
4. In a medium bowl, stir together the coconut milk, olive oil, lime juice, ginger and turmeric juices, garlic, and the remaining 1½ teaspoons salt. Stir in the reserved 3 tablespoons spice blend. Set aside about ½ cup of the marinade and refrigerate, then pour the remaining marinade over the chicken. Cover the chicken and refrigerate for at least 3 hours or up to overnight, if you have the time.
5. When ready to cook the chicken, preheat the oven to 350°F (180°C). Line a large baking sheet with parchment paper. Remove the marinated chicken from the refrigerator and let it come to room temperature.
6. Put the chicken, with its marinade, on the prepared baking sheet and bake for 30 minutes, or until starting to turn golden. Remove the baking sheet from the oven.
7. Without disturbing the chicken, carefully pour the juices from the pan into a small bowl. Baste the chicken by spooning the juices over, then return the chicken to the oven and bake for 15 minutes more, or until it starts to turn golden brown, then baste again with the juices, and if needed, carefully pour off any excess juices once more into the bowl. Increase the oven temperature to 375°F (190°C) and bake for 5 to 10 minutes, until golden brown and bubbly and the bones of the thighs begin to stick through the skin. If you like the skin crispier, turn on the convection function, or turn up the oven temperature to 400°F (205°C) if you don't have a convection oven, and bake for 5 minutes.
8. Pour the reserved marinade into a small saucepan and simmer over medium heat until it has reduced by half.
9. Serve the chicken drizzled with the reduced sauce and sprinkled with parsley.

Butter Chicken Thighs

Prep time: 5 minutes | Cook time: 15 minutes | Serves 4

1½ pounds (680 g) boneless, skinless chicken thighs
2 teaspoons kosher salt
1 teaspoon freshly ground black pepper
¼ cup plus 2 tablespoons extra-virgin olive oil
2 tablespoons fresh lemon juice
1 tablespoon finely chopped garlic
2 teaspoons paprika
1 teaspoon red pepper flakes
¼ cup plus 1 tablespoon clarified butter
3 tablespoons hot sauce

1. Spread the chicken out in a shallow container good for marinating. Season with 1 teaspoon of the salt and ½ teaspoon of the black pepper. Set aside.
2. In a small bowl, combine the remaining 1 teaspoon salt, remaining ½ teaspoon black pepper, ¼ cup of the olive oil, the lemon juice, garlic, paprika, and red pepper flakes and stir until combined well. Pour the mixture over the chicken, tossing to thoroughly coat. Cover and refrigerate for at least 2 hours or up to overnight, if you have the time.
3. When ready to cook, remove the chicken from the refrigerator and let it come to room temperature.
4. Heat a large, dry cast-iron skillet over high heat. Once hot, reduce the heat to medium and heat the remaining 2 tablespoons olive oil. When the oil is warm, add the chicken thighs to the skillet and cook until browned and crispy, about 4 minutes, then flip and cook until cooked through and browned, 5 to 7 minutes more, depending on the thickness of the thighs. Test for doneness. Set the pan aside.
5. In a small pan, melt the clarified butter over low heat. Transfer the butter to a blender, add the hot sauce, and blend until emulsified. Spoon the sauce over the chicken in the pan, coating the chicken thoroughly.
6. Serve immediately.

Asian Chicken Curry with Bok Choy

Prep time: 15 minutes | Cook time: 40 minutes | Serves 4

- 2 pounds (907 g) ground chicken (half dark meat and half white meat, if you can find it)
- ½ cup chopped fresh basil, plus ½ cup sliced into ribbons for garnish, if desired
- 2 tablespoons minced garlic (about 8 cloves)
- 3 scallions, thinly sliced
- 4 tablespoons coconut aminos
- ¼ cup plus 1 tablespoon red curry paste
- 2½ teaspoons kosher salt
- 2 tablespoons coconut oil
- 1¼ cups chicken stock, warmed
- 3 tablespoons extra-virgin olive oil
- ¾ cup finely diced yellow onion
- 1 (14-ounce / 397-g) can full-fat unsweetened coconut milk, blended
- 3 tablespoons fresh lime juice
- 1 tablespoon arrowroot starch
- 1 tablespoon very cold water
- 2 teaspoons red pepper flakes
- ½ teaspoon cayenne pepper
- 4 heads baby bok choy, coarsely chopped
- ½ cup chopped fresh cilantro, for garnish (optional)

1. In a large bowl, mix the chicken, the chopped basil, 1 tablespoon of the garlic, the scallions, 3 tablespoons of the coconut aminos, 1 tablespoon of the red curry paste, and the salt until combined well.
2. In a large skillet with high sides, melt the coconut oil over medium-high heat. Using a large spoon, transfer the chicken mixture, spoonful by spoonful (rather than dumping it in), to the skillet. Using a wooden spoon, cook, stirring continuously and breaking up the chicken as it cooks, until cooked through, about 5 minutes. Remove the chicken from the pan and set aside.
3. Return the skillet to the heat and add ¼ cup of the warm stock, stirring and scraping up all the bits of goodness from the bottom of the pan. Pour everything from the skillet over the cooked chicken.
4. In a bowl, stir together the remaining ¼ cup curry paste and 1 cup stock until the curry paste has dissolved. Set aside.
5. In the same skillet, heat 2 tablespoons of the olive oil over medium heat. Add the onion and cook, stirring continuously, until soft, about 2 minutes. Add the remaining 1 tablespoon garlic and cook, stirring, until fragrant, about 1 minute more. Add a bit of the curry-stock mixture and stir, scraping up any bits of loveliness from the bottom of the pan. Add the remainder of the curry-stock mixture and stir to combine well.
6. Add the coconut milk to the skillet and whisk until everything is dissolved and smooth. Add the lime juice and the remaining 1 tablespoon coconut aminos, then stir to combine.
7. Make a slurry by mixing together the arrowroot and cold water in a small bowl, then add to the skillet and stir to combine well.
8. Return the chicken with the juices to the skillet and add the red pepper flakes and cayenne. Stir to combine, and bring to a simmer, stirring occasionally, for 20 minutes.
9. In a medium sauté pan, heat the remaining 1 tablespoon olive oil over medium-high heat. Add the bok choy and cook, stirring continuously, until the leaves are bright green and the bok choy has released some of its liquid, about 2 minutes.
10. Plate the bok choy and spoon the chicken curry over the top. Garnish with the basil ribbons and cilantro, if desired, and serve.

Oregano Chicken Thighs with Parsnips

Prep time: 25 minutes | Cook time: 6 hours | Serves 4

- 2 teaspoons garlic powder
- 2 teaspoons dried oregano
- 1 teaspoon salt
- ½ teaspoon paprika
- ½ teaspoon black pepper
- 8 boneless, skinless chicken thighs (about 2 pounds (907 g) / 907 g total)
- 1 lemon, thinly sliced
- ½ cup chopped Whole30-compliant pitted green olives
- 2 medium parsnips, peeled and sliced ½-inch thick
- 2 medium russet potatoes, peeled and sliced ½-inch thick
- ¼ cup melted clarified butter or ghee
- 2 tablespoons tapioca flour

1. In a small bowl, combine the garlic powder, oregano, salt, paprika, and pepper. Sprinkle 2 teaspoons of the garlic seasoning over the chicken. Place the chicken in a slow cooker. Add ½ cup water, the lemon slices, and olives.
2. In a medium bowl, combine the parsnips and potatoes; sprinkle with the remaining garlic seasoning. Add to the slow cooker and pour the melted butter over all.
3. Cover and cook on low for 6 hours or on high for 3 hours. Transfer the chicken, potatoes, and parsnips to a platter; cover and keep warm.
4. Turn the slow cooker to high if using the low setting. In a small bowl, stir together the tapioca powder and ¼ cup water; add to the cooking liquid. Stir until the sauce is thickened, about 3 minutes. Serve the sauce over the chicken, potatoes, and parsnips.

It is never too late.

Chipotle Chicken with Roasted Tomatoes

Prep time: 15 minutes | Cook time: 5 hours | Serves 4

1 (14½-ounce / 411-g) can Whole30-compliant fire-roasted crushed tomatoes
1 medium yellow bell pepper, coarsely chopped
2 cloves garlic, minced
2 teaspoons chili powder
1 teaspoon chipotle powder
½ teaspoon salt
8 boneless, skinless chicken thighs (1½ to 2 pounds (907 g) / 680 to 907 g total)
1 (12-ounce / 340-g) package frozen cauliflower rice, prepared according to package directions or 3 cups raw cauliflower rice
Sliced green onions, for serving
Lime wedges, for serving

1. In a slow cooker, stir together the tomatoes, bell pepper, garlic, chili powder, chipotle powder, and salt. Add the chicken and turn to coat. Cover and cook on low for 5 to 6 hours or on high for 2½ to 3 hours.
2. Serve the chicken on cauliflower rice and top with green onions. Serve with lime wedges.

Herby Roast Chicken and Vegetables

Prep time: 30 minutes | Cook time: 6 hours | Serves 4

1. 1 lemon, quartered
2. 4 sprigs fresh herbs (rosemary, thyme, and/or oregano); plus more for serving (optional)
3. 1 whole chicken (3 to 3½ pounds / 1.4 to 1.6 kg)
4. 1 tablespoon extra-virgin olive oil
5. 1 tablespoon grated lemon zest
6. 1½ teaspoons fresh lemon juice
7. ½ teaspoon salt
8. ¼ teaspoon black pepper
9. 2 large onions, cut into wedges
10. 1 pound (454 g) baby Yukon Gold potatoes
11. 6 medium carrots, peeled and cut into 1-inch slices
12. Lemon wedges (optional)

1. Place the lemon quarters and the herb sprigs in the cavity of the chicken. In a small bowl, combine the olive oil, lemon zest, lemon juice, salt, and pepper. Rub the mixture all over the chicken. Tie the legs together with cotton kitchen string.
2. In a slow cooker, combine the onions, potatoes, and carrots. Place the chicken, breast side up, on the vegetables. Cover and cook on low for 6 to 7 hours or on high for 3 to 3½ hours, or until the chicken is no longer pink and a thermometer registers 170°F (77°C) when inserted into a thigh.
3. Preheat the oven to broil.
4. Carefully transfer the chicken to a broiler-safe 13 × 6-inch baking pan. Remove and discard the lemon and herbs from the cavity. Use a slotted spoon to transfer the vegetables to the baking pan; discard the cooking liquid. Broil the chicken and vegetables until the chicken skin is golden brown and crispy, about 5 minutes. Serve the chicken with the vegetables. If desired, top with additional fresh herb leaves and/or serve with lemon wedges.

Chicken Thighs and Artichoke Stew

Prep time: 10 minutes | Cook time: 55 minutes | Serves 4 to 6

10 bone-in, skin-on chicken thighs
2 teaspoons kosher salt
1 teaspoon freshly ground black pepper
1½ tablespoons duck fat
1¼ cups chicken stock
1 (14½-ounce / 411-g) can whole tomatoes, with juices
2 tablespoons balsamic vinegar
5 garlic cloves, pressed
1 teaspoon dried oregano
¾ cup green Cerignola olives, pitted and halved lengthwise
1 cup drained canned artichoke hearts, halved

1. Preheat the oven to 375°F (190°C).
2. Thoroughly season the chicken thighs with the salt and pepper.
3. In a large Dutch oven, melt the duck fat over medium heat. Add the chicken thighs, skin-side down, and fry until golden, 4 to 6 minutes. Flip the chicken and fry until golden on the second side, about 4 minutes more. When done, transfer the chicken thighs to a large plate and set aside.
4. Add the stock to the pan and stir to scrape up any browned bits from the bottom of the pot. Bring the stock to a simmer and cook for 2 minutes. Add the tomatoes, crushing them with your hands, then add the juices from the can. Bring to a simmer and cook for 2 minutes more. Add the vinegar, garlic, and oregano and bring to a boil. Reduce the heat and simmer for 1 minute.
5. Return the chicken to the Dutch oven and cover. Transfer the pot to the oven and bake for 15 minutes. Then remove the lid and bake for 20 minutes more. Return the pot to the stovetop.
6. Remove the chicken from the pot and set aside. Add the olives and artichokes to the pot and stir to combine. Bring the stew to a boil, then reduce the heat and simmer for 1 minute. Return the chicken to the pot. Serve.

Lemony Chicken with Green Beans

Prep time: 15 minutes | Cook time: 8 hours | Serves 4

1 cup Whole30-compliant chicken broth
¾ pound (340 g) green beans, trimmed and halved crosswise
1 small white onion, diced
3 Roma (plum) tomatoes, cored and quartered
8 bone-in chicken thighs (2 to 2½ pounds / 907 g to 1.1 kg total), skin removed
¾ teaspoon salt
½ teaspoon black pepper
½ teaspoon dried thyme
2 lemons, cut into ¼-inch-thick slices, seeds removed

1. In a slow cooker, combine the broth, green beans, onion, and tomatoes. Place the chicken on the vegetables and sprinkle with the salt, pepper, and thyme. Top the chicken with the lemon slices.
2. Cover and cook on low for 8 hours or on high for 4 hours. Serve the chicken with the vegetables.

Thai Curried Chicken Bowls

Prep time: 30 minutes | Cook time: 4½ hours | Serves 6

3 tablespoons Whole30-compliant red curry paste
4 tablespoons olive oil
1 tablespoon grated fresh ginger
1 teaspoon grated lemon zest
12 small bone-in chicken thighs, skin removed
6 medium carrots, peeled and cut into 1½-inch pieces
1 small red onion, cut into thin wedges
⅔ cup Whole30-compliant chicken broth
2 (10.7-ounce / 303-g) packages zucchini noodles or 3 medium zucchini, spiralized, long noodles snipped if desired
1 tablespoon sesame seeds, toasted
⅓ cup chopped fresh cilantro
¼ cup slivered almonds, toasted
Lemon wedges, for serving

1. In a small bowl, combine the curry paste, 2 tablespoons of the olive oil, the ginger, and lemon zest. Place half the chicken in a large bowl. Spoon half the curry mixture on the chicken and rub all over. Repeat with remaining chicken and curry mixture. (If desired, cover and marinate the chicken in the refrigerator for up to 2 hours.)
2. Transfer the chicken to a slow cooker. Top with the carrots and onion. Pour the broth over all. Cover and cook on low for 4½ to 5 hours or on high for 2¼ to 2½ hours.
3. Meanwhile, in a large skillet, cook the zucchini noodles in the remaining 2 tablespoons olive oil over medium heat, stirring frequently, until the noodles are crisp, 3 to 4 minutes. Remove from the heat. Stir in 2 teaspoons of the sesame seeds.
4. In a small bowl, combine the cilantro, almonds, and remaining 1 teaspoon sesame seeds. Serve the chicken and vegetables over the zucchini noodles; spoon some of the cooking juices on top. Sprinkle with the cilantro-almond-sesame mixture and serve with lemon wedges.

Turkey Meatballs with Squash

Prep time: 30 minutes | Cook time: 5 hours | Serves 4

1 large egg
½ cup finely chopped onion
¼ cup almond flour
½ teaspoon fennel seeds, finely crushed
½ teaspoon ground coriander
1 teaspoon salt
¼ teaspoon black pepper
1 pound (454 g) ground turkey
2 cups Whole30-compliant canned crushed tomatoes, undrained
⅓ cup finely chopped drained Whole30-compliant roasted red peppers
¼ cup Whole30-compliant tomato paste
3 cloves garlic, minced
1 bay leaf
1 spaghetti squash (about 2 pounds (907 g) / 907 g), halved lengthwise and seeds removed
1 tablespoon extra-virgin olive oil
⅓ cup coarsely chopped Whole30-compliant pitted green olives
2 tablespoons fresh lemon juice
½ cup chopped flat-leaf parsley

1. Preheat the oven to 400°F (205°C).
2. In a large bowl, whisk the egg together with 2 tablespoons water. Stir in the onion, almond flour, fennel seeds, coriander, ¾ teaspoon of the salt, and the pepper. Add the turkey and mix well. Shape into 12 meatballs and place in a foil-lined rimmed baking pan. Bake for 10 minutes.
3. Meanwhile, in a medium bowl, stir together the crushed tomatoes, roasted peppers, tomato paste, garlic, and bay leaf. Pour about half of the sauce into a slow cooker. Place the squash halves, cut sides down, on the sauce. (If necessary to fit in the slow cooker, cut squash halves in half.) Place the meatballs around and on top of the squash. Spoon the remaining sauce over the meatballs.
4. Cover and cook on low for 5 hours or on high for 2½ hours. Use a large spoon to transfer the squash halves to a cutting board; cool for about 10 minutes. Use a fork to scrape the strands into a large bowl. Drizzle the squash strands with the olive oil and sprinkle with the remaining ¼ teaspoon salt. Toss to coat.
5. Remove and discard the bay leaf. Gently stir the olives and lemon juice into the sauce and meatballs. Serve the meatballs and sauce over the squash. Sprinkle with parsley.

Chicken Legs with Artichoke and Olives

Prep time: 20 minutes | Cook time: 6 hours | Serves 4

2 teaspoons garlic powder
1 teaspoon salt
½ teaspoon black pepper
8 chicken legs, skin removed
2 medium white onions, roughly chopped
2 (14-ounce / 397-g) cans Whole30-compliant whole artichoke hearts, drained and halved
1½ cups pitted Whole30-compliant Kalamata olives
1 lemon, cut into wedges
3 sprigs fresh thyme, plus additional leaves for garnish

1. In a small bowl, combine the garlic powder, salt, and pepper. Rub the chicken with the seasoning. Place the onions, artichoke hearts, and olives in a slow cooker. Add the chicken. Top with lemon wedges and thyme sprigs.
2. Cover and cook on low for 6 to 7 hours or on high for 3 to 3½ hours. Remove and discard the lemon wedges and thyme. Serve the chicken with the artichokes, onions, and olives. Sprinkle with additional thyme.

Chinese Five-Spice Chicken Wings

Prep time: 20 minutes | Cook time: 3 hours | Serves 4

3 pounds (1.4 kg) chicken wings
2 tablespoons Whole30-compliant five-spice powder
1 teaspoon cayenne pepper
1 teaspoon salt
3 green onions, trimmed
½ cup unsweetened pineapple juice
2 tablespoons coconut aminos
1 tablespoon grated fresh ginger
1 tablespoon sesame seeds, toasted
½ to 1 teaspoon red pepper flakes
Whole30-compliant creamy ranch dressing
Mixed salad greens (optional)

1. Use kitchen shears or a very sharp chef's knife to remove the tips of the chicken wings (discard the tips or save them for making stock). Cut along the edge of the drumette through the joint to separate the wingette and the drumette (you should have 8 of each). Place the chicken pieces in a large bowl.
2. In a small bowl, combine the five-spice powder, cayenne, and salt. Sprinkle over the chicken and toss to coat.
3. Slice and set aside the green tops of the green onions. Trim the root of the white ends. Add the white green onion ends, pineapple juice, coconut aminos, and ginger to a slow cooker. Add the wings and toss to coat.
4. Cover and cook on high for 3 hours. Using a slotted spoon, transfer the chicken to a large bowl and carefully toss with the sliced green onion tops, sesame seeds, and red pepper flakes. Discard the cooking liquid. Serve the wings with the ranch salad dressing for dipping and, if desired, drizzled over mixed greens.

Grapefruit Whole Chicken

Prep time: 10 minutes | Cook time: 2 hours | Serves 4

1 tablespoon plus 2½ teaspoons kosher salt
1½ teaspoons freshly ground black pepper
1 teaspoon granulated garlic
1 teaspoon dried marjoram
1 teaspoon paprika
¼ teaspoon cayenne pepper
1 whole chicken (about 4 pounds / 1.8 kg)
4 tablespoons extra-virgin olive oil
¾ cup fresh grapefruit juice (reserve one of the juiced halves)
3 large carrots, halved lengthwise and cut into thirds
3 cups quartered red potatoes (about 1 pound (454 g) / 454 g)
1 medium yellow onion, cut into 8 wedges
5 garlic cloves

1. In a small bowl, stir together 1 tablespoon plus 1½ teaspoons of the salt, 1 teaspoon of the black pepper, the granulated garlic, marjoram, paprika, and cayenne. Set aside.
2. Put the chicken on a baking sheet or large plate and coat the skin with 1 tablespoon of the olive oil. Sprinkle the spice blend on all sides of the chicken to liberally and evenly coat. Cover the chicken and refrigerate for at least 2 hours or up to overnight.
3. When ready to cook the chicken, preheat the oven to 350ºF (180ºC). Line a baking sheet with parchment paper.
4. Set the chicken on the lined baking sheet.
5. In a small bowl, stir together the grapefruit juice and 2 tablespoons of the olive oil. Set aside.
6. In a medium bowl, combine the carrots, potatoes, onion, and garlic cloves with the remaining 1 tablespoon olive oil, 1 teaspoon salt, and ½ teaspoon black pepper and toss to coat evenly. Distribute the vegetables evenly on the baking sheet around the chicken. Fold the juiced grapefruit half and stuff it inside the chicken.
7. Bake the chicken for 30 minutes, then baste it with the grapefruit juice mixture. Return it to the oven and bake for a total time of 80 to 90 minutes (or 20 minutes per pound), basting every 15 minutes. If the chicken becomes too brown, loosely cover it with aluminum foil.
8. Serve.

Roasted Pepper Chicken Breast

Prep time: 10 minutes | Cook time: 4 hours | Serves 4

1 (12-ounce / 340-g) jar Whole30-compliant roasted red peppers, drained and sliced
1 cup thinly sliced onion
½ cup Whole30-compliant chicken broth
2 cloves garlic, minced
½ teaspoon salt
1½ pounds (680 g) boneless, skinless chicken breasts
2 teaspoons Whole30-compliant garlic and herb seasoning
¼ cup pitted Whole30-compliant Kalamata olives, quartered
1 tablespoon chopped flat-leaf parsley
1 teaspoon grated lemon zest
1 tablespoon extra-virgin olive oil

1. In a slow cooker, combine the red peppers, onion, broth, garlic, and salt. Top with the chicken; sprinkle with the garlic and herb seasoning. Cover and cook on low for 4 hours or on high for 2 hours.
2. Transfer the chicken and vegetables to a serving platter. Discard the cooking liquid. Top the chicken with the olives, parsley, and lemon zest. Drizzle with the olive oil.

Chicken Legs Cacciatore

Prep time: 15 minutes | Cook time: 40 minutes | Serves 2

4 tablespoons cooking fat
1 pound (454 g) chicken legs (bone-in, skin-on)
½ pound (227 g) chicken thighs (boneless)
½ teaspoon salt
½ teaspoon black pepper
½ onion, minced
½ red bell pepper, finely diced
1 cup mushrooms, sliced
2 cloves garlic, minced
1 tablespoon Whole30-compliant capers, drained
1 (14½-ounce / 411-g) can diced tomatoes
1 cup chicken broth or water
1 tablespoon fresh basil leaves, rough chopped

1. In a large skillet with high edges, heat 2 tablespoons of the cooking fat over medium-high heat, swirling to coat the bottom of the pan. Season the chicken with the salt and pepper and place in the pan. Sear the chicken until golden brown, about 3 minutes on each side. Remove the chicken from the pan and set aside.
2. With the same pan still on medium-high heat, add the remaining 2 tablespoons of cooking fat, onions, and peppers and sauté for 2 to 3 minutes, until the onion becomes translucent. Add the mushrooms and continue to cook, stirring for 2 minutes. Add the garlic and stir until aromatic, about 1 minute. Add the capers and diced tomatoes.
3. Return the chicken to the pan and cover everything with the chicken broth or water. Reduce the heat to medium and bring everything to a simmer. Turn the heat down to low and continue to simmer (not boil) until the chicken reaches an internal temperature of 160ºF (71ºC), about 30 minutes.
4. Garnish with the chopped basil and serve.

Comforting Chicken Breast Fricassée

Prep time: 5 minutes | Cook time: 20 minutes | Serves 4

4 boneless, skinless chicken breasts (about 2½ pounds / 1.1 kg total)
2¼ teaspoons kosher salt
1 teaspoon freshly ground black pepper
4 tablespoons clarified butter
4 cups finely julienned carrots (3 or 4 medium carrots)
1 cup chicken stock
1 teaspoon arrowroot starch
4 teaspoons apple cider vinegar
2 tablespoons full-fat unsweetened coconut milk, blended
1½ tablespoons chopped fresh tarragon leaves

1. Remove the tender from each chicken breast and set them aside for another use (such as a stir-fry or chicken salad). Season the chicken liberally with 2 teaspoons of the salt and the pepper.
2. In a large sauté pan, melt 3 tablespoons of the clarified butter over medium-high heat. Add the chicken and cook until browned, 4 minutes per side. Reduce the heat to medium, cover the pan, and cook until the chicken is cooked through, 3 to 5 minutes more. Transfer the chicken to a bowl and set aside.
3. In the same pan, melt the remaining 1 tablespoon clarified butter over medium heat. Add the carrots and the remaining ¼ teaspoon salt and cook, stirring, until tender, 3 to 4 minutes. Remove the carrots from the pan and set aside with the chicken.
4. Stir together the stock and arrowroot, then add the mixture to the pan and stir to scrape up any browned bits from the bottom. Add the vinegar and coconut milk and stir to combine. Return the chicken and the carrots to the pan, along with any juices that have collected in the bowl. Bring to a boil. Reduce the heat to medium and simmer for 2 minutes more. Top with the tarragon leaves and serve.

It is never too late. -Chapter 7 Poultry

Sticky Apricot Chicken Drumsticks

Prep time: 15 minutes | Cook time: 5 hours | Serves 4

½ cup water
2 tablespoons coconut aminos
2 tablespoons Whole30-compliant Dijon mustard
1 clove garlic, minced
½ teaspoon salt
¼ teaspoon red pepper flakes
8 chicken drumsticks (1½ to 2 pounds (907 g) / 680 to 907 g total), skin removed
6 ounces (170 g) dried apricots, chopped
1 shallot, thinly sliced (about ⅓ cup)
2 packages (12 ounces / 340 g each) frozen riced cauliflower, prepared according to package directions, or 3 cups raw cauliflower rice
Chopped fresh parsley (optional)

1. In a slow cooker, combine the water, coconut aminos, mustard, garlic, salt, and red pepper flakes. Add the chicken, apricots, and shallot and toss to coat.
2. Cover and cook on low for 5 to 6 hours or on high for 2½ to 3 hours. Transfer the chicken to a plate and cover to keep warm. Use an immersion blender to blend the mixture in the cooker until smooth. Add water, 1 tablespoon at a time, if needed for desired consistency. Return the chicken to the slow cooker and toss gently with tongs to coat.
3. Serve the drumsticks over the cauliflower rice. Top with the sauce and chopped parsley, if desired.

Garlic Herb Chicken and Vegetable

Prep time: 15 minutes | Cook time: 6 hours | Serves 4

1 pound (454 g) new red potatoes, halved
4 medium carrots, peeled, halved lengthwise, and cut into 1-inch pieces
1 medium onion, cut into thin wedges
½ cup Whole30-compliant chicken broth
1 teaspoon salt
½ teaspoon black pepper
8 bone-in chicken thighs, skin removed
1½ teaspoons Whole30-compliant Italian seasoning
½ teaspoon garlic powder
Chopped fresh flat-leaf parsley, for serving

1. In a slow cooker, combine the potatoes, carrots, onion, broth, ½ teaspoon of the salt, and ¼ teaspoon of the pepper. Top with the chicken. Sprinkle with the Italian seasoning, garlic powder, and remaining salt and pepper.
2. Cover and cook on low for 6 to 8 hours or on high for 3 to 4 hours.
3. Strain the cooking liquid. Serve the chicken and vegetables drizzled with some of the cooking liquid. Top with parsley.

ChickenWings with Green Chile Sauce

Prep time: 15 minutes | Cook time: 45 minutes | Serves 8

16 chicken wings
½ cup fresh lime juice
6 tablespoons extra-virgin olive oil
3 cloves garlic, minced
2½ teaspoons salt
1 tablespoon grated lime zest
1 tablespoon ground cumin
2½ teaspoons ground coriander
1 large poblano pepper, halved lengthwise and seeded
1 serrano chile, halved lengthwise and seeded (if desired)
½ cup lightly packed fresh cilantro
2 green onions, chopped
2 tablespoons 100% pineapple juice

1. Use kitchen shears or a very sharp chef's knife to remove the tips of the chicken wings (discard the tips or save them for making stock). Cut the rest of the wings at the joint to make two pieces each. Place the wings in a large resealable plastic bag.
2. In a glass measuring bowl or small bowl, whisk together the lime juice, olive oil, garlic, salt, lime zest, cumin, and coriander. Pour ½ cup over the wings in the bag and reserve the remaining mixture. Seal the bag and refrigerate for 4 to 12 hours, turning the bag once or twice.
3. Meanwhile, preheat the oven to 450°F (235°C). Line a large rimmed baking pan with foil. Place the peppers on the baking pan, skin sides up. Roast, about 15 minutes for the poblano and 10 minutes for the serrano, until the peppers are charred and crisp tender.
4. Peel the loose skin from the peppers and roughly chop. Transfer the peppers to a blender. Add the reserved lime juice mixture, the cilantro, green onions, and pineapple juice. Cover and blend until smooth. Cover and chill the sauce for at least 1 hour or up to 24 hours.
5. Preheat the oven to 425°F (220°C). Line two large rimmed baking pans with foil. Place a wire rack on each baking pan.
6. Drain and discard the marinade from the chicken pieces. Arrange the pieces on the rack. Roast for 20 minutes. Turn each chicken piece and roast until cooked through and lightly browned, about 20 minutes. Brush the wings on both sides with some of the sauce and roast for 10 minutes more. Serve the wings with the remaining sauce.

Italian Chicken Thighs with Fennel

Prep time: 10 minutes | Cook time: 4 hours | Serves 4

¼ cup Whole30-compliant tomato paste
5 cloves garlic, minced
1 teaspoon dried oregano
¾ teaspoon salt
¼ teaspoon black pepper
8 bone-in chicken thighs, skin removed
1 bulb fennel, cored and cut into thin wedges
1 medium red, orange, or yellow bell pepper, cut into 1-inch pieces
1 (14½-ounce / 411-g) can Whole30-compliant fire-roasted diced tomatoes
¼ cup Whole30-compliant capers, drained
Chopped fresh flat-leaf parsley, for serving

1. In a slow cooker, stir together the tomato paste, garlic, oregano, salt, and pepper. Add the chicken and turn to coat. Place the fennel under the chicken. Top the chicken with the bell pepper and tomatoes.
2. Cover and cook on low for 4 to 5 hours or on high for 2 to 2½ hours. Serve the chicken and vegetables topped with the capers and fresh parsley.

Creamy Spinach Artichoke Chicken Breast

Prep time: 5 minutes | Cook time: 20 minutes | Serves 4

4 (6-ounce / 170-g) boneless, skinless chicken breasts
Kosher salt and freshly ground black pepper, to taste
2 tablespoons extra-virgin olive oil
2 garlic cloves, finely chopped
½ cup chicken stock
1 cup full-fat coconut milk
1 tablespoon Dijon mustard
⅓ cup loosely packed baby spinach
1 (14-ounce / 397-g) can artichoke hearts packed in water, drained and sliced in half

1. Set the chicken breasts on a cutting board. Place one hand flat on one chicken breast and extend your fingers away from the board for safety. With your knife blade held parallel to the cutting board, slice the chicken breast in half horizontally. Repeat with the remaining chicken breasts. Pat the chicken slices dry with paper towels and season both sides with salt and pepper.
2. In a large skillet, heat the olive oil over medium-high heat. Add the chicken and cook until golden brown on both sides and cooked through, 4 to 5 minutes per side. Transfer the chicken to a plate and set aside.
3. Add the garlic to the skillet and cook, stirring continuously, for 30 seconds. Add the stock and cook, scraping up any browned bits from the bottom of the pan with your spoon, for 1 to 2 minutes. Add the coconut milk, ¼ teaspoon salt, and ¼ teaspoon pepper and cook until the sauce has reduced by half, 3 to 4 minutes. Stir in the mustard.
4. Add the spinach and artichokes and cook until the spinach has wilted, about 2 minutes. Taste and season with salt and pepper as desired. Return the chicken to the pan and serve immediately.

Skillet Seasoned Chicken Piccata

Prep time: 10 minutes | Cook time: 22 minutes | Serves 4

2 pounds (907 g) skinless, boneless chicken cutlets
1 teaspoon kosher salt
½ teaspoon freshly ground black pepper
¼ cup arrowroot starch
2 tablespoons extra virgin olive oil, plus more as needed
1 tablespoon ghee
3 garlic cloves, minced
2 heaping tablespoons capers, drained and rinsed, plus more for serving
1 cup low-sodium chicken broth
2 tablespoons fresh lemon juice (1 lemon), plus lemon slices for garnish (optional)
1 tablespoon chopped fresh flat-leaf parsley leaves, for serving

1. Season the chicken cutlets on both sides with the salt and pepper and set aside.
2. Pour the arrowroot onto a large plate or a wide bowl. Lightly dredge each individual cutlet in the arrowroot until evenly coated, then shake off any excess. Place the dredged cutlets on a clean plate and continue until all are complete.
3. In a large skillet over medium-high heat, heat the oil. Working in batches so as to not overcrowd the skillet, carefully add the cutlets and cook until golden brown on both sides, 3 to 4 minutes per side. The chicken does not need to be completely cooked through, just golden brown. Transfer to a parchment-lined plate. Repeat with the remaining chicken, adding more oil to the pan if necessary.
4. Reduce the heat to low, add the ghee to the skillet, and swirl to evenly coat the bottom of the pan. Add the garlic and cook until fragrant, stirring to prevent burning, about 30 seconds. Stir in the capers, chicken broth, and lemon juice. Increase the heat to a simmer. Nestle the chicken into the sauce and cook, uncovered and stirring occasionally, until the sauce has thickened and the chicken is tender, about 15 minutes. Taste and adjust the seasoning with salt and pepper, if desired. Garnish with the parsley and fresh lemon slices, if desired, and serve.

It is never too late. -Chapter 7 Poultry

Smoky Butternut Spanish Chicken Meatballs

Prep time: 30 minutes | Cook time: 6 hours | Serves 6

1 (15-ounce / 425-g) can Whole30-compliant tomato sauce
1 (14½-ounce / 411-g) can Whole30-compliant diced fire-roasted tomatoes
¼ cup fresh orange juice
1 teaspoon Spanish (sweet) paprika
½ teaspoon smoked paprika
⅓ cup almond meal
1 large egg, lightly beaten
2 tablespoons chopped Whole30-compliant green olives
1 serrano chile pepper, seeded and finely chopped
½ teaspoon grated orange zest
2 cloves garlic, minced
½ teaspoon salt
1½ pounds (680 g) ground chicken
1 tablespoon extra-virgin olive oil
2 packages (10 ounces / 283 g each) frozen riced butternut squash, prepared according to package directions
Chopped fresh parsley, for serving

1. In a slow cooker, combine the tomato sauce, tomatoes, orange juice, Spanish paprika, and smoked paprika. In a medium bowl, combine the almond meal, egg, olives, serrano, orange zest, garlic, and salt. Add the chicken and, using wet hands, mix well. Shape into 1½-inch meatballs. Arrange the meatballs over the sauce in the cooker. Drizzle with the olive oil. Cover and cook on low for 6 hours or on high for 3 hours.
2. Serve the meatballs and sauce over the riced squash. Sprinkle with parsley.

Chicken Stir Fry with Green Beans

Prep time: 10 minutes | Cook time: 10 minutes | Serves 2

3 tablespoons cooking fat
1 pound (454 g) chicken breast or thighs (boneless, skinless)
1 clove garlic, minced
1 tablespoon ginger, grated
1 head broccoli florets
2 cups mushrooms, sliced
2 carrots, julienned
½ pound (227 g) green beans, cut into 1-inch pieces
2 green onions, minced
½ lime, juiced
1 tablespoon minced fresh cilantro

1. Heat 2 tablespoons of the cooking fat in a large skillet over medium heat, swirling to coat the bottom of the pan. Place the chicken in the pan and sear until the outside is browned and it lifts easily from the bottom of the skillet, about 3 minutes on each side. Add the garlic and ginger. Cook and stir until aromatic, about 1 minute. Remove the chicken from the pan and slice into thin strips. Set the sliced chicken aside.
2. Wipe the pan clean and dry.
3. Heat the remaining 1 tablespoon of cooking fat in the skillet over medium-high heat. Add the broccoli, mushrooms, carrots, and green beans and quickly stir-fry until the vegetables begin to soften, 2 to 3 minutes. Add the chicken strips to the pan; mix, and continue to cook for 2 to 3 minutes until everything is heated through.
4. Top with the green onions, lime juice, and cilantro. Serve immediately.

Chicken Breast Schnitzel

Prep time: 5 minutes | Cook time: 10 minutes | Serves 2

2 (6-ounce / 170-g) boneless, skinless chicken breasts
¼ cup arrowroot starch
¼ cup cassava flour
2 large eggs
¼ teaspoon kosher salt
⅛ teaspoon freshly ground black pepper
3 tablespoons avocado oil
1 teaspoon sesame seeds, for serving
Flaky sea salt, for serving

1. Line a baking sheet with a wire rack.
2. Set the chicken breasts on a cutting board. Place one hand flat on one chicken breast and extend your fingers away from the board for safety. With your knife blade held parallel to the cutting board, slice the chicken breast in half horizontally. Repeat with the second chicken breast. Lay the chicken slices flat on the cutting board, cover them with plastic wrap, and pound them with a meat mallet or rolling pin until they are approximately ¼ inch thick.
3. Place the arrowroot starch, cassava flour, and eggs into three separate bowls. Season the cassava flour with the salt and pepper. Add 2 tablespoons water to the eggs and whisk vigorously until frothy.
4. Dredge each piece of chicken in the arrowroot starch to coat both sides, then dip into the egg wash, letting any excess drip off. Dredge in the seasoned cassava flour to coat and set aside on a large plate.
5. In a large nonstick skillet, heat the avocado oil over medium-high heat for 1 to 2 minutes, until it shimmers. Carefully add the breaded chicken to the hot oil and cook until golden brown, about 4 minutes. Flip and cook for 2 minutes more, until browned on the second side. Transfer the cooked schnitzel to the wire rack. Sprinkle them evenly with the sesame seeds and season each with a tiny pinch of flaky sea salt. Serve immediately.

Chicken Thighs with Walnuts

Prep time: 15 minutes | Cook time: 5 to 10 minutes | Serves 2

2 tablespoons cooking fat
1 pound (454 g) boneless, skinless chicken thighs, cut into 1-inch dice
½ teaspoon salt
½ teaspoon black pepper
¼ cup chopped walnuts
1 sweet potato, peeled and grated
1 Granny Smith apple, cored, peeled, and diced
½ teaspoon red pepper flakes
¼ cup apple cider
2 generous handfuls arugula or baby spinach

1. In a large skillet, heat the cooking fat over medium-high heat, swirling to coat the bottom of the pan. When the fat is hot, add the chicken, being sure not to crowd the pieces. Season the chicken with the salt and pepper. Cook until browned, 2 to 3 minutes. Turn the chicken to brown the other sides, add the walnuts, and cook until the chicken is browned and the walnuts are toasted, 2 to 3 minutes. (Shake the pan occasionally so the walnuts don't burn.) Add the sweet potato, apple, and red pepper flakes and cook, stirring often, until the chicken is fully cooked, 3 to 4 minutes.
2. Add the apple cider and mix all the ingredients together, scraping the bottom of the pan with a wooden spoon to bring up any tasty bits. Add the arugula and cook for another 30 seconds, gently stirring to the wilt leaves. Serve immediately.

Turkey Stuffed Bell Peppers with Guacamole

Prep time: 30 minutes | Cook time: 2½ hours | Serves 4

Peppers:
4 medium red, green, or yellow bell peppers
1 pound (454 g) ground turkey
2 cups chopped button mushrooms
1 stalk celery, thinly sliced
½ cup chopped onion
3 cloves garlic, minced
Guacamole:
1 medium avocado, halved, pitted, and peeled
1 tablespoon fresh lemon juice
1 clove garlic, minced
1 teaspoon paprika
½ teaspoon ground coriander
½ teaspoon coarse salt
¼ to ½ teaspoon cayenne pepper
1 large Roma (plum) tomato, finely chopped

½ teaspoon coarse salt
⅛ teaspoon black pepper
2 tablespoons chopped flat-leaf parsley

1. Make the peppers: Place a small rack in a slow cooker. Add ¼ cup water to the slow cooker. Cut a thin slice across the top of each pepper to remove the stem. Use a small sharp knife to cut out the seeds and membranes, keeping the pepper intact. Set the peppers, cut sides up, on the rack in the cooker.
2. In a large skillet over medium heat, cook the turkey, mushrooms, celery, and onion, stirring occasionally and breaking up the meat with a wooden spoon, until the turkey is browned. Drain off the fat. Add the 3 cloves minced garlic, the paprika, coriander, ½ teaspoon salt, and the cayenne pepper. Cook, stirring, over medium heat for 30 seconds. Remove from the heat. Stir in the tomato. Spoon the turkey mixture into the peppers.
3. Cover and cook on low for 2½ to 3 hours. Carefully transfer the stuffed peppers to serving plates.
4. Make the guacamole: In a medium bowl combine the avocado, lemon juice, 1 clove minced garlic, ½ teaspoon salt, and the black pepper. Mash with a fork or potato masher until almost smooth. Stir in the parsley. Top the peppers with the guacamole and serve.

Garlic Chicken Thighs Primavera

Prep time: 15 minutes | Cook time: 27 minutes | Serves 2

2 tablespoons cooking fat
½ cup diced onions
2 cloves garlic, minced
1 teaspoon minced fresh oregano
1 teaspoon fresh thyme
3 cups diced seeded tomatoes (about 3 large tomatoes)
1 pound (454 g) boneless, skinless chicken thighs, 1-inch diced
2 cups green beans, cut into 1-inch pieces
1½ cups medium-diced zucchini
1½ cup medium-diced yellow squash
¼ teaspoon red pepper flakes
1 teaspoons salt
½ teaspoon black pepper
1 to 2 tablespoons minced fresh basil leaves

1. In a large pot or Dutch oven, heat the cooking fat on medium-high heat and swirl to coat the bottom of the pan. Add the onions, garlic, oregano, and thyme and cook until the onions are translucent and the garlic is fragrant, 2 to 3 minutes.
2. Add the tomatoes and chicken to the pot and cook, stirring occasionally, until the tomatoes have softened, 3 to 4 minutes. Add the green beans, zucchini, and squash and cook, stirring occasionally, until the vegetables are crisp-tender and the chicken is cooked through (with no pink remaining in the center), 5 to 6 minutes. Add the red pepper flakes, salt, and pepper, sprinkle on the basil, stir for 30 seconds to incorporate, and serve immediately.

Chapter 8 Vegetables and Sides

Cabbage, Carrot, and Cashew Slaw

Prep time: 10 minutes | Cook time: 0 minutes | Serves 2

1 clove garlic, minced
Juice of 1 lemon
¼ cup extra-virgin olive oil
1 medium head green cabbage, finely shredded
1 cup shredded carrots
2 tablespoons chopped cashews
1 teaspoon sesame seeds
½ teaspoon salt
½ teaspoon black pepper
1 tablespoon ribbon-chopped fresh basil

1. Whisk the garlic and lemon juice in a mixing bowl. While whisking, slowly add the olive oil in a steady stream until fully blended.
2. In a large bowl, combine the cabbage, carrots, cashews, and sesame seeds. Mix with a wooden spoon to combine, then toss with the lemon oil. Adjust the seasoning with the salt and pepper and top with the basil.

Spicy Broccoli, Mushrooms, and Squash

Prep time: 10 minutes | Cook time: 12 minutes | Serves 2

1 head broccoli, cut into florets
2 tablespoons coconut oil or extra-virgin olive oil
¼ small onion, finely chopped
½ pint button, cremini, or portabella mushrooms, quartered
1 medium yellow squash, cut into large dice
2 cloves garlic, minced
Salt and black pepper
½ cup roasted red peppers sauce

1. Bring 1 cup of water to a boil in a large pot. Place a colander or steamer inside the pot. Add the broccoli, cover, and steam until the broccoli is fork tender, 5 to 6 minutes. Remove the broccoli from the pot and set aside.
2. While you wait for the water to boil, heat the oil in a large skillet over medium heat, swirling to coat the bottom of the pan. When the oil is hot, add the onion and mushrooms and cook, stirring occasionally, until the onion is translucent, 2 to 3 minutes. Add the yellow squash and garlic and continue to cook, stirring, until the squash is slightly softened, about 5 minutes. Remove the pan from the heat.
3. Add the broccoli to the skillet and toss with the squash mixture. Lightly dust with salt and pepper, as the roasted red peppers sauce is also seasoned. Transfer the contents of the pan to a serving bowl or individual plates and top with the roasted red peppers sauce.

Grilled Lemony Asparagus

Prep time: 5 minutes | Cook time: minutes | Serves 2

1 pound (454 g) asparagus, trimmed
1 tablespoon clarified butter, ghee, or coconut oil, melted
½ teaspoon salt
Grated zest and juice of 1 lemon

1. Preheat a grill to medium-high heat 400ºF (205ºC). Line a baking sheet with foil.
2. Place the asparagus on the baking sheet, drizzle with the melted cooking fat, and sprinkle with the salt. With tongs, transfer the asparagus to the grill, laying the spears horizontally across the grate, and grill until tender, 4 to 6 minutes.
3. Transfer the asparagus to a serving plate. Drizzle the lemon juice over the top and sprinkle with the lemon zest just before serving.

Oven-Roasted Cauliflower

Prep time: 5 minutes | Cook time: 50 minutes | Serves 4

1 head cauliflower, preferably with leaves still attached
2 tablespoons plus 1 teaspoon kosher salt
2 tablespoons ghee, at room temperature
2 tablespoons extra-virgin olive oil
Flaky sea salt, for garnish

1. Preheat the oven to 425ºF (220ºC). Line a baking sheet with parchment paper.
2. Trim the stem of the cauliflower so the cauliflower will stand upright on the board. If the cauliflower has leaves still attached, do not trim them off.
3. Bring a large pot of water to a boil over high heat. Add 2 tablespoons of the salt and submerge the cauliflower in the water, stem-side up. Boil until the florets have slightly softened but are still intact, 10 to 12 minutes. Place the cauliflower stem-side down on a wire rack to drain and let air-dry for 5 minutes.
4. Stand the cauliflower on the prepared baking sheet and, using your hands, spread apart the florets to create some crevices. Rub the florets with the ghee and season with the remaining 1 teaspoon salt. Roast until the florets are golden brown and fork-tender, 40 to 45 minutes.
5. Drizzle the roasted cauliflower with the olive oil and finish with a sprinkle of flaky salt. Serve immediately.

Balsamic and Wine-Glazed Red Onions

Prep time: 10 minutes | Cook time: 40 minutes | Serves 4

2 red onions, unpeeled
½ cup balsamic vinegar
1 tablespoon white wine
½ teaspoon your favorite spice blend
1 tablespoon drained and rinsed Whole30-compliant capers
2 tablespoons chopped fresh parsley

1. Preheat the oven to 400ºF (205ºC). Line an 8-inch square baking dish with parchment paper.
2. Cut the tops off the onions and remove their skins. Slice the onions lengthwise into eighths but leave the root end intact to hold the onion together.
3. Place the onions in the prepared baking dish and pour ¼ cup of the vinegar and the wine over the top. Sprinkle with the spice blend. Cover with foil and bake for 30 minutes.
4. Remove from the oven and carefully remove the foil. Rearrange the onion slices so each resembles a flower that has opened up. Spoon any juices in the bottom of the pan over the onions. Pour the remaining ¼ cup vinegar over the onions and bake, uncovered, until the onions are tender and the flower shapes open up completely and crisp a little at the edges, about 10 minutes.
5. Transfer to a serving dish and scatter the capers and parsley over the onions. Spoon any pan juices over the top and serve.

Pan-Roasted Brussels Sprouts and Butternut Squash

Prep time: 10 minutes | Cook time: 12 minutes | Serves 2

3 tablespoons extra-virgin olive oil
½ pound (227 g) Brussels sprouts, trimmed and cut in half
½ red onion, cut into 1-inch pieces
1 teaspoon dried sage
½ teaspoon nutmeg
½ teaspoon black pepper
¼ teaspoon salt
3 cups diced peeled butternut squash

1. Heat the olive oil in a large skillet over medium heat and swirl to coat the bottom of the pan. When the oil is hot, add the Brussels sprouts and onion and season with the sage, nutmeg, pepper, and salt. Cover and cook, shaking the pan occasionally, until the sprouts begin to brown, 5 to 7 minutes. Turn the sprouts and add the squash and cook everything until the squash is fork-tender, an additional 7 to 10 minutes.
2. Transfer to a serving dish or plates and serve immediately.

Oven-Roasted Spaghetti Squash

Prep time: 5 minutes | Cook time: 1 hour | Serves 2

1 whole spaghetti squash
2 tablespoons extra-virgin olive oil
2 teaspoons fresh thyme leaves (or ¼ teaspoon dried)
½ teaspoon salt
¼ teaspoon black pepper

1. Preheat the oven to 425ºF (220ºC). Line a baking sheet with foil or parchment paper.
2. Cut the squash in half lengthwise and remove the seeds with a large spoon. Drizzle the insides evenly with the olive oil. Place the squash flesh-side down on the baking sheet.
3. Roast the squash for 1 hour, until fork-tender. Carefully turn the squash flesh-side up and let cool until cool enough to handle.
4. Use a fork to gently scrape out the flesh; the squash will come out in noodle-like strands. Season evenly with the thyme, salt, and pepper, and serve immediately.

Smashed Potatoes with Dried Herb

Prep time: 10 minutes | Cook time: 36 minutes | Serves 10

10 baby Yukon Gold potatoes
½ cup clarified butter or ghee
4 cloves garlic, minced
1 teaspoon dried thyme
1 teaspoon dried rosemary
¾ teaspoon salt
½ teaspoon coarse black pepper
¼ teaspoon smoked paprika
3 tablespoons chopped fresh chives or parsley

1. Preheat the oven to 400ºF (205ºC). Line a large rimmed baking pan with parchment paper.
2. Place the potatoes in a large pot; add water to cover. Bring to a boil over high heat; cook until just tender, about 15 minutes. Drain. Let cool slightly while making the herbed butter.
3. Melt the butter in a small saucepan over medium heat. Add the garlic, thyme, rosemary, salt, pepper, and smoked paprika. Cook, stirring constantly, 1 minute. Remove from the heat.
4. Place the potatoes on the baking pan. Use the bottom of a glass to smash each potato until about ½ inch thick. Drizzle with herbed butter. Roast for 17 to 20 minutes, until tender. Turn the oven to broil. Broil for about 3 minutes, until the potatoes are crisp on top. Sprinkle with chives.

Twice-Fried Green Plantains

Prep time: 5 minutes | Cook time: 8 minutes | Serves 4

½ cup avocado oil, plus more as needed
3 large green plantains, peeled and cut on an angle into ½-inch-thick discs
Flaky sea salt, to taste

1. In a 10-inch nonstick skillet, heat ¼ cup of the avocado oil over medium-high heat to 350ºF (180ºC). Line a baking sheet with paper towels and place it near your frying station.
2. Working in batches, if needed, carefully lay the plantains in the hot oil and fry until golden, 2 to 3 minutes per side. Transfer the parcooked plantains to the baking sheet and repeat to fry the remaining plantains, adding more oil as needed.
3. One at a time, place the plantain slices between two sheets of waxed paper and gently smash them to ½ inch thick using a flat-bottomed cup, ramekin, or tortilla press.
4. Bring the oil back to 350ºF (180ºC). Again working in batches, carefully lay the smashed plantains in the hot oil and fry until golden brown and crispy, 2 to 3 minutes per side. Add more oil to the pan as needed. Transfer the tostones to the baking sheet and season with flaky salt. Serve immediately.

Sautéed Lemony Kale with Almonds

Prep time: 10 minutes | Cook time: 5 minutes | Serves 2

1 head kale, stemmed, leaves cut into 1-inch ribbons
3 tablespoons cooking fat
1 clove garlic, minced
¼ cup raw sliced almonds
½ teaspoon salt
½ teaspoon black pepper
Grated zest and juice of ½ lemon

1. Bring 1 cup of water to a boil in a large pot. Place a colander or steamer inside the pot. Add the kale, cover, and steam until the kale is tender but not soft, 3 to 5 minutes. Remove the colander or steamer from the pot and transfer to a dish towel to catch any dripping water.
2. Heat the cooking fat in a large skillet over medium-high heat, swirling to coat the bottom of the pan. When the fat is hot, add the garlic and almonds and cook until the garlic is aromatic, about 1 minute. Increase the heat to high, add the kale, and cook for 1 minute, tossing to combine the kale with the garlic and almonds. Transfer to a serving dish and season with the salt, pepper, and lemon juice. Top with the lemon zest and serve.

Green Beans with Bacon

Prep time: 5 minutes | Cook time: 30 minutes | Serves 4

1 pound (454 g) fresh green beans
5 cloves garlic, peeled
½ teaspoon fine Himalayan salt
5 slices bacon, cut into ½-inch pieces

1. Preheat the oven to 400ºF (205ºC).
2. Trim the green beans. To be efficient, I like to hold a bunch in my hand and use kitchen shears to snip off the ends. Spread them out on a sheet pan so none are overlapping. Add the garlic cloves to the pan and sprinkle everything with the salt. Distribute the bacon pieces evenly over the green beans.
3. Roast for 15 minutes. Open the oven, use a kitchen towel to hold the sheet pan firmly in one hand, and give it a shake so the green beans and bacon move around a bit. Close the oven and roast the beans for another 15 minutes, or until they are slightly shriveled with crispy ends.
4. Store leftovers in an airtight container in the fridge for up to 4 days. To reheat, sauté over high heat for 5 minutes.

Grilled Zucchini with Italian Herbs

Prep time: 10 minutes | Cook time: 4 minutes | Serves 4

Spray oil (for grill)
¼ teaspoon freshly ground black pepper
10 to 12 baby zucchini, halved, or 2 mature zucchini, cut into long planks
6 thin lemon slices
1 orange wedge
1 teaspoon grated orange zest
1 teaspoon grated lemon zest
3 tablespoons pine nuts, toasted
2 tablespoons mixed chopped fresh herbs (such as oregano, basil, and parsley)
¼ teaspoon flaky sea salt, such as Maldon (optional)

1. Heat grill to high or heat a grill pan over high heat. Reduce the heat to medium-high, then spray the grill grate or pan lightly with oil.
2. Sprinkle the black pepper all over the zucchini. Place the zucchini cut-side down on the grill or pan and grill until browned on each side, 2 to 3 minutes per side. Transfer to a small platter, arranging the pieces decoratively on the platter.
3. Place the lemon slices among the grilled zucchini pieces. Squeeze the juice from the orange wedge over the top and finish with the orange and lemon zests, pine nuts, fresh herbs, and salt (if using).

Butter Parsley Stuffed Mushrooms

Prep time: 5 minutes | Cook time: 25 minutes | Serves 4

4 large portobello mushroom caps
¼ cup grass-fed butter or ghee, at room temperature
¼ cup finely chopped fresh parsley leaves, plus more for garnish
1½ teaspoons finely chopped garlic
Kosher salt and freshly ground black pepper, to taste

1. Preheat the oven to 425ºF (220ºC). Line a rimmed baking sheet with parchment paper.
2. Wipe the mushrooms clean with a damp paper towel and place them gill-side up on the prepared baking sheet.
3. In a medium bowl, stir together the butter, parsley, and garlic until well combined. Evenly spread the butter over the gill side of each mushroom and season each with a pinch each of salt and pepper. Bake until the mushrooms are deeply browned and sizzling, 22 to 25 minutes. Garnish with parsley and serve immediately.

Paprika Cashews

Prep time: 5 minutes | Cook time: 6 minutes | Makes 1 cup

1 cup raw unsalted cashews
1 tablespoon avocado oil
1 tablespoon nutritional yeast powder or flakes
1 teaspoon sweet paprika
1 teaspoon flaky sea salt
⅛ teaspoon cayenne pepper, plus more to taste

1. In a dry nonstick skillet, toast the cashews over medium-low heat, stirring occasionally, until warm, about 4 minutes. Add the avocado oil, toss to coat the nuts, and cook, stirring occasionally, until the cashews are golden, 2 to 3 minutes more. Add the nutritional yeast, paprika, flaky salt, and cayenne and toss to coat. Taste the nuts for seasoning and adjust the salt and cayenne pepper as desired.
2. Transfer the nuts to a serving dish. Let cool for at least 5 minutes before serving. Store in an airtight container at room temperature for up to 1 week.

Sweet Potato Croutons Baked

Prep time: 5 minutes | Cook time: 30 minutes | Makes 2 cups

2 cups cubed peeled sweet potatoes (½-inch cubes)
1 tablespoon extra-virgin olive oil
½ teaspoon kosher salt
¼ teaspoon freshly ground black pepper

1. Preheat the oven to 375ºF (190ºC). Line a baking sheet with parchment paper.
2. In a medium bowl, combine the sweet potato cubes, olive oil, salt, and pepper and toss until thoroughly coated. Spread them out on the prepared baking sheet and bake for 30 minutes, flipping halfway through, until cooked through and crispy. Transfer to a platter for serving.

Garlicky Cherry Tomatoes

Prep time: 5 minutes | Cook time: 20 minutes | Serves 4

1 pint cherry tomatoes, halved lengthwise
10 garlic cloves, smashed
Freshly ground black pepper, to taste
Leaves from 1 large sprig thyme

1. Preheat the oven to 375ºF (190ºC). Line a rimmed baking sheet with parchment paper.
2. Spread the tomatoes, cut-sides up, over the baking sheet and scatter the garlic cloves among them. Sprinkle everything with pepper and the thyme leaves.
3. Roast until the tomatoes collapse and char a bit on the edges, about 20 minutes. Use immediately, or let cool and refrigerate in an airtight container for up to 2 days.

Loaded Roasted Carrots with Ginger Sauce

Prep time: 10 minutes | Cook time: 40 minutes | Serves 4

8 medium carrots with greens
2 tablespoons unsalted butter, ghee, or lard
1 teaspoon poppy seeds
1 teaspoon sesame seeds
1 teaspoon dried cilantro or thyme leaves
½ teaspoon fine Himalayan salt
¼ cup ginger sauce

1. Preheat the oven to 400ºF (205ºC).
2. Trim the carrot greens so there are about 3 inches left. Cut the carrots in half lengthwise and rub them with the butter. Lay them out evenly on a sheet pan. Sprinkle the seeds, cilantro, and salt all over the carrots.
3. Roast for 40 to 45 minutes. Remove from the oven and drizzle the sauce over the carrots. Serve immediately. Store leftover carrots in separate airtight containers for up to 4 days. Reheat in a preheated 350ºF (180ºC) oven for 8 minutes.

Golden Oven Fries

Prep time: 5 minutes | Cook time: 30 minutes | Serves 2 to 4

2 pounds (907 g) yellow or white potatoes
2 tablespoons avocado oil
¾ teaspoon kosher salt
¼ teaspoon freshly ground black pepper

1. Preheat the oven to 425ºF (220ºC). Line a baking sheet with parchment paper.
2. Rinse and scrub the potatoes to remove any dirt. After patting them dry, cut them into ¼-inch-thick matchsticks and arrange them on the prepared baking sheet. Drizzle the avocado oil over the potatoes and season with about half the salt and all the pepper. Toss to coat, then spread the fries into a single layer over the baking sheet.
3. Roast on the bottom rack of the oven until the fries are golden brown and fork-tender, 30 to 35 minutes—no need to flip them halfway. Season with the remaining salt and serve immediately.

Balsamic Sweet Potato and Brussels Sprouts

Prep time: 10 minutes | Cook time: 39 minutes | Serves 2

1 cup balsamic vinegar
1 sweet potato, peeled and cut into large dice
3 tablespoons melted ghee, clarified butter, coconut oil, or extra-virgin olive oil
½ pound (227 g) Brussels sprouts, trimmed and cut in half
½ red onion, thinly sliced
3 cloves garlic, minced
½ teaspoon salt
¼ teaspoon black pepper

1. Preheat the oven to 400ºF (205ºC). Line a baking sheet with parchment paper.
2. Bring the vinegar to a boil in a small saucepan over medium-high heat. Turn the heat down to medium low and simmer until the balsamic is reduced by about half, 20 to 30 minutes. Remove from the heat, allow to cool, and reserve. (You can do this up to a week ahead of time; store in a covered container at room temperature.)
3. While the glaze is reducing, combine the sweet potato and 1 tablespoon of the cooking fat in a medium bowl and stir or toss to coat evenly. Spread the coated sweet potatoes on the prepared baking sheet.
4. Meanwhile, add the remaining 2 tablespoons of fat to a large skillet over medium-high heat and swirl to coat the bottom of the pan. When the fat is hot, add the Brussels sprouts and cook, shaking the pan occasionally as they start to brown, for 3 to 4 minutes. Add the onion and garlic and continue to cook, stirring, until the garlic is aromatic, an additional minute. Season with the salt and pepper.
5. Add the Brussels sprout mixture to the sweet potatoes on the pan, spreading them evenly without crowding. Put the baking sheet in the oven and roast for 15 to 18 minutes, until the sweet potatoes are golden brown and soft and the sprouts are tender.
6. Plate the Brussels sprouts and sweet potato mixture and drizzle with the balsamic sauce.

Brussels Sprouts and Shallots Bowl

Prep time: 10 minutes | Cook time: 15 minutes | Serves 2

1 pound (454 g) Brussels sprouts, quartered or shaved on a mandoline
1 cup quartered or shaved shallots
½ teaspoon cracked black pepper
¼ teaspoon sea salt
3 tablespoons unseasoned rice vinegar
¼ teaspoon togarashi
¼ cup chopped green onion
1 small red Thai chile or other hot pepper, thinly sliced

1. In a medium bowl, combine the Brussels sprouts, shallots, black pepper, salt, vinegar, and togarashi. Toss until sprouts are evenly coated, then cover the bowl and let rest at room temperature for 1 hour.
2. Preheat the oven to 400ºF (205ºC). Line a rimmed baking sheet with parchment paper.
3. Spread the sprouts over the prepared pan in a single layer and pour any liquid from the bowl over the sprouts. Roast until tender, 15 to 20 minutes.
4. Transfer to a serving bowl and fold in the green onion and chile.

Pumpkin-Spiced Sweet Potato

Prep time: 5 minutes | Cook time: 12 minutes | Serves 4

1 (10-ounce / 283-g) sweet potato
3 tablespoons clarified butter or ghee, melted
¾ teaspoon pumpkin pie spice

1. Preheat the oven to 375ºF (190ºC). Place a wire rack on each of two large rimmed baking pans.
2. Use a mandoline set at 1/16 or 1/8 inch or a sharp knife to thinly slice the potatoes. Place the potato slices in a bowl and drizzle with the butter. Sprinkle with the pumpkin pie spice; toss to coat. Arrange the slices in a single layer on the wire racks.
3. Bake for 12 to 15 minutes, until the potatoes are lightly browned and crisp around the edges.

Warm Fennel Olives

Prep time: 10 minutes | Cook time: 7 minutes | Serves 10

2 teaspoons fennel seeds
¾ cup extra-virgin olive oil
1 lemon
4 large cloves garlic, smashed
1 tablespoon ground Aleppo pepper
4 cups assorted Whole30-compliant olives with pits, such as Castelvetrano, Cerignola, and/or Kalamata
Fresh thyme or rosemary sprigs

1. In a large skillet, heat the fennel seeds over medium heat, stirring occasionally, until toasted and fragrant, 2 to 3 minutes. Add the olive oil.
2. Use a vegetable peeler to remove wide strips of peel from the lemon (be sure to not remove the bitter pith). Add the peel to the fennel seeds.
3. Add the garlic and Aleppo pepper; stir to combine. Add the olives and thyme or rosemary sprigs. Simmer over medium-low heat, 5 to 10 minutes. Do not let boil.
4. Serve the olives warm.

Whole Roasted Hot Spiced Cauliflower

Prep time: 10 minutes | Cook time: 1¼ hours | Serves 4

½ cup pitted dates
¼ cup garlic cloves
1 cup canned no-added-sodium crushed tomatoes
1 cup low-sodium vegetable broth
¼ cup roasted red peppers
1½ teaspoons onion granules
1 to 1½ teaspoons red pepper flakes
½ teaspoon smoked paprika
¼ teaspoon sea salt
½ cup lightly packed fresh cilantro leaves
1 large head cauliflower, trimmed

1. Preheat the oven to 375°F (190°C).
2. In a small saucepan, combine the dates and garlic and add water to cover. Bring to a simmer over medium heat and simmer until softened, about 15 minutes. Drain the dates and garlic and transfer to a food processor or a (preferably high-speed) blender.
3. Add the tomatoes, ½ cup of the broth, the roasted peppers, onion granules, red pepper flakes, paprika, and salt. Blend until smooth. Pulse in all but a few cilantro leaves (set those leaves aside for garnish).
4. Place the cauliflower cut-side down in a Dutch oven or deep roasting pan. Spoon half the sauce over the cauliflower, coating it completely. Pour the remaining ½ cup broth into the bottom of the pan. Cover with a lid or foil, making sure the foil does not touch the food. Roast for 25 minutes.
5. Remove the cauliflower from the oven and baste it with the drippings from the bottom of the pan. Spoon on the remaining sauce and roast, uncovered, until the cauliflower is easily pierced with a knife, 30 to 45 minutes more, depending on the size of your cauliflower. Remove from the oven and let cool.
6. Transfer the cauliflower to a cutting board and slice it into thick slabs. Serve with the pan juices drizzled over the top and garnish with the reserved cilantro leaves.

Celeriac, Carrot, and Potato Pot Roast

Prep time: 15 minutes | Cook time: 3½ hours | Serves 8

2 onions, quartered
2 large carrots, quartered
3 large russet potatoes, scrubbed and quartered
5 garlic cloves, smashed
½ cup low-sodium vegetable broth
½ teaspoon smoked paprika
½ teaspoon red pepper flakes
2 teaspoons freshly ground black pepper
½ teaspoon sea salt
1 large celeriac (celery root), trimmed and scrubbed
1 tablespoon onion granules
Juice of 1 lime
2 bay leaves
1 tablespoon chopped fresh thyme
1 tablespoon chopped fresh rosemary
½ cup lightly packed small fresh flat-leaf parsley leaves

1. If using the oven, preheat the oven to 400°F (205°C). If using a slow cooker, set the slow cooker to High.
2. In a Dutch oven or in the slow cooker, combine the onions, carrots, potatoes, garlic, ¼ cup of the broth, the paprika, red pepper flakes, 1 teaspoon of the black pepper, and the salt. Gently toss to completely coat the vegetables with the seasonings.
3. In a medium bowl, combine the whole celeriac, onion granules, lime juice, remaining ¼ cup broth, and 1 teaspoon black pepper. Gently toss to coat, then put the celeriac in the Dutch oven or slow cooker, nestling it into the other vegetables. Scrape the contents of the bowl into the Dutch oven or slow cooker. Add the bay leaves.
4. Cover, place the Dutch oven in the oven, and reduce the oven temperature to 300°F (150°C); if using a slow cooker, set it to Low. Cook until the celeriac is tender enough to be easily pierced with a knife, 3½ to 4 hours in the oven or 4 to 6 hours in the slow cooker, depending on size of celeriac.
5. Remove and discard the bay leaves. Carve the celeriac into slices and serve it with the vegetables and pan juices. Garnish with the thyme, rosemary, and parsley.

Chili Brussels Sprouts

Prep time: 5 minutes | Cook time: 28 minutes | Serves 4

2 tablespoons extra-virgin olive oil
1 clove garlic, thinly sliced
4 cups Brussels sprouts, trimmed and halved
½ teaspoon coarse salt
¼ teaspoon black pepper
⅛ teaspoon chipotle powder or cayenne pepper

1. Preheat the oven to 425ºF (220ºC). Line a large baking pan with parchment paper.
2. In a saucepan, heat the olive oil and garlic over medium heat, until the garlic is fragrant and starts to brown, 3 to 4 minutes. Remove from the heat; cool for 5 minutes. Remove the garlic from the oil; discard the garlic.
3. Place the Brussels sprouts in a large bowl. Drizzle with the garlic oil and sprinkle with the salt, pepper, and chipotle powder; toss to coat. Arrange the sprouts in a single layer on the pan. Roast for about 25 minutes, stirring once halfway through, until lightly browned and just tender. Transfer the pan to a wire rack to cool. Place the Brussels sprouts in an airtight container. Chill for at least 2 hours before traveling.

Golden Onion Rings with Aioli

Prep time: 15 minutes | Cook time: 20 minutes | Serves 8

For the Onion Rings:
1 cup almond flour
1 teaspoon paprika
1 teaspoon dried oregano, crushed
1 teaspoon coarse salt
½ teaspoon garlic powder
2 large eggs
2 medium yellow onions, sliced ½ inch thick
¼ cup extra-virgin olive oil

For the Aioli:
2 green onions, chopped
1 egg, at room temperature
1 clove garlic
1 teaspoon Whole30-compliant Dijon mustard
1 tablespoon fresh lemon juice
1 to 1¼ cups light-tasting olive oil
1 teaspoon cracked black pepper

1. Line two large rimmed baking pans with parchment paper.
2. Make the Onion Rings
3. In a large bowl, combine the almond flour, paprika, oregano, salt, and garlic powder. In another large bowl, whisk the 2 eggs. Stir ¼ cup of the flour mixture into the eggs.
4. Separate the onion slices into rings. Add 3 to 4 onion rings at a time to the egg mixture and turn to coat. Use your hands or a slotted spoon to transfer the onions to the flour mixture; turn to coat.
5. Transfer the onions to the baking pans in a single layer. Refrigerate for at least 1 hour or up to 4 hours.
6. Make the Aioli
7. In a blender, combine the green onions, egg, garlic, mustard, and lemon juice. Cover and pulse to combine. With the blender running, slowly add the light olive oil until creamy. Add the pepper and pulse to combine. Transfer to a serving bowl; cover and refrigerate until ready to serve.
8. Preheat the oven to 450ºF (235ºC). Drizzle the onion rings with the extra-virgin olive oil. Bake until the onions are tender and the coating is golden and crisp, about 20 minutes. Transfer to a serving platter and serve with the aioli.

Chili Roasted Zucchini Slices

Prep time: 10 minutes | Cook time: 15 minutes | Serves 8

6 medium zucchini, halved lengthwise and cut into ¾-inch slices
Grated zest and juice of 2 small limes
¼ cup extra-virgin olive oil
1 tablespoon Whole30-compliant chili powder
1½ teaspoons salt
½ teaspoon black pepper

1. Preheat the oven to 400ºF (205ºC). Line 2 large rimmed baking pans with parchment paper.
2. Place the zucchini in an extra-large bowl. In a small bowl, whisk together ¼ cup lime juice with the olive oil, chili powder, salt, and pepper. Drizzle over the zucchini and toss to coat.
3. Arrange the zucchini in a single layer in the two pans.
4. Roast for about 15 minutes, until just tender, rotating pans halfway through.
5. Transfer the zucchini to a large serving bowl. Sprinkle with 2 teaspoons of the lime zest and gently stir to combine.

Super Easy Zucchini Noodles

Prep time: 30 minutes | Cook time: 0 minutes | Serves 2

4 zucchini
1 teaspoon kosher salt

1. Trim the ends of the zucchini and pass them through a spiralizer to create noodles. Transfer the zucchini noodles to a colander set over a bowl, sprinkle with the salt, and massage the noodles to coat. Let the zucchini noodles sit until drained of excess moisture, about 30 minutes, or up to 1 hour.
2. Drain the zucchini noodles and serve as desired.

Sautéed Kale with Pine Nuts

Prep time: 5 minutes | Cook time: 15 minutes | Serves 3 or 4

1 pound (454 g) Tuscan kale
Kosher salt, to taste
¼ cup pine nuts
3 tablespoons extra-virgin olive oil, plus more for finishing
2 garlic cloves, thinly sliced
1 teaspoon red pepper flakes
½ lemon, cut into wedges, for serving

1. Trim the lower parts of the kale stems and use your hands to strip the leaves from the stems. Finely chop the stems and set aside. Stack the leaves on top of one another, cut them crosswise into 1-inch ribbons, and set aside.
2. Fill a large bowl with ice and water and set it nearby.
3. Bring a large pot of water to a boil over high heat. Season the water with 2 tablespoons salt, add the kale leaves, and cook until tender and bright green, about 3 minutes. Transfer the kale to the ice water and let stand for 3 minutes to stop the cooking and set the vivid green color. Drain the kale very well before cooking.
4. In a large sauté pan, toast the pine nuts over medium heat until lightly browned and fragrant, 3 to 4 minutes. Transfer the nuts to a bowl or plate and set aside.
5. In the same pan, heat the olive oil over medium heat. Add the chopped kale stems and the garlic and season with a pinch of salt. Cook, stirring, until the kale stems soften, about 3 minutes. Add the red pepper flakes and cook for 1 minute. Add the kale leaves and season with another small pinch of salt. Toss the kale to coat in the oil. Add 2 tablespoons water and quickly cover the pan to trap the steam. Cook until wilted and tender, 3 minutes, stirring once about halfway through. Taste and adjust the seasoning.
6. Transfer the cooked kale to a serving platter, garnish with the toasted pine nuts, drizzle with a bit more olive oil, and serve with the lemon wedges alongside for squeezing over the top.

Sweet Potatoes Mash

Prep time: 10 minutes | Cook time: 15 minutes | Serves 4

Kosher salt and freshly ground black pepper, to taste
4 sweet potatoes, peeled and cut into 1-inch cubes
3 tablespoons extra-virgin olive oil, plus more for finishing
2 garlic cloves, finely chopped
1 tablespoon ghee (optional)
Flaky sea salt, for finishing

1. Bring a large saucepan of water to a boil over high heat. Season the water with 1 tablespoon salt and add the sweet potatoes. Boil until the potatoes are fork-tender, about 15 minutes, then drain them and return them to the pot.
2. Add the olive oil, garlic, and ghee (if using) to the pot with the sweet potatoes. Season with a pinch each of salt and pepper and mash the potatoes with a fork or potato masher until smooth.
3. Transfer the mashed sweet potatoes to a serving bowl, drizzle with a bit more olive oil, and season with a pinch of flaky salt. Serve immediately.

Broccoli Soup

Prep time: 15 minutes | Cook time: 25 minutes | Serves 4

2 tablespoons extra-virgin olive oil
1 yellow onion, diced
1 carrot, diced
Kosher salt and freshly ground black pepper, to taste
2 garlic cloves, coarsely chopped
1 teaspoon sweet paprika
½ teaspoon cayenne pepper (optional)
4 cups chicken stock
3 small sweet potatoes, peeled and cut into 2-inch cubes (about 3½ cups)
2 heads broccoli (about 1½ pounds / 680 g), finely chopped, including stems
¼ cup nutritional yeast powder or flakes

1. In a large Dutch oven or heavy-bottomed pot, heat the olive oil over medium-high heat. Add the onion and carrot and season with ¼ teaspoon each salt and black pepper. Cook, stirring, until the vegetables are slightly softened, 5 to 6 minutes. Add the garlic and cook, stirring, for an additional minute, followed by the paprika and cayenne (if using), and cook, stirring, for 1 minute more so everything is evenly coated with the spices.
2. Add the stock, sweet potatoes, and all but 1½ cups of the broccoli. Add 4 cups water and bring to a boil. Cook at a boil until the sweet potatoes are fork-tender, about 12 minutes. Stir in the nutritional yeast. Remove from the heat and use an immersion blender to blend the soup until smooth and creamy. (Alternatively, let the soup cool slightly, carefully transfer it to a blender, and blend until smooth and creamy, then return the soup to the pot.) Taste and adjust the salt and pepper, as desired.
3. Stir in the remaining florets and cook over medium heat until the broccoli is just tender, 2 to 3 minutes. Let the soup cool for 5 to 10 minutes, then ladle it into individual bowls and serve.

Zucchini Ribbons

Prep time: 10 minutes | Cook time: 10 minutes | Serves 4

2 medium zucchini, sliced lengthwise into about 6 (¼-inch-thick) planks each
⅛ teaspoon plus ¼ teaspoon kosher salt
¼ teaspoon freshly ground black pepper
2 tablespoons plus 1 teaspoon extra-virgin olive oil
2 tablespoons fresh lime juice
2 tablespoons chopped scallions
1 tablespoon pressed garlic
Juice from 1 tablespoon grated fresh ginger

1. Season the zucchini planks with ⅛ teaspoon of the salt and the pepper.
2. In a large sauté pan or grill pan, heat 1 teaspoon of the olive oil over high heat. When the oil is hot, reduce the heat to medium and spread the zucchini planks in the pan in a single layer (work in batches if they don't all fit at the same time). Cook until the zucchini is fork-tender but not mushy, about 1½ minutes per side.
3. In a bowl, stir together the remaining 2 tablespoons olive oil, the lime juice, scallions, garlic, ginger juice, and remaining ¼ teaspoon salt.
4. Pour the marinade over the zucchini. Serve.

Green Beans with Almonds

Prep time: 5 minutes | Cook time: 8 minutes | Serves 4

1 tablespoon plus ¼ teaspoon kosher salt
1 pound (454 g) French green beans
1 tablespoon extra-virgin olive oil
3 tablespoons slivered almonds
6 garlic cloves, thinly sliced (about 4 tablespoons)
¼ teaspoon freshly ground black pepper

1. Fill a large pot with water, add 1 tablespoon of the salt, and bring to a boil over high heat. Prepare a large bowl of ice water.
2. Add the green beans to the boiling water and cook for 3 minutes. Drain and plunge into the ice water; let cool for 5 minutes. Drain again and dry the beans. Set aside.
3. In a medium sauté pan, heat the olive oil over medium-high heat. Add the almonds and cook, stirring, until golden, 1 to 2 minutes.
4. Increase the heat to high, add the green beans, garlic, ¼ teaspoon salt, and the pepper, and stir to combine well. Cook, stirring, until the garlic is golden and the green beans are tender, about 2 minutes more.
5. Serve.

Carrots with Fennel and Shallots

Prep time: 10 minutes | Cook time: 20 minutes | Serves 4

3 tablespoons clarified butter
1 cup thinly sliced fennel
½ cup chopped shallots
4 large carrots, cut on the bias into ¼-inch-thick slices (4 cups)
1 teaspoon kosher salt

1. In a large sauté pan, melt 2 tablespoons of the clarified butter over medium heat. Add the fennel and shallots and cook, stirring continuously, until soft and lightly golden, about 8 minutes. Using a slotted spoon, transfer the shallots and fennel to a bowl and set aside.
2. Add the remaining 1 tablespoon clarified butter to butter remaining in the pan and melt over medium heat. Add the carrots and cook, stirring, until the soft, about 9 minutes. Add the salt and stir to combine. Return the fennel and shallots to the pan and stir together. Serve.

Red Cabbage with Apple and Bacon

Prep time: 5 minutes | Cook time: 15 minutes | Serves 4

8 ounces (227 g) sliced bacon
5 cups thinly sliced red cabbage (about ⅔ of a small head)
1 cup peeled and thinly sliced apple
1 tablespoon white vinegar
1 teaspoon kosher salt
¼ teaspoon freshly ground black pepper

1. Bring a large pot of water (about 4 quarts) to a boil over high heat.
2. Meanwhile, in a large skillet over medium-high heat, fry the bacon until done, 6 to 8 minutes. Transfer the bacon to a cutting board, leaving as much bacon fat in the pan as possible, and slice into ½-inch pieces. Set aside.
3. Pour the bacon fat into a bowl. Measure 2 tablespoons of the bacon fat, return it to the pan, and discard the remaining fat. Set the pan aside.
4. Add the red cabbage to the boiling water and cook until tender but still a bit crunchy, about 3 minutes. Drain the cabbage and set aside.
5. Heat the reserved bacon fat over medium-high heat. Add the apple and cook, stirring, until just soft, about 1 minute. Add the cabbage, bacon, vinegar, salt, and pepper and stir to combine thoroughly. Serve.

Brussels Sprouts with Lemon Tahini

Prep time: 10 minutes | Cook time: 10 minutes | Serves 2

2 cups Brussels sprouts, trimmed and halved (or quartered if large)
2 tablespoons clarified butter or ghee, melted
1 teaspoon paprika
½ to 1 teaspoon red pepper flakes
¼ teaspoon salt
¼ black pepper
2 teaspoons fresh lemon juice
2 tablespoons Whole30-compliant tahini

1. Preheat the oven to 400ºF (205ºC). Line a baking sheet with parchment paper.
2. Combine the Brussels sprouts, butter, paprika, pepper flakes, salt, and black pepper in a large bowl. Place the Brussels sprouts in a single layer on the pan.
3. Roast the Brussels sprouts, stirring once halfway through cooking, until the outer leaves are crispy and lightly browned, 8 to 10 minutes. Drizzle the lemon juice over the Brussels sprouts and serve with the tahini for dipping.

Sautéed Lemony Kale

Prep time: 5 minutes | Cook time: 4 minutes | Serves 8

4 tablespoons clarified butter or ghee
2½ bunches kale, stalks removed, leaves torn into bite-size pieces
3 tablespoons fresh lemon juice
3 cloves garlic, finely minced
½ teaspoon salt
¼ teaspoon black pepper

1. In an extra-large skillet, melt the butter over medium-high heat. Add the kale; use tongs to turn to coat in the butter. Reduce the heat to medium. Add the lemon juice and garlic. Cook, stirring occasionally, until the kale is slightly wilted, 4 to 5 minutes. Season with the salt and pepper.

Kale with Garlic

Prep time: 8 minutes | Cook time: 5 minutes | Serves 2

2 tablespoons extra-virgin olive oil
5 garlic cloves, chopped or sliced
1 pound (454 g) kale, stemmed, leaves cut crosswise into ½-inch-wide slices
½ teaspoon kosher salt

1. In a medium sauté pan, heat 1 tablespoon of the olive oil over medium heat. Add the garlic and cook, stirring continuously, until it begins to turn brown, making sure not to burn the garlic, about 45 seconds. Immediately remove the garlic and set aside.
2. Increase the heat to medium-high and add the remaining 1 tablespoon olive oil to the pan. Add the greens and ½ teaspoon salt and cook, stirring continuously, until the greens have wilted to your liking, 1½ to 2 minutes. Serve.

Chile Roasted Sweet Potatoes

Prep time: 5 minutes | Cook time: 20 minutes | Serves 4

1 (16-ounce / 454-g) bag frozen cubed sweet potatoes
2 tablespoons coconut oil, melted
½ jalapeño, seeded and finely chopped; or ¼ to ½ teaspoon chipotle powder
1 teaspoon ground cumin
½ teaspoon salt
Lime wedges, for serving

1. Preheat the oven to 450ºF (235ºC). Line a large baking sheet with parchment paper.
2. Place the sweet potatoes in a medium bowl, cover with microwave-safe plastic wrap, and pull back a small section of the plastic wrap so the steam can escape. Microwave on high for 2 minutes.
3. Add the coconut oil, jalapeño, cumin, and salt and toss to coat. Place the sweet potatoes on the pan and roast, stirring once halfway through, until golden, about 20 minutes. Serve with the lime wedges.

Baby Beet and Red Cabbage Salad

Prep time: 10 minutes | Cook time: 0 minutes | Serves 4

1 (8-ounce / 227-g) package refrigerated cooked baby beets; or 1 (15-ounce / 425-g) can whole beets, drained
1 (10-ounce / 283-g) bag shredded red cabbage
⅓ cup finely chopped shallot
½ cup Whole30-compliant dried dark sweet cherries, chopped
¼ cup roasted salted sunflower seeds
¼ cup chopped fresh parsley
3 tablespoons red wine vinegar
1 tablespoon balsamic vinegar
¼ cup extra-virgin olive oil
¼ teaspoon salt
¼ teaspoon black pepper

1. Slice the beets and cut into thin strips. Combine the beets, cabbage, shallot, cherries, sunflower seeds, and parsley in a large bowl. Drizzle with both of the vinegars and toss to coat. Drizzle with the olive oil, sprinkle with the salt and black pepper, and toss again.
2. Serve immediately or store in an airtight container in the refrigerator for up to 24 hours.

Parsnips with Lemony Dill

Prep time: 20 minutes | Cook time: 20 minutes | Serves 4

2 pounds (907 g) parsnips, peeled and cut into 3 × ¼-inch matchsticks
3 tablespoons extra-virgin olive oil
3 cloves garlic, thinly sliced
½ teaspoon salt
⅛ teaspoon black pepper
2 tablespoons fresh lemon juice
2 teaspoons snipped fresh dill or ½ teaspoon dried dill

1. Preheat the oven to 425°F (220°C).
2. Combine the parsnips, olive oil, garlic, salt, and pepper in a large bowl and toss to coat. Place the parsnips in an even layer on two baking sheets.
3. Roast, uncovered, stirring twice, until the parsnips are tender and starting to brown, 20 to 30 minutes. Drizzle with the lemon juice and sprinkle with the dill; toss to coat and serve.

Zucchini with Basil

Prep time: 10 minutes | Cook time: 25 minutes | Serves 4

4 small zucchini
2 tablespoons extra-virgin olive oil
2 cloves garlic, minced
1 teaspoon grated lemon zest
2 tablespoons finely chopped fresh basil
½ teaspoon salt

1. Preheat the oven to 425°F (220°C). Line a baking sheet with foil.
2. Arrange two chopsticks or wooden spoons lengthwise on opposite sides of one zucchini. Cut the zucchini crosswise into ¼-inch-thick slices, stopping when the knife reaches the chopsticks to prevent slicing all the way through. Carefully fan the slices slightly. Repeat with the remaining zucchini. Place the zucchini on the pan.
3. In a small bowl, combine the olive oil, garlic, lemon zest, basil, and salt. Carefully spoon the gremolata between the zucchini slices and over the tops.
4. Roast the zucchini just until tender, 25 to 30 minutes.

Quick Sugar Snap Peas

Prep time: 5 minutes | Cook time: 5 minutes | Serves 2

1 tablespoon clarified butter or ghee
2 tablespoons finely chopped shallot
1 teaspoon minced fresh ginger
⅛ teaspoon red pepper flakes
1 (8-ounce / 227-g) bag fresh stringless sugar snap peas
2 teaspoons coconut aminos

1. Heat the butter in a medium skillet over medium heat. Add the shallot, ginger, and pepper flakes and cook, stirring, until fragrant, about 1 minute. Add the sugar snap peas and cook until crisp-tender, 3 to 5 minutes longer. Stir in the coconut aminos and serve.

Sweet Potato and Cauliflower Mash

Prep time: 5 minutes | Cook time: 15 minutes | Serves 4

1 pound (454 g) sweet potatoes, peeled and chopped
3 cups cauliflower florets
2 cloves garlic, peeled
3 tablespoons clarified butter or ghee
½ teaspoon salt
¼ teaspoon black pepper

1. Place the sweet potatoes, cauliflower, and garlic in a large saucepan, add enough water to cover, and bring to a boil. Reduce the heat, cover, and simmer until the vegetables are tender, 12 to 15 minutes. Drain.
2. Using a potato masher, mash the vegetables until desired consistency. Stir in the butter, salt, and pepper and serve.

Pistachio Over Kale Salad

Prep time: 10 minutes | Cook time: 30 minutes | Serves 2 or 3

Dressing:
3 tablespoons extra-virgin olive oil
2 anchovy fillets
2 teaspoons fresh lemon juice
2 cloves garlic
1 teaspoon Whole30-compliant Dijon mustard
⅛ teaspoon cayenne pepper
1 hard-cooked egg, yolk and white separated
Salt and black pepper, to taste

Salad:
1 bunch curly leafed or Tuscan kale, stemmed and leaves sliced
⅓ cup roasted salted pistachios, chopped

1. Make the dressing: In a blender, combine the olive oil, anchovy fillets, lemon juice, garlic, mustard, cayenne, and the hard-cooked egg yolk (reserve the egg white for another use or chop it and add it to the finished salad). Cover and blend until smooth. (Alternatively, place the ingredients in a bowl and use an immersion blender.) Season with salt and black pepper.
2. Make the salad: Place the kale in a large bowl; add the dressing. Using your hands, work the dressing into the kale for 15 seconds. Chill for 30 minutes or up to 2 hours. Sprinkle the pistachios over the salad just before serving.

Balsamic Roasted Root Veggie

Prep time: 15 minutes | Cook time: 35 minutes | Serves 2

Vegetables:

1 medium red, golden, or Chioggia beet, peeled and cut into 1-inch pieces (8 ounces / 227 g)
1 small turnip, peeled and cut into 1-inch pieces (8 ounces / 227 g)
1 bunch radishes, trimmed and halved lengthwise (8 ounces / 227 g)
1 small onion, cut into 1-inch pieces
3 tablespoons extra-virgin olive oil
½ teaspoon salt
¼ teaspoon black pepper

Vinaigrette:

2 tablespoons extra-virgin olive oil
1 tablespoon balsamic vinegar
1 tablespoon minced shallot
¼ teaspoon salt
⅛ teaspoon black pepper
½ cup roughly chopped fresh parsley

1. Make the vegetables: Preheat the oven to 425°F (220°C). In a large bowl, combine the beet, turnip, radishes, onion, olive oil, salt, and pepper; toss to coat. Transfer the vegetables to a large rimmed baking sheet and spread them into a single layer. Roast for 35 to 45 minutes, stirring once and rotating the baking sheet halfway through the cooking time, until all the vegetables are tender and browned.
2. Make the vinaigrette: In a small bowl, whisk together the olive oil, vinegar, shallot, salt, and pepper.
3. Transfer the roasted vegetables to a large bowl. Drizzle with the vinaigrette and sprinkle with the parsley. Gently toss to coat.

Curry Carrot and Sweet Potato Soup

Prep time: 20 minutes | Cook time: 4 to 5 hours | Serves 4

1 tablespoon coconut oil
1 large leek, white and light green parts only, thinly sliced
½ pound (227 g) carrots, sliced
1 tablespoon Madras curry powder
½ teaspoon sea salt
1 teaspoon grated fresh ginger
3 cloves garlic, minced
Pinch of cayenne pepper
2 Japanese sweet potatoes, peeled and chopped
3 cups chicken bone broth or Whole30-compliant chicken broth
2 cups full-fat coconut milk
Chopped fresh chives, for serving
Red pepper flakes, for serving

1. Heat the coconut oil in a large skillet over medium heat. Add the leek and carrots and cook, stirring frequently, until the leek is soft, 5 to 7 minutes.
2. Add the curry powder, salt, ginger, garlic, and cayenne to the skillet. Cook, stirring, until the garlic is fragrant, about 1 minute. Transfer the leek mixture to a slow cooker. Add the sweet potatoes, broth, and coconut milk to the slow cooker. Cover and cook on low for 4 to 5 hours.
3. Turn off the slow cooker and remove the lid; let the soup cool slightly. Using an immersion blender, purée the soup until smooth. Ladle the soup into bowls and top with chives and red pepper flakes.

Green Beans with Almond

Prep time: 5 minutes | Cook time: 8 minutes | Serves 4

1 tablespoon coconut oil
1 pound (454 g) fresh green beans, trimmed
1 teaspoon grated lemon zest
1 to 2 teaspoons fresh lemon juice
¼ teaspoon salt
¼ teaspoon black pepper
¼ cup sliced almonds, toasted

1. Heat the coconut oil in a large skillet over medium-high heat. Add the green beans and cook, without stirring, until the beans begin to blister, about 2 minutes. Stir and continue to cook, stirring occasionally, until crisp-tender and blistered in spots, 5 to 6 minutes.
2. Remove the skillet from the heat and stir in the lemon zest and juice, salt, and black pepper. Sprinkle with the almonds and serve.

Greek Spiced Potatoes

Prep time: 15 minutes | Cook time: 1½ hours | Serves 6

½ cup chicken bone broth or Whole30-compliant chicken broth
½ cup fresh lemon juice
⅓ cup extra-virgin olive oil
1 tablespoon dried thyme, crushed
1 tablespoon dried oregano, crushed
3 cloves garlic, minced
½ teaspoon sea salt
6 medium russet potatoes, peeled, if desired, and cut into ½-inch-thick wedges

1. Preheat the oven to 400°F (205°C).
2. Combine the broth, lemon juice, olive oil, thyme, oregano, garlic, and salt in a large bowl. Mix well.
3. Arrange the potato wedges in a single layer in a large baking dish. Pour the broth mixture over the potatoes. Cover with aluminum foil and bake, stirring once, for 1 hour 30 minutes.

Romaine Heart with Tahini Dressing

Prep time: 10 minutes | Cook time: 6 minutes | Serves 2

1 tablespoon fresh lemon juice
1 teaspoon tahini
½ to 1 teaspoon coconut aminos
¼ teaspoon olive oil
1 clove garlic, minced
Pinch of salt
4 teaspoons avocado oil
1 romaine heart, halved lengthwise
Fresh cilantro leaves (optional)
Chopped toasted almonds (optional)

1. Preheat a grill to medium heat.
2. In a small bowl, whisk together the lemon juice, tahini, coconut aminos, olive oil, garlic, and salt. Slowly whisk in 3 teaspoons of the avocado oil.
3. Brush the romaine halves with the remaining 1 teaspoon avocado oil.
4. Grill the romaine, cut sides down, over direct heat for 4 to 6 minutes, until slightly charred. Place the romaine on salad plates, cut sides up. Drizzle with the dressing. Sprinkle with cilantro and almonds, if desired.

Butternut Squash and Kale Salad

Prep time: 20 minutes | Cook time: 0 minutes | Serves 4

1 teaspoon grated lime zest
1 tablespoon fresh lime juice
¾ cup full-fat coconut milk
2 tablespoons fresh orange juice
1 teaspoon white wine vinegar
Salt, to taste
½ butternut squash (8 ounces / 227 g), peeled and seeded
1 bunch curly leafed or Tuscan kale, stemmed and leaves cut into bite-size pieces (2 cups lightly packed)
¾ cup pomegranate seeds
⅓ cup slivered almonds
⅓ cup roasted unsalted pepitas (pumpkin seeds)

1. In a small bowl, combine lime zest, lime juice, coconut milk, orange juice, vinegar, and salt to taste. Set the dressing aside.
2. Use a vegetable peeler to shave the squash into thin strips (you should have 4 cups lightly packed). In a large bowl, combine the squash, kale, pomegranate seeds, almonds, and pepitas. Drizzle with ½ cup of the dressing and gently toss to coat. Season with salt. Store the remaining dressing in the refrigerator for up to 1 week.

Mustard Brussels Sprout Slaw

Prep time: 30 minutes | Cook time: 0 minutes | Serves 2

2 pounds (907 g) Brussels sprouts, trimmed
1 small apple, cored and chopped
¼ cup chopped walnuts, toasted
¼ cup thinly sliced green onions
2 tablespoons extra-virgin olive oil
1 tablespoon white wine vinegar
2 teaspoons snipped fresh thyme
1 teaspoon Whole30-compliant coarse-grain mustard
¼ teaspoon coarse salt

1. Cut the Brussels sprouts in half lengthwise. Place the halves, cut sides down, on a cutting board and thinly slice the halves. (You should have about 10 cups sliced sprouts.) Transfer 1½ cups of the sliced sprouts to a medium bowl. Place the remaining sprouts in an airtight container or plastic bag; seal and store in the refrigerator for up to 3 days.
2. Add the apple, walnuts, and green onions to the bowl with the Brussels sprouts and toss to combine. In a small bowl, whisk together the oil, vinegar, thyme, mustard, and salt. Drizzle the dressing over the slaw and toss to coat. Let stand for 5 to 10 minutes before serving; toss again before serving.

Red Curried Cauliflower

Prep time: 5 minutes | Cook time: 35 minutes | Serves 4

6 cups cauliflower florets
3 tablespoons clarified butter or ghee, melted
2 teaspoons Whole30-compliant red curry powder
½ teaspoon salt
¼ teaspoon black pepper
2 tablespoons chopped fresh cilantro
Lime wedges, for serving

1. Preheat the oven to 400°F (205°C). Line a large rimmed baking sheet with parchment paper.
2. Place the cauliflower in a large bowl and drizzle it with the melted butter; mix well. Add the curry powder, salt, and pepper and toss to evenly coat the cauliflower. Spread the cauliflower evenly on the prepared baking sheet.
3. Roast for 20 minutes, then stir. Roast for 15 to 20 minutes more, until the cauliflower is tender and browned. Transfer to a serving bowl. Sprinkle with the cilantro and serve with lime wedges.

Chapter 9 Salads and Wraps

Tropically-Inspired Chicken Salad

Prep time: 10 minutes | Cook time: 2 hours | Serves 4

1½ pounds (680 g) boneless, skinless chicken breasts
1 (20-ounce / 567-g) can crushed pineapple in 100% pineapple juice, drained
1 green bell pepper, diced
1 red onion, finely chopped
1 clove garlic, minced
2 tablespoons coconut aminos
½ teaspoon salt
¼ teaspoon black pepper
8 chard leaves, stems removed and leaves sliced into ribbons
1 avocado, halved, pitted, peeled, and sliced
1 jalapeño, seeded, if desired, and sliced
Lime wedges

1. In a 4-quart slow cooker, combine the chicken, pineapple, bell pepper, onion, garlic, coconut aminos, salt, and pepper. Turn the chicken to coat. Cover and cook on low for 4 to 5 hours or on high for 2 to 3 hours.
2. Transfer the chicken to a cutting board. Use two forks to shred the chicken, then return to the slow cooker and stir.
3. Divide the chard among four bowls; top with the chicken mixture, avocado, and jalapeño. Serve with lime wedges.

Barbecue-Pulled-Chicken Lettuce Wraps

Prep time: 5 minutes | Cook time: 17 minutes | Serves 4

1 pound (454 g) boneless, skinless chicken breasts or boneless, skinless chicken thighs
½ to ¾ cup Whole30-compliant barbecue sauce
1 cup packaged shredded carrots or 2 medium carrots, shredded
2 tablespoon chopped fresh cilantro
2 tablespoons fresh lime juice
8 Bibb or romaine lettuce leaves

1. Place the chicken in a medium saucepan and add enough water to cover. Bring to a boil. Reduce the heat to low, cover, and simmer until the chicken is cooked through, 15 to 20 minutes.
2. Transfer the chicken to a cutting board and let cool slightly. Discard the water in the pan and wipe dry with paper towels. Use two forks to shred the chicken. Return the chicken to the pan and stir in the barbecue sauce. Cook over medium heat until heated through, about 2 minutes.
3. In a small bowl, combine the carrots, cilantro, and lime juice. Serve the BBQ chicken and some of the shredded carrot mixture in the lettuce leaves.

Toasty Sesame Chicken Wraps

Prep time: 10 minutes | Cook time: 2½ hours | Serves 4

¼ cup apple cider
¼ cup coconut aminos
2 teaspoons toasted sesame oil
2 cloves garlic, minced
½ teaspoon ground ginger
½ teaspoon red pepper flakes
1½ pounds (680 g) boneless, skinless chicken thighs
12 leaves butterhead lettuce
¼ cup sliced green onions
4 teaspoons sesame seeds, toasted

1. In a 3½- to 4-quart slow cooker, stir together the apple cider, coconut aminos, sesame oil, garlic, ginger, and red pepper flakes. Add the chicken and turn to coat the pieces.
2. Cover and cook on low for 5 to 6 hours or on high for 2½ to 3 hours. Transfer the chicken to a bowl. Use two forks to shred the chicken. Strain the cooking liquid. Add enough cooking liquid to the chicken to moisten. Serve the chicken in the lettuce leaves, sprinkled with the green onions and sesame seeds.

Mediterranean Chicken Breast Wraps

Prep time: 15 minutes | Cook time: 2½ hours | Serves 4

1 medium onion, finely chopped
2 pounds (907 g) boneless, skinless chicken breasts
1 teaspoon salt
½ teaspoon coarsely ground black pepper
1 (15-ounce / 425-g) jar roasted red peppers, drained and roughly chopped
½ cup Whole30-compliant Kalamata olives
3 tablespoons Whole30-compliant capers, drained
2 tablespoons fresh lemon juice
1 tablespoon extra-virgin olive oil
2 large cloves garlic, minced
2 teaspoons Whole30-compliant Italian seasoning
16 Bibb lettuce leaves
Fresh chopped basil

1. Place the onion in a 4-quart slow cooker. Season the chicken with salt and pepper and place on the onion. Add the roasted red peppers, olives, and capers. In a small bowl, whisk together the lemon juice, olive oil, garlic, and Italian seasoning; pour over the chicken.
2. Cover and cook on high for 2½ to 3 hours.
3. Use a slotted spoon to transfer the chicken and vegetables to a bowl. Use two forks to shred the chicken; moisten with some of the cooking liquid. Serve the chicken and vegetables in the lettuce leaves, topped with basil.

Teriyaki Skirt Steak Wraps

Prep time: 15 minutes | Cook time: 3 hours | Serves 4

2 red, yellow, orange, and/or green bell peppers, cut into strips
1 medium red onion, cut into wedges
¼ cup coconut aminos
¼ cup chopped pitted dates
1 piece (2 inches) fresh ginger, peeled and minced
1 teaspoon red pepper flakes
1 (1½- to 2-pound / 680- to 907-g) skirt steak
½ teaspoon salt
½ teaspoon black pepper
2 teaspoons arrowroot powder
1 head leaf lettuce, separated into leaves
2 green onions, green tops sliced
Sesame seeds, toasted

1. In a 6-quart slow cooker, combine the bell peppers, onion, coconut aminos, dates, ginger, and red pepper flakes. Season the steak with salt and pepper, add to the cooker, and turn to coat.
2. Cover and cook on low for 6 hours or on high for 3 hours. Use a slotted spoon to transfer the steak, peppers, and onion to a cutting board or platter. Cover and let the steak rest 5 minutes.
3. Meanwhile, skim the fat from the cooking liquid. Turn the slow cooker to high if using the low setting. Whisk the arrowroot into 2 tablespoons water, then stir into the cooking liquid. Cook, uncovered, until the sauce is thickened, about 5 minutes. Pour the sauce into individual small bowls.
4. Slice the steak against grain. Spoon the steak, peppers, and onion into the lettuce leaves and sprinkle with the green onions and sesame seeds. Serve with the sauce for dipping.

Bacon, Egg, and Veggie Salad

Prep time: 10 minutes | Cook time: 15 minutes | Serves 4

½ cup slivered red onion
⅓ cup cider vinegar
½ teaspoon coarse salt
6 strips Whole30-compliant bacon, chopped
1- to 1¼-pound (454- to 567-g) sweet potatoes, peeled and cut into 1-inch cubes
8 large eggs
2 teaspoons Whole30-compliant coarse-grain mustard
½ cup avocado oil or walnut oil
6 cups arugula, tough stems trimmed
½ cup chopped walnuts, toasted

1. In a small bowl, toss together the onion, vinegar, and ¼ teaspoon of the salt. Cover and let stand at room temperature while preparing the salad.
2. On a 6-quart Instant Pot, select Sauté and adjust to Normal/Medium. Add the bacon. Cook, stirring occasionally, until the bacon is crisp, about 8 minutes. Press Cancel. Use a slotted spoon to transfer the bacon to paper towels to drain. Crumble the bacon when cool enough to handle.
3. Carefully pour 1 cup water into the bacon grease in the pot. Add the sweet potatoes and place the eggs on the potatoes (the eggs should not touch each other). Lock the lid in place.
4. Select Manual and cook on high pressure for 5 minutes. Use quick release.
5. Meanwhile, combine water and ice in a large bowl to fill halfway. Carefully transfer the eggs to the ice water to cool, about 10 minutes. Use a slotted spoon to transfer the sweet potatoes to another large bowl; set aside. Peel the eggs and thinly slice or cut into halves or quarters.
6. Drain the onion, reserving the vinegar. In a medium bowl, whisk together ¼ cup of the vinegar, the mustard, and remaining ¼ teaspoon salt. Slowly whisk in the oil until the dressing is well combined and thickened. Drizzle the potatoes with about ¼ cup of the dressing. Toss gently to coat.
7. To serve, divide the arugula among four serving plates. Top with the sweet potatoes, eggs, drained onion, and bacon. Drizzle with the remaining dressing. Sprinkle with the walnuts.

Mexican Picadillo with Lettuce

Prep time: 15 minutes | Cook time: 3½ hours | Serves 4

1 pound (454 g) extra-lean ground beef
1 medium russet potato, peeled and chopped into ½-inch cubes
1 cup diced yellow onion, plus more for serving
1 cup diced peeled carrot
½ medium green bell pepper, diced
½ cup Whole30-compliant salsa
4 cloves garlic, thinly sliced
1 jalapeño, seeded and diced
1 teaspoon chili powder
1 teaspoon salt
1 teaspoon ground cumin
½ teaspoon dried oregano
¼ teaspoon black pepper
16 Bibb lettuce leaves
Chopped fresh cilantro

1. In a large skillet, cook the beef over medium-high heat, stirring with a wooden spoon to break it up, until no longer pink, 5 to 8 minutes. Use a slotted spoon to transfer the meat to a 4-quart slow cooker. Add 1 cup water, the potato, onion, carrot, bell pepper, salsa, garlic, jalapeño, chili powder, salt, cumin, oregano, and pepper.
2. Cover and cook on low for 7 to 8 hours or on high for 3½ to 4 hours.
3. Serve in lettuce leaves, topped with cilantro and chopped onion.

Hot-and-Sour Salmon Fillet Salad

Prep time: 15 minutes | Cook time: 3 minutes | Serves 4

1 cup cider vinegar
½ cup thinly sliced radishes
½ cup matchstick carrots
½ cup thinly sliced cucumber
½ teaspoon salt
4 (4-ounce / 113-g) skinless salmon fillets
Cracked black pepper, to taste
2 tablespoons avocado oil
2 tablespoons fresh lemon juice
3 tablespoons Whole30-compliant hot sauce
1 (5-ounce / 142-g) package mixed salad greens
2 tablespoons chopped fresh chives

1. In a small bowl, combine the vinegar, radishes, carrots, cucumber, and ¼ teaspoon of the salt. Let sit while preparing the salmon.
2. Add the rack and 1 cup water to a 6-quart Instant Pot. Season the salmon with remaining ¼ teaspoon salt and the pepper. Place the salmon on the rack. Lock the lid in place.
3. Select Manual and cook on high pressure for 3 minutes. Use quick release. Remove the salmon.
4. For the dressing, whisk together the oil, lemon juice, and hot sauce in another small bowl. Drain the vegetables; discard the vinegar. Arrange the greens on serving plates and top with the vegetables. Use a fork to break the salmon into chunks. Add the salmon to the salads. Drizzle with the dressing and sprinkle with the chives.

Prosciutto and Shrimp Cabbage Cups

Prep time: 10 minutes | Cook time: 6 minutes | Serves 4

2 tablespoons extra-virgin olive oil
2 ounces (57 g) sliced prosciutto, chopped
1 pound (454 g) peeled and deveined large shrimp
1 red bell pepper, chopped
3 cloves garlic, chopped
2 teaspoons Italian seasoning
½ teaspoon salt
½ teaspoon black pepper
½ cup chopped fresh basil
1 tablespoon white wine vinegar
1 small head red cabbage or Bibb lettuce

1. Heat the olive oil in a large skillet over medium heat. Add the prosciutto and cook, stirring, until crisp, 2 to 3 minutes. Transfer the prosciutto with a slotted spoon to paper towels to drain.
2. Increase the heat to medium-high. Add the shrimp and bell pepper and cook, stirring occasionally, until the shrimp are almost opaque and the pepper is softened, about 2 minutes. Add the garlic, Italian seasoning, salt, and black pepper. Cook, stirring, until the shrimp are opaque, 2 to 3 minutes longer. Remove from the heat. Stir in the basil and vinegar.
3. Separate the leaves from the cabbage and arrange on a platter. Spoon the shrimp filling into the leaves, top with the prosciutto, and serve.

Roast Beef and Avocado Salad Wraps

Prep time: 10 minutes | Cook time: 0 minutes | Serves 2

12 large Bibb lettuce leaves
8 ounces Whole30-compliant sliced roast beef, cut into ½-inch strips
For the Dressing:
¼ cup Whole30-compliant mayonnaise
1 clove garlic, minced
1 tablespoon chopped fresh basil
1 medium avocado, halved, pitted, peeled, and diced
1 cup quartered or halved cherry tomatoes
½ teaspoon grated lemon zest
1 teaspoon fresh lemon juice

1. In a small bowl, stir together the mayonnaise, garlic, basil, and lemon zest and juice.
2. Arrange the lettuce leaves on two serving plates. Divide the roast beef strips, avocado, and tomatoes among the leaves. Drizzle with the dressing and serve.

Vegetable Wraps with Lemony Zucchini Dressing

Prep time: 10 minutes | Cook time: 0 minutes | Serves 2

2 cups assorted thinly sliced vegetables, such as cucumbers, carrots, bell peppers, radishes, and/ or green onions
10 ounces (283-g) cooked chicken, beef, or shrimp, chopped or sliced
12 Bibb lettuce leaves
2 tablespoons chopped fresh dill
For the Dressing:
1 medium unpeeled zucchini, chopped
¼ cup almond butter
3 tablespoons fresh lemon juice
1 tablespoon extra-virgin olive oil
1 clove garlic, minced
½ teaspoon salt

1. In a food processor, combine the zucchini, almond butter, lemon juice, olive oil, garlic, and salt. Process until smooth.
2. Arrange the lettuce leaves on two plates. Divide the vegetables and the chicken, beef, or shrimp among the leaves. Drizzle with some of the dressing, sprinkle with fresh dill, and serve.

Pork, Apple, and Fennel Radicchio Wraps

Prep time: 10 minutes | Cook time: 5 minutes | Serves 2

1 small fennel bulb
1 tablespoon extra-virgin olive oil
8 ounces (227 g) ground pork
1 small cooking apple (such as Granny Smith or McIntosh), cored and diced
1 teaspoon dried sage, crushed
¼ teaspoon salt
2 tablespoons finely chopped unsulfured dried apricots
2 tablespoons Whole30-compliant mayonnaise
1 tablespoon cider vinegar
8 medium radicchio, cabbage, butterhead lettuce, or Bibb lettuce leaves
¼ cup chopped walnuts, toasted

1. Trim the fennel bulb, reserving the feathery tops (fronds). Remove the core and then coarsely chop the bulb. Heat the olive oil in a medium skillet over medium heat. Add the chopped fennel and the pork and cook, stirring, until the pork is almost cooked through, 3 to 4 minutes.
2. Add the apple, sage, and salt. Cook, stirring, until the pork is no longer pink and the apple is crisp-tender, 2 to 3 minutes. Stir in the apricots. Remove from the heat. In a small bowl, whisk together the mayonnaise and vinegar. Add to the pork mixture and stir until combined.
3. Place the radicchio leaves on a large serving plate. Spoon the pork filling into the center of the leaves. Sprinkle with the walnuts. Chop some of the reserved fennel fronds and sprinkle over the walnuts.

Chicken Breast, Bacon and Kale Salad

Prep time: 15 minutes | Cook time: 17 minutes | Serves 2

For the Chicken:
Extra-virgin olive oil
1 large egg
½ cup almond flour
⅓ cup finely chopped raw cashews
½ teaspoon salt
½ teaspoon black pepper
6 (2-ounce / 57-g) boneless, skinless chicken breast tenderloins

For the Salad:
3 slices Whole30-compliant bacon, chopped
4 cups torn fresh kale
1 small red onion, slivered
½ cup packaged shredded carrot
½ cup grape tomatoes, halved
¼ cup raw cashews, toasted and chopped

Make the Chicken
1. Preheat the oven to 425ºF (220ºC). Lightly brush olive oil on a medium baking sheet.
2. Whisk together the egg and 1 tablespoon olive oil in a shallow dish. In another shallow dish, stir together the flour, cashews, salt, and pepper. Dip each tenderloin into the egg, turning to coat. Allow the excess to drip off, then dip into the cashew mixture, turning to coat. Place on the prepared pan.
3. Bake the chicken, turning once halfway through cooking, until the internal temperature is 165ºF (74ºC) and the chicken is no longer pink, 15 to 18 minutes.

Make the Salad
1. Meanwhile, in a large skillet, cook the bacon, stirring, until browned and crisp. Using a slotted spoon, transfer the bacon to a plate lined with paper towels, reserving the bacon fat in the skillet. Add the kale and onion to the skillet with the bacon fat. Cook, tossing frequently with tongs, until the kale is wilted and tender, 2 to 3 minutes.
2. Remove the skillet from the heat. Stir in the cooked bacon, carrot, and tomatoes. Serve the chicken on top of the kale salad. Sprinkle with the cashews.

Lime Watermelon Salad

Prep time: 5 minutes | Cook time: 0 minutes | Serves 4

2 pounds (907 g) watermelon, cut into large dice
2 tablespoons extra-virgin olive oil
Juice of 2 limes
Leaves from 4 sprigs fresh mint, finely chopped
½ serrano chile pepper, seeded, finely sliced (optional)

1. Place all of the ingredients in a large non-reactive bowl and use a wooden spoon to combine. Cover and chill in the refrigerator for at least 20 minutes before serving. The salad can also be made up to one day ahead of time.

Balsamic Tomato Salad

Prep time: 5 minutes | Cook time: 0 minutes | Serves 4

2 pounds (907 g) assorted ripe tomatoes (gorgeous ones of any size)
½ teaspoon kosher salt
¼ teaspoon freshly ground black pepper
1 tablespoon extra-virgin olive oil
1 tablespoon high-quality balsamic vinegar
1 tablespoon red wine vinegar

1. Slice any large tomatoes into rounds, smaller tomatoes into quarters, and cherry tomatoes in half.
2. Arrange the sliced tomatoes on a platter. Sprinkle them with the salt and pepper. Drizzle them first with the olive oil, then with the balsamic and red wine vinegars.

Greek Olives Salad

Prep time: 10 minutes | Cook time: 0 minutes | Serves 2

- 1 head romaine lettuce, chopped
- 4 tomatoes, seeded and cut into large dice
- 1 cucumber, peeled and cut into large dice
- ½ red onion, thinly sliced
- 30 pitted Kalamata olives, halved
- ¼ cup extra-virgin olive oil
- 2 tablespoons red wine vinegar
- 1 clove garlic, minced
- ¼ teaspoon salt
- ¼ teaspoon black pepper
- Juice of ½ lemon

1. Combine the lettuce, tomatoes, cucumber, onion, and olives in a large serving bowl.
2. Combine the olive oil, vinegar, garlic, salt, and pepper in a small bowl and whisk together.
3. Pour the dressing over the salad ingredients and top with the lemon juice.

Tangy Brown Rice Salad with Jalapeño

Prep time: 15 minutes | Cook time: 0 minutes | Serves 4

- 2 cups cooked brown rice, cooled
- 2 tablespoons minced shallot
- 1 garlic clove, minced
- ¼ cup chopped red bell pepper
- 2 seedless mandarin oranges, peeled and chopped
- 3 tablespoons sunflower seeds or shelled pistachios, toasted
- Grated zest and juice of ½ lemon
- 2 tablespoons finely chopped fresh mint
- 2 tablespoons chopped fresh parsley leaves
- 1 jalapeño, seeded, if less heat is desired, and minced
- ½ teaspoon sea salt
- ¼ teaspoon freshly ground black pepper

1. Combine all the ingredients in a large bowl and mix gently.

Cilantro-Lime Pork Tenderloin Salad

Prep time: 20 minutes | Cook time: 5 hours | Serves 4

Pork:
- 2 teaspoons chili powder
- ½ teaspoon salt
- ¼ teaspoon ground cumin
- ¼ teaspoon black pepper
- Dash cayenne pepper
- 1 Whole30-compliant pork tenderloin (about 1¼ pounds / 567 g), trimmed
- ½ cup Whole30-compliant chicken broth

Salad:
- ½ cup Whole30-compliant mayonnaise
- ½ teaspoon grated lime zest
- 1 tablespoon fresh lime juice
- 2 tablespoons chopped fresh cilantro
- 6 cups chopped butterhead lettuce
- 1 medium avocado, halved, pitted, peeled, and diced
- 1 cup grape tomatoes, halved
- ¼ cup sliced green onions

1. Make the pork: In a small bowl, combine the chili powder, salt, cumin, pepper, and cayenne; sprinkle over the pork. Add the pork to a slow cooker. Pour the broth around the pork.
2. Cover and cook on low for 5 to 6 hours or on high for 2½ to 3 hours. Transfer the pork to a cutting board; cut into ½-inch slices. Discard the cooking liquid.
3. Make the salad: In a small bowl, combine the mayonnaise, lime zest, lime juice, and cilantro. If the dressing is too thick, stir in water, 1 teaspoon at a time, to reach desired consistency. Arrange the lettuce on plates. Top with the pork, avocado, tomatoes, and green onions. Spoon the dressing on top. Season with additional pepper, if desired.

Jerusalem Veggie Salad

Prep time: 15 minutes | Cook time: 0 minutes | Serves 4

- 2 garlic cloves, finely chopped
- ¾ teaspoon kosher salt
- ¼ cup tahini (sesame paste)
- ¼ cup extra-virgin olive oil
- ¼ cup fresh lemon juice
- ½ teaspoon freshly ground black pepper
- 2 cups halved cherry tomatoes
- 2 cups cubed English cucumber
- 2 cups quartered radishes
- 1 teaspoon finely grated lemon zest
- 3 tablespoons chopped fresh parsley
- 2 tablespoons smoky hot pepitas
- ¼ cup drained caper berries (optional)

1. On a cutting board, use the side of a chef's knife to mash the chopped garlic. When it starts to become juicy, add ½ teaspoon of the salt and mash it with the garlic until combined and broken down into a paste. Set aside.
2. Put the tahini in a medium bowl and stir until smooth. While stirring continuously with a fork or a whisk, add the olive oil, 1 tablespoon at a time, and stir until the mixture has a creamy consistency. Add the lemon juice, 1 tablespoon at a time and stir until incorporated. Add the remaining ¼ teaspoon salt, the pepper, and the garlic paste and stir to mix well. If the mixture is too thick or not combining well, stir in 2 tablespoons water. Set aside.
3. In a separate large bowl, gently toss the tomatoes, cucumber, radishes, lemon zest, parsley, and pepitas. Drizzle with dressing to your liking and toss to coat.
4. Top with the caper berries, if desired. Serve.

Chicken Breast Salad

Prep time: 15 minutes | Cook time: 35 minutes | Serves 4

For the Chicken:
- 3 bone-in, skin-on chicken breasts
- 1 tablespoon extra-virgin olive oil
- 1 teaspoon kosher salt
- ¼ teaspoon freshly ground black pepper

For the Sauce:
- ¾ cup Whole30-compliant mayonnaise
- ¼ cup whole jarred Peppadew peppers, plus ¼ cup brine from the jar

To Assemble:
- ½ cup finely chopped celery
- ½ cup finely chopped pitted green Cerignola olives
- ½ cup finely chopped jarred Peppadew peppers
- ½ cup finely chopped yellow onions
- ¼ cup finely chopped fresh chives
- 1 teaspoon kosher salt
- ½ teaspoon freshly ground black pepper
- ¼ teaspoon granulated garlic

1. Preheat the oven to 350ºF (180ºC). Line a baking sheet with parchment paper.
2. For the chicken: Evenly coat the chicken breasts with the olive oil. Sprinkle them with the salt and pepper. Put them on the prepared baking sheet and bake for 30 minutes. Remove from the oven and baste the chicken breasts with the juices from the bottom of the pan, then return the pan to the oven and bake for 5 to 10 minutes more, until the chicken is cooked through and the skin is browned and crispy. Remove and let cool.
3. Meanwhile, for the sauce: In a blender, combine the mayonnaise, the whole Peppadews, and the brine and blend until well combined. Set aside.
4. Assemble the salad: When the chicken is cool, remove the skin and set it aside, then use your hands to meticulously pull the meat off the bones, discarding the imperfections like soft tendons, cartilage, and red pieces. Coarsely chop the crispiest bits of skin and reserve to use as croutons on top of the salad. Measure out 3 cups of the chicken, reserving the rest for a different recipe. Divide the 3 cups of chicken into two groups: perfect, moist pieces in one group, and dry, not-so-perfect pieces in another. Coarsely chop the perfect, moist pieces and put them in a large bowl. Put the dry, not-so-perfect pieces in the food processor and pulse for 5 seconds, then transfer to the bowl with the perfect pieces and mix.
5. Add the celery, olives, chopped Peppadews, onion, chives, salt, black pepper, and granulated garlic to the bowl and toss to combine. Top with three-quarters of the sauce and toss very well to thoroughly coat. If desired, add more of the sauce and mix again to combine. Top with the bits of crispy skin.

Oregano Lamb Chop Salad

Prep time: 15 minutes | Cook time: 4 minutes | Serves 4

For the Lamb:
- ¼ cup plus 2 tablespoons extra-virgin olive oil
- 1 tablespoon fresh lemon juice
- 1 tablespoon red wine vinegar
- 1 teaspoon dried oregano
- 1 garlic clove, pressed
- 1½ teaspoons kosher salt
- 1 teaspoon freshly ground black pepper
- 8 skinny (¼- to ½-inch-thick) lamb chops

For The Salad:
- ½ teaspoon kosher salt
- ¼ teaspoon freshly ground black pepper
- 12 ounces (340 g) romaine lettuce, chopped
- ½ cup sliced cucumber
- ½ cup quartered cherry tomatoes
- 12 jarred pepperoncini
- ¼ cup Niçoise olives
- Marinated red onion, with their oil

Make the Lamb
1. In a medium bowl, combine ¼ cup of the olive oil, the lemon juice, vinegar, oregano, garlic, ½ teaspoon of the salt, and ½ teaspoon of the pepper and stir until combined thoroughly.
2. Put the lamb chops in a shallow container good for marinating and thoroughly season them with the remaining 1 teaspoon salt and ½ teaspoon pepper. Pour the marinade over the lamb and cover. Refrigerate for 30 minutes, or overnight if you have the time.
3. In a large cast-iron pan, heat the remaining 2 tablespoons oil over medium-high heat. Add the lamb chops and cook until seared and cooked to medium-rare or medium doneness, 2 to 3 minutes per side.

Assemble the Salad

4. In a bowl, thoroughly season the cucumbers and tomatoes with the salt and pepper. Arrange a bed of lettuce on each plate, then top with the cucumber, tomatoes, pepperoncini, and olives, dividing them evenly. Arrange the chops on top, drizzle each plate with marinated onion oil, and top with marinated onions.

Smoked Salmon Salad

Prep time: 15 minutes | Cook time: 12 minutes | Serves 2

2 large eggs
½ head iceberg lettuce, finely shredded, or 2 cups mixed greens
2 vine-ripened tomatoes, cut into 8 wedges
½ English cucumber, thinly sliced
1 avocado, cut into wedges
4 radishes, thinly sliced
½ small red onion, thinly sliced
4 ounces (113 g) no-sugar-added smoked salmon
1 tablespoon capers packed in brine, drained
2 tablespoons extra-virgin olive oil
1 tablespoon fresh lemon juice
1 tablespoon bagel be gone seasoning

1. Fill a large bowl with ice and water and set it nearby.
2. Bring a small pot of water to a boil over high heat. Using a slotted spoon, slowly lower the eggs into the water, being careful not to crack them on the bottom of the pot. Cook the eggs for exactly 12 minutes for hard yolks and whites. Transfer the eggs to the ice bath and let cool for at least 5 minutes.
3. Peel the eggs and slice them into quarters.
4. Arrange the eggs, lettuce, tomatoes, cucumber, avocado, radishes, onion, salmon, and capers side by side on a large serving platter. Drizzle the salad with the olive oil and lemon juice and sprinkle with the Bagel Be Gone Seasoning. Serve immediately.

Broiled Salmon Steak Salad

Prep time: 10 minutes | Cook time: 6 minutes | Serves 2

For the Salmon:
1 tablespoon cooking fat
2 (3-ounce / 85-g) salmon steaks
1 teaspoon fine Himalayan salt
Grated zest of 1 lime

For the Salad:
2 cups fresh arugula
1 medium Hass avocado, peeled, pitted, and sliced
1 green onion, sliced
6 slices bacon, chopped

For Serving:
¼ cup raspberry vinaigrette or other dressing
Lime wedges

1. Turn on the broiler and set the oven rack 3 to 5 inches from the heat source.
2. Spread half of the cooking fat on a sheet pan and place the salmon steaks on it skin side down. Sprinkle the salt and lime zest evenly over the salmon steaks and then add the rest of the cooking fat to the tops of the salmon steaks.
3. Broil for 6 minutes, or longer if the steaks are very thick. The salmon will be ready when you can flake the thickest part of it easily with a fork. After 6 minutes, check for doneness in 1-minute intervals.
4. While the salmon cooks, make the salad: Place the arugula, avocado, green onion, and bacon in a large bowl. Gently toss to combine, then divide evenly between two plates.
5. When the salmon is ready, remove it from the oven and use a spatula to gently separate the salmon fillet from the skin. You should be able to do this quite easily just by running the spatula under the meat.
6. Place a salmon steak on each salad and drizzle with 2 tablespoons of dressing. Serve with lime wedges on the side.
7. If you're preparing this to eat later, store the salad base, dressing, and salmon in separate airtight containers in the fridge for up to 3 days. Toss all together to eat.

Oven-Roast Vegetable Salad

Prep time: 10 minutes | Cook time: 40 minutes | Serves 6

3 cups halved Brussels sprouts
2 cups broccoli florets
5 cloves garlic, sliced
3 tablespoons avocado oil
1 teaspoon fish sauce
1 teaspoon fine Himalayan salt
1 teaspoon ground black pepper
1 teaspoon ground cumin
1 teaspoon turmeric powder
½ teaspoon ginger powder
¼ cup Whole30-compliant mayonnaise

1. Preheat the oven to 400°F (205°C).
2. Spread the Brussels sprouts, broccoli, and garlic evenly on a sheet pan. Drizzle with the avocado oil and fish sauce and sprinkle the salt, pepper, cumin, turmeric, and ginger powder over them. Toss to combine, massaging the oil and seasonings into the Brussels and broccoli. Then spread them out again on the sheet pan. Wash your yellow hands so the turmeric doesn't stain them!
3. Roast the vegetables on the middle rack of the oven for 40 minutes. Remove from the oven and let cool to room temperature.
4. Transfer the roasted vegetables to a bowl. Add the mayo and stir to combine. Store in the fridge for up to 5 days, until ready to serve or for meal prep.

Kale and Green Olives Salad

Prep time: 5 minutes | Cook time: 0 minutes | Serves 4

1 pound (454 g) dinosaur or curly kale
1 teaspoon fine Himalayan salt
¼ cup ripe green olives, pitted
2 tablespoons garlic confit
2 tablespoons Toum or Whole30-compliant mayonnaise
Juice of 1 lemon

1. Tear the kale leaves into 1- to 2-inch pieces and place in a bowl with the salt. With your hands, massage the salt into the kale for 2 minutes, or until the kale begins to release some liquid and has become very tender.
2. Add the olives, garlic confit, toum, and lemon juice. Toss to combine and serve, or store in a quart-sized jar in the fridge for up to 4 days.

Asian Cabbage Salad

Prep time: 10 minutes | Cook time: 0 minutes | Serves 6

¼ medium head red cabbage
¼ medium head green cabbage
2 green onions, minced
Leaves from 2 sprigs
For The Dressing:
Juice of 4 limes
3 tablespoons avocado oil
2 tablespoons coconut aminos
fresh basil, minced
Leaves from 4 sprigs fresh cilantro, minced
1 teaspoon fine Himalayan salt

4 cloves garlic, minced
1 (1-inch) piece ginger, peeled and minced

1. Lay one of the cabbage wedges on the cutting board and use a sharp knife to trim off the core on the diagonal. Then slice the cabbage as thinly as possible. Repeat with the second wedge. Combine the shredded red and green cabbage in a large bowl.
2. Add the green onions, basil, and cilantro and toss with the cabbage. Sprinkle in the salt and toss to combine.
3. Make the dressing: Place the lime juice, avocado oil, and coconut aminos in a small bowl. Add the garlic and ginger and whisk to combine.
4. If you're serving the salad right away, pour the dressing over the cabbage and toss to thoroughly distribute the dressing.
5. If you're not serving the salad right away, store the salad in an airtight container in the fridge with a folded paper towel to absorb moisture. Store the dressing in a separate airtight container in the fridge. Both the salad and the dressing will keep for up to 5 days.

Rosemary Cauliflower

Prep time: 10 minutes | Cook time: 1 hour | Serves 4

1 medium head cauliflower
½ cup garlic confit
1 tablespoon fish sauce
1 teaspoon dried rosemary needles
1 teaspoon fine Himalayan salt
1½ cups bone broth
1 teaspoon turmeric powder
½ teaspoon ground black pepper

1. Preheat the oven to 400ºF (205ºC).
2. Trim the leaves and stem off the head of cauliflower. Then use a paring knife to pierce it all over, a few stabs around the side and a cross on the top. Set on a sheet pan.
3. Place the garlic confit, fish sauce, rosemary, and salt in a blender and blend until a chunky paste forms. (When you measure the confit, make sure you pour out some oil as well!) Use a spatula to scrape it out of the blender and smear it all over the cauliflower.
4. Roast the cauliflower for 1 hour. Meanwhile, in a small bowl, combine the broth, turmeric, and pepper. Every 20 minutes, baste the cauliflower with ¼ cup of the broth mixture.
5. Remove the cauliflower from the oven and serve warm. Slice it up like pie! Store leftovers in an airtight container in the fridge for up to 5 days. To reheat, pan-sear in a hot skillet for 4 to 5 minutes.

Salmon and Baby Yellow Potato Salad

Prep time: 10 minutes | Cook time: 15 minutes | Serves 4

1½ pounds (680 g) baby yellow potatoes, halved
⅓ cup avocado oil
1 tablespoon Whole30-compliant Dijon mustard
1 tablespoon fresh lemon juice
½ teaspoon salt
½ teaspoon black pepper
1 (6-ounce / 170-g) can salmon, drained
2 cups arugula
3 green onions, sliced
2 tablespoons snipped fresh chives
1 tablespoon minced fresh parsley

1. Place the potatoes in a medium pot and add enough cold water to cover. Bring to a low boil and cook until tender, about 15 minutes. Drain.
2. In a large bowl, whisk together the avocado oil, mustard, lemon juice, salt, and pepper. Add the potatoes, salmon, arugula, green onions, chives, and parsley. Gently toss until the potatoes are coated. Serve warm.

Tomato and Cucumber Salad

Prep time: 15 minutes | Cook time: 0 minutes | Serves 2 to 4

4 Persian cucumbers, diced
2 Roma (plum) tomatoes, diced
½ red onion, diced
¼ cup loosely packed fresh parsley leaves, finely chopped
2 tablespoons extra-virgin olive oil
1 tablespoon fresh lemon juice
2 teaspoons ground sumac
Kosher salt and freshly ground black pepper, to taste

1. In a large bowl, combine the cucumbers, tomatoes, onion, parsley, olive oil, lemon juice, and sumac. Taste and season with salt and pepper as desired. Serve, or cover and refrigerate for 2 to 3 days.

Beef Steak Fajita Salad

Prep time: 20 minutes | Cook time: 6 hours | Serves 6

2 beef flank steaks (1 pound (454 g) / 454 g each)
¼ cup plus 1 tablespoon fresh lime juice
¼ cup plus 1 tablespoon avocado oil
¼ cup finely chopped shallots
2 cloves garlic, minced
1 teaspoon paprika
½ teaspoon ground cumin
1 medium red onion, cut into ½-inch-thick slices
3 medium red, green, or yellow bell peppers, quartered
1 medium avocado, halved, pitted, peeled, and chopped
¾ cup quartered cherry tomatoes or chopped seeded tomatoes
¼ cup thinly sliced green onion tops
⅛ teaspoon salt
⅛ teaspoon cayenne pepper
6 cups torn romaine lettuce
½ cup chopped fresh cilantro

1. Using a sharp knife, score the flank steaks on both sides with shallow diagonal cuts 1 inch apart. Place the steaks in a large shallow baking dish. In a small bowl, whisk together ¼ cup of the lime juice, ¼ cup of the oil, the shallots, garlic, paprika, and cumin. Pour over the steaks in the baking dish, turning to coat the steaks all over with the marinade. Cover and marinate at room temperature for 30 minutes, turning once. (For even more flavor, marinate the steaks, covered, in the refrigerator for up to 8 hours.)
2. Place the red onion slices in a slow cooker. Top with the marinated steaks. Top the steaks with the peppers. Cover and cook on low for 6 to 7 hours or on high for 3 to 3½ hours.
3. In a medium bowl, combine the remaining 1 tablespoon lime juice, remaining 1 tablespoon avocado oil, the avocado, tomatoes, green onion tops, salt, and cayenne.
4. Using a slotted spoon, transfer the peppers and onions to a cutting board; cut the peppers into thin strips. Transfer the steaks to the cutting board; thinly slice across the grain. Arrange the lettuce on six serving plates. Top with the beef, pepper strips, onion slices, guacamole, and cilantro.

Carne Asada Salad

Prep time: 20 minutes | Cook time: 4 hours | Serves 4

Steak:
1 cup fresh orange juice
¼ cup fresh lemon juice
¼ cup fresh lime juice
2 tablespoons olive oil
2 tablespoon minced jalapeño
6 cloves garlic, minced
1 tablespoon chopped fresh cilantro
¼ teaspoon salt
1 pound (454 g) flank or sirloin steak

Dressing:
1 avocado, halved, pitted, and peeled
3 tablespoons extra-virgin olive oil
1 tablespoon minced jalapeño
1 tablespoon fresh lime juice
2 tablespoons chopped fresh cilantro
⅛ teaspoon ground cumin
¼ teaspoon salt
½ cup water

Salad:
6 cups mixed salad greens
¼ cup sliced radishes
1 cup halved grape or cherry tomatoes
½ cup coarsely chopped green bell pepper
¼ cup sliced green onions

1. Make the steak: In a slow cooker, combine the orange, lemon, and lime juices, olive oil, jalapeño, garlic, cilantro, and salt. Place the steak in the slow cooker; turn to coat both sides.
2. Cover and cook for 4 hours on low or 2 hours on high, turning the steak once halfway through cooking. Transfer the steak to a cutting board; tent with foil while preparing the salad dressing.
3. Make the dressing: In a food processor, combine the avocado, olive oil, jalapeño, lime juice, cilantro, cumin, and salt. Process until smooth. Continue to process, slowly adding water until the dressing reaches the desired consistency.
4. Assemble the salad: Arrange the salad greens, radishes, tomatoes, and bell pepper on four serving plates. Slice the steak thinly and add to the salads. Drizzle with the avocado dressing and top with sliced green onions.

Fattoush

Prep time: 20 minutes | Cook time: 0 minutes | Serves 3 or 4

Vinaigrette:
¼ cup extra-virgin olive oil
Juice of ½ lemon
1 tablespoon red wine vinegar
1 garlic clove, finely chopped
1 teaspoon ground sumac
1 teaspoon dried parsley
¼ teaspoon kosher salt, plus more as needed
⅛ teaspoon freshly ground black pepper, plus more as needed

Salad:
2 heads romaine lettuce, coarsely chopped into 2-inch pieces
6 radishes, thinly sliced into rounds
3 Persian cucumbers, sliced into thin half-moons
2 vine-ripened tomatoes, cut into 1-inch pieces
½ red onion, thinly sliced
12 fresh mint leaves, thinly sliced
¼ cup loosely packed fresh parsley leaves, coarsely chopped

1. Make the vinaigrette: In a mason jar, combine the olive oil, lemon juice, vinegar, garlic, sumac, parsley, salt, and pepper. Cover tightly with a lid and shake until combined. Taste and adjust the salt and pepper as desired.
2. Make the salad: In a large bowl, combine the lettuce, radishes, cucumbers, tomatoes, onion, mint, and parsley. Drizzle the vinaigrette over the top and toss to coat. Let sit for 10 to 15 minutes before serving.

Oregano Chicken Breast and Kale Salad

Prep time: 20 minutes | Cook time: 6 hours | Serves 6

Chicken:
3 bone-in, skin-on chicken breast halves
3 sprigs fresh oregano
2 teaspoons grated orange zest
2 cloves garlic, minced
1½ teaspoons dried oregano
½ teaspoon salt
½ teaspoon black pepper
¼ cup fresh orange juice
2 tablespoons extra-virgin olive oil

Dressing:
2 tablespoons red wine vinegar
1 tablespoon fresh orange juice
½ teaspoon salt
½ teaspoon black pepper
3 tablespoons extra-virgin olive oil
½ cup thinly sliced red onion
1 bunch kale, stems removed and torn into bite-size pieces

1. Make the chicken: Use your fingers to loosen the skin from the meat of the chicken but do not remove the skin. Place an oregano sprig underneath the skin of each breast half. In a small bowl, combine the orange zest, minced garlic, oregano, salt, and pepper; rub over the chicken. Place the chicken in a slow cooker. Drizzle with the orange juice, then the olive oil.
2. Cover and cook on low for 6 to 7 hours or on high for 3 to 3½ hours. Remove the chicken; let cool until easy to handle. Remove the chicken from the bones; discard the skin, bones, and herb sprigs. Use two forks to shred the chicken. Moisten the chicken with the cooking liquid.
3. Make the dressing: Meanwhile, in a small bowl, combine the vinegar, orange juice, salt, and pepper. Whisk in the olive oil. Add the onion; cover and let stand for at least 1 hour.
4. Place the kale in a large bowl. Drizzle with the dressing and toss to coat. Add the chicken and toss to combine (the kale will wilt slightly).

Chicken Thighs Taco Salad

Prep time: 15 minutes | Cook time: 5 hours | Serves 4

1 tablespoon minced fresh cilantro
1 teaspoon grated lime zest
¼ cup fresh lime juice
½ teaspoon salt
1 medium onion, cut into wedges
1½ pounds (680 g) bone-in chicken thighs, skin removed
1 tablespoon chili powder
1 teaspoon ground cumin
2 tablespoons extra-virgin olive oil
8 cups torn romaine lettuce
1 medium tomato, chopped
1 avocado, halved, pitted, peeled, and thinly sliced
Chopped fresh cilantro, for serving (optional)

1. In a small bowl, combine the cilantro, lime zest, lime juice, and salt until well blended. Divide the lime juice mixture into two small bowls; set aside.
2. In a slow cooker, layer the onion and chicken thighs. To one of the bowls of the lime juice mixture, add the chili powder and cumin and pour over the chicken and onions. Cover and refrigerate the remaining lime juice mixture for the dressing.
3. Cover and cook on low for 5 to 6 hours or on high for 2½ to 3 hours. Transfer the chicken and onions to a cutting board. Using two forks, pull the chicken apart into large shreds.
4. Meanwhile, whisk the olive oil into the reserved lime juice mixture until well combined.
5. Layer the lettuce, chicken, onions, tomato, and avocado on serving plates. Drizzle with the dressing and top with cilantro, if desired.

Pork and Olives Greek Salad

Prep time: 10 minutes | Cook time: 10 minutes | Serves 4

Pork:
- 1 pound (454 g) ground pork
- 1 teaspoon Greek seasoning

Salad:
- 3 tablespoons red wine vinegar
- 1 or 2 cloves garlic, minced
- 1 teaspoon Greek seasoning
- ½ cup thinly sliced red onion
- ½ cup sliced pitted Kalamata olives
- ¼ cup extra-virgin olive oil
- 8 cups chopped romaine lettuce
- 1 medium cucumber, chopped

1. Cook the pork: In a large nonstick skillet, cook the pork and Greek seasoning over medium-high heat, stirring occasionally, until browned and crispy, 6 to 8 minutes. Turn off the heat. Stir in the red onion and olives. Let stand for 2 minutes to soften the onion.
2. Make the salad: Meanwhile, in a small bowl, combine the vinegar, garlic, and Greek seasoning. Whisk in the olive oil until well combined.
3. Layer the lettuce, cucumber, and pork in bowls. Drizzle with the dressing and serve.

Chimichurri Pork Shoulder and Cabbage Salad

Prep time: 30 minutes | Cook time: 9 hours | Serves 6

- 1 teaspoon salt
- 1 teaspoon garlic powder
- 1 teaspoon ground cumin
- 1 teaspoon black pepper
- 2½ to 3 pounds (1.1 to 1.4 kg) boneless pork shoulder, trimmed and cut into 3 pieces
- 1 cup packed fresh cilantro, large stems removed, plus extra for serving
- 1 cup packed fresh flat-leaf parsley, large stems removed, plus extra for serving
- ¼ cup chopped shallots
- 3 cloves garlic, chopped
- ¼ cup plus 3 tablespoons extra-virgin olive oil
- 3 tablespoons white wine vinegar
- ¼ teaspoon red pepper flakes
- 8 cups coarsely shredded cored savoy or green cabbage
- 1 cup purchased shredded carrots
- ½ cup thinly sliced green onion tops
- ½ cup unsulfured golden raisins
- 3 tablespoons fresh lemon juice
- 3 tablespoons extra-virgin olive oil
- ½ cup chopped walnuts or pecans, toasted

1. In a small bowl, combine ½ teaspoon of the salt, the garlic powder, cumin, and pepper. Sprinkle all over the pork pieces; rub in with your fingers. Place the pork in a slow cooker. Add ½ cup water.
2. Cover and cook on low for 9 to 10 hours or on high for 4½ to 5 hours. Transfer the pork to a cutting board; cool for about 10 minutes. Using two forks, coarsely shred the pork; transfer to a large bowl.
3. Meanwhile, in a blender or food processor, combine the cilantro, parsley, shallots, garlic, ¼ cup of the olive oil, the vinegar, and red pepper flakes. Cover and blend or process until almost smooth. Pour over the shredded pork and stir to combine. Set aside.
4. In a large bowl, toss together the cabbage, carrots, green onion tops, and raisins. In a small bowl, whisk together the remaining 3 tablespoons olive oil, remaining ½ teaspoon salt, and the lemon juice. Pour over the cabbage salad and toss to coat. Stir in the pork. Sprinkle with the walnuts and additional cilantro and/or parsley.

Mediterranean Chicken and Veggie Salad

Prep time: 15 minutes | Cook time: 5 hours | Serves 4

Dressing:
- ½ cup extra-virgin olive oil
- ¼ cup fresh lemon juice
- 2 cloves garlic, minced
- 2 teaspoons Whole30-compliant Italian seasoning
- ¼ teaspoon salt

Chicken and Salad:
- 1 pound (454 g) bone-in, skinless chicken thighs
- 1 medium red onion, cut into wedges
- 8 cups torn romaine lettuce
- 1 red bell pepper, chopped
- 1 medium cucumber, chopped
- ¼ cup sliced pitted Whole30-compliant Kalamata olives

1. Make the dressing: In a small bowl, combine the olive oil, lemon juice, garlic, Italian seasoning, and salt until well blended; set aside.
2. Make the chicken: In a slow cooker, layer the chicken and onion. Pour half the dressing over the chicken and onions. Cover and refrigerate the remaining dressing.
3. Cover and cook on low for 5 to 6 hours or on high for 2½ to 3 hours. Transfer the chicken and onions to a cutting board. Using two forks, pull the chicken apart into large shreds.
4. Arrange the lettuce, chicken and onion, bell pepper, cucumber, and olives on serving plates. Drizzle with the reserved dressing.

Potato Salad with Chicken Sausage

Prep time: 20 minutes | Cook time: 5 hours | Serves 4

1½ pounds (680 g) small red potatoes, sliced ¼-inch thick
1 small sweet onion, chopped
2 stalks celery, chopped
1 green bell pepper, chopped
2 slices Whole30-compliant bacon, chopped into 1-inch pieces
1 tablespoon olive oil
½ teaspoon salt
½ teaspoon black pepper
1½ packages (24 ounces / 680 g total) Whole30-compliant chicken-apple sausage, halved
¼ cup Whole30-compliant chicken broth
3 tablespoons cider vinegar
¼ cup chopped Whole30-compliant dill pickles
3 tablespoons chopped fresh dill
6 cups baby spinach

1. In a slow cooker, combine the potatoes, onion, celery, bell pepper, bacon, olive oil, salt, and pepper. Add the sausages and broth. Cover and cook on low for 5 to 6 hours or on high for 2½ to 3 hours, until the potatoes are tender.
2. Remove the sausages from the slow cooker; cover to keep warm. Add the vinegar, pickles, and dill to the potato mixture in the cooker; toss to combine.
3. Divide the spinach among four serving bowls; top each with some of the potato mixture and three sausage halves.

Steak Salad with Charred Onions

Prep time: 15 minutes | Cook time: 20 minutes | Serves 4

Steak and Onions:
1 flank steak or skirt steak (16 to 20 ounces / 454 to 567 g)
1 tablespoon cumin seeds, lightly crushed

Dressing:
¾ cup Whole30-compliant mayonnaise
Grated zest and juice of 1 lime
2 teaspoons Whole30-compliant hot sauce
8 cups chopped
1 teaspoon salt
1 teaspoon black pepper
1 large onion
2 tablespoons extra-virgin olive oil

butterhead or iceberg lettuce
2 avocadoes, halved, pitted, peeled, and diced
Chopped fresh cilantro, for serving

1. Preheat a grill to medium-high heat or a grill pan over medium-high heat.
2. Grill the steak and onions: Season the steak with the cumin seeds, salt, and pepper. Cut the onion into ½-inch-thick slices. Drizzle the steak and onions with the olive oil.
3. Grill the steak and onion slices over direct heat, turning once, until the onion is lightly charred, 5 to 6 minutes, and the steak is cooked to desired doneness, 15 to 20 minutes for medium (160°F / 71°C). Remove the steak and onion and let rest for 5 minutes.
4. Make the dressing: Meanwhile, in a small bowl, combine the mayonnaise, lime zest and juice, and hot sauce.
5. Thinly slice the steak against the grain and coarsely chop the onions. Place the lettuce in a serving bowl and top with the steak and onions. Drizzle the dressing over the salad. Top with the avocado and cilantro.

Turkey Meatball and Lemon-Avocado Salad

Prep time: 15 minutes | Cook time: 20 minutes | Serves 2

Meatballs:
1 large egg
¼ cup almond flour
3 cloves garlic, minced
1 teaspoon dried oregano, crushed
½ teaspoon salt
¼ teaspoon black pepper
8 ounces (227 g) ground turkey

Lemon-Avocado Salad:
½ small avocado, pitted and peeled
¼ cup unsweetened flax milk or Whole30-compliant coconut milk
1 to 2 tablespoons fresh lemon juice
1 clove garlic, minced
¼ teaspoon salt
⅛ teaspoon black pepper
2 tablespoons chopped fresh mint
1 (9-ounce / 255-g) bag hearts of romaine
½ English cucumber, sliced, slices quartered
⅔ cup drained roasted red pepper, patted dry and chopped

1. Make the meatballs: Preheat the oven to 400°F (205°C). Line a baking pan with parchment paper.
2. In a medium bowl, whisk the egg until lightly beaten. Stir in the almond flour, garlic, oregano, salt, and black pepper. Add the ground turkey and gently mix to combine. Shape the mixture into 8 meatballs and place on the pan. Bake for 18 to 20 minutes, until the internal temperature is 165°F (74°C).
3. Make the lemon-avocado salad: Meanwhile, in a blender combine the avocado, flax milk, lemon juice, garlic, salt, and black pepper. Cover and blend until smooth. Transfer the dressing to a small bowl and stir in the mint.
4. Arrange the romaine on serving plates. Top with the cucumber, roasted pepper, and meatballs. Drizzle with the dressing and serve.

Chicken Larb Salad

Prep time: 20 minutes | Cook time: 5 hours | Serves 4

½ cup Whole30-compliant chicken broth
1½ pounds (680 g) boneless, skinless chicken thighs, cut into ½-inch pieces
½ cup minced shallots
1 stalk lemongrass, bruised
1 Thai chile pepper, seeded (if desired) and finely chopped
4 tablespoons fresh lime juice
3 teaspoons Whole30-compliant fish sauce
½ teaspoon salt
2 green onions, thinly sliced
¼ cup chopped fresh mint, plus extra for serving
2 tablespoons chopped fresh cilantro, plus extra for serving
1 (5-ounce / 142-g) package mixed salad greens
2 medium carrots, peeled and cut into matchsticks
½ English cucumber, sliced

1. In a slow cooker, combine the broth, chicken, shallots, lemongrass, Thai chile, 2 tablespoons of the lime juice, 2 teaspoons of the fish sauce, and the salt.
2. Cover and cook on low for 5 to 6 hours or on high for 2½ to 3 hours. Remove and discard the lemongrass.
3. Use a slotted spoon to transfer the chicken to a medium bowl. (Discard the cooking liquid.) Add the remaining 2 tablespoons lime juice, remaining 1 teaspoon fish sauce, the green onions, mint, and cilantro to the chicken.
4. Top the greens with the chicken mixture, carrots, cucumber, and additional cilantro and mint. Serve.

Warm Chicken Romaine Salad

Prep time: 20 minutes | Cook time: 4 hours | Serves 4

4 green onions
2½ pounds (1.1 kg) bone-in chicken thighs, skin removed
½ cup Whole30-compliant chicken broth
3 cloves garlic, minced
1 medium red bell pepper, diced
2 stalks celery, thinly sliced
1 tablespoon Whole30-compliant Dijon mustard
2 tablespoons cider vinegar
½ cup Whole30-compliant mayonnaise
1 (16-ounce / 454-g) package hearts of romaine, chopped

1. Thinly slice the green onions; separate the white bottoms from the green tops. In a slow cooker, combine the green onion whites, chicken, broth, and garlic.
2. Cover and cook on low for 4 hours or on high for 2 hours. Add the bell pepper and celery. Turn the slow cooker to high if using low setting. Cover and cook for 20 to 30 minutes, or until the pepper and celery are tender. Using a slotted spoon, transfer the chicken, pepper, and celery to a large bowl.
3. Let the chicken cool slightly. Remove the chicken from the bones; discard the bones. Use two forks to shred the chicken. Stir the mustard, vinegar, and mayonnaise into the shredded chicken.
4. Arrange the lettuce on four plates; top with the warm chicken salad. Sprinkle with the reserved sliced green onion tops.

Chicken, Watermelon, and Spinach Salad

Prep time: 15 minutes | Cook time: 10 minutes | Serves 2

Chicken:
2 boneless, skinless chicken breasts (about 6 ounces / 170 g each)
1 teaspoon red pepper flakes
½ teaspoon garlic powder
½ teaspoon salt
½ teaspoon black pepper
2 tablespoons extra-virgin olive oil

Salad:
4 cups baby spinach
2 cups chopped seedless watermelon
¼ cup finely chopped shallot
3 tablespoons extra-virgin olive oil
2 tablespoons red wine vinegar
½ teaspoon salt
½ teaspoon black pepper
⅓ cup roasted salted pistachios, chopped

1. Make the chicken: Place the chicken breasts between two pieces of plastic wrap and use the flat side of a meat mallet to flatten to a ¼-inch thickness. (You can ask your butcher to do this for you.) Combine the pepper flakes, garlic powder, salt, and pepper in a small bowl. Sprinkle the seasoning over the chicken.
2. Heat the olive oil in a large skillet over medium-high heat. Add the chicken and cook, turning once, until browned and cooked through, about 8 minutes. Place the chicken on a cutting board and let rest for 5 minutes. Thinly slice the chicken.
3. Make the salad: Combine the spinach, watermelon, and shallot in a large bowl. Drizzle with the olive oil and vinegar. Sprinkle with the salt and black pepper. Toss the salad to coat with the dressing.
4. Arrange the salad on two serving plates. Top with the sliced chicken, sprinkle with the pistachios, and serve.

Fruity Chicken Chopped Salad

Prep time: 10 minutes | Cook time: 0 minutes | Serves 2

Dressing:
2 tablespoons fresh orange juice
1 tablespoon white wine vinegar
¼ cup extra-virgin olive oil
⅛ teaspoon salt
⅛ teaspoon black pepper

Salad:
1 medium orange, peeled and white pith removed
6 cups chopped romaine lettuce
1½ cups coarsely chopped cooked chicken
¼ cup pomegranate seeds
¼ cup coarsely chopped roasted cashews
2 green onions, sliced

1. Make the dressing: In a small bowl, whisk together the orange juice, vinegar, olive oil, salt, and pepper.
2. Make the salad: Divide the orange into segments. Arrange the lettuce in serving bowls. Top with the orange segments, chicken, pomegranate seeds, cashews, and green onions. Drizzle with the dressing and serve.

Italian Chopped Salad with Grated Yolk

Prep time: 20 minutes | Cook time: 5 minutes | Serves 4

For the Dressing:
¼ cup red wine vinegar
½ cup extra-virgin olive oil
2 teaspoons Italian seasoning (check label for compliance if doing Whole30)
2 teaspoons red pepper flakes
½ teaspoon kosher salt

For the Salad:
1 tablespoon extra-virgin olive oil
12 ounces (340 g) precooked Italian sausages, quartered lengthwise and chopped
12 ounces (340 g) romaine lettuce, chopped
2 slices prosciutto (check label for compliance if doing Whole30), rolled lengthwise and thinly sliced crosswise into small ribbons
12 jarred pepperoncini, stemmed and cut in half lengthwise
½ cup sliced hearts of palm
½ cup quartered artichoke hearts, sliced into strips
¼ cup small olives, such as Niçoise or Kalamata
¾ cup Marinated red onion
Yolks from 4 large hard-boiled eggs, grated (optional)

For the Dressing
1. Put the vinegar in a medium bowl. While whisking continuously, slowly add the olive oil and whisk until emulsified. Add the Italian seasoning, red pepper flakes, and salt and whisk until combined well. Set aside.

For the Salad
1. In a medium sauté pan, heat the olive oil over medium-high heat. Add the sausages and cook, stirring, until golden brown, 5 to 7 minutes. Set aside.
2. On a large platter, make a bed of the lettuce, then arrange the sausages, prosciutto, pepperoncini, hearts of palm, artichokes, and olives in separate mounds on top.
3. Top with the marinated onions, the dressing, and the grated egg yolks, if desired, and serve. (Alternatively, toss all the ingredients together in a large bowl as you would a traditional chopped salad and serve with the grated egg yolk over the top.)

Ahi Tuna Mango Poke

Prep time: 20 minutes | Cook time: 0 minutes | Serves 4

Dressing:
3 tablespoons coconut aminos
1 tablespoon rice vinegar
1 teaspoon olive oil
1 teaspoon grated fresh ginger
¼ teaspoon salt
⅛ teaspoon black pepper

Salad:
1½ pounds (680 g) sushi-grade ahi tuna, cut into bite-sized pieces
1 (5-ounce / 142-g) package baby spinach
1 ripe avocado, halved, pitted, peeled, and chopped
1 ripe mango, pitted, peeled, and chopped
1 small unpeeled cucumber, sliced
1 cup packaged shredded carrots, or 2 medium carrots, shredded
Black sesame seeds (optional)
Sliced green onions (optional)

1. Make the dressing: In a small bowl, stir together the dressing ingredients.
2. Make the salad: In a medium bowl, gently toss the tuna with 2 tablespoons of the dressing to coat. Let stand and marinate while you assemble the salads.
3. Divide the spinach among four plates. Arrange the avocado, mango, cucumber, and carrots on the spinach. Top with the marinated tuna and drizzle the salads with the remaining dressing. Top with black sesame seeds and sliced green onions, if desired, and serve.

Mayo Chicken Salad

Prep time: 15 minutes | Cook time: 0 minutes | Serves 3 to 4

½ cup Whole30-compliant mayonnaise
1 tablespoon fresh lime juice
2 tablespoons fresh cilantro
2 teaspoons Whole30-compliant curry powder
¼ teaspoon salt
2 cups diced cooked chicken
½ medium apple, diced
1 celery stalk, finely diced
3 tablespoons finely diced red onion
¼ cup roughly chopped Whole30-compliant dry-roasted cashews
Sliced green onions, shredded cabbage, shredded carrots, and/or chopped cashews (optional)

1. In a medium bowl, stir together the mayonnaise, lime juice, cilantro, curry powder, and salt. Add the chicken, apple, celery, and onion and toss to coat. Fold in the cashews. If desired, top the salad with green onions, cabbage, carrots, and/or additional cashews.

Beef Taco Salad

Prep time: 15 minutes | Cook time: 2 hours | Serves 6

1½ pounds (680 g) lean ground beef
1 medium white onion, diced
2 cloves garlic, minced
2 Anaheim chile peppers, seeded and finely chopped
1 tablespoon ground cumin
1 teaspoon dried oregano
1 teaspoon chili powder
1 teaspoon coriander
1 teaspoon salt
1 teaspoon black pepper
1 (10-ounce / 283-g) bag chopped romaine or 1 head romaine lettuce, chopped
3 green onions, sliced
2 tomatoes, diced
2 jalapeños, seeded if desired, and sliced
Whole30-compliant salsa (optional)
¼ cup chopped fresh cilantro (optional)
2 limes, cut into wedges

1. In a large skillet, cook the beef, onion, and garlic over medium-high heat, stirring with a wooden spoon to break up the beef, until no longer pink, 5 to 8 minutes. Use a slotted spoon to transfer to a slow cooker. Add the Anaheim chiles, cumin, oregano, chili powder, coriander, salt, and pepper. Stir to combine.
2. Cover and cook on high for 2 hours.
3. Serve the taco meat on top of the chopped lettuce. Top servings with green onions, tomatoes, and jalapeños, along with salsa and cilantro, if desired. Serve with the lime wedges.

Balsamic Peach Arugula Salad

Prep time: 20 minutes | Cook time: 15 minutes | Serves 8

Peaches and Vegetables:
3 ripe peaches, peeled and sliced, or 1 (16-ounce / 454-g) bag frozen peaches, thawed
2 tablespoons clarified butter or ghee, melted
2 tablespoons balsamic vinegar
1 small red onion, thinly sliced into rings
2 teaspoons extra-virgin olive oil
¼ teaspoon salt
¼ teaspoon black pepper
24 thin asparagus spears, trimmed

Arugula Salad:
½ cup balsamic vinegar
3 (5-ounce / 142-g) containers baby arugula
3 tablespoons extra-virgin olive oil
½ teaspoon salt
¼ teaspoon pepper
½ cup coarsely chopped roasted pistachios

1. Preheat the oven to 425°F (220°C). Line two large rimmed baking pans with parchment paper.
2. Make the peaches and vegetables: Arrange the peach slices on half of one pan; brush with the butter. Drizzle vinegar over the slices. Arrange the onion on the other half of the pan. Drizzle with 1 teaspoon olive oil. Sprinkle with ⅛ teaspoon each salt and pepper. Roast for 5 minutes.
3. Meanwhile, arrange the asparagus on the other pan. Drizzle with 1 teaspoon olive oil. Sprinkle with the remaining ⅛ teaspoon each salt and pepper. Add the asparagus to the oven. Stir the onions. Roast both pans 10 minutes more.
4. Make the arugula salad: Meanwhile, in a small saucepan, bring the vinegar to a boil over medium-high heat. Reduce the heat to medium-low and simmer until reduced by half, 8 to 10 minutes. Cool completely.
5. Place the arugula in an extra-large bowl. Drizzle with the olive oil and sprinkle with ½ teaspoon salt and ¼ teaspoon pepper; toss to coat.
6. Divide the arugula, asparagus, peaches, and onions among 8 salad plates. Drizzle the salads with about 1 teaspoon of the reduced vinegar. Sprinkle with the pistachios.

Tuna, Snow Pea, and Broccoli Salad

Prep time: 10 minutes | Cook time: 0 minutes | Serves 4

Dressing:
1 teaspoon grated orange zest
3 tablespoons extra-virgin olive oil
3 tablespoons rice vinegar

Salad:
1 orange, peeled and cut into bite-size pieces
1 (12-ounce / 340-g) bag broccoli slaw
1 (8-ounce / 227-g) package fresh snow peas, trimmed and halved diagonally
2 (5-ounce / 142-g) cans water-packed wild albacore tuna, drained and broken into chunks

1. Make the dressing: In a small bowl, combine the orange zest, olive oil, and vinegar.
2. Make the salad: In a large bowl, combine the orange pieces with the broccoli slaw, snow peas, and tuna. Drizzle with the dressing and gently toss.

Shrimp and Mango Salad

Prep time: 15 minutes | Cook time: 5 minutes | Serves 2

Dressing:
½ teaspoon grated lime zest
2 tablespoons fresh lime juice
¼ cup extra-virgin olive oil
1 tablespoon chopped fresh cilantro
2 teaspoons finely chopped seeded jalapeño
⅛ teaspoon salt

Salad:
1 tablespoon extra-virgin olive oil
8 ounces (227 g) peeled and deveined large shrimp
1 teaspoon chili powder
⅛ teaspoon salt
6 cups torn Bibb lettuce leaves
1 medium ripe mango, peeled, pitted, and diced
1 medium ripe avocado, halved, pitted, peeled, and diced

1. Make the dressing: In a small bowl, combine the lime zest and juice. While whisking, drizzle in the olive oil until combined. Stir in the cilantro, jalapeño, and salt.
2. Make the salad: In a large skillet, heat the olive oil over medium-high heat. Add the shrimp, chili powder, and salt. Cook, stirring, until the shrimp are opaque, about 5 minutes.
3. Arrange the lettuce on serving plates. Top with the mango, avocado, and shrimp. Drizzle the salads with the dressing and serve.

Beef Steak and Broccoli Salad

Prep time: 15 minutes | Cook time: 15 minutes | Serves 4

1 pound (454 g) boneless beef sirloin steak or stir-fry meat
½ teaspoon salt
¼ teaspoon black pepper
2 teaspoons grated lemon zest
6 tablespoons Whole30-compliant lemon-garlic dressing
3 cups broccoli florets
1 large orange or red bell pepper, seeded and thinly sliced
1 (9-ounce / 255-g) package spring mix/baby spinach
¼ cup snipped fresh chives

1. Thinly slice the meat across the grain into bite-size pieces and season both sides with the salt, pepper, and lemon zest. In a medium bowl, toss the meat with 2 tablespoons of the dressing.
2. In a large bowl, combine the broccoli, bell pepper, and 3 tablespoons of the dressing. Toss to coat.
3. In a large skillet, cook the broccoli and bell pepper over medium-high heat, stirring, for 3 minutes. Return the vegetables to the large bowl. Add the meat to the hot skillet and cook, stirring, until slightly pink in center, 1 to 2 minutes. Add the vegetables to the skillet and stir to combine with the meat.
4. In a large bowl, toss the greens with the remaining 1 tablespoon dressing. Serve the meat and vegetables over the greens. Sprinkle the salad with the snipped chives.

Chapter 10 Soups, Stews, and Noodle Bowls

Chili Beef with Sweet Potato

Prep time: 15 minutes | Cook time: 4 hours | Serves 6

1½ pounds (680 g) lean ground beef
1 medium red onion, chopped
1 poblano pepper, seeded and diced
4 cups large sweet potatoes, peeled and cut into ½-inch cubes
1 (10¾-ounce / 304.8-g) can Whole30-compliant tomato puree
1 (15-ounce / 425.2-g) can Whole30-compliant crushed tomatoes
2 cups Whole30-compliant tomato juice
2 tablespoons cider vinegar
1 tablespoon chili powder
1½ teaspoons smoked paprika
1 teaspoon cumin
1 teaspoon garlic powder
½ teaspoon allspice
¼ teaspoon cayenne pepper
1 teaspoon smoked salt or regular salt
Finely chopped red onion (optional)

1. In a large skillet, cook the beef over medium-high heat, stirring with a wooden spoon, until browned, about 10 minutes. Drain off the fat.
2. Transfer the beef to a 4- to 5-quart slow cooker. Add the onion, poblano pepper, sweet potatoes, tomato puree, crushed tomatoes, tomato juice, vinegar, chili powder, smoked paprika, cumin, garlic powder, allspice, cayenne, and salt to the cooker. Stir to combine.
3. Cover and cook on low for 8 hours or on high for 4 hours.
4. If desired, top servings with chopped onions.

Brazilian Cod and Shrimp Stew

Prep time: 20 minutes | Cook time: 25 minutes | Serves 4

For the Seasoning and Seafood:
1 teaspoon smoked paprika
½ teaspoon salt
½ teaspoon garlic powder
½ teaspoon ground cumin
¼ teaspoon ground coriander
1 pound (454 g) red snapper, halibut, or cod fillets, cut into 1-inch pieces
1 pound (454 g) peeled and deveined medium shrimp

For the Stew:
2 tablespoons extra-virgin olive oil
1 medium yellow onion, chopped
2 cloves garlic, minced
1 red bell pepper, sliced into matchsticks
1 (10-ounce / 283-g) package frozen sweet potatoes
1 (14-ounce / 397-g) can Whole30-compliant fire-roasted diced tomatoes, undrained
1 (13½-ounce / 383-g) can Whole30-compliant coconut milk
½ teaspoon red pepper flakes
2 teaspoons sweet paprika
1 lime, cut into wedges

1. Season the seafood: In a small bowl, combine the smoked paprika, salt, garlic powder, cumin, and coriander. Place the cod and shrimp in a large bowl and sprinkle with the seasoning. Set aside.
2. Make the stew: On a 6-quart Instant Pot, select Sauté and adjust to Normal/Medium. Add the olive oil to the pot. When it's hot, add the onion and garlic and cook, stirring occasionally, until the onion is softened, about 2 minutes. Press Cancel.
3. Add the bell pepper, sweet potatoes, tomatoes, coconut milk, red pepper flakes, and sweet paprika; stir. Add the fish and shrimp to the pot. Stir gently. Lock the lid in place.
4. Select Manual and cook on high pressure for 2 minutes. Use quick release.
5. Serve the stew with lime wedges.

Curry Pork and Carrot Noodle Bowls

Prep time: 15 minutes | Cook time: 15 minutes | Serves 4

2½ pounds (1.1 kg) Whole30-compliant boneless pork shoulder, trimmed and cut into 1-inch pieces
¾ teaspoon salt
½ teaspoon black pepper
2 tablespoons coconut oil
1 (13½-ounce / 383-g) can Whole30-compliant coconut milk
¼ cup Whole30-compliant green curry paste
1 small onion, chopped
2 medium red, yellow, or green bell peppers, chopped
1 piece (1 inch) fresh ginger, peeled and grated
3 cloves garlic, minced
1 (12-ounce / 340-g) package frozen carrot spirals or 4 large carrots, spiralized, long noodles snipped
¼ cup unsweetened shredded coconut, lightly toasted
¼ cup chopped fresh cilantro or basil
1 lime, cut into wedges

1. Sprinkle the pork with the salt and pepper. In a 6-quart Instant Pot, use the Sauté setting and heat 1 tablespoon of the coconut oil. Add half the pork and cook until browned, about 5 minutes. Transfer the pork to a plate. Repeat with the remaining 1 tablespoon oil and pork. Return all the pork to the pot. Add the coconut milk, curry paste, onion, bell pepper, ginger, and garlic.
2. Lock the lid in place. Select Manual and cook for 10 minutes on high pressure. Use natural release. Stir in the carrot noodles. Cover and let sit for 5 minutes to soften the noodles.
3. Spoon the curry into bowls, top with lightly toasted coconut and cilantro or basil, and serve with lime wedges.

Thai Chicken and Potato-Noodle Bowls

Prep time: 10 minutes | Cook time: 3 minutes | Serves 4

For the Cashew-Coconut Cream:
1 cup raw unsalted cashews
¾ cup Whole30-compliant coconut milk
⅛ teaspoon salt

For the Sweet Potato Noodles and Chicken:
6 cups Whole30-compliant chicken or vegetable broth or chicken bone broth
¼ teaspoon salt
1 (10-ounce / 283-g) package sweet potato spirals or 1 medium sweet potato, spiralized
1 medium red bell pepper, seeded and cut into bite-size pieces
½ jalapeño, seeded and finely chopped
3 cups shredded cooked chicken breast
1 cup coarsely chopped fresh basil and/or mint

Make the Cashew-Coconut Cream
1. Rinse the cashews and drain. Place in a bowl and add enough water to cover by 1 inch. Cover the bowl and let stand for 4 hours or up to overnight. Drain the cashews and rinse under cold water. Place the cashews, coconut milk, and salt in a high-speed blender. Cover and blend until smooth. Add cold water, 1 tablespoon at a time, to reach drizzling consistency.

Make the Sweet Potato Noodles and Chicken
1. In a large saucepan, bring the broth and salt to a boil. Add the sweet potato, bell pepper, and jalapeño and simmer for 3 minutes. Remove from the heat and stir in the chicken. Let stand until heated through, 2 minutes.
2. Divide the herbs among four bowls. Ladle the soup over the herbs. Drizzle each with about 1 tablespoon of the cashew-coconut cream.

Steak, Mushrooms, and Rutabaga-Noodle Bowls

Prep time: 15 minutes | Cook time: 10 minutes | Serves 6

1½ pounds (680 g) beef stir-fry strips
2 teaspoons Whole30-compliant Italian seasoning
½ teaspoon salt
½ teaspoon black pepper
2 tablespoons olive oil
1 (14-ounce / 397-g) bag frozen bell pepper and onion blend
4 cups Whole30-compliant beef broth or Beef Bone Broth
1 (14½-ounce / 411-g) can Whole30-compliant diced tomatoes with garlic and onion
2 portobello mushrooms, gills removed, halved and sliced
1 medium rutabaga, spiralized or diced
1 cup fresh basil leaves

1. Season the meat with the Italian seasoning, salt, and pepper. Heat 1 tablespoon of the olive oil over medium-high heat in a large pot. Add half of the meat and cook, stirring occasionally, until browned but still pink in the center, 2 to 3 minutes. Transfer the meat to a bowl. Add the remaining 1 tablespoon olive oil to the pot and cook the remaining meat. Transfer the meat to the bowl.
2. Add the frozen bell pepper and onion blend to the pot. Cook over medium heat, stirring occasionally, until tender, 3 to 4 minutes. Add the broth and tomatoes and bring to a boil.
3. Add the mushrooms and rutabaga noodles and bring to a low boil. Cook until the mushrooms and rutabaga are just tender, 6 to 7 minutes. Return the meat to the pot, stir in the basil, and serve.

Smoky Scallop and Zucchini Noodle Bowls

Prep time: 10 minutes | Cook time: 8 minutes | Serves 2

1 pound (454 g) small sea scallops
1 tablespoon smoked paprika
½ teaspoon salt
2 tablespoons clarified butter, ghee, or extra-virgin olive oil
2 cloves garlic, sliced
2 cups cherry tomatoes
1 cup Whole30-compliant chicken broth or chicken bone broth
1 tablespoon fresh lemon juice
2 (11-ounce / 311.8-g) packages zucchini noodles; or 2 medium zucchini, spiralized, long noodles snipped if desired
1 tablespoon chopped fresh parsley

1. Rinse the scallops and pat dry with a paper towel. Sprinkle the paprika and salt on the scallops. In a large heavy skillet, heat 1 tablespoon of the butter over medium-high heat. Add the scallops and sear on each side for 1 minute. (The scallops will not be cooked through at this point.) Remove the scallops from the skillet and cover to keep warm.
2. Add the garlic and tomatoes to the skillet and cook over medium-high heat, stirring, until the tomatoes are lightly charred and start to burst, about 3 minutes. Add the broth, lemon juice, and scallops and cook until the scallops are just cooked, about 2 minutes.
3. Meanwhile, in a large skillet, cook the zucchini noodles in the remaining 1 tablespoon butter until just tender, 1 to 2 minutes. Serve the scallops, tomatoes, and broth over the noodles in bowls. Top with the fresh parsley and serve.

Mexican Shrimp and Zucchini Noodles Soup

Prep time: 15 minutes | Cook time: 12 minutes | Serves 4

- 1 tablespoon extra-virgin olive oil
- 1 large onion, chopped
- 2 large jalapeños, seeded and finely chopped
- ¼ teaspoon kosher salt
- ¼ cup Whole30-compliant tomato paste
- 1 tablespoon Whole30-compliant Mexican seasoning or chili powder
- 5 cups Whole30-compliant chicken broth or chicken bone broth
- 1 pound (454 g) peeled and deveined small shrimp
- 1 (11-ounce / 311.8-g) package zucchini noodles; or 2 small zucchini, spiralized, long noodles snipped if desired
- 1 cup chopped fresh cilantro
- Chopped avocado
- Lime wedges

1. Heat the olive oil in a 4-quart Dutch oven or stockpot over medium heat. Add the onion, jalapeños, and salt and cook, stirring occasionally, until softened, 6 to 8 minutes. Stir in the tomato paste and Mexican seasoning. Cook, stirring, for 1 minute. Add the broth and bring to a boil.
2. Stir in the shrimp and zucchini noodles. Cook until the shrimp are opaque and the zucchini is crisp-tender, about 5 minutes. Stir in the chopped cilantro. Serve the soup with chopped avocado and lime wedges.

Pork and Carrot-Noodle Bowls

Prep time: 10 minutes | Cook time: 15 minutes | Serves 4

For the Pork:
- 1 pound (454 g) ground pork
- 2 teaspoons toasted sesame oil
- 2 green onions, sliced
- 2 teaspoons minced fresh ginger
- 2 cloves garlic, minced
- ⅛ teaspoon red pepper flakes
- 2 tablespoons coconut aminos

For the Carrot Noodles:
- 4 large carrots, peeled
- 1 tablespoon clarified butter or ghee
- ⅛ teaspoon salt
- Chopped fresh cilantro
- Lime wedges

Make the Pork
1. In a large nonstick skillet, cook the pork over medium-high heat, breaking it up with a wooden spoon, until browned, about 10 minutes. Transfer to a bowl. Drain any fat from the skillet.
2. Heat the sesame oil in the same skillet over medium heat. Add the green onions, ginger, garlic, and pepper flakes. Cook, stirring, until fragrant, 1 to 2 minutes. Stir in the pork and coconut aminos and heat through, about 1 minute.

Make the Carrot Noodles
1. Meanwhile, use a vegetable peeler to cut the carrots lengthwise into long, thin noodles. Heat the butter in a large skillet over medium heat. Add the carrot noodles and salt and cook, stirring occasionally, until just tender, 3 to 4 minutes.
2. Serve the pork mixture on top of the carrot noodles. Top with cilantro and serve with lime wedges.

Vegetable Soup with Basil-Nuts Pesto

Prep time: 30 minutes | Cook time: 15 minutes | Serves 4

Pesto:
- 1 cup lightly packed fresh basil leaves
- ¼ cup roasted almonds or toasted pine nuts
- 1 tablespoon nutritional yeast (optional)
- ¼ teaspoon salt
- ¼ teaspoon black pepper
- 1 clove garlic, chopped
- ⅓ cup extra-virgin olive oil

Soup:
- 1 tablespoon extra-virgin olive oil
- 1 medium onion, chopped
- 1 clove garlic, minced
- 4 cups Whole30-compliant chicken broth or chicken bone broth
- 1 (14½-ounce / 411-g) can Whole30-compliant diced tomatoes, undrained
- ½ pound (227 g) fresh green beans, trimmed and cut into 1-inch pieces
- ½ teaspoon salt
- ¼ teaspoon black pepper
- 2 large, thick carrots, spiralized
- 1 (16-ounce / 454-g) package very small cooked peeled deveined shrimp
- 1 (10.7-ounce / 303-g) package zucchini noodles; or 2 small zucchini, spiralized

1. Make the pesto: In a food processor, combine the basil leaves, almonds, nutritional yeast (if using), salt, pepper, and garlic. Cover and pulse until finely chopped. With the food processor running, add the oil and process until well combined and nearly smooth.
2. Make the soup: In a large pot, heat the olive oil over medium-high heat. Add the onion and garlic and cook, stirring frequently, until the onions are softened, about 3 minutes. Stir the broth, tomatoes, green beans, salt, and pepper into the pot and bring to a boil. Reduce the heat, cover, and simmer until the beans are crisp-tender, about 5 minutes. Add the carrot noodles and cook for 3 minutes. Add the shrimp and the zucchini noodles and cook until noodles are just tender, about 2 minutes more. Ladle the soup into bowls and top with some of the pesto.

Pork Tenderloin and Pepper Paprikash

Prep time: 10 minutes | Cook time: 24 minutes | Serves 4

¾ cup chopped unsalted raw cashews
1¼ pounds (567 g) pork tenderloin, cut into 1-inch pieces
½ teaspoon salt
½ teaspoon black pepper
2 tablespoons extra-virgin olive oil
1 (14.5-ounce / 411.1-g) package frozen pepper stir-fry blend
2 tablespoons sweet paprika
1 teaspoon dried marjoram
3 tablespoons Whole30-compliant tomato paste
4 cups Whole30-compliant chicken broth or chicken bone broth
Chopped fresh parsley

1. For cashew cream, place the cashews in a small bowl and add boiling water to cover. Cover and let stand for 15 minutes. Drain and rinse the cashews. Combine the cashews and ½ cup fresh water in a blender. Puree until smooth, 3 to 4 minutes.
2. Meanwhile, season the pork with the salt and black pepper. In a Dutch oven or large pot, heat the olive oil over medium-high heat. Add the pork and cook, stirring occasionally, until the pork begins to brown, about 5 minutes. Add the pepper stir-fry, paprika, and marjoram. Continue to cook, stirring occasionally, until the peppers are softened, about 5 minutes. Stir in the tomato paste and cook, stirring, 1 minute. Stir in the broth and bring to a boil. Reduce the heat to medium-low and simmer for 10 minutes. Remove from the heat. Stir in the cashew cream. Top each serving with parsley.

Spring Asparagus Cream Soup

Prep time: 10 minutes | Cook time: 24 minutes | Serves 4

2 tablespoons coconut oil
1 medium onion, chopped
2 (1 pound / 454-g) bunches asparagus
5 cups Whole30-compliant chicken broth or chicken bone broth
1 tablespoon chopped fresh tarragon
½ cup Whole30-compliant coconut milk
2 tablespoons fresh lemon juice
½ teaspoon salt
¼ teaspoon black pepper
2 slices Whole30-compliant prosciutto, rolled up and cut into thin ribbons

1. Heat the coconut oil in a large pot over medium heat. Add the onion and cook, stirring occasionally, until tender, about 5 minutes.
2. Meanwhile, cut the tips off the asparagus and set aside. Cut the asparagus stalks into 1-inch pieces, discarding any woody ends. Add the stalk pieces, broth, and tarragon to the onion and bring to a boil. Reduce the heat to low and cook for 15 minutes. Place the asparagus tips in a metal steamer and lower into the broth mixture. Cook, uncovered, just until tender, about 4 minutes. Carefully remove the strainer and run the tips under cold water; set aside. Remove the pot from the heat and stir in the coconut milk and lemon juice.
3. Carefully transfer the soup in batches to a blender, in batches if necessary, and let cool briefly; pulse a few times, then blend until smooth. (Or use an immersion blender to blend the soup directly in the pot.) Season with salt and pepper. Top servings with the asparagus tips and prosciutto ribbons.

Mexican-Style Pork Shoulder Stew

Prep time: 30 minutes | Cook time: 6 hours | Serves 6

1½ teaspoons chipotle powder
1 teaspoon ground cumin
1 teaspoon oregano
1 teaspoon garlic powder
½ teaspoon paprika
1 teaspoon sea salt
½ teaspoon black pepper
2½ to 3 pounds (1.1 to 1.4 kg) pork shoulder or butt roast
1 pound (454 g) baby red potatoes
½ cup chopped onion
4 ounces (113 g) button mushrooms, halved (about 2 cups)
1 (14½-ounce / 411-g) can Whole30-compliant whole tomatoes, drained
1 large zucchini (about 5 ounces / 142 g), halved and cut into 2-inch chunks
2 cups packed chopped spinach
2 tablespoons tapioca flour

1. In a small bowl, combine the chipotle powder, cumin, oregano, garlic powder, paprika, salt, and pepper. Sprinkle half of the seasoning on the pork. Place the pork in a slow cooker. Add ¼ cup water, the potatoes, onion, and mushrooms.
2. In a large bowl, crush the tomatoes with your hands. Add the remaining seasoning mix to the tomatoes; pour into the slow cooker. Cook for 6 hours on low or 3 hours on high, or until the pork and potatoes are tender. Transfer the pork to a platter and keep warm.
3. Turn the slow cooker to high if using the low setting. Stir the zucchini and spinach into the cooking liquid in the slow cooker.
4. In a small bowl, stir the tapioca flour into 2 tablespoons water. Add to the stew and cook, stirring, for 3 minutes. Using two forks, shred the pork and stir it into the stew.

Beef and Root Vegetable Stew

Prep time: 25 minutes | Cook time: 6 hours | Serves 4

- 2 tablespoons extra-virgin olive oil
- 1½ pounds (680 g) beef stew meat, cut into ¾-inch pieces
- 4 medium carrots, peeled and diagonally sliced 1 inch thick
- 8 baby red potatoes, quartered
- 1 medium yellow onion, cut into thin wedges
- 2 cloves garlic, minced
- ½ teaspoon salt
- ½ teaspoon black pepper
- 1 bay leaf
- 2 cups Whole30-compliant beef broth
- 2 cups Whole30-compliant vegetable juice
- 2 tablespoons coconut aminos
- 2 tablespoons tapioca flour (optional for a thicker stew)

1. In a large skillet, heat the olive oil over medium-high heat. Add the beef and cook in batches if necessary, stirring occasionally, until browned on all sides.
2. Transfer the beef to a slow cooker. Add the carrots, potatoes, onion, garlic, salt, pepper, bay leaf, broth, vegetable juice, and coconut aminos; stir to combine. Cover and cook on low for 6 to 8 hours or on high for 3 to 4 hours, or until the beef and vegetables are tender.
3. If using the tapioca flour, turn the slow cooker to high if using the low setting. In a small bowl, stir together the tapioca flour and 2 tablespoons water. Stir into the stew. Cover and cook for 10 minutes. Remove and discard the bay leaf before serving.

Moroccan Beef Meatball Stew

Prep time: 30 minutes | Cook time: 5 hours | Serves 4

- 1 large shallot, finely chopped
- 1 large egg, lightly beaten
- ⅓ cup almond meal
- 1 teaspoon ground cumin
- 1 teaspoon ground coriander
- 1 teaspoon salt
- ½ teaspoon black pepper
- ½ teaspoon ground ginger
- ½ teaspoon ground cinnamon
- 1½ pounds (680 g) ground beef
- 1 onion, chopped
- 2 carrots, peeled and chopped
- 4 cloves garlic, minced
- 1 teaspoon ground turmeric
- 2 (14½-ounce / 411-g) cans Whole30-compliant beef broth
- 1 (14½-ounce / 411-g) can Whole30-compliant diced tomatoes, undrained
- 8 cups chopped greens, such as kale, mustard greens, chard, and/or spinach
- ½ cup chopped fresh cilantro

1. Preheat the oven to 400°F (205°C).
2. In a medium bowl, combine the shallot, egg, almond meal, cumin, coriander, salt, pepper, ginger, and cinnamon. Add the ground beef and mix just until combined. Form into 1½-inch meatballs. Place the meatballs on a foil-lined shallow baking pan. Bake for 10 minutes.
3. In a slow cooker, combine the onion, carrots, garlic, and turmeric. Add the broth and tomatoes. Arrange the meatballs in an even layer in the slow cooker. Cover and cook on low for 5 hours or on high for 2½ hours.
4. Turn the slow cooker to high if using the low setting. Gently stir in the greens. Cover and cook just until the greens are tender, 5 to 10 minutes. Stir in the cilantro just before serving.

Pork Shoulder and Green Chile Stew

Prep time: 10 minutes | Cook time: 1 hour | Serves 6

- 2 pounds (907 g) boneless pork shoulder, cut into 1-inch pieces
- ½ teaspoon coarse salt
- ½ teaspoon black pepper
- 3 tablespoons clarified butter, ghee, or coconut oil
- 1 medium onion, chopped
- 2 cloves garlic, minced
- 4 cups Whole30-compliant chicken broth or chicken bone broth
- 2 (4½-ounce / 128-g) cans chopped green chiles, undrained
- 1 pound (454 g) small red potatoes, cut into ¾-inch pieces
- 1 small red bell pepper, cut into matchsticks
- Snipped fresh cilantro (optional)

1. Season the pork with the salt and black pepper. Heat 1 tablespoon of the butter in a large pot over medium-high heat. Add half of the pork and cook, stirring occasionally, until browned on all sides, about 5 minutes. Transfer the pork to a plate. Add 1 tablespoon butter to the pot and repeat to cook the remaining pork.
2. Add the remaining 1 tablespoon butter to the pot. Add the onion and cook, stirring, until tender, 2 to 3 minutes. Add the garlic and cook, stirring frequently, until fragrant, about 30 seconds. Add the broth, green chiles, and pork, bring to a boil, then reduce the heat to medium-low. Cook, covered, until the pork is tender, about 30 minutes.
3. Add the potatoes and bell pepper to the pot and bring the stew to a boil. Cook, uncovered, until the potatoes are tender and the stew is slightly thickened, 8 to 10 minutes. Top servings with cilantro.

It's never too late to change old habits.

Chicken, Bacon and Mushroom Soup

Prep time: 10 minutes | Cook time: 25 minutes | Serves 4

2 slices Whole30-compliant bacon, chopped
1 (8-ounce / 227-g) package fresh cremini or button mushrooms, sliced
½ cup chopped onion
2 cloves garlic, minced
½ teaspoon salt
⅛ teaspoon red pepper flakes
4 cups Whole30-compliant chicken broth or chicken bone broth
3 medium sweet potatoes, peeled and chopped
3 cups coarsely chopped cooked chicken
2 teaspoons chopped fresh thyme

1. Cook the bacon in a large pot over medium heat, stirring frequently, until crisp, about 5 minutes. Transfer with a slotted spoon to paper towels to drain.
2. Heat the bacon drippings in the pot over medium heat. Add the mushrooms, onion, garlic, salt, and pepper flakes and cook, stirring frequently, until the mushrooms are tender, 4 to 6 minutes. Stir in the broth and sweet potatoes. Bring to a boil then reduce the heat. Simmer, covered, until the sweet potatoes are tender, about 15 minutes.
3. Add the chicken and thyme and heat through, about 1 minute. Top servings with the bacon.

Italian Beef and Veggie Soup

Prep time: 10 minutes | Cook time: 15 minutes | Serves 4

1 pound (454 g) ground beef
½ cup chopped onion
2 cloves garlic, minced
4 cups Whole30-compliant beef broth or beef bone broth
1 medium yellow or red bell pepper, chopped
1 medium zucchini, quartered lengthwise, then slice the quarters
1 teaspoon salt
¼ teaspoon black pepper
⅛ teaspoon red pepper flakes
3 medium Roma (plum) tomatoes, coarsely chopped
2 tablespoons chopped fresh basil

1. In a large pot, cook the ground beef, onion, and garlic over medium heat, stirring to break up the meat, until the meat is browned, about 5 minutes. Drain off any fat.
2. Stir the broth, bell pepper, zucchini, salt, pepper, and pepper flakes into the pot and bring the soup to a boil. Reduce the heat and simmer until the vegetables are tender, 8 to 10 minutes. Add the tomatoes and cook until heated through, about 2 minutes more. Stir in the fresh basil and serve.

Carrot-Parsnip Soup with Bacon Crumble 10

Prep time: 10 minutes | Cook time: 20 minutes | Serves 4

1 (12-ounce / 340-g) package petite baby carrots
1 small onion, peeled and quartered
1 tablespoon extra-virgin olive oil
4 cups Whole30-compliant chicken broth or chicken bone broth
2 large parsnips, peeled and coarsely chopped
2 apples, peeled, cored, and chopped
1 tablespoon curry powder
½ teaspoon salt
1 cup apple cider
Balsamic vinegar
2 slices Whole30-compliant bacon, cooked and finely chopped

1. Using a food processor, coarsely chop the carrots and onion. Heat the olive oil in a large pot over medium heat. Add the onion and carrots and cook, stirring frequently, until the onion is softened, about 5 minutes. Stir in the broth, parsnips, apples, curry powder, and salt and bring to a boil. Reduce the heat and simmer until the parsnips are tender, about 15 minutes. Stir in the cider.
2. Carefully transfer the soup to a blender, in batches if necessary, and let cool briefly; blend until the soup is smooth. (Or use an immersion blender to blend the soup in the pot.) Ladle the soup into bowls, drizzle with balsamic vinegar, and sprinkle with the bacon.

Italian Chicken Sausage Soup

Prep time: 10 minutes | Cook time: 4 hours | Serves 4

1 pound (454 g) Whole30-compliant sweet Italian chicken sausage, diagonally sliced ½ inch thick
4 cups Whole30-compliant chicken broth
1 (14½-ounce / 411-g) can Whole30-compliant diced tomatoes, undrained
½ cup chopped onion
2 cloves garlic, minced
1½ teaspoons Whole30-compliant Italian seasoning
¼ teaspoon salt
¼ teaspoon red pepper flakes
1½ cups cauliflower rice or cauliflower crumbles
4 cups baby spinach

1. In a slow cooker, combine the sausage, broth, tomatoes, onion, garlic, Italian seasoning, salt, and red pepper flakes. Cover and cook on low for 4 to 5 hours or on high for 2 to 2½ hours.
2. Turn the slow cooker to high if using the low setting. Stir in the cauliflower. Cover and cook until the cauliflower is tender, 15 to 20 minutes. Stir in the baby spinach. Serve.

Gazpacho Shrimp and Zucchini Noodle Soup

Prep time: 10 minutes | Cook time: 0 minutes | Serves 4

1 (16-ounce / 454-g) package very small cooked peeled deveined shrimp	tomato juice or 100% vegetable juice
1 (11-ounce / 311.8-g) package zucchini noodles; or 2 small zucchini, spiralized and long noodles snipped	1½ cups fresh medium-hot salsa
	¼ cup fresh lemon juice
	¼ cup chopped fresh parsley and/or basil
4 cups Whole30-compliant	⅓ cup sliced almonds, toasted

1. In a large non-metal bowl, stir together the shrimp, zucchini, tomato juice, salsa, lemon juice, and half of the parsley. Cover and chill for 2 to 24 hours.
2. To serve, top servings with the remaining parsley and almonds.

Southwest Chicken and Potato Noodle Bowl

Prep time: 10 minutes | Cook time: 7 minutes | Serves 4

1 pound (454 g) boneless, skinless chicken breast halves, thinly sliced	1 large red and/or yellow bell pepper, chopped
1 tablespoon Whole30-compliant Southwest seasoning	4 green onions, trimmed and cut diagonally into 1-inch pieces
2 tablespoons extra-virgin olive oil	1 medium russet potato, peeled and spiralized
4 cups Whole30-compliant chicken broth or chicken bone broth	1 cup fresh Whole30-compliant salsa
	2 tablespoons fresh lime juice

1. Sprinkle the chicken all over with the Southwest seasoning. Heat 1 tablespoon of the olive oil in an extra-large skillet over medium-high heat. Add half the chicken and cook, stirring occasionally, until no longer pink on the outside, about 2 minutes (the chicken will not be cooked through). Transfer the chicken to a plate. Add the remaining olive oil and chicken to the skillet. Cook the chicken until no longer pink, 2 to 3 minutes. Return all of the chicken to the skillet.
2. Add the broth and bring to a boil. Stir in the bell peppers, green onions, and potato noodles and return to a boil. Reduce the heat and simmer, stirring occasionally, until the vegetables are tender and the chicken is cooked through, 3 minutes. Gently stir in the salsa and lime juice and serve.

Chinese-Style Egg Drop Soup

Prep time: 10 minutes | Cook time: 11 minutes | Serves 2

2 teaspoons clarified butter or ghee	fresh shiitake mushrooms
2 green onions, chopped, white and green parts separated	½ teaspoon salt
	3 cups Whole30-compliant chicken broth or chicken bone broth
2 teaspoons minced fresh ginger	2 tablespoons coconut aminos
½ pound (227 g) ground chicken or turkey	½ teaspoon ground cumin
	3 large eggs
1 cup sliced stemmed	Toasted sesame oil

1. Heat the butter in a medium saucepan over medium-high heat. Add the white parts of the green onions and the ginger and cook, stirring, until fragrant, about 2 minutes. Add the ground chicken, mushrooms, and salt and cook until the chicken is no longer pink and the mushrooms are tender, 8 to 10 minutes. Add the broth, coconut aminos, and cumin, bring to a boil, then reduce the heat to a simmer.
2. In a small bowl, whisk the eggs for 30 seconds. Holding a fork over the saucepan, slowly pour the eggs through the tines of the fork and whisk the broth gently as you pour. Let the soup stand for a few seconds to finish cooking the eggs.
3. Top with the green parts of the green onions, drizzle with sesame oil, and serve.

Roasted Veggie Soup

Prep time: 10 minutes | Cook time: 30 minutes | Serves 2

2 medium carrots, peeled	2 tablespoons coconut oil
1 cup baby Brussels sprouts	2 cups bone broth
1 rib celery	½ medium Hass avocado, peeled, pitted, and sliced
¼ medium head cabbage	1 green onion, minced
2 teaspoons fine Himalayan salt, divided	4 sprigs fresh cilantro, minced

1. Preheat the oven to 400ºF (205ºC).
2. Cut all of the vegetables into small pieces and spread out on a sheet pan. Sprinkle with 1 teaspoon of the salt and toss with the coconut oil. Roast for 30 minutes.
3. While the vegetables are roasting, heat the broth in a saucepan over medium heat.
4. When the vegetables are ready, divide them between two serving bowls. Add the avocado, green onion, and cilantro and sprinkle in the remaining teaspoon of salt. Divide the broth between the bowls.
5. Serve immediately. Store leftovers in an airtight container in the fridge for up to 4 days.

Italian Chicken and Vegetable Soup

Prep time: 15 minutes | Cook time: 6 hours | Serves 4

- 1¼ pounds (567 g) bone-in chicken thighs, skin removed
- 1 medium onion, chopped
- 1 medium zucchini, cut into ½-inch pieces
- 4 medium carrots, cut into ½-inch pieces (2 cups)
- 4 cups Whole30-compliant chicken broth
- ½ teaspoon salt
- ¼ teaspoon black pepper
- 1½ cups sliced button mushrooms
- 1 (28-ounce / 794-g) can Whole30-compliant fire-roasted diced tomatoes, undrained
- ¼ cup chopped fresh basil

1. In a slow cooker, combine the chicken, onion, zucchini, carrots, broth, salt, and pepper. Cover and cook on low for 6 to 7 hours or on high for 3 to 3½ hours.
2. Remove the chicken from the slow cooker. Use two forks to coarsely shred the chicken; discard the bones. Return the chicken to the cooker. Stir in the mushrooms and tomatoes. Cover and cook on high for 30 minutes. Serve topped with basil.

Thyme Chicken and Zoodle Soup

Prep time: 25 minutes | Cook time: 6 hours | Serves 6

- 2 pounds (907 g) boneless, skinless chicken thighs, cut into 1-inch pieces
- 6 cups Whole30-compliant chicken broth
- 3 carrots, peeled and sliced
- 3 stalks celery with leaves, chopped ¼ inch thick
- 1 large white onion, coarsely chopped
- 1 tablespoon fresh lemon juice
- 1 teaspoon dried thyme
- 1 teaspoon dried marjoram
- 1 bay leaf
- 1 teaspoon salt
- ½ teaspoon black pepper
- 1 (10.7-ounce / 303-g) package zucchini noodles or 2 small zucchini, spiralized
- Coarse ground black pepper (optional)
- Fresh thyme leaves (optional)

1. In a slow cooker, combine the chicken, broth, carrots, celery, onion, lemon juice, dried thyme, marjoram, bay leaf, salt, and pepper. Stir to combine.
2. Cover and cook on low for 6 hours or on high for 3 hours. Remove and discard the bay leaf. Turn the slow cooker to high if using the low setting. Add the zucchini noodles. Cover and cook for 5 minutes or until the noodles are tender.
3. If desired, top servings with coarse ground black pepper and fresh thyme.

Chicken Thighs and Dumplings Soup

Prep time: 20 minutes | Cook time: 39 minutes | Serves 4

- 2 tablespoons avocado oil
- 1 medium onion, diced
- 3 ribs celery, diced
- 3 small radishes, diced
- 1 small carrot, sliced
- 4 cloves garlic, minced
- 1 pound (454 g) boneless, skinless chicken thighs
- 1 bay leaf
- 3 sprigs fresh oregano
- 4 cups bone broth
- 1 teaspoon fine Himalayan salt
- 1 teaspoon ground black pepper

For the Dumplings:
- 2 large eggs
- 2 tablespoons coconut oil or melted unsalted butter
- 3 tablespoons coconut flour
- Pinch of fine Himalayan salt
- Pinch of ground nutmeg
- Fresh parsley, for garnish (optional)

1. Heat a 5-quart pot over medium heat. Pour in the avocado oil and add the onions, celery, radishes, carrots, and garlic. Sauté, stirring often, for 8 minutes, until the onions are aromatic and translucent.
2. Push the sofrito to the side and place the chicken thighs flat on the bottom of the pot with the bay leaf and the oregano sprigs on top. Brown for 3 minutes on each side, then mix the chicken thighs well with the sofrito and pour in the broth. Stir in the salt and pepper. Bring the soup to a boil and cook for 20 minutes.
3. While the soup cooks, make the dumplings: In a medium-sized bowl, whisk together the eggs and coconut oil. Add the coconut flour, salt, and nutmeg and mix until a dry dough forms. Shape into eight equal-sized balls.
4. Reduce the heat to low and stir the soup, bringing it down to a simmer. Use tongs to gently tear apart the chicken thighs.
5. Carefully add the dumplings to the soup one at a time. Simmer for about 5 minutes, turning them over with tongs once. They're done when they begin to puff up a little—do not let them swell too much.
6. Remove the soup from the heat, garnish with fresh parsley if desired, and serve right away. I like to give each serving two dumplings, but you can hoard them if you like.
7. I do not recommend storing this soup with the dumplings; the longer they sit in the soup, the more they will disintegrate. We like to eat up all the dumplings on first go-round and enjoy the lighter chicken soup, sans dumplings, for leftovers. Store the soup in an airtight container in the refrigerator for up to 6 days. To reheat, bring to a simmer on the stovetop.

Chicken Sausage and Kale Stew

Prep time: 20 minutes | Cook time: 6 hours | Serves 4

1 pound (454 g) boneless, skinless chicken breast, cut into 1-inch pieces
4 cups Whole30-compliant chicken broth
1 (14½-ounce / 411-g) can Whole30-compliant fire-roasted diced tomatoes, undrained
1 large yellow onion, cut into thin wedges
2 cloves garlic, minced
2 teaspoons grated lemon zest, plus extra for serving
1½ teaspoons fennel seeds, crushed
8 ounces (227 g) Whole30-compliant smoked kielbasa or chicken-apple sausage, sliced into ½-inch pieces
2 cups packed chopped fresh kale

1. In a slow cooker, combine the chicken, broth, tomatoes, onion, garlic, lemon zest, and fennel seeds.
2. Cover and cook on low for 6 to 7 hours or on high for 3 to 3½ hours. Add the sausage and kale. Cover and let stand for 5 minutes or until the sausage is heated through and the kale is wilted. Serve, topped with additional lemon zest if desired.

Beef Fajita Soup

Prep time: 10 minutes | Cook time: 6 hours | Serves 4

1 pound (454 g) ground beef
1 cup chopped onion
2 cloves garlic, minced
1 medium green bell pepper, coarsely chopped
1 medium red bell pepper, coarsely chopped
1 serrano chile pepper, seeded and chopped
4 cups Whole30-compliant beef broth
1 (14½-ounce / 411-g) can Whole30-compliant fire-roasted diced tomatoes, undrained
2 teaspoons chili powder
½ teaspoon salt
Chopped fresh cilantro, for serving
Lime wedges, for serving

1. In a large skillet, cook the beef, onion, and garlic over medium-high heat, breaking up the meat with a wooden spoon, until browned. Drain off any fat and transfer the beef mixture to a slow cooker. Add the bell peppers, serrano pepper, broth, tomatoes, chili powder, and salt. Cover and cook on low for 6 to 7 hours or on high for 3 to 3½ hours.
2. Serve the soup with cilantro and lime wedges.

Beef and Bell Pepper Soup

Prep time: 25 minutes | Cook time: 5 hours | Serves 4

1 pound (454 g) lean ground beef
1 medium onion, chopped
1 (14½-ounce / 411-g) can Whole30-compliant diced tomatoes, undrained
1 (15-ounce / 425-g) can Whole30-compliant tomato sauce
2 medium red or orange bell peppers, chopped
2 cloves garlic, minced
2 teaspoons Whole30-compliant Italian seasoning
½ teaspoon fennel seeds, crushed
½ teaspoon salt
2½ cups Whole30-compliant beef broth
Fresh basil leaves (optional)

1. In a large skillet, cook the beef and onion over medium heat, stirring occasionally and breaking up the beef with a wooden spoon, until browned, 8 to 10 minutes. Drain off the fat. Transfer to a slow cooker.
2. Stir in the tomatoes, tomato sauce, bell peppers, garlic, Italian seasoning, fennel seeds, and salt, and then the broth.
3. Cover and cook on low for 5 to 6 hours or on high for 2½ to 3 hours. Top servings with fresh basil, if desired.

Turkey Sausage and Root Vegetable Soup

Prep time: 10 minutes | Cook time: 18 minutes | Serves 4

1¼ pounds (567 g) ground turkey
2 teaspoons fennel seeds, crushed
2 teaspoons ground paprika
4 cloves garlic, minced
1 tablespoon extra-virgin olive oil
4 cups Whole30-compliant chicken broth or chicken bone broth
1 (16-ounce / 454-g) package frozen fire-roasted sweet potatoes
1 (15-ounce / 425-g) can Whole30-compliant fire-roasted tomatoes with garlic
2 teaspoons Whole30-compliant Italian seasoning
½ cup chopped fresh basil

1. Combine the turkey, fennel seeds, paprika, and garlic in a large bowl. Use your hands to mix well.
2. Heat the olive oil in a large pot over medium heat. Add the turkey and cook, stirring frequently, until lightly browned, 8 to 10 minutes. Add the broth, sweet potatoes, tomatoes, and Italian seasoning and bring to a boil. Reduce the heat and simmer, stirring occasionally, until the sweet potatoes are tender, about 10 minutes. Stir in the basil and serve.

It's never too late to change old habits. -Chapter 10 Soups, Stews, and Noodle Bowls

Creamy Broccoli and Kale Soup

Prep time: 10 minutes | Cook time: 14 minutes | Serves 4

1 tablespoon extra-virgin olive oil
2 leeks, white parts only, cut into 1-inch pieces
2 cloves garlic, minced
1 pound (454 g) broccoli, trimmed and coarsely chopped
1 bunch kale, stalks removed, leaves chopped
½ teaspoon salt
⅛ teaspoon red pepper flakes
5 cups Whole30-compliant chicken broth or chicken bone broth
1 can (13½-ounce / 382.7-g) Whole30-compliant coconut milk

1. In a large pot, heat the olive oil over medium heat. Add the leeks and garlic and cook, stirring frequently, until the leeks are softened, 3 to 5 minutes.
2. Stir in the broccoli, kale, salt, pepper flakes, and broth. Bring to a boil. Reduce the heat to low. Cover and simmer, stirring occasionally, until the broccoli is tender, about 10 minutes. Add 1 cup of the coconut milk and cook until heated through, about 1 minute.
3. Carefully transfer the soup to a blender, in batches if necessary, and let cool briefly; pulse a few times, then blend until smooth and return to the pot. (Or use an immersion blender and blend directly in the pot.) Top servings of the soup with a swirl of the remaining coconut milk.

Sweet Potatoes Pork Stew

Prep time: 30 minutes | Cook time: 6 hours | Serves 6

2 pounds (907 g) lean ground pork
1 quart Whole30-compliant vegetable broth
3 medium sweet potatoes, peeled and cut into 1-inch pieces
1 Braeburn apple, cored and cut into 1-inch pieces
2 jalapeños, seeded and diced
1 large shallot, minced
1 tablespoon fresh thyme, plus extra for serving
2 teaspoons ground ginger
½ teaspoon salt
½ teaspoon white pepper
Paprika, for serving

1. In an extra-large skillet, cook the pork over medium-high heat, stirring, until no longer pink, about 10 minutes. Using a slotted spoon, transfer the pork to a slow cooker. Add the broth, sweet potatoes, apple, jalapeños, shallot, thyme, ginger, salt, and white pepper.
2. Cover and cook on low for 6 hours or on high for 3 hours. Use a potato masher or fork to gently mash the sweet potatoes to thicken the stew.
3. Serve, sprinkled with paprika and fresh thyme.

Butternut Squash Pureed Soup

Prep time: minutes | Cook time: 20 minutes | Serves 2

3 tablespoons clarified butter, ghee, or coconut oil
½ cup diced onion
3 cups diced seeded peeled butternut squash
2 cloves garlic, minced
½ teaspoon ground ginger
4 cups chicken broth
1 teaspoon salt
½ teaspoon black pepper

1. In a large pot, melt the cooking fat over medium heat, swirling to coat the bottom of the pot. When the fat is hot, add the onion and cook, stirring, until translucent, 2 to 3 minutes. Add the squash, garlic, and ginger and stir until the garlic becomes aromatic, about 1 minute.
2. Add the chicken broth and bring to a boil over high heat. Boil until the butternut squash is soft, about 10 minutes. Remove the pot from the heat.
3. In one or two batches, transfer the soup to a food processor or blender and blend on high speed until smooth in texture. Return the pureed soup to the pot.
4. Heat the soup over medium-high heat until it thickens enough to coat the back of a wooden spoon, 7 to 10 minutes. Season with the salt and pepper.

Simple Egg Drop Soup

Prep time: 10 minutes | Cook time: 20 minutes | Serves 4

2 tablespoons toasted sesame oil
1 (2-inch) piece fresh ginger, peeled
4 cloves garlic, peeled
4 cups bone broth
1 tablespoon coconut aminos
1 tablespoon fish sauce
Pinch of fine Himalayan salt
4 large eggs, whisked
2 green onions, sliced, for garnish
4 sprigs fresh cilantro, minced, for garnish

1. In a 6- or 8-quart pot, heat the sesame oil over medium heat. Add the ginger and garlic and stir until lightly browned.
2. Add the broth, coconut aminos, fish sauce, and salt. Bring to a low simmer, reduce the heat to low, cover, and cook for 20 minutes.
3. Slowly drizzle in the eggs while stirring the soup so the eggs cook instantly in ribbons as they hit the broth.
4. Garnish with the green onions and cilantro and serve hot. Store leftovers in an airtight container in the fridge for up to 5 days. I don't recommend freezing this soup.

Chicken and Vegetable Soup

Prep time: 15 minutes | Cook time: 1¼ hours | Serves 6 to 8

4 chicken quarters
4 large carrots, unpeeled
2 yellow onions, unpeeled, cut in half
2 celery stalks, cut in half
1 large parsnip, unpeeled, cut in half
1 chayote squash, cut in half
1 small bunch dill, plus more for garnish
1 (2-inch) piece fresh ginger
1 head garlic, bottom trimmed and discarded
3 bay leaves
2 tablespoons kosher salt, plus more if needed
1 teaspoon whole black peppercorns
Freshly ground black pepper

1. In a 7½-quart stockpot or Dutch oven, combine the chicken, carrots, onions, celery, parsnip, squash, dill, ginger, garlic, bay leaves, salt, and peppercorns. Add enough water to fill the pot. Bring the water to a gentle simmer over medium heat. Cover and cook for 1¼ hours, using a spoon to skim off any foam that rises to the surface.
2. Remove the pot from the heat and use a large slotted spoon or spider to transfer the chicken to a bowl; let cool slightly. Discard all the vegetables except the carrots. Peel the carrots and slice them into 1-inch-thick discs. Set aside.
3. When the chicken is cool enough to handle, shred the meat with your hands or two forks. Discard the bones, skin, and cartilage. Return the shredded chicken to the pot along with the sliced carrots. Taste the soup and season with additional salt, if desired.
4. Ladle into individual bowls, garnish with dill and freshly ground black pepper, and serve.

Matzo Ball Soup with Dill and Parsley

Prep time: 10 minutes | Cook time: 20 minutes | Serves 3 to 6

¼ cup Manischewitz matzo meal
2 large eggs
2 tablespoons avocado oil
2 tablespoons water or chicken stock
¼ cup loosely packed fresh dill, finely chopped, plus more for garnish
¼ cup loosely packed fresh parsley leaves, finely chopped, plus more for garnish
2 quarts chicken soup
Kosher salt, to taste

1. In a medium bowl, stir together the matzo meal, eggs, avocado oil, water, dill, and parsley with a fork until just combined. Cover the bowl and refrigerate for 20 minutes.
2. Pour the chicken soup into a medium pot and warm it through over medium-high heat.
3. Fill a large sauté pan with water (I prefer using a wider pot so the matzo balls have room to expand without getting crowded). Bring the water to a boil and season with 2 tablespoons salt.
4. Wet your hands with some water and roll the matzo meal mixture into golf ball–size balls. Carefully drop the matzo balls into the boiling water, reduce the heat to medium, cover, and cook until you can easily pierce through to the center of a matzo ball with a knife, 20 to 30 minutes. If the matzo balls are still firm, cook for 10 minutes more, then test again; repeat as needed until the matzo balls are tender.
5. Use a slotted spoon to transfer the matzo balls into individual serving bowls and ladle chicken soup over them. Serve garnished with dill and parsley.

Autumn Pumpkin Chili

Prep time: 15 minutes | Cook time: 28 minutes | Serves 4

1 tablespoon unsalted butter, ghee, or avocado oil
1 medium onion, diced
3 radishes, diced
2 cloves garlic, minced
4 ribs celery, diced
1 teaspoon dry mustard
1 teaspoon fine Himalayan salt
1 teaspoon garam masala
1 teaspoon ground black pepper
1 pound (454 g) ground beef (85% lean)
½ cup canned unsweetened pumpkin puree
2 cups bone broth
¼ cup Whole30-compliant mayonnaise
¼ cup minced fresh cilantro, for garnish

1. Heat a large pot over medium-high heat. Melt the butter in the pot, then add the onions, radishes, garlic, and celery. Sauté, stirring often, until the onions are translucent and aromatic, about 8 minutes.
2. Add the seasonings, mix well, and cook until they become fragrant, about 2 minutes.
3. Add the ground beef, crumbling it up as you go. Use a whisk to make sure it breaks apart well.
4. Cook, stirring often, until all of the ground beef is browned and crumbly, about 8 minutes.
5. Add the pumpkin puree and the broth and bring to a simmer. Reduce the heat to low and simmer for 10 to 15 minutes.
6. Stir in the mayo until well dissolved and remove from the heat. Sprinkle with the cilantro. Enjoy!
7. Store in an airtight container in the fridge for up to 5 days or in the freezer for up to 30 days. To reheat, bring to a simmer on the stovetop.

Spicy and Sour Shrimp Soup

Prep time: 15 minutes | Cook time: 4 hours | Serves 4

6 cups Whole30-compliant chicken broth
1 pound (454 g) peeled and deveined large shrimp
2 cups quartered cremini mushrooms
2 medium carrots, peeled and grated (½ cup)
2 cups thinly sliced green cabbage
½ cup canned sliced bamboo shoots, rinsed, drained, and cut into strips
½ to 1 serrano chile pepper, seeded, if desired, and minced
2 tablespoons minced fresh ginger
4 cloves garlic, minced
⅛ teaspoon ground white pepper
¼ cup rice wine vinegar
½ teaspoon olive oil
1 large egg, lightly beaten
2 tablespoons sliced green onions

1. In a slow cooker, combine the broth, shrimp, mushrooms, carrots, cabbage, bamboo shoots, serrano chile, ginger, garlic, and white pepper. Cover and cook for 4 hours on low or 2 hours on high, or until the shrimp are pink and opaque and the cabbage is tender.
2. Turn the slow cooker to high if using the low setting. Add the vinegar and olive oil, and then the beaten egg. Stir the soup until the egg is cooked and slightly thickens the soup.
3. Serve, topped with the green onions and additional serrano pepper, if desired.

Pork and Napa Cabbage Soup

Prep time: 10 minutes | Cook time: 6 hours | Serves 4

⅓ cup almond meal
1 large egg, lightly beaten
2 green onions, thinly sliced
1 tablespoon sesame seeds
2 cloves garlic, minced
1 teaspoon salt
½ teaspoon black pepper
1½ pounds (680 g) lean ground pork
4 cups Whole30-compliant chicken broth
2 shallots, chopped
4 cloves garlic, thinly sliced
2 tablespoons coconut aminos
2 tablespoons minced fresh ginger
1 teaspoon olive oil
4 cups thinly sliced Napa cabbage
2 tablespoons sliced fresh basil

1. Preheat the oven to 400ºF (205ºC).
2. In a medium bowl, combine the almond meal, egg, green onions, sesame seeds, garlic, salt, and pepper. Add the pork and mix just until combined. Form into 8 meatballs and place on a foil-lined rimmed baking sheet. Bake for 10 minutes.
3. In a slow cooker, combine the broth, shallots, garlic, coconut aminos, ginger, and olive oil. Place the meatballs in the cooker in a single layer. Cover and cook on low for 6 to 7 hours or on high for 3 to 3½ hours.
4. Turn the slow cooker to high if using the low setting. Transfer the meatballs to serving bowls. Stir the cabbage into the liquid in the slow cooker. Cook on high for 5 minutes. Ladle the soup over the meatballs. Top servings with the basil.

Lush Chicken and Carrot Stew

Prep time: 30 minutes | Cook time: 6 hours | Serves 4

1 medium onion, cut into wedges
2 cloves garlic, minced
4 slices Whole30-compliant bacon, chopped
4 medium carrots, peeled and cut into 1-inch pieces
1 large leek, white part only, sliced
12 small red potatoes (about 12 ounces / 340 g)
Grated zest and juice of 1 lemon
½ cup Whole30-compliant chicken broth
1 tablespoon tapioca flour
1 teaspoon salt
½ teaspoon coarsely ground black pepper
8 meaty bone-in chicken pieces (breast halves, thighs, and drumsticks), skin removed
2 tablespoons extra-virgin olive oil
2 teaspoons herbes de Provence
2 tablespoons Whole30-compliant Dijon mustard
1 cup Whole30-compliant Kalamata olives or other black olives
Fresh tarragon leaves, for serving

1. In a slow cooker, combine the onion, garlic, bacon, carrots, leek, and potatoes. In a small bowl, stir together the lemon juice, broth, and tapioca flour; stir into the slow cooker. In another small bowl, combine the lemon zest, salt, and pepper. Coat the chicken with the olive oil and rub with the salt mixture. Add to the slow cooker. Sprinkle the herbes de Provence over the chicken.
2. Cover and cook on low for 6 to 7 hours or on high for 3 to 3½ hours.
3. Transfer the chicken to shallow serving bowls. Stir the mustard and olives into the cooking liquid. Ladle some of the cooking liquid over the chicken. Sprinkle with fresh tarragon leaves and serve.

Chicken Breast and Avocado Soup

Prep time: 25 minutes | Cook time: 8 hours | Serves 6

2 quarts Whole30-compliant chicken broth
1 (14½-ounce / 411-g) can Whole30-compliant diced tomatoes
1 medium white onion, finely diced
1 jalapeño, seeded and finely diced
3 cloves garlic, minced
1 tablespoon chipotle powder or regular chili powder
1 teaspoon ground cumin
1 teaspoon dried oregano
½ teaspoon salt
½ teaspoon black pepper
4 boneless, skinless chicken breasts (2 pounds (907 g) / 907 g)
½ cup chopped fresh cilantro
½ cup fresh lime juice, plus lime wedges for serving
3 avocados, halved, pitted, peeled, and diced

1. In a slow cooker, stir together the broth, tomatoes, onion, jalapeño, garlic, chipotle powder, cumin, oregano, salt, and pepper. Add the chicken.
2. Cover and cook on low for 8 to 10 hours or on high for 4 to 5 hours.
3. Use tongs to transfer the chicken to a cutting board. Use two forks to shred the chicken. Return the chicken to the cooker and stir in the cilantro and lime juice.
4. Top servings with avocado and serve with lime wedges.

Silky Broccoli Soup

Prep time: 10 minutes | Cook time: 25 minutes | Serves 4

6 slices bacon, chopped
4 heaping cups broccoli florets
5 cloves garlic, peeled
¼ cup nutritional yeast
1 teaspoon dried dill weed
1 teaspoon fine Himalayan salt
1 teaspoon onion powder
½ teaspoon ground black pepper
3 cups bone broth
3 tablespoons mayonnaise or coconut cream

1. Heat a large pot over medium heat. Add the bacon and cook until crispy, stirring occasionally. Remove half of the crispy bacon with a slotted spoon and set aside—it will be used later as a garnish. Leave the rendered bacon fat and the other half of the bacon at the bottom of the pot.
2. Add the broccoli and garlic. Sauté for about 10 minutes, until the garlic becomes aromatic and the broccoli is bright green, then mix in all of the seasonings and pour in the broth.
3. Bring to a simmer, stir well, and cook for 15 minutes. Remove from the heat and carefully transfer the mix to a blender.
4. Add the mayo or coconut cream and blend to your desired consistency. I like mine silky smooth.
5. Ladle the soup into four small bowls and garnish with the reserved crispy bacon. Store leftovers in an airtight container in the fridge for up to 5 days or in the freezer for up to 30 days. To reheat, bring to a simmer on the stovetop.

Cauliflower Soup with Sausage and Spinach

Prep time: 10 minutes | Cook time: 30 minutes | Serves 4

1 pound (454 g) Whole30-compliant spicy ground pork sausage
1 tablespoon extra-virgin olive oil
4 cups cauliflower florets
1 medium onion, coarsely chopped
3 stalks celery, coarsely chopped
1 fennel bulb, trimmed, cored, and coarsely chopped
2 cloves garlic, coarsely chopped
5 cups Whole30-compliant chicken broth or chicken bone broth
¼ teaspoon paprika
½ teaspoon black pepper
5 ounces (142 g) fresh baby spinach leaves

1. In a large heavy pot, brown the sausage over medium heat. Using a slotted spoon, transfer the sausage to a plate lined with paper towels to drain. Drain off any fat in the skillet.
2. Heat the olive oil in the same pot over medium-high heat. Add the cauliflower, onion, celery, fennel, and garlic and cook, stirring occasionally, for 5 to 6 minutes. Stir in the broth, scraping up any browned bits on the bottom. Bring to a boil, reduce the heat, and simmer for 15 minutes.
3. Carefully transfer the soup to a blender, in batches if necessary, and let cool briefly; blend until the soup is smooth and creamy. (Or use an immersion blender to blend the soup in the pot.) Return the soup to the pot and add the paprika and black pepper. Just before serving, stir the spinach and sausage into the soup.

It's never too late to change old habits. -Chapter 10 Soups, Stews, and Noodle Bowls

Turnip Leek Soup

Prep time: 10 minutes | Cook time: 35 minutes | Serves 4

- 4 slices Whole30-compliant bacon, diced
- 2 leeks, white parts only, cut into 1-inch pieces
- 2 turnips, peeled and chopped (about 3½ cups)
- 1 medium zucchini, ends removed and diced
- 1 (14½-ounce / 411-g) can Whole30-compliant coconut milk
- 1 cup Whole30-compliant chicken broth or chicken bone broth
- 1 teaspoon garlic powder
- 1 teaspoon onion powder
- 1 teaspoon dried rosemary
- 1 teaspoon salt
- 2 green onions, minced

1. In a large pot, cook the bacon over medium-high heat until crisp, about 3 minutes. Use a slotted spoon to remove the bacon and drain on paper towels. Reserve the drippings in the pot.
2. Reduce the heat to medium. Add the leeks to the pot and cook, stirring, until softened, about 3 minutes. Add the turnips and zucchini and continue to cook, stirring, until tender, about 5 minutes. Stir in the coconut milk, broth, garlic powder, onion powder, rosemary, and salt. Simmer the soup, covered, for 20 minutes.
3. Carefully transfer the soup to a blender, in batches if necessary, and let cool briefly; blend until the soup is smooth and creamy. (Or use an immersion blender to blend the soup in the pot.) Top servings with the bacon and green onions.

Almond Chicken and Sweet Potatoes Stew

Prep time: 30 minutes | Cook time: 6 hours | Serves 6

- 1½ pounds (680 g) boneless, skinless chicken thighs, cut into 1½-inch pieces
- 2 medium sweet potatoes (about 1¼ pounds / 567 g total), peeled and cut into 1½-inch pieces
- 1 (14½-ounce / 411-g) can Whole30-compliant stewed tomatoes, undrained
- 1 medium yellow onion, chopped
- 3 cloves garlic, minced
- 1 piece (1 inch) fresh ginger, peeled and finely chopped
- ¼ teaspoon cayenne pepper
- 2½ cups Whole30-compliant chicken broth
- 1 bunch collard greens, trimmed and coarsely chopped
- ¼ cup Whole30-compliant sunflower seed butter
- ½ cup chopped almonds, toasted
- ½ cup chopped fresh cilantro or flat-leaf parsley

1. In a slow cooker, combine the chicken, sweet potatoes, tomatoes, onion, garlic, ginger, and cayenne. Add the broth. Cover and cook on low for 6 to 7 hours or on high for 3 to 3½ hours.
2. Turn the slow cooker to high if using the low setting. Use a ladle to remove ½ cup of the cooking liquid from the cooker; set aside. Stir the collard greens into the stew; cover and cook 15 minutes longer. Whisk the sunflower butter into the reserved ½ cup cooking liquid until smooth. Stir into the stew.
3. Serve, sprinkled with almonds and cilantro.

Winter Greens and Potato Soup

Prep time: 10 minutes | Cook time: 30 minutes | Serves 4

- 2 tablespoons extra-virgin olive oil, plus more for serving
- 2 small to medium leeks, halved lengthwise and sliced (1½ cups)
- ½ teaspoon salt
- ½ teaspoon black pepper
- 3 cloves garlic, minced
- 6 cups Whole30-compliant chicken broth or chicken bone broth
- 3 medium russet potatoes, peeled and diced
- 6 cups chopped greens, such as kale, collard greens, or mustard greens
- ½ cup packed chopped fresh parsley
- Grated zest and juice of 1 lemon
- 8 large eggs

1. Heat the olive oil over medium heat in a large pot. Add the leeks, salt, and pepper and cook, stirring occasionally, until the leeks are softened but not browned, about 4 minutes. Add the garlic and cook, stirring, for 1 minute. Stir in the broth and potatoes and bring to a boil. Reduce the heat, cover, and simmer until the potatoes are tender, about 10 minutes.
2. Add the greens and cook over medium-high heat, stirring occasionally, until the greens are wilted, about 2 minutes. Reduce the heat to low and stir in the parsley and lemon zest. Break an egg into a small bowl and slide it into the soup. Repeat with the remaining eggs. Cover and simmer until the eggs are cooked to desired doneness, 4 to 6 minutes.
3. Drizzle each serving with lemon juice and olive oil. Season with salt and pepper to taste.

Pork Loin Stew

Prep time: 25 minutes | Cook time: 6 hours | Serves 6

1½ pounds (680 g) Whole30-compliant boneless pork loin, cut into 1-inch pieces
½ small butternut squash, peeled and cut into 1-inch pieces (about 2 cups)
3 medium carrots, peeled and cut into ½-inch pieces
2 medium parsnips, peeled and cut into ½-inch pieces
1 medium yellow onion, chopped
2 teaspoons fresh thyme
½ teaspoon salt
½ teaspoon black pepper
4 cups Whole30-compliant chicken broth
Chopped fresh parsley, for serving

1. In a slow cooker, combine the pork, squash, carrots, parsnips, onion, thyme, salt, pepper, and broth. Cover and cook on low for 6 to 7 hours or on high 3 to 3½ hours.
2. Serve, topped with parsley.

Lush Shrimp Coconut Bowl

Prep time: 25 minutes | Cook time: 11 minutes | Serves 4

1¼ pounds (567 g) large shell-on shrimp, deveined
2 tablespoons grated fresh ginger
3 tablespoons grated fresh turmeric
2 tablespoons clarified butter
2 cups sliced Broccolini (stems sliced, florets kept whole)
1 cup chopped green beans (1-inch pieces)
1½ teaspoons kosher salt
¾ teaspoon freshly ground black pepper
2 tablespoons coconut oil
¼ cup thinly sliced shallots
1 garlic clove, thinly sliced
½ cup thinly sliced scallions
2 tablespoons finely chopped lemongrass
2 cups chicken stock, warmed
2 Kaffir lime leaves (optional)
1 red Thai chile or other spicy fresh red chile, seeded and sliced, or 1 dried Thai chile
1 cup full-fat unsweetened coconut milk, blended
¼ teaspoon cayenne pepper
2 tablespoons coconut aminos
1 tablespoon fresh lime juice
1 cup spinach leaves
Fresh cilantro leaves, for garnish
Lime wedges, for garnish

1. Put the shrimp in a large bowl and squeeze the juice from the ginger and the juice from 2 tablespoons of the grated turmeric over the shrimp. Toss well, then cover with plastic wrap and refrigerate for 10 minutes.
2. In a medium pot, melt the clarified butter over medium heat. Add the Broccolini, green beans, ½ teaspoon of the salt, and ¼ teaspoon of the black pepper, stir to combine, and cook until the vegetables turn bright green and tender but are still crisp, about 3 minutes. Remove the beans and Broccolini from the pot and set aside.
3. In the same pot, melt the coconut oil over medium heat. Add the shallots and garlic and cook, stirring, until fragrant but not browned, about 30 seconds. Add the scallions, lemongrass, and ½ teaspoon of the salt and cook until softened, about 1 minute more. Add 2 cups of the stock and stir well, scraping up all the caramelized bits from the bottom of the pan. Add the lime leaves and chile, stir, and bring to a simmer. Cook for 2 to 3 minutes.
4. Stir in the coconut milk, then add the shrimp, remaining ½ teaspoon salt, remaining ½ teaspoon black pepper, and the cayenne and stir to combine well. Bring back to a simmer and cook until the shrimp are just cooked through, about 3 minutes.
5. In a small bowl, combine the coconut aminos, lime juice, and the juice from the remaining 1 tablespoon grated turmeric. Mix well, then add to the pot. Add the sautéed vegetables and the spinach to the pot and cook, stirring gently, for 1 minute more.
6. Serve garnished with cilantro, with lime wedges alongside.

Mexican-Style Chicken Soup

Prep time: 10 minutes | Cook time: 20 minutes | Serves 4

1 tablespoon extra-virgin olive oil
½ cup chopped onion
1 medium poblano pepper, seeded and chopped
1 medium yellow or red bell pepper, chopped
2 cloves garlic, minced
½ teaspoon salt
4 cups Whole30-compliant chicken broth or chicken bone broth
1 (14½-ounce / 411-g) can Whole30-compliant fire-roasted diced tomatoes, undrained
2 teaspoons chili powder
3 cups shredded cooked chicken
Chopped fresh cilantro, for serving
1 avocado, halved, pitted, peeled, and sliced
Lime wedges, for serving

1. Heat the olive oil in a large pot over medium-high heat. Add the onion, poblano, bell pepper, garlic, and salt. Cook, stirring frequently, until the vegetables are crisp-tender, 3 to 5 minutes.
2. Stir the broth, tomatoes, and chili powder into the pot and bring to a boil. Reduce the heat and simmer for 10 minutes. Add the chicken and heat through, about 1 minute.
3. Serve the soup with cilantro, avocado, and lime wedges.

Chapter 11 Sauces, Dressings, and Dips

5-Ingredient Mayonnaise

Prep time: 5 minutes | Cook time: 0 minutes | Makes 1½ cups

- 1¼ cups light olive oil
- 1 large egg
- ½ teaspoon dry mustard
- ½ teaspoon salt
- Juice of ½ lemon

1. Place ¼ cup of the olive oil, the egg, mustard, and salt in a blender, food processor, or mixing bowl. Blend, process, or mix thoroughly. While the food processor or blender is running (or while mixing in a bowl with an immersion blender), slowly drizzle in the remaining 1 cup olive oil until the mayonnaise has emulsified. Add the lemon juice and blend on low or stir to incorporate.

Eggless Mayonnaise

Prep time: 5 minutes | Cook time: minutes | Makes 1¼ cups

- ½ cup coconut butter, slightly warmed
- ½ cup warm water
- ¼ cup light olive oil
- 2 cloves garlic, peeled
- 1 tablespoon fresh lemon juice (optional)
- ¼ teaspoon salt

1. Place all the ingredients in a food processor or blender and blend on high until the mixture thickens, 1 to 2 minutes.

Caesar-Style Salad Dressing

Prep time: 10 minutes | Cook time: 0 minutes | Makes 2 cups

- 1 cup cashews
- 2 cups plus 6 tablespoons water
- ¼ cup fresh lemon juice
- 2 cloves garlic, minced
- 4 anchovy fillets
- 2 teaspoons coconut aminos
- 1 teaspoon Whole30-compliant Dijon mustard
- ½ teaspoon salt
- ¼ teaspoon black pepper
- ½ cup extra-virgin olive oil

1. Place the cashews in a medium bowl; cover with 2 cups of the water and soak for 8 hours or overnight. Drain and rinse the cashews. In a high-speed blender, combine the cashews, lemon juice, remaining 6 tablespoons water, the garlic, anchovy fillets, coconut aminos, mustard, salt, and pepper. Blend on low, then increase the speed to high and blend until smooth. With the blender running, slowly add the olive oil and blend until the dressing is smooth.
2. Refrigerate the dressing for at least 2 hours before using. If the dressing becomes too thick after chilling, whisk in water, 1 teaspoon at a time, until it reaches the desired consistency.

Ketchup For Whole30

Prep time: 5 minutes | Cook time: 5 minutes | Makes 1 cup

- 1 cup Whole30-compliant tomato paste
- ½ cup apple cider
- ½ cup apple cider vinegar
- 1 teaspoon garlic powder
- ½ teaspoon salt
- ⅛ teaspoon ground cloves (optional)

1. Heat a medium saucepan over medium heat. Add the tomato paste, apple cider, and vinegar. Stir to combine and let the mixture come to a simmer, but do not allow it to boil. Add the garlic powder, salt, and cloves (if using) and cook, stirring frequently to prevent scorching—you may need to turn the heat down to low or simmer here— until the ketchup has thickened enough to evenly coat the back of a spoon, 5 to 8 minutes. Remove from the heat and allow to cool. Serve when cool, or store in an airtight container in the refrigerator for up to 2 weeks.

Creamy Caramelized Green Onion Sauce

Prep time: 10 minutes | Cook time: 11 minutes | Makes ½ cup

- 1 tablespoon coconut oil
- 2 green onions, thinly sliced, white and green parts kept separate
- ¾ cup thinly sliced quartered red onion
- 2 medium shallots, thinly sliced
- 2 cloves garlic, minced
- ¼ cup white wine vinegar
- 1 teaspoon Whole30-compliant coarse-grain mustard
- ¼ teaspoon coarse salt
- ⅛ teaspoon black pepper
- ⅓ cup extra-virgin olive oil

1. Heat the coconut oil in a medium skillet over medium heat. Add the white parts of the green onions, the red onion, and the shallots and cook, stirring occasionally, until tender and golden brown, 10 to 15 minutes. If the onions start to brown too quickly, reduce the heat. Add the garlic and cook, stirring, for 1 minute. Remove the skillet from the heat. Add the vinegar and stir to scrape up any browned bits from the bottom of the skillet.
2. Transfer the onion mixture to a blender. Add the mustard, salt, and pepper. Cover and blend until nearly smooth. With the blender running, slowly add the olive oil through the opening in the lid and blend until the sauce is well combined and smooth. Transfer to a small bowl. Stir in some of the green onion tops. Use immediately or cover and store the sauce in the refrigerator for up to 1 week.

Arugula and Walnut Pesto

Prep time: 10 minutes | Cook time: 0 minutes | Makes ¾ cup

1½ cups packed arugula
¾ cup packed fresh basil leaves
½ cup chopped walnuts, toasted
1 tablespoon fresh lemon juice
1 clove garlic, minced
¼ teaspoon salt
⅓ cup extra-virgin olive oil

1. In a food processor or blender, combine the arugula, basil, walnuts, lemon juice, garlic, and salt and process or blend until combined. With the motor running, add the olive oil through the opening in the lid in a thin, steady stream until the pesto is smooth and reaches the desired consistency.

Jalapeño and Seeds Harissa Sauce

Prep time: 10 minutes | Cook time: 10 minutes | Makes 1 cup

8 ounces (227 g) jalapeños, halved and seeded
1 medium red bell pepper, halved and seeded
1½ teaspoons cumin seeds
1 teaspoon coriander seeds
1 teaspoon caraway seeds
1 tablespoon fresh lemon juice
2 cloves garlic, minced
1 teaspoon salt
½ teaspoon smoked paprika
¼ cup extra-virgin olive oil

1. Preheat the broiler. Line a large baking sheet with aluminum foil. Lightly grease the foil.
2. Arrange the jalapeños and bell pepper halves, cut sides down, on the prepared baking sheet. Broil 3 to 4 inches from the heat for 5 to 10 minutes, until the skins are very charred. (If the jalapeño halves char before the bell pepper, transfer them to a bowl and continue broiling the bell pepper.) Let the peppers cool until easy to handle.
3. Toast the cumin, coriander, and caraway seeds in a small skillet over medium heat, shaking the skillet often, until fragrant, about 5 minutes.
4. Use a sharp knife to peel off the charred skin from the peppers (you do not need to remove every bit of the skins). Roughly chop the peppers. In a food processor, combine the peppers, toasted spices, lemon juice, garlic, salt, and paprika. Pulse until the peppers are chopped. With the food processor running, drizzle the olive oil through the opening in the lid to form a thick paste.
5. Store the sauce in an airtight container in the refrigerator for up to 1 month.

Asian Barbecue Sauce

Prep time: 10 minutes | Cook time: 13 minutes | Makes 3 cups

1 cup diced onion
1 cup canned no-added-sodium crushed tomatoes
⅓ cup apple cider vinegar
3 tablespoons low-sodium tamari or soy sauce
¼ cup no-added-sodium tomato paste
¼ cup date paste
2 tablespoons minced fresh ginger
2 garlic cloves
¾ teaspoon freshly ground black pepper
½ teaspoon smoked paprika
½ teaspoon ground cinnamon
1 bay leaf
½ serrano chile, minced (optional)

1. Heat a medium saucepan over medium-high heat. When hot, add the onion and dry sauté, stirring often, until it begins to stick to the pan and lightly brown, 3 to 4 minutes. Add the remaining ingredients, reduce the heat to medium-low, and bring to a slow simmer. Cook for 10 minutes, until reduced in volume and slightly thickened.
2. Remove from the heat and remove the bay leaf. Carefully transfer the sauce to a high-speed blender or food processor and blend until smooth. Use immediately as a stir-fry sauce or dipping sauce, or refrigerate in an airtight container for up to 1 week.

Chile-Grapefruit and Cilantro Vinaigrette

Prep time: 10 minutes | Cook time: 0 minutes | Makes 1 cup

1 teaspoon grated grapefruit zest
½ cup fresh grapefruit juice
1 serrano chile pepper, seeded, if desired, and minced
3 tablespoons finely chopped fresh cilantro
1 clove garlic, minced
1 teaspoon Whole30-compliant Dijon mustard
½ teaspoon salt
¼ cup avocado oil
¼ cup extra-virgin olive oil

1. In a bowl, whisk together the grapefruit zest and juice, the serrano pepper, cilantro, garlic, mustard, and salt. While whisking, drizzle in the avocado oil and olive oil in a steady stream until emulsified.
2. Transfer the vinaigrette to a bottle, jar, or storage container. Store in the refrigerator for up to 3 days.

Everything you need is within you. -Chapter 11 Sauces, Dressings, and Dips

Lemon Tahini Sauce

Prep time: 10 minutes | Cook time: 0 minutes | Makes ⅔ cup

¼ cup tahini
3 tablespoons fresh lemon juice
2 to 3 tablespoons warm water
¼ teaspoon grated lemon zest
1 garlic clove, minced
¼ teaspoon salt
Dash of cayenne pepper
1 tablespoon chopped fresh parsley

1. In a small bowl, whisk together the tahini and lemon juice until combined. (The mixture will be thick.) Whisk in the warm water, 1 tablespoon at a time, until the mixture is smooth and pourable. Add the lemon zest, garlic, salt, and cayenne; mix well.
2. Cover and refrigerate for at least 1 hour, allowing the flavors to blend. Stir in the parsley before serving.

Strawberry-Chile Summer Vinaigrette

Prep time: 10 minutes | Cook time: 23 minutes | Makes 1¼ cups

1 poblano chile
1 jalapeño
2 cups ripe fresh strawberries, stemmed
½ apple, peeled, cored, and chopped
3 tablespoons unseasoned rice vinegar
8 large fresh mint leaves
Leaves from ½ bunch cilantro

1. Preheat the broiler. Line a baking sheet with parchment paper.
2. Put the poblano and jalapeño on the prepared baking sheet and broil until their skins are charred all over, 8 to 10 minutes, turning them to blacken all sides. Transfer them to a bowl, cover with plastic wrap, and set aside to steam for 15 minutes. When cool enough to handle, use a clean dishtowel or paper towel to wipe off the charred skin; discard the skin. Use a paring knife to remove and discard the stems, cores, and seeds and place the flesh of both chiles in a high-speed blender.
3. Add the strawberries, apple, and vinegar and blend until smooth, 30 to 40 seconds. Add the mint and cilantro and pulse just until finely chopped, to give you those bursts of flavor.
4. Use immediately or refrigerate in an airtight container for up to 1 day.

Sherry-Citrus Vinaigrette

Prep time: 10 minutes | Cook time: 0 minutes | Makes 1 cup

1 teaspoon grated orange zest
2 tablespoons fresh orange juice
2 tablespoons sherry vinegar
1 teaspoon dry mustard
1 clove garlic, minced
¾ cup extra-virgin olive oil
1 teaspoon chopped fresh thyme
½ teaspoon salt
¼ teaspoon black pepper

1. In a small bowl, combine the orange zest, orange juice, vinegar, mustard, and garlic. While whisking, drizzle in the olive oil until emulsified. Add the thyme, salt, and pepper and whisk until blended.
2. Store the vinaigrette in an airtight container in the refrigerator for up to 3 days.

Tangy Barbecue Sauce

Prep time: 10 minutes | Cook time: 30 minutes | Makes 2 cups

2 tablespoons ghee or clarified butter
1 small onion, diced
3 cloves roasted garlic
1 large sweet potato, peeled and cut into 1-inch dice
½ cup apple cider
1 (3-ounce / 85-g) can tomato paste
1 tablespoon apple cider vinegar
1 teaspoon paprika
1 teaspoon salt
½ teaspoon chipotle powder

1. Heat the ghee in a medium skillet over medium heat. When the ghee is hot, add the onion and cook, stirring occasionally, until they start to brown and caramelize, 15 to 20 minutes.
2. Meanwhile, combine the roasted garlic, sweet potato, and apple cider in a medium saucepan. Add enough water to just barely cover the sweet potatoes—do not over-cover. Bring to a boil, then reduce the heat to a simmer and cook until the sweet potato is fork-tender, about 15 minutes. Strain and reserve the liquid from the pan.
3. Combine the sautéed onion and sweet potato mixture in a food processor or blender. Add the tomato paste, vinegar, paprika, salt, and chipotle powder. Add ¼ cup of the reserved cooking liquid and blend on low to medium speed. If the mixture is still too thick, add more liquid, ¼ cup at a time, while blending until you arrive at the desired consistency. (The sauce should pour like ketchup.)
4. Store in the refrigerator for up to 2 to 3 days.

Cashew Ranch Salad Dressing

Prep time: 10 minutes | Cook time: 0 minutes | Makes 2½ cups

1 cup raw cashews
¾ cup unsweetened soy milk or other nondairy milk
1 tablespoon distilled white vinegar
Juice of ½ lemon
1 garlic clove
2 teaspoons onion powder
1 teaspoon cracked black pepper
Pinch of dry mustard
1½ teaspoons chopped fresh chives
1 tablespoon chopped fresh dill

1. Soak cashews in water to cover at room temperature for at least 3 hours or up to overnight. Drain and rinse the cashews, then transfer them to a (preferably high-speed) blender. Add the nondairy milk, vinegar, lemon juice, garlic, onion powder, pepper, and mustard. Process until very smooth, 1 to 2 minutes.
2. Add the fresh herbs and briefly pulse until just incorporated. Use immediately or refrigerate in an airtight container for up to 2 days.

Citrus-White Miso Dressing

Prep time: 10 minutes | Cook time: 0 minutes | Makes 1½ cups

2 oranges, preferably mandarins or tangerines, peeled
½ cup white miso paste
1 tablespoon tahini
1 tablespoon unseasoned rice vinegar
1 tablespoon chopped fresh ginger
1 teaspoon low-sodium tamari

1. Combine all the ingredients in a high-speed blender and blend until smooth, 1 to 2 minutes. Use immediately or refrigerate in an airtight container for up to 1 day.

Punchy Fig-Balsamic Dressing

Prep time: 10 minutes | Cook time: 0 minutes | Makes 2 cups

¾ cup balsamic vinegar
¼ cup fig paste
¼ cup low-sodium tamari
1 tablespoon minced shallot
1½ teaspoons minced fresh parsley
2 teaspoons minced fresh rosemary
¼ teaspoon freshly ground black pepper

1. Combine all the ingredients and ¼ cup water in a bowl or glass jar. Whisk or cover and shake well until combined. Use immediately or refrigerate for up to 4 days.

Almond Butter-Chile Sauce

Prep time: 10 minutes | Cook time: 0 minutes | Makes 1½ cups

½ cup smooth almond butter (no added oil, salt, or sugar)
¾ cup warm water
2½ tablespoons fresh lime juice
2½ tablespoons low-sodium tamari or soy sauce
1 tablespoon minced fresh ginger
½ teaspoon minced fresh garlic
¼ to ½ teaspoon red pepper flakes

1. Combine all the ingredients in a high-speed blender and blend until smooth, 1 to 2 minutes. Use immediately or store in an airtight container in the refrigerator for up to 2 weeks.

Hot BBQ Tahini Sauce

Prep time: 10 minutes | Cook time: 0 minutes | Makes 1½ cups

½ cup tahini
⅓ cup hot pepper sauce, such as Tabasco
1 tablespoon no-added-sodium tomato paste
1 tablespoon nutritional yeast
1 teaspoon ground cumin
1 teaspoon chili powder
½ teaspoon smoked paprika
½ teaspoon coarse sea salt
½ teaspoon freshly ground black pepper

1. Combine all the ingredients and ⅓ cup water in a blender or bowl and blend or mix until smooth. Use immediately or refrigerate in an airtight container for up to 3 days.

Light Garlic Paste

Prep time: 5 minutes | Cook time: 4 minutes | Makes ½ cup

½ cup garlic cloves
¼ teaspoon sea salt
½ teaspoon freshly ground black pepper

1. Bring 1 cup water to a boil in a small saucepan. Add the garlic and simmer until soft, about 4 minutes. Remove from the heat.
2. Drain the garlic and transfer it to a small bowl or a mortar. Add the salt and pepper and mash with a fork or the pestle until very smooth. Spoon into an airtight container and store in the refrigerator for up to 1 week.

Everything you need is within you. -Chapter 11 Sauces, Dressings, and Dips

Oil-Free Herb and Pine Nuts Pesto

Prep time: 10 minutes | Cook time: minutes | Makes 2 cups

2 cups lightly packed chopped fresh basil leaves
¼ cup chopped fresh parsley leaves
¼ cup chopped leeks
2 garlic cloves
½ cup toasted pine nuts
2 tablespoons nutritional yeast
½ avocado, pitted and peeled
½ teaspoon sea salt

1. Combine all the ingredients in a food processor and pulse until finely chopped. Pulse in just enough water, 1 tablespoon at a time, to get things moving and break the mixture down to a coarse and chunky puree—it should not be completely smooth. You should only need a tablespoon or two of water. Refrigerate for up to 5 days.

No-Oil Great Red Sauce

Prep time: 10 minutes | Cook time: 1 hour | Makes 10 cups

2 onions, finely chopped
2 carrots, finely grated or chopped
½ cup low-sodium vegetable broth
1 (15-ounce / 425-g) jar roasted red peppers, drained
2 (28-ounce / 794-g) cans no-added-sodium whole plum tomatoes, with their juices
¼ cup no-added-sodium tomato paste
¼ cup garlic cloves, smashed
1½ teaspoons freshly ground black pepper
½ teaspoon sea salt
3 bay leaves
½ cup fresh basil leaves, torn by hand (optional)

1. Heat a large saucepan over medium-high heat. Add onions and carrots and dry sauté, stirring often, until the onions begin to stick to the pan and lightly brown, 3 to 4 minutes. Add the broth and stir to deglaze the pan. Cook, stirring now and then, until the onions are translucent, 2 to 3 minutes.
2. Stir in the roasted peppers, whole tomatoes with their juices, tomato paste, garlic, black pepper, and salt. Bring to a simmer, then reduce the heat to low and simmer for 1 to 2 hours. (The longer the sauce simmers, the more concentrated the flavors become.)
3. Remove from the heat and let cool slightly. Blend directly in the pot with an immersion blender until smooth (or carefully transfer to an upright blender and blend until smooth, then return the sauce to the pot). Add the bay leaves. Bring to a simmer over medium heat and simmer gently for 20 minutes.
4. Remove the pot from the heat, remove the bay leaves, and stir in the basil (if using). Use immediately or transfer to airtight containers and refrigerate for up to 5 days or freeze for up to 2 months.

Rich Cashew Cream Sauce

Prep time: 5 minutes | Cook time: 5 minutes | Makes 4 cups

1½ cups raw cashews
3 cups low-sodium vegetable broth
1 cup chopped onion
¼ cup garlic cloves
2 tablespoons nutritional yeast (optional)
1 teaspoon sea salt (optional)

1. Soak the cashews in warm water to cover for at least 3 hours or up to overnight. Drain and rinse the cashews, then transfer to a (preferably high-speed) blender.
2. In a small saucepan, combine the broth, onion, and garlic. Bring to a simmer over medium-high heat and simmer until the garlic and onion are very soft, 5 to 8 minutes. Remove from the heat and let cool slightly, then transfer the contents (liquid and vegetables) of the pan to the blender with the cashews. Add the nutritional yeast and sea salt, if desired. Blend until very smooth, a few minutes in a high-speed blender like a Vitamix or slightly longer in a standard blender.
3. Use immediately or transfer to an airtight container and refrigerate for up to 1 week or freeze for up to 3 months.

Roasted Red Peppers Sauce

Prep time: 10 minutes | Cook time: 0 minutes | Makes 2 cups

1 jar (16-ounce / 454-g) roasted red peppers, drained
¼ cup extra-virgin olive oil
¼ onion, roughly chopped
2 cloves garlic, minced
2 tablespoons chopped
fresh parsley
1 tablespoon capers, drained
Juice of ½ lemon
½ teaspoon salt
½ teaspoon black pepper

1. Combine all ingredients in a food processor and pulse 5 to 10 times to combine, then blend on high speed until smooth.
2. Store in the refrigerator for up to 5 days.

Roasted Red Bell Pepper Sauce

Prep time: 10 minutes | Cook time: 9 minutes | Makes 3 cups

3 cups chopped roasted red bell peppers
3 tablespoons pine nuts, toasted
⅔ cup chopped onion
½ teaspoon red pepper flakes
3 garlic cloves, minced
¼ cup low-sodium vegetable broth
½ cup unsweetened soy milk
¼ cup chopped fresh basil
¼ teaspoon sea salt
¼ teaspoon freshly ground black pepper

1. Combine the roasted peppers and pine nuts in a high-speed blender and blend until smooth, 1 to 2 minutes.
2. Heat a large skillet over medium heat. When hot, add the onion and red pepper flakes and dry sauté, stirring often, until the onion begins to stick to the pan and lightly brown, 3 to 4 minutes, stirring often. Stir in the garlic and cook for 1 minute. Add the broth and cook until the liquid evaporates, 2 to 3 minutes.
3. Whisk in the red pepper puree and soy milk until thoroughly combined. Simmer, stirring a few times to prevent burning, until the mixture is heated through and bubbling, 3 to 4 minutes. Remove from the heat and stir in basil, salt, and black pepper. Refrigerate for up to 5 days.

Delicious Steak Sauce

Prep time: 20 minutes | Cook time: 10 minutes | Makes 2 cups

¾ cup water
½ cup balsamic vinegar
2 cloves garlic, smashed
1 teaspoon grated orange zest
⅓ cup fresh orange juice
⅓ cup unsulfured black or golden raisins
¼ cup finely chopped yellow onion
¼ cup Whole30-compliant ketchup
¼ cup Whole30-compliant Dijon or brown mustard
2 tablespoons coconut aminos
2 tablespoons fresh lemon juice
½ teaspoon celery seeds
½ teaspoon salt
¼ teaspoon black pepper
⅛ teaspoon ground cinnamon
⅛ teaspoon ground cloves
⅛ teaspoon ground ginger
Dash of cayenne pepper

1. Combine all the ingredients in a medium saucepan. Bring to a boil. Reduce the heat and simmer, uncovered, until the garlic is tender, 10 to 12 minutes. Let cool for 10 minutes.
2. Transfer the cooled mixture to a blender. Cover and blend until completely smooth.
3. Store in an airtight container in the refrigerator for up to 2 weeks.

Caramelized Garlic Paste

Prep time: 5 minutes | Cook time: 25 minutes | Makes ½ cup

4 whole heads garlic
Spray oil
¼ teaspoon sea salt
½ teaspoon freshly ground black pepper

1. Preheat the oven to 400ºF (205ºC).
2. Slice off the top of each head of garlic just enough to expose the very tops of the garlic cloves. Place each head of garlic cut-side up on a piece of foil. Very lightly spray the exposed garlic cloves with spray oil to help prevent scorching. Loosely wrap each bulb in the foil. Place the foil packets on a rimmed baking sheet and roast until the garlic cloves are fork-tender, 25 to 35 minutes. Remove them from the oven and let cool in the foil.
3. When cool enough to handle, unwrap the heads of garlic. Holding one over a small bowl, squeeze the entire head of garlic to force the individual cloves from their papery skins into the bowl (or a mortar). Repeat with the remaining heads of garlic. Add the salt and pepper and mash with a fork (or the pestle) until very smooth. Spoon into an airtight container and store in the refrigerator for up to 1 week.

Mexican Guacamole

Prep time: 10 minutes | Cook time: 0 minutes | Makes 3 cups

3 ripe avocados, split lengthwise, pitted, and peeled
Juice of 1 lime
1 teaspoon salt
½ onion, finely diced
1 tomato, finely diced
½ jalapeño, seeded and finely diced
3 tablespoons chopped fresh cilantro
1 clove garlic, minced

1. In a medium bowl, mix together the avocados, lime juice, and salt. Mash with a fork or potato masher if you like it chunky; use an immersion blender or food processor if you prefer a creamy texture. Mix in the onion, tomato, jalapeño, cilantro, and garlic.
2. Serve immediately, or store in an airtight container and refrigerate before serving. Your guacamole will keep in the fridge for up to 3 days.

Everything you need is within you. -Chapter 11 Sauces, Dressings, and Dips

Spanish Romesco Sauce

Prep time: 10 minutes | Cook time: 9 minutes | Makes 2 cups

2 tablespoons cooking fat
½ cup almonds, chopped
1 small onion, diced
3 cloves garlic, minced
1 teaspoon chili powder
1 teaspoon paprika
2 tomatoes, seeded and chopped
2 tablespoons extra-virgin olive oil
1½ teaspoons red wine vinegar
1 teaspoon salt
½ teaspoon black pepper

1. Melt the cooking fat in a large skillet over medium-high heat. When the fat is hot, add the almonds and toast for 3 minutes, stirring often. Add the onion and cook, stirring, for 2 minutes. Add the garlic and cook until aromatic, about 1 minute. Add the chili powder and paprika and cook until the flavors open up, about 30 seconds. Finally, add the tomatoes, mix into the ingredients, and cook, stirring to bring up the tasty bits from the bottom of the pan, until the tomatoes are warmed through, about 2 minutes.
2. Transfer the sauce mixture to a food processor. Add the rest of the ingredients and blend on low speed until the sauce is smooth, then pour into a serving dish or glass storage container.
3. Allow to cool before refrigerating; the sauce will keep for up to 5 days.

Flavorful Ginger Sauce

Prep time: 10 minutes | Cook time: 0 minutes | Makes 1½ cups

½ cup full-fat coconut milk
¼ cup coconut aminos
¼ cup peeled and minced fresh ginger
4 cloves garlic, peeled
2 tablespoons coconut vinegar or red wine vinegar
2 tablespoons sesame oil
1 tablespoon Dijon mustard
1 tablespoon fish sauce
1 teaspoon minced lemongrass or grated lemon zest

1. Place all of the ingredients in a blender and blend on high until the mixture is smooth and light brown. You can also make this sauce in a jar with an immersion blender.
2. Store in an airtight container in the refrigerator for up to 10 days. Shake before using.

Simmered Classic Chili

Prep time: 15 minutes | Cook time: 1¼ hours | Severs 2

1 pound (454 g) ground meat (beef, lamb, bison)
1 onion, finely chopped
3 cloves garlic, minced
1 teaspoon cumin
1 teaspoon chili powder
½ teaspoon paprika
½ teaspoon mustard powder
½ teaspoon salt
1 red bell pepper, finely chopped
1 green bell pepper, finely chopped
1 can (14½-ounce / 411-g) diced tomatoes
2 cups beef broth

1. Heat a large pot or high-walled skillet over medium-high heat (without cooking fat). Add the ground meat and cook until the meat is fully browned, 7 to 10 minutes. Remove the meat from the pot with a slotted spoon and transfer it to a side dish, keeping the leftover fat in the pot.
2. Add the onions, garlic, cumin, chili powder, paprika, mustard powder, and salt to the pot. Reduce the heat to medium low and cook until the onions are translucent, 4 to 5 minutes.
3. Add the bell peppers, tomatoes, and broth. Turn the heat up to high. When the chili reaches a boil, reduce the heat to low and simmer uncovered for 1 hour.

Versatile Chimichurri

Prep time: 10 minutes | Cook time: 0 minutes | Makes 2½ cups

¼ cup red wine vinegar
¼ cup lime juice
2 cloves garlic, minced
½ shallot, minced
1½ cups extra-virgin olive oil
¼ cup fresh cilantro
¼ cup fresh parsley leaves
½ teaspoon salt
½ teaspoon black pepper

1. Combine the vinegar, lime juice, garlic, and shallot in a food processor and mix on low speed. Drizzle in the olive oil while mixing; the dressing will begin to emulsify. Add the cilantro, parsley, salt, and pepper and continue to mix on low until the dressing is uniform in texture and the herb pieces are chopped quite small.
2. Chimichurri will last 2 to 3 days in the refrigerator. If making ahead, bring it to room temperature before serving. If the dressing has separated, gently whisk to reblend.

Dump Ranch Dressing

Prep time: 10 minutes | Cook time: 0 minutes | Makes 2 cups

- 1 large egg, at room temperature
- 1 cup light olive oil
- ½ cup full-fat coconut milk
- ½ cup packed fresh cilantro, parsley, and/or other herbs
- 2 tablespoons red wine vinegar
- 1 tablespoon fresh lemon juice
- 1 teaspoon salt
- ¾ teaspoon onion powder
- ¾ teaspoon garlic powder
- ½ teaspoon black pepper

1. In a wide-mouth quart-size jar, combine the egg, olive oil, coconut milk, fresh herbs, vinegar, lemon juice, salt, onion powder, garlic powder, and pepper. Blend with an immersion blender for 1 minute. Store in the refrigerator for up to 1 week.

Homemade Fiery Cocktail Sauce

Prep time: 10 minutes | Cook time: 50 minutes | Makes 1¼ cups

- 1 large red bell pepper, quartered, stemmed, and seeded
- 1 small head garlic
- 2 tablespoons plus ½ teaspoon extra-virgin olive oil
- 2 dried ancho chiles
- 3 dates, pitted
- Boiling water
- 3 tablespoons fresh lemon juice
- ¾ teaspoon coarse salt
- ¼ teaspoon cayenne pepper

1. Preheat the oven to 425°F (220°C). Line a baking pan with aluminum foil.
2. Place the bell pepper quarters, skin side up, in the baking pan. Cut a thin slice off the top of the head of garlic to reveal the individual cloves. Leave the outer peel around the garlic head. Place the garlic head on a small square of foil, cut side up. Drizzle with ½ teaspoon of the olive oil. Enclose the garlic in the foil and place it in the pan with the peppers. Roast for 25 to 30 minutes, until the pepper skins are charred and the garlic cloves are tender. Wrap the foil up around the pepper quarters to fully enclose. Let the peppers and garlic cool. When the peppers are cool enough to handle, use a sharp knife to peel off and discard the pepper skin.
3. Combine the chiles and dates in a medium bowl. Add enough boiling water to cover by about 1 inch. Cover and let stand for 15 minutes. Drain the chiles and dates, reserving the water. Remove and discard the stems and seeds from the chiles. Chop the chiles.
4. Use your fingers to squeeze the garlic cloves from their peels. Place the garlic cloves in a blender. Add the roasted bell pepper, chiles, and dates. Add ½ cup of the reserved soaking liquid, the lemon juice, the remaining 2 tablespoons olive oil, the salt, and cayenne. Blend until smooth.
5. Serve the sauce warm or cold with cooked shrimp, fish, or meat. Store the sauce in an airtight container in the refrigerator for up to 1 week.

Whole30- and Paleo-compliant mayonnaise

Prep time: 5 minutes | Cook time: 0 minutes | Makes 1 cup

- 1 cup avocado oil
- 1 large egg, at room temperature
- 2 teaspoons fresh lemon juice
- 1 teaspoon Dijon mustard
- Sea salt, to taste

1. In a widemouthed mason jar, combine the avocado oil, egg, lemon juice, and mustard. Center the head of the immersion blender over the egg yolk and blend on the lowest speed (if your blender has multiple speeds), without moving the blender, for a count of 15 Mississippis, until the bottom half of the oil is emulsified.
2. Slowly move the immersion blender up and down for an additional 15 Mississippis to gradually emulsify the remaining oil. Taste the mayonnaise and season with salt to taste (it likely won't take more than a pinch). Blend to combine. Cover the jar with a lid and refrigerate for at least 1 hour before using.

Salsa Sauce

Prep time: 10 minutes | Cook time: 0 minutes | Makes 3 cups

- 6 tomatoes, cored, seeded, and diced
- ½ cup chopped fresh cilantro
- ½ onion, finely diced
- 3 cloves garlic, minced
- 1 jalapeño, finely diced
- ½ teaspoon salt
- ¼ teaspoon black pepper
- Grated zest and juice of ½ lime

1. Mix all the ingredients together in a small bowl and stir gently to combine. Serve immediately, or allow the flavors to come together in the refrigerator for 1 to 3 hours.
2. Store your salsa in the refrigerator for up to 1 week.

Everything you need is within you. -Chapter 11 Sauces, Dressings, and Dips

Sunshine Dip

Prep time: 10 minutes | Cook time: 0 minutes | Makes 1 cup

½ cup unsweetened sunflower seed butter
½ cup coconut milk
Juice of 1 lime
1 tablespoon coconut aminos (optional)

1 clove garlic, minced
½ teaspoon crushed red pepper flakes
½ teaspoon rice vinegar or apple cider vinegar

1. Mix all the ingredients together in a small bowl and stir to combine. Store in an air-tight container in the refrigerator for up to 3 days.

Pearl Onion, Mushroom, and Caper Sauce

Prep time: 10 minutes | Cook time: 16 minutes | Makes 3 cups

2 tablespoons extra-virgin olive oil
1 (8-ounce / 227-g) package frozen pearl onions, thawed and patted dry
2 cloves garlic, minced
½ teaspoon dried thyme, crushed
12 ounces (340 g) cremini or button mushrooms, cleaned and sliced
vW

1 cup beef bone broth or Whole30-compliant beef or vegetable broth
2 teaspoons arrowroot powder
1 tablespoon capers, drained
¼ to ½ teaspoon black pepper
Salt, to taste

1. Heat 1 tablespoon of the olive oil in a large nonstick skillet over medium heat. Add the pearl onions and cook, stirring occasionally, until golden, 6 to 8 minutes. Add the garlic and thyme and cook, stirring, for 1 minute. Move the onions to the edge of the skillet and add the remaining 1 tablespoon olive oil to the center of the skillet. Raise the heat to medium-high. Add the mushrooms and cook, stirring occasionally, until tender, 5 to 8 minutes.
2. Meanwhile, in a small bowl, whisk together 1 table-spoon of the broth and the arrowroot powder; set aside. Stir the remaining broth into the mushroom mixture; raise the heat and bring to a boil. Reduce the heat and simmer for 3 minutes. Stir in the arrowroot mixture, capers, and pepper. Cook, stirring, for 1 minute. Season with additional pepper and salt to taste.
3. Serve the sauce over steak, pork, cooked vegetables, or mashed potatoes. To serve with chicken, prepare as directed except substitute chicken broth for the beef broth.

Chapter 12 Spices and Rub

Vibrant and Umami-Rich Spice Blend

Prep time: 10 minutes | Cook time: 0 minutes | Makes ¾ cup

2 tablespoons smoked paprika
2 tablespoons garlic powder
1 tablespoon onion powder
1 tablespoon dried parsley
1 tablespoon dried basil
1 tablespoon dried oregano
1 tablespoon dried thyme
1 teaspoon cayenne pepper
⅛ teaspoon dried lemon peel
1 teaspoon sea salt (optional)

1. Combine everything in a small airtight container, cover, and shake well. Store at room temperature away from heat and light for up to 4 months.

Go-To Spice Rub for BBQ

Prep time: 5 minutes | Cook time: 0 minutes | Makes 2 tablespoons

1 tablespoon granulated onion
1 tablespoon granulated garlic
1 tablespoon sweet paprika
2 teaspoons kosher salt
1 teaspoon cayenne pepper

1. In a small jar, combine all the ingredients. Seal the jar and shake to combine. Store in a cool, dry place for up to 1 month.

Super Spicy Jerk Rub

Prep time: 10 minutes | Cook time: 0 minutes | Makes 1 cup

6 scallions, white and light green parts only, coarsely chopped
¼ cup coconut aminos
2 Scotch bonnet chiles, seeded
2 tablespoons apple cider vinegar
2 tablespoons avocado oil
3 garlic cloves, coarsely chopped
1 tablespoon grated fresh ginger
1 tablespoon fresh thyme leaves
1 tablespoon whole allspice berries
1 teaspoon freshly grated nutmeg

1. In a food processor or blender, combine all the ingredients and blend on medium speed until smooth. (Alternatively, combine all the ingredients in a widemouthed mason jar and blend with an immersion blender until smooth.) Transfer to a jar, cover, and store in the refrigerator for up to 1 week.

Italian-Style Umami Spice Blend

Prep time: 10 minutes | Cook time: 0 minutes | Makes ½ cup

½ cup dried mushrooms, such as porcini or portobello
2 teaspoons dried rosemary
1 teaspoon dried thyme
1 teaspoon salt-free lemon pepper seasoning
1 tablespoon garlic granules
1 tablespoon onion granules
½ teaspoon red pepper flakes
½ teaspoon freshly ground black pepper

1. In a spice grinder, grind the mushrooms to a fine powder (you should have about ¼ cup). Transfer the powder to a small bowl.
2. Put the rosemary, thyme, and lemon pepper seasoning in the grinder and grind to a fine powder. Transfer to the bowl with the mushroom powder.
3. Stir in the remaining ingredients and transfer the blend to a shaker or spice jar. Store at room temperature away from heat and light for up to 3 weeks.

Adobo Spice Blend

Prep time: 5 minutes | Cook time: 0 minutes | Makes 3 tablespoons

1 tablespoon granulated onion
1 tablespoon granulated garlic
1 teaspoon dried oregano
1 teaspoon ground turmeric
1 teaspoon kosher salt
½ teaspoon freshly ground black pepper

1. In a small jar, combine all the ingredients. Seal the jar and shake to combine. Store in a cool, dry place for up to 1 month.

Bagel Be Gone Spice Blend

Prep time: 10 minutes | Cook time: 0 minutes | Makes 3½ tablespoons

1 tablespoon white sesame seeds
1 tablespoon black sesame seeds
1½ teaspoons flaky sea salt, such as Maldon
1 teaspoon poppy seeds
1 teaspoon dehydrated garlic flakes
1 teaspoon dehydrated onion flakes

1. In a small jar, combine all the ingredients. Seal the jar and shake to combine. Store in a cool, dry place for up to 1 month.

What you plant now, you will harvest later.

All-Purpose Blackening Spice

Prep time: 10 minutes | Cook time: 0 minutes | Makes 1⅔ tablespoons

1 teaspoon granulated garlic
1 teaspoon sweet paprika
1 teaspoon kosher salt
½ teaspoon freshly ground black pepper
½ teaspoon smoked paprika
½ teaspoon dried oregano or thyme
½ to 1 teaspoon cayenne pepper (use the higher quantity if you like more heat)

1. In a small jar, combine all the ingredients. Seal the jar and shake to combine. Store in a cool, dry place for up to 1 month.

Montreal Steak Spice Blend

Prep time: 5 minutes | Cook time: 0 minutes | Makes 2½ tablespoons

2 teaspoons coarse sea salt
2 teaspoons dehydrated onion flakes
2 teaspoons dehydrated garlic flakes
2 teaspoons red pepper flakes
1 teaspoon dill seeds
½ teaspoon coarsely ground black pepper

1. In a small jar, combine all the ingredients. Seal the jar and shake to combine. Store in a cool, dry place for up to 1 month.

Asian-Style Umami Spice Blend

Prep time: 10 minutes | Cook time: 0 minutes | Makes ⅔ cup

½ cup dried mushrooms, such as shiitake or portobello
¼ cup sesame seeds, toasted
2 teaspoons ground ginger
2 tablespoons garlic granules
2 tablespoons onion granules
1 teaspoon cayenne pepper
1 teaspoon nori or kelp granules or powder

1. In a spice grinder, grind the mushrooms to a fine powder (you should have about ¼ cup). Transfer the mushroom powder to a small bowl.
2. Pour the toasted sesame seeds into the grinder and grind to a coarse powder. Transfer to the bowl with the mushroom powder.
3. Stir in the remaining ingredients and transfer the blend to a shaker or spice jar. Store at room temperature away from heat and light for up to 3 weeks.

Mexican Taco Seasoning

Prep time: 10 minutes | Cook time: 0 minutes | Makes 3½ tablespoons

1 tablespoon granulated onion
1 teaspoon sweet paprika
1 teaspoon ground coriander
1 teaspoon chili powder or dried ground chile of your choice, such as ancho
1 teaspoon dried oregano, preferably Mexican
1 teaspoon ground cumin
¾ teaspoon kosher salt
½ to 1 teaspoon cayenne pepper (use the higher quantity if you like more heat)
¼ teaspoon freshly ground black pepper

1. In a small jar, combine all the ingredients. Seal the jar and shake to combine. Store in a cool, dry place for up to 1 month.

Spicy Seeds Blend

Prep time: minutes | Cook time: minutes | Makes ⅔ cup

2 tablespoons sunflower seeds, toasted
¼ cup sesame seeds, toasted
2 tablespoons hemp seeds, toasted
2 tablespoons finely ground nutritional yeast
1½ teaspoons onion granules
½ teaspoon jalapeño powder or hot pepper of your choice

1. Pour the toasted sunflower seeds into a spice grinder and grind to a coarse meal. Transfer the meal to a small bowl and stir in the remaining ingredients.
2. Transfer the blend to a shaker or spice jar and store at room temperature away from heat and light for up to 3 weeks.

Shawarma Spice Blend 10

Prep time: 10 minutes | Cook time: 0 minutes | Makes 2 tablespoons

1 teaspoon granulated onion
1 teaspoon ground cumin
1 teaspoon ground coriander
1 teaspoon kosher salt
½ teaspoon ground turmeric
½ teaspoon cayenne pepper
½ teaspoon ground cinnamon
½ teaspoon ground cardamom

1. In a small jar, combine all the ingredients. Seal the jar and shake to combine. Store in a cool, dry place for up to 1 month.

Chapter 13 Basics

Chicken Bone Broth

Prep time: 10 minutes | Cook time: 12 hours | Makes 1 gallon

- Carcass from a roasted (3- to 4-pound / 1.4- to 1.8-kg) chicken
- 2 carrots, roughly chopped
- 3 stalks celery, roughly chopped
- 2 onions, roughly chopped
- 5 or 6 sprigs fresh parsley
- 1 sprig fresh thyme
- 2 tablespoons cider vinegar
- 10 whole black peppercorns
- 1 teaspoon salt

1. Combine all the ingredients in a large stockpot, add water to cover, and bring to a boil over high heat. Cover, reduce the heat to low, and simmer for 12 to 24 hours without stirring. (You can also do this in a slow cooker: Set the cooker to high until the water comes to a boil, then turn the temperature down to low and simmer for 12 to 24 hours.)
2. Strain the broth through a fine-mesh strainer set over a large bowl or clean pot. Discard the solids. Transfer the broth to multiple containers to speed up cooling—don't freeze or refrigerate the broth while it's hot! Allow the broth to sit in the fridge, uncovered, for several hours, until the fat rises to the top and hardens. Scrape off the fat with a spoon and discard it.
3. Refrigerate the broth in airtight containers for 3 to 4 days or freeze for up to 6 months.

Beef Bone Broth

Prep time: 10 minutes | Cook time: 12 hours | Makes 1 gallon

- 3- to 4-pound (1.4- to 1.8-kg) beef bones
- 2 carrots, roughly chopped
- 3 stalks celery, roughly chopped
- 2 onions, roughly chopped
- 5 or 6 sprigs fresh parsley
- 1 sprig fresh thyme
- 2 tablespoons cider vinegar
- 10 whole black peppercorns
- 1 teaspoon salt

1. Combine all the ingredients in a large stockpot, add water to cover, and bring to a boil over high heat. Cover, reduce the heat to low, and simmer for 12 to 24 hours without stirring. (You can also do this in a slow cooker: Set the cooker to high until the water comes to a boil, then turn the temperature down to low and simmer for 12 to 24 hours.)
2. Strain the broth through a fine-mesh strainer set over a large bowl or clean pot. Discard the solids. Transfer the broth to multiple containers to speed up cooling—don't freeze or refrigerate the broth while it's hot! Allow the broth to sit in the fridge, uncovered, for several hours, until the fat rises to the top and hardens. Scrape off the fat with a spoon and discard it.
3. Refrigerate the broth in airtight containers for 3 to 4 days or freeze for up to 6 months.

Marinated Red Onion

Prep time: 5 minutes | Cook time: 0 minutes | Makes 1¼ cups

- 1 small, ½ medium, or ¼ large red onion, thinly sliced into rounds
- ¾ cup extra-virgin olive oil
- 1 tablespoon red wine vinegar
- 1 tablespoon dried oregano

1. Put the onion in a small, shallow bowl.
2. In a separate small bowl, mix the olive oil, vinegar, and oregano together until combined well. Pour the mixture over the onions. The marinade should completely cover the onions; if any are peeking out, then you have too many in the bowl.
3. Cover and let the onions marinate on the counter for at least 12 hours before using. They will keep for up to 3 days. Do not refrigerate. (But you may refrigerate the oil after the onions are gone!).

Clarified Butter

Prep time: 5 minutes | Cook time: 20 minutes | Makes 1½ cups

1 pound (454 g) unsalted butter

1. Cut the butter into 1-inch cubes. In a small pot or saucepan, melt the butter over medium-low heat and let it come to a simmer without stirring. As the butter simmers, foamy white dairy solids will rise to the surface. With a spoon or ladle, gently skim the dairy solids off the top and discard, leaving just the pure clarified butter in the pan.
2. Once you've removed the majority of the milk solids, strain the butter through cheesecloth into a glass storage jar, discarding the milk solids and cheesecloth when you are done. Allow the butter to cool before storing.
3. clarified butter can be stored in the refrigerator for up to 6 months or at room temperature for up to 3 months. (With the milk solids removed, clarified butter is shelf-stable for a longer period of time than regular butter.)

When you eat crap, you feel crap.

Smoky Hot Pepitas

Prep time: 5 minutes | Cook time: minutes | Makes ½ cup

- ½ teaspoon kosher salt
- ½ teaspoon smoked paprika
- ½ teaspoon granulated garlic
- 1 teaspoon extra-virgin olive oil
- ½ cup raw hulled pepitas (pumpkin seeds)

1. In a small bowl, stir together the salt, smoked paprika, and granulated garlic until combined well. Set aside.
2. In medium stainless steel sauté pan, heat the olive oil over medium to medium-high heat. Add the pepitas and cook, stirring continuously, until browned, 4 to 5 minutes; watch them closely—if they char a little or start to burn, it's okay, just turn the heat down to low. Turn off the heat and add the spice mixture to the pepitas, stirring to coat well. Cool and store in an airtight container for up to 8 weeks.

Roasted Chicken Breasts and Thighs

Prep time: 5 minutes | Cook time: 45 minutes | Makes 6 cups

- 4 bone-in, skin-on chicken breasts
- 4 bone-in, skin-on chicken thighs
- 2 tablespoons extra virgin olive oil
- 2 teaspoons kosher salt
- 1 teaspoon freshly ground pepper black pepper

1. Preheat the oven to 375°F (190°C). Cover a large baking sheet with parchment paper.
2. Place the chicken breasts and thighs on top of the parchment paper and drizzle with the olive oil. Rub the olive oil all over the chicken pieces to coat evenly. Season the tops with the salt and pepper.
3. Place the baking sheet in the preheated oven and bake until the thighs are cooked through, about 35 minutes.
4. Keep the oven on and, using tongs, carefully transfer the chicken thighs to a large cutting board to let rest. Return the baking sheet with the breasts back to the oven and continue to cook for about 10 more minutes, or until the meat is no longer pink and the juices run clear.
5. Allow all of the chicken to rest for about 10 minutes before eating it as-is or, to use in recipes, let cool enough to handle with your hands. Peel and discard the skin and, using your hands, pull/shred the chicken into bite-size pieces.

Speedy Mayo Base

Prep time: 5 minutes | Cook time: 0 minutes | Makes 1 cup

- 1 cup avocado oil or other light-flavored oil
- 1 large egg
- 1 clove minced garlic (optional)
- 1 teaspoon fresh lemon juice (optional)
- 2 teaspoons mustard powder (optional)
- Kosher salt, to taste (optional)

1. Pour the oil into a wide-mouth glass jar with an opening a little bit wider than the head of your immersion blender. Crack the egg into the oil and let settle into the bottom of the jar.
2. Place the immersion blender into the jar and position the blade directly over the egg yolk. Turn the immersion blender on low and hold in place, while the blender is running, until the bottom of the jar starts to turn into a creamy emulsion, about 10 seconds. Once you see that creamy emulsion at the bottom, start lifting the blender up a bit and pressing it back down, essentially emulsifying the mixture above the mayo at the bottom, bit by bit, until you reach the top and the entire jar is emulsified. Use as-is in the recipes throughout this book.

Compound Butter

Prep time: 5 minutes | Cook time: 5 minutes | Serves 4 to 8

- ½ cup clarified butter or ghee
- ¼ cup hazelnuts
- 1 clove garlic, minced
- 2 teaspoons fresh thyme leaves
- ½ teaspoon salt
- ¼ teaspoon black pepper

1. Place the butter in a small bowl and leave it on the counter until it reaches room temperature.
2. Heat a dry pan over medium heat. When the pan is hot, add the hazelnuts and toast, shaking the pan often to prevent burning, until lightly browned, about 5 minutes. Transfer the hazelnuts to a cutting board, allow to cool, then chop.
3. Gently fold the chopped hazelnuts, garlic, thyme, salt, and pepper into the softened butter. Place a large piece of plastic wrap on a flat surface and place the butter mixture in the center. Form the butter into a rough log about 1½ inches in diameter. Wrap the plastic wrap tightly around the butter and refrigerate until firm, about 2 hours. You can do this ahead of time if prepping for an event or dinner party—wrapped in plastic, compound butter made with fresh ingredients will keep in the fridge for 2 to 3 days.

Oven-Roasted Spaghetti Squash

Prep time: 5 minutes | Cook time: 30 minutes | Serves 4

1 (2- to 3-pound / 0.9- to 1.4-kg) medium-size spaghetti squash
2 tablespoons extra virgin olive oil
1 teaspoon kosher salt

1. Preheat the oven to 400ºF (205ºC) and line a baking sheet with parchment paper.
2. Using a sharp knife, first trim off a small slice from each end of the spaghetti squash and discard. Next, cut the spaghetti squash in half crosswise. Using a sharp spoon (I use an ice cream scoop), scoop out the seeds and stringy bits from the center of each cavity and discard.
3. Place the squash, cavity-side up, on the prepared baking sheet and brush the inside all over with the olive oil. Sprinkle with salt and roast until fork-tender, 30 to 35 minutes.
4. Remove the squash from oven and allow to cool enough to handle. Using a fork, gently scrape out the strands that resemble spaghetti. Serve as desired.

Raspberry and Rosemary Smash

Prep time: 5 minutes | Cook time: 0 minutes | Serves 2

¼ cup raspberries (fresh or frozen)
1 sprig fresh rosemary leaves
½ lemon, juiced
12 ounces (340 g) sparkling water

1. Muddle raspberries and rosemary leaves in a large glass. Add the lemon juice and sparkling water, and shake or mix thoroughly. Strain the mixture into a new glass, discarding the rosemary leaves. Add ice if desired.

Freshly Lemon Brewed Iced Tea

Prep time: 5 minutes | Cook time: 0 minutes | Serves 6

6 black tea bags
24 ounces Whole30-compliant lemon-flavored sparkling water, chilled
Ice

1. Bring 3 cups water to a boil. Add the tea bags and steep for 10 minutes. Remove the bags. Allow the tea to cool to room temperature, about 30 minutes. Transfer to an airtight pitcher.
2. To serve, pour ½ cup of the tea concentrate into an ice-filled glass. Add ½ cup sparkling water. Stir gently.

Garlic Confit Baked

Prep time: 5 minutes | Cook time: 1 hour | Makes ½ cup

Garlic cloves, peeled
Olive oil or avocado oil
Himalayan salt
Fresh herb sprigs, such as thyme, rosemary, oregano, or sage

1. Preheat the oven to 250ºF (121ºC).
2. Put as many garlic cloves as you like in a small baking dish with a lid (a cocotte is perfect for this), leaving at least an inch of space at the top.
3. Pour in the olive oil until the garlic is just submerged. Sprinkle in a little salt and place a few sprigs of herbs on top. Cover with the lid and place on a sheet pan to prevent a mess.
4. Pop it in the oven and bake for 1 hour, or until you can easily pierce the garlic cloves with a fork. Remove from the oven and let it cool to room temperature.
5. Transfer all of the garlic with the oil and herbs to an airtight glass or ceramic storage container. Store in the fridge for up to 3 months. Always use a clean spoon to remove garlic cloves or oil.

Citrus Zinger

Prep time: 5 minutes | Cook time: 0 minutes | Serves 2

½ lemon, juiced
½ lime, juiced
1 teaspoon fresh ginger
zest
12 ounces (340 g) sparkling water

1. Squeeze the lemon and lime into a glass and add ginger zest. Top with ice and the sparkling water. Give it a quick stir before serving.

South Africa Fruity Rooibos Iced Tea

Prep time: 5 minutes | Cook time: 1 minutes | Serves 8

1½ cups frozen cranberries
1 large ripe pear, peeled, cored, and thinly sliced
¼ cup loose rooibos tea leaves or 10 rooibos tea bags
Ice

1. In a large saucepan, bring 2 quarts of water to a boil. Add 1 cup of the cranberries and the pear slices. Boil for 1 minute. Remove the pan from the heat; cover and steep for 10 minutes.
2. Bring the water to a boil again; remove from the heat. Add the tea; cover and steep for 5 minutes. Strain to remove the tea leaves and fruit. Transfer the tea to a large heatproof pitcher. Cover and chill until cold, at least 4 hours.
3. To serve, pour the tea into ice-filled glasses. Garnish each with 1 tablespoon frozen cranberries.

Chapter 14 Beverages

Pickled Red Onion

Prep time: 5 minutes | Cook time: 8 minutes | Makes 4 cups

2 cups filtered water
1 cup apple cider vinegar
1 teaspoon fine Himalayan salt
2 bay leaves
2 red onions, thinly sliced and cut into half-moons

1. Combine the water, vinegar, salt, erythritol (if using), and bay leaves in a small saucepan over medium heat. Bring to a light simmer and cook for about 8 minutes. Stir to make sure the salt and sweetener have dissolved.
2. Put all the onion slices in a jar with the bay leaves and then pour the hot brine over the onions until they are fully submerged. Let the onions steep for 30 minutes at room temperature before using. Seal the jar and store in the fridge for up to 1 month.

Bubbly Melon-Berry Lemonade

Prep time: 5 minutes | Cook time: 0 minutes | Serves 4

¾ cup chopped seedless watermelon
¾ cup coarsely chopped, hulled fresh strawberries
½ cup frozen unsweetened dark sweet cherries, thawed
1 (25-ounce / 708.7-g) bottle Whole30-compliant lemon-flavored sparkling water, chilled
Ice

1. In a blender, combine the watermelon, strawberries, cherries, and ¼ cup water. Cover and blend until smooth.
2. Place a fine-mesh strainer over a large measuring cup or bowl; line with cheesecloth. Pour the fruit mixture into the sieve. Press the fruit with a large spoon to squeeze out the juice; discard the seeds and pulp.
3. Pour the fruit juice into a 2-quart pitcher. Cover and chill for 1 hour or up to 24 hours.
4. Slowly pour the sparkling water into the pitcher with the fruit juice; stir gently to combine. Pour into ice-filled glasses.

Pink Fizzy Mocktail

Prep time: 5 minutes | Cook time: 0 minutes | Serves 8

1 (6-ounce / 170-g) container fresh raspberries
½ cup peaches, fresh or frozen
⅔ cup fresh orange juice
Whole30-compliant orange-flavored sparkling water
Ice

1. Place the raspberries, peaches, and orange juice in a blender. Cover and blend until smooth.
2. Place a fine-mesh strainer over a large bowl. Pour the fruit mixture into the strainer. Gently press the fruit with the back of a large spoon to remove the seeds. Discard the seeds and pulp.
3. To serve, add 3 tablespoons fruit puree and 1 cup sparkling water to each ice-filled glass. Store the fruit puree in an airtight container in the refrigerator for up to 1 week.

Iced Peach Tea

Prep time: 5 minutes | Cook time: 2 minutes | Serves 8

6 black tea bags
2 ripe peaches, pitted and sliced
1 sprig fresh mint, leaves bruised
Ice
Fresh mint leaves, for garnish

1. In a large saucepan, bring 4 cups of water to a boil. Remove from the heat; add the tea bags.
2. Cover and steep for 5 to 6 minutes. Remove and discard the tea bags. Add 8 cups water, the peaches, and the mint sprig. Cover and chill for 1 to 2 hours.
3. Using a slotted spoon, remove the mint and peach slices, reserving the peach slices for garnish.
4. To serve, pour the tea into ice-filled glasses. Garnish with fresh mint leaves and a reserved peach slice.

Choco-Vanilla Rooibos Hot Tea

Prep time: 5 minutes | Cook time: 2 minutes | Serves 8

2 (3-inch) cinnamon sticks, plus more for garnish (optional)
½ vanilla bean, split lengthwise
1 tablespoon cacao nibs
¼ cup loose rooibos tea leaves or 10 rooibos tea bags

1. In a large saucepan, bring 2 quarts of water to a boil. Add the 2 cinnamon sticks, vanilla bean halves, and cacao nibs. Remove from the heat; cover and steep for 10 minutes.
2. Bring the water to a boil again; remove from the heat. Add the tea; cover and steep for 5 minutes. Strain the tea through a fine-mesh sieve into a large heatproof glass pitcher or teapot.
3. Serve hot. Garnish each serving with a cinnamon stick, if desired.

Blood Orange and Lime Paloma

Prep time: 5 minutes | Cook time: 0 minutes | Serves 2

1 blood orange, juiced
½ lime, juiced
12 ounces (340 g) sparkling water

1. Add the blood orange and lime into a glass. Top with ice and the sparkling water.

Peach-Orange Agua Fresca

Prep time: 10 minutes | Cook time: 0 minutes | Serves 4

4 cups ripe cubed, peeled peaches (about 4 peaches)
2 cups fresh orange juice
2 tablespoons fresh lemon juice
1¼ cups water
8 large fresh basil leaves, torn, plus whole leaves for serving
Orange slices, for serving

1. Combine the peaches, orange juice, and lemon juice in a blender. Cover and blend until smooth. Pour the peach mixture into a pitcher. Stir in the water. Add the torn basil leaves. Cover and steep in the refrigerator for at least 2 hours.
2. To serve, remove and discard the torn basil leaves. Serve in ice-filled glasses with orange slices and whole basil leaves.

Raspberry-Lime Sparkling Water

Prep time: 5 minutes | Cook time: 0 minutes | Serves 10

2 pints fresh raspberries or 1 (16-ounce / 454-g) package frozen raspberries, thawed
⅓ cup fresh lime juice
2 teaspoons grated lime zest
4 cups 100% pineapple juice, chilled
2 (25-ounce / 708.7-g) bottles Whole30-compliant sparkling water, chilled
Fresh raspberries and/or mint leaves for garnish

1. In a blender, combine the raspberries, 1 cup water, lime juice, and zest. Cover and blend until smooth. Place a fine-mesh strainer over a large measuring cup or bowl; pour the fruit mixture into the sieve. Press the fruit with a large spoon to remove the seeds. Discard the seeds.
2. Add the fruit puree to a 4-quart pitcher or a punch bowl, then whisk in the pineapple juice. Add the sparkling water; stir gently to combine. Pour or ladle into 10- to 12-ounce glasses. Garnish with fresh raspberries and/or mint leaves.

Watermelon Puree and Lime Sparkling Water

Prep time: 5 minutes | Cook time: 0 minutes | Serves 6

6 cups cubed watermelon
½ cup fresh lime juice
¼ cup mint leaves, plus more for garnish
1 (12-ounce / 340-g) can Whole30-compliant sparkling water, chilled
Ice
Thinly sliced watermelon wedges, for garnish

1. In a blender, combine the watermelon, lime juice, and mint leaves. Cover and blend until smooth (in batches if necessary). Pour the watermelon mixture into a large pitcher. Stir in the sparkling water.
2. To serve, pour the watermelon mixture over ice-filled glasses. Garnish with a wedge of watermelon and fresh mint leaves

White Tea and Fruit Sangria

Prep time: 5 minutes | Cook time: 0 minutes | Serves 2

1 white tea bag
1 ginger tea bag
1 cup boiling water
¼ cup halved white grapes
¼ cup diced golden delicious apple
8 ounces (227 g) sparkling water
Lemon slices, for garnish

1. Heat 1 cup of water to boiling, let it cool for 5 minutes. Add the tea bags to the hot water and steep for 7 to 10 minutes; remove and discard the tea bags. Chill in the refrigerator for 25 minutes.
2. Place the fruit into a large glass and add ice if desired. Pour tea over the fruit and top with sparkling water. Garnish with lemon slices.

Refreshing Mocktail Mule

Prep time: 5 minutes | Cook time: 0 minutes | Serves 4

1 (16-ounce / 454-g) bottle Whole30-compliant ginger kombucha, chilled
1 (12-ounce / 340-g) can Whole30-compliant lime-flavored sparkling water, chilled
1 tablespoon fresh lime juice
Ice
Lime slices
Fresh mint leaves

1. In a large pitcher, stir together the kombucha, sparkling water, and lime juice. Add ice to four 8-ounce glasses. Pour the mixture over the ice, and garnish with lime slices and mint leaves.

Appendix 1: Measurement Conversion Chart

VOLUME EQUIVALENTS (DRY)

US STANDARD	METRIC (APPROXIMATE)
1/8 teaspoon	0.5 mL
1/4 teaspoon	1 mL
1/2 teaspoon	2 mL
3/4 teaspoon	4 mL
1 teaspoon	5 mL
1 tablespoon	15 mL
1/4 cup	59 mL
1/2 cup	118 mL
3/4 cup	177 mL
1 cup	235 mL
2 cups	475 mL
3 cups	700 mL
4 cups	1 L

VOLUME EQUIVALENTS (LIQUID)

US STANDARD	US STANDARD (OUNCES)	METRIC (APPROXIMATE)
2 tablespoons	1 fl.oz.	30 mL
1/4 cup	2 fl.oz.	60 mL
1/2 cup	4 fl.oz.	120 mL
1 cup	8 fl.oz.	240 mL
1 1/2 cup	12 fl.oz.	355 mL
2 cups or 1 pint	16 fl.oz.	475 mL
4 cups or 1 quart	32 fl.oz.	1 L
1 gallon	128 fl.oz.	4 L

WEIGHT EQUIVALENTS

US STANDARD	METRIC (APPROXIMATE)
1 ounce	28 g
2 ounces	57 g
5 ounces	142 g
10 ounces	284 g
15 ounces	425 g
16 ounces (1 pound)	455 g
1.5 pounds	680 g
2 pounds	907 g

TEMPERATURES EQUIVALENTS

FAHRENHEIT (F)	CELSIUS (C) (APPROXIMATE)
225 °F	107 °C
250 °F	120 °C
275 °F	135 °C
300 °F	150 °C
325 °F	160 °C
350 °F	180 °C
375 °F	190 °C
400 °F	205 °C
425 °F	220 °C
450 °F	235 °C
475 °F	245 °C
500 °F	260 °C

Appendix 2: Recipe Index

A
Adobo Spice Blend 157
Ahi Tuna Mango Poke 130
Ahi Tuna with Tangy Fruit Salsa 79
All-Purpose Blackening Spice 158
Almond Butter-Chile Sauce 151
Almond Chicken and Sweet Potatoes Stew 146
Apple-Pork Chops and Spinach 59
Arugula and Walnut Pesto 149
Asian Barbecue Sauce 149
Asian Beef and Zucchini Noddles Soup 28
Asian Cabbage Salad 124
Asian Chicken Curry with Bok Choy 95
Asian Shrimp and Zucchini Noodles 75
Asian-Style Umami Spice Blend 158
Autumn Pumpkin Chili 143

B
Baby Back Ribs with Brussels Sprouts 42
Baby Back Ribs with Spiced Rub 49
Baby Beet and Red Cabbage Salad 113
Baby Spinach and Tomato Frittata 15
Bacon and Brussels Sprouts Frittata 8
Bacon and Kale Frittata 14
Bacon-Wrapped Beef Meatloaf 41
Bacon, Egg, and Veggie Salad 118
Bacon, Spinach, and Tomato Breakfast Salad 16
Bagel Be Gone Spice Blend 157
Baked Sausage Scotch Eggs 11
Balsamic and Herb Pork Tenderloin 42
Balsamic and Wine-Glazed Red Onions 105
Balsamic Chuck Roast and Veggies 36
Balsamic Peach Arugula Salad 131
Balsamic Roasted Root Veggie 115
Balsamic Sweet Potato and Brussels Sprouts 108
Balsamic Tomato Salad 120
Balsamic-Glazed Salmon and Sweet Potatoes 65
Barbecue-Pulled-Chicken Lettuce Wraps 117
Basil Pork Tenderloin and Cauliflower Curry 54
Basil Roasted Salmon Fillet with Broccoli 81
Basil Sirloin Medallions with Veggie 30
Bavarian Pot Rump Roast 49
Beef and Bell Pepper Soup 141
Beef and Root Vegetable Stew 137
Beef and Sweet Potato Chili 25
Beef Arm with Mushrooms and Snow Peas 27
Beef Bone Broth 159
Beef Brisket Braised with Potatoes 28
Beef Brisket with Celery Root Slaw 22
Beef Fajita Soup 141
Beef Hamburger Soup 32
Beef Short Ribs with Cauliflower Rice 22
Beef Short Ribs with Two Mushrooms 31
Beef Short Ribs with Vegetable and Parsley 23
Beef Steak and Broccoli Salad 132
Beef Steak Fajita Salad 125
Beef Steaks with Garlic-Shallot Purée 34
Beef Stroganoff with Coconut Sour Cream 30
Beef Taco Salad 131
Bistro Curly Endive and Egg Salad 12
Black Pepper Beef and Coleslaw Stir-Fry 36
Blood Orange and Lime Paloma 163
Borscht 29
Braised Beef Brisket 34
Brazilian Cod and Shrimp Stew 133
Broccoli Soup 111
Broiled Salmon Steak Salad 123
Brussels Sprouts and Shallots Bowl 108
Brussels Sprouts with Lemon Tahini 113
Bubbly Melon-Berry Lemonade 162
Buffalo Chicken and Veggie Frittata 10
Butter Chicken Thighs 94
Butter Parsley Stuffed Mushrooms 107
Butternut Squash and Kale Salad 116
Butternut Squash Frittata 16
Butternut Squash Pureed Soup 142

C
Cabbage and Pork Sausage Casserole 44
Cabbage, Carrot, and Cashew Slaw 104
Caesar-Style Salad Dressing 148
Cajun Chicken Wings 87
Caramelized Garlic Paste 153
Carne Asada Salad 125
Carrot-Parsnip Soup with Bacon Crumble 10 138
Carrots with Fennel and Shallots 112
Cashew Ranch Salad Dressing 151
Cassava-Crusted Calamari 75
Catalina Beef Tacos 29
Cauliflower Soup with Sausage and Spinach 145
Celeriac, Carrot, and Potato Pot Roast 109
Ceviche with Avocado 71
Charred Tomatillo Salsa Over Omelet 13
Cherry and Banana Cocoa Smoothie 20
Chia Seeds Pudding 21
Chicken and Vegetable Soup 143
Chicken Bone Broth 159
Chicken Breast and Avocado Soup 145
Chicken Breast Salad 122

Chicken Breast Schnitzel 102
Chicken Breast with Ginger and Basil 85
Chicken Breast, Bacon and Kale Salad 120
Chicken Larb Salad 129
Chicken Legs Cacciatore 99
Chicken Legs with Artichoke and Olives 98
Chicken Meatballs with Tomato Cream Sauce 88
Chicken Sausage and Kale Stew 141
Chicken Stir Fry with Green Beans 102
Chicken Thighs and Artichoke Stew 96
Chicken Thighs and Dumplings Soup 140
Chicken Thighs Taco Salad 126
Chicken Thighs with Walnuts 103
Chicken Tikka Masala with Cauliflower Rice 83
Chicken with Jerk Rub 87
Chicken with Kielbasa Stuffed Mushrooms 92
Chicken with Red Bell Pepper 86
Chicken with Sweet Potatoes and Mushrooms 92
Chicken, Bacon and Mushroom Soup 138
Chicken, Watermelon, and Spinach Salad 129
ChickenWings with Green Chile Sauce 100
Chile Roasted Sweet Potatoes 113
Chile-Grapefruit and Cilantro Vinaigrette 149
Chili Beef with Sweet Potato 133
Chili Brussels Sprouts 110
Chili Roasted Zucchini Slices 110
Chili Verde Pork Tenderloin 58
Chimichurri Pork Shoulder and Cabbage Salad 127
Chinese Five-Spice Chicken Wings 98
Chinese-Style Egg Drop Soup 139
Chipotle Chicken with Roasted Tomatoes 96
Choco-Vanilla Rooibos Hot Tea 162
Churrasco with Chimichurri 24
Cider Pulled Pork Butt 57
Cider-Brined Roasted Pork Tenderloin 47
Cilantro-Lime Pork Tenderloin Salad 120
Citrus Beef Short Ribs 23
Citrus Cod with Spinach 72
Citrus Zinger 161
Citrus-Ginger Glazed Halibut Fillet 79
Citrus-White Miso Dressing 151
Clarified Butter 159
Classic Shakshuka 12
Cod Fillet in Tomato and Pepper Sauce 80
Cod Fillet with Olive Relish and Pilaf 82
Cod Fillet with Spinach Cream Sauce 69
Comforting Chicken Breast Fricassée 99
Compound Butter 160
Coriander-Crusted Pork Tenderloin 43
Creamy Broccoli and Kale Soup 142
Creamy Caramelized Green Onion Sauce 148
Creamy Spinach Artichoke Chicken Breast 101
Cuban Beef and Bell Peppers 27

Curried Lamb and Potatoes 61
Curry Carrot and Sweet Potato Soup 115
Curry Pork and Carrot Noodle Bowls 133

D
Delicious Steak Sauce 153
Deviled Eggs with Smoked Paprika 11
Dijon Salmon with Cashews 69
Dried Apricot Stuffed Pork Chops 60
Dump Ranch Dressing 155

E-F
Egg Florentine Cups 12
Egg Salad with Fresh Dill 9
Eggless Mayonnaise 148
Eggs with Cabbage and Prosciutto 11
Fajita Beef Skillet Over the Cauliflower 24
Fattoush 126
Fingerling Potatoes with Spring Asparagus 19
Fish and Vegetable Stir-Fry 82
Fish en Papillote 81
Fish Fillet en Papillote 76
Flavorful Ginger Sauce 154
Fresh Rosemary Whole Chicken 86
Freshly Lemon Brewed Iced Tea 161
Fried Eggs with Veggie 17
Fruity Chicken Chopped Salad 130

G-H
Garlic Chicken Thighs Primavera 103
Garlic Confit Baked 161
Garlic Herb Chicken and Vegetable 100
Garlic-Roasted Leg of Lamb Roast 62
Garlicky Cherry Tomatoes 107
Garlicky Pork Butt Roast with Collards 42
Gazpacho Shrimp and Zucchini Noodle Soup 139
Ginger Snapper Fillet with Shiitake Mushrooms 77
Go-To Spice Rub for BBQ 157
Golden Onion Rings with Aioli 110
Golden Oven Fries 108
Grapefruit Whole Chicken 98
Greek Olives Salad 121
Greek Spiced Potatoes 115
Greek Whole Chicken and Potatoes 89
Green Beans with Almond 115
Green Beans with Almonds 112
Green Beans with Bacon 106
Green Chile Chicken Thigh Stew 92
Green Chile Pork Shoulder 57
Green Curry Lamb Stew Meat 62
Green Vegetable and Fruit Smoothie 18
Green-Chile Squash with Seeds-Crusted Fish 66
Grilled Beef Skirt 31
Grilled Lemony Asparagus 104
Grilled Zucchini with Italian Herbs 106

Gyro-Inspired Skillet Sausages 64
Harissa Salmon Fillets with Warm Salad 79
Hawaii Lazy Moco 41
Hawaiian Chicken and Pineapple Burgers 87
Hearty Pacific Northwest Mushroom Hash 20
Herb Beef Eye of Round Roast 38
Herb Pork Loin and Spiced Cauliflower 45
Herby Roast Chicken and Vegetables 96
Homemade Fiery Cocktail Sauce 155
Hot BBQ Tahini Sauce 151
Hot Beef Arm Roast 26
Hot-and-Sour Salmon Fillet Salad 119

I-J

5-Ingredient Mayonnaise 148
Iced Peach Tea 162
Indian Masala Steak Stir-Fry 35
Instant Pot Turkey Chili with Avocado 84
Italian Beef and Veggie Soup 138
Italian Chicken and Vegetable Soup 140
Italian Chicken Sausage Soup 138
Italian Chicken Thighs with Fennel 101
Italian Chopped Salad with Grated Yolk 130
Italian Turkey Meatballs with Marinara Sauce 84
Italian-Style Umami Spice Blend 157
Jalapeño and Seeds Harissa Sauce 149
Jamaican Jerk Salmon with Fruity Salsa 78
Jerusalem Veggie Salad 121

K

Kale and Green Olives Salad 124
Kale with Garlic 113
Ketchup For Whole30 148
Korean-Style Pot Roast with Jicama Salad 45
Kung Pao Chicken Lettuce Cups 88

L

Lamb Chops and Potatoes with Pesto 63
Lamb Loaves with Cauliflower and Apricots 62
Lemon Dill Salmon Fillet 77
Lemon Tahini Sauce 150
Lemony Chicken with Green Beans 97
Light Garlic Paste 151
Light Taco Breakfast Casserole 10
Light Tuna Lettuce Wraps 73
Lime Watermelon Salad 120
Loaded Roasted Carrots with Ginger Sauce 107
Lobster Mac Skillet 78
Lush Chicken and Carrot Stew 144
Lush Shrimp Coconut Bowl 147

M-N

Mango and Pistachio Millet with Raspberry 19
Marinated Lamb Leg 61
Marinated Red Onion 159
Matzo Ball Soup with Dill and Parsley 143
Mayo Chicken Salad 131
Meat Loaf with Sweet-Sour Glaze 24
Mediterranean Calamari with Veggie 67
Mediterranean Chicken and Veggie Salad 127
Mediterranean Chicken Breast Wraps 117
Mexican Guacamole 153
Mexican Picadillo with Lettuce 118
Mexican Shrimp and Zucchini Noodles Soup 135
Mexican Taco Seasoning 158
Mexican-Style Chicken Soup 147
Mexican-Style Pork Shoulder Stew 136
Mexican-Style Tuna Boats 78
Mici with Mustard Dipping 26
Mojo Pork Shoulder 53
Mojo Roast Chicken Wings 93
Mongolian Beef and Mixed Greens 35
Montreal Steak Spice Blend 158
Moroccan Beef Meatball Stew 137
Mushroom Stuffed Sirloin Roulade 32
Mushroom, Leek, and Spinach Frittata 10
Mussels and Squash in Spicy Tomato Sauce 76
Mustard Brussels Sprout Slaw 116
Mustard Chicken Salad Lettuce Cups 89
No-Oil Great Red Sauce 152

O

Oil-Free Herb and Pine Nuts Pesto 152
Onion Chicken Meatballs 93
Orange Chicken Breast with Cauliflower Rice 86
Oregano Chicken Breast and Kale Salad 126
Oregano Chicken Thighs with Parsnips 95
Oregano Lamb Chop Salad 122
Oven-Roast Vegetable Salad 123
Oven-Roasted Cauliflower 104
Oven-Roasted Spaghetti Squash 105
Oven-Roasted Spaghetti Squash 161

P-Q

Pan-Roasted Brussels Sprouts and Butternut Squash 105
Pan-Seared Beef Rib-Eye with Arugula 37
Pan-Seared Cod Fillet 73
Pan-Seared Sea Scallops with Orange Sauce 74
Paprika Cashews 107
Paprika Salmon 70
Parsnips with Lemony Dill 114
Patrick's Golden Chicken Fingers 85
Peach-Orange Agua Fresca 163
Pearl Onion, Mushroom, and Caper Sauce 156
Pepperoncini-Flavour Skirt Steak 39
Perfect Jammy Eggs 8
Persian Herby Frittata 14
Picadillo-Style Beef Chuck Roast 23
Pickled Red Onion 162

Pineapple Beef Steak Kabobs 33
Pineapple Salmon Fillet 74
Pink Fizzy Mocktail 162
Pink Shrimp and Tomatoes with Pesto 68
Piri Piri Whole Chicken 91
Pistachio Over Kale Salad 114
Poached Pear 20
Pomegranate Braised Lamb Shanks with Almonds 63
Pork and Carrot-Noodle Bowls 135
Pork and Napa Cabbage Soup 144
Pork and Olives Greek Salad 127
Pork and Veggie Stuffed Cabbage 51
Pork Carnitas 57
Pork Char Siu with Vegetable Medley 47
Pork Chops with Mashers and Pesto 59
Pork Chops with Parsnip Purée 54
Pork Chops with Spiced Applesauce 55
Pork Chops with Sweet Potato Colcannon 48
Pork Loin and Vegetable Yellow Curry 43
Pork Loin Back Ribs with Mole Verde 46
Pork Loin Chops with Watermelon Salad 52
Pork Loin Chops with Zucchini Noodles 49
Pork Loin Stew 147
Pork Loin with Potato and Fruit Smash 46
Pork Patties with Ginger Sauce 52
Pork Sausage 45
Pork Sausage Potato Hash 55
Pork Sausage with Sweet Potatoes 58
Pork Scaloppini with Cremini Mushrooms 55
Pork Shoulder and Green Chile Stew 137
Pork Shoulder Curry with Asparagus 53
Pork Shoulder Lettuce Wraps with Salsa 56
Pork Shoulder with Butternut Squash 54
Pork Shoulder with Pear Sauce 50
Pork Tenderloin and Bell Pepper Stir-Fry 48
Pork Tenderloin and Pepper Paprikash 136
Pork Tenderloin with Squash and Shallots 42
Pork with White BBQ Sauce and Collard Greens 44
Pork, Apple, and Fennel Radicchio Wraps 120
Potato Croutons 20
Potato Salad with Chicken Sausage 128
Potato, Pork Sausage, and Kale Soup 52
Potato, Sausage and Bacon Breakfast Bites 21
Poultry Breast-Asparagus Roll-Ups 89
Prosciutto and Shrimp Cabbage Cups 119
Pumpkin-Spiced Sweet Potato 108
Punchy Fig-Balsamic Dressing 151
Quick Sugar Snap Peas 114

R

Raspberry and Rosemary Smash 161
Raspberry-Lime Sparkling Water 163
Red Cabbage with Apple and Bacon 112

Red Curried Cauliflower 116
Refreshing Mocktail Mule 163
Rich Cashew Cream Sauce 152
Ritzy Short Rib Ragù 40
Roast Beef and Avocado Salad Wraps 119
Roasted Chicken Breasts and Thighs 160
Roasted Pepper Chicken Breast 99
Roasted Red Bell Pepper Sauce 153
Roasted Red Peppers Sauce 152
Roasted Veggie Soup 139
Romaine Heart with Tahini Dressing 116
Rosemary Cauliflower 124
Rosemary Pork with Red Potatoes 53
Russian Beef Stew Meat 28

S

Salmon and Baby Yellow Potato Salad 124
Salmon and Bluebrry Salad in Avocado Boats 71
Salmon Fillet with Lemon-Basil Pesto 69
Salmon Fillet with Mustard-Dill Cream Sauce 70
Salmon with Cauliflower and Spinach Salad 80
Salsa Sauce 155
Salsa Verde Chicken Breast 90
Sausage with Eggs and Home Fries 18
Sautéed Kale with Pine Nuts 111
Sautéed Lemony Kale 113
Sautéed Lemony Kale with Almonds 106
Scallops with Ginger-Blueberry Sauce 77
Scrambled Egg with Salmon 14
Scrambled Eggs Breakfast Tacos 17
Scrambled Eggs with Mushrooms and Greens 8
Sea Scallops and Veggie with Aioli 68
Seared Scallops with Bacon and Spinach 72
Seared Sirloin Steak with Asparagus 37
Shawarma Spice Blend 10 158
Sheet Pan Shrimp with Roasted Broccoli 67
Sherry-Citrus Vinaigrette 150
Shrimp and Fish Cakes with Snap Peas 75
Shrimp and Mango Salad 132
Shrimp and Vegetable Sauce over Squash 67
Shrimp and Vegetable with Lemon Sauce 66
Shrimp Gumbo with Cauliflower 65
Shrimp on Cauliflower Grits with Bacon 68
Shrimp with Mashed Potatoes 73
Shrimp with Pine Nuts 76
Shrimp with Vinaigrette and Salad 65
Silky Broccoli Soup 145
Simmered Classic Chili 154
Simple Egg Drop Soup 142
Sirloin Steak and Broccoli Stir-Fry 36
Sirloin with Beans 25
Sirloin, Zucchini, and Mushroom Stir-Fry 27
Skillet Buttered Chicken Thighs 85

Skillet Potatoes with Herbs 21
Skillet Seasoned Chicken Piccata 101
Slow Cooked Beef Short Ribs 25
Slow-Cooked Shawarma 26
Smashed Potatoes with Dried Herb 105
Smoked Salmon Salad 123
Smoky Butternut Spanish Chicken Meatballs 102
Smoky Hot Pepitas 160
Smoky Scallop and Zucchini Noodle Bowls 134
Smoky Shrimp Omelet with Arugula 13
Soft-Boiled Scotch Eggs 15
Sole Fillet with Olives, Pistachios, and Tarragon 71
South Africa Fruity Rooibos Iced Tea 161
Southern Fall Smoothie 18
Southwest Chicken and Potato Noodle Bowl 139
Southwest Egg Breakfast Bowls 19
Southwest Scrambled Eggs with Avocado 9
Southwest Turkey Legs with Fruit Salad 84
Spaghetti Squash with Pork Arrabbiata Sauce 48
Spanish Chicken Breast Cauliflower Skillet 90
Spanish Romesco Sauce 154
Speedy Mayo Base 160
Speedy Shrimp Scampi 80
Spice-Crusted Roast Pork Tenderloin 56
Spicy and Sour Shrimp Soup 144
Spicy Broccoli, Mushrooms, and Squash 104
Spicy Seeds Blend 158
Spinach and Arugula Breakfast Hash 21
Spring Asparagus Cream Soup 136
Steak au Poivre with Green Peppercorn Sauce 39
Steak Fajita Bowls with Veggie 35
Steak Salad with Charred Onions 128
Steak, Mushrooms, and Rutabaga-Noodle Bowls 134
Sticky Apricot Chicken Drumsticks 100
Stir-Fried Chicken Breast and Bok Choy 90
Strawberry-Chile Summer Vinaigrette 150
Stuffed Bell Peppers with Beef 33
Stuffed Bell Peppers with Turkey 83
Summer in A Glass 18
Sunshine Dip 156
Super Easy Zucchini Noodles 110
Super Spicy Jerk Rub 157
Sweet and Sour Red Snapper 74
Sweet Potato and Cauliflower Mash 114
Sweet Potato Croutons Baked 107
Sweet Potato Stacks with Hot Sauce 15
Sweet Potatoes Mash 111
Sweet Potatoes Pork Stew 142

T

Tahini Lamb with Almonds and Parsley 61
Tangy Barbecue Sauce 150
Tangy Brown Rice Salad with Jalapeño 121
Tangy Chicken Skewers 93
Tarragon Grilled Pork Chops 60
Tender Beef Pot Roast 33
Teriyaki Pork Tenderloin 43
Teriyaki Skirt Steak Wraps 118
Thai Chicken and Potato-Noodle Bowls 134
Thai Curried Chicken Bowls 97
Thai-Style Beef Curry with Green Beans 34
Thai-Style Red Curry Shrimp 81
Thyme Chicken and Zoodle Soup 140
Toasted Coconut Salmon Fillet 70
Toasty Sesame Chicken Wraps 117
Tomato and Cucumber Salad 125
Traditional Caldo Verde 50
Traditional Picadillo 38
Tropically- Inspired Chicken Salad 117
Tuna, Snow Pea, and Broccoli Salad 132
Tunisian-Style Lamb and Squash Stew 64
Turkey and Veggie Chili 87
Turkey Meatball and Lemon-Avocado Salad 128
Turkey Meatballs with Squash 97
Turkey Sausage and Root Vegetable Soup 141
Turkey Stuffed Bell Peppers with Guacamole 103
Turkey Tenderloins with Pepper 90
Turkish-Inspired Poached Eggs 9
Turmeric Chicken 94
Turnip Leek Soup 146
Twice-Fried Green Plantains 106

V

Vegetable Soup with Basil-Nuts Pesto 135
Vegetable Wraps with Lemony Zucchini Dressing 119
Versatile Chimichurri 154
Vibrant and Umami-Rich Spice Blend 157

W

Walnut-Crusted Pork Tenderloin with Greens 46
Warm Chicken Romaine Salad 129
Warm Fennel Olives 109
Watermelon Puree and Lime Sparkling Water 163
West African Suya Stir-Fry 40
White Tea and Fruit Sangria 163
Whole Chicken with Steak Spice 88
Whole Roasted Hot Spiced Cauliflower 109
Whole30 Fauxsole Verde con Pollo 91
Whole30- and Paleo-compliant mayonnaise 155
Winter Greens and Potato Soup 146

Z

Zucchini Ribbons 112
Zucchini with Basil 114
Zucchini-Basil Chicken Thighs Hash 83
Zucchini-Wrapped Cod Fillet with Brussels Sprouts 66

CPSIA information can be obtained
at www.ICGtesting.com
Printed in the USA
BVHW061224130421
604816BV00004B/953